SPECULATIONS

An Anthology for Reading, Writing, and Research

SECOND EDITION

Edited by

Paula Farca

Matthew Wynn Sivils

Constance Squires

KENDALL/HUNT PUBLISHING COMPANY
4050 Westmark Drive Dubuque, Iowa 52002

Contents

Chapter Four: What's in the Future?   231

CHAPTER ONE

How Does the Mind Work?

Introduction

The idea of Artificial Intelligence presupposes that we can understand enough of how the human mind works to duplicate it, and cloning aspires to the perfect duplication of a functioning human. So how does the mind work? At its most basic level, human consciousness must constantly mediate between itself and the world outside, between "me" and everything that is "not me." The subject of the fundamental barrier between these two worlds stands at the core of every selection in this section. As citizens, students, writers, readers, and consumers, all of us have probably at one time or another become aware of the impossibility of seeing the world outside ourselves without the mind imposing its own order on what it perceives.

We encounter this difficulty at every level, from the personal to the professional. It affects our thinking on many questions, from what kind of learning environment is best for different kinds of intelligence to whether or not the Internet changes how effectively we connect with other people. How does our ability to imagine walking a mile in someone else's shoes determine how we understand societal issues, and subsequently, how we vote? How do the stories we tell about ourselves form and sustain our sense of self? Do objective standards of art, culture, politics, or religion help us to understand our world, or do they artificially impose objective standards where there are none?

None of the pieces appearing in this section claims to settle the question of how the mind works. The writing in this section ranges from ancient philosophy to contemporary poetry and fiction, from modern philosophy to psychology and medicine. Each piece suggests the fascinating complexity of the human mind and offers ways of approaching the subject that will facilitate further exploration.

Thomas R. Smith, "Learning to Read"

Thomas R. Smith is the author of three collections of poetry, *Keeping the Star, Horse of Earth,* and *The Dark Indigo Current.* He has conducted poetry workshops in schools and often visited schools during his tenure as director of Artspeople, a community arts organization in western Wisconsin.

 Before You Read:

What is your earliest memory of learning to read? What emotions are attached to it?

Learning to Read

Thomas R. Smith

How tired the elbows grew,
bones thrusting against skin.
Flesh took the brunt,
pressed into the carved desk.

In front of the room, a woman—
old, pretty, ugly, young,
she was ours and we were
hers. We hoped for kindness.

Around us, other faces in that
same balance of anticipation
and dread. Large black letters
floated unanchored on the page.

The boy and girl in the pictures looked
friendly, but only those who could
fit the sounds into words
were allowed to join their play.

The ones who couldn't learn
smoldered with a fatal resentment
I rarely noticed before it gushed
a bloody nose on the playground.

Meanwhile my mind turned a word,
grasped it, used it as a key
to open the door to a refuge
beyond hard desks and fists.

 For Discussion:

1. How does Smith's image of language as a "key" compare with the images given by Plato, Brennan, Hofstadter, or Schank?
2. Compare the form of this poem to the form of "Advice to Young Writers." Why do you think Smith breaks the poem into six stanzas? What do you notice about the stanzas?
3. Notice how learning to read immediately creates division between children on the playground. Compare this to the educational hierarchies offered by Hofstadter and Plato.
4. Why do you think Smith uses the word "fatal" in the 5th stanza?

 For Fact-Finding, Research, and Writing:

1. Using a reliable online encyclopedia, like Wikipedia, look up "blank verse" and "free verse." Which is Smith using in this poem?
2. Using on online database like google.com/unclesam or Statistical Lexis-Nexis (through the library A–Z index), find current statistics about literacy in Oklahoma.

Ron Padgett, "Advice to Young Writers"

Ron Padgett is the author of more than twenty-five books of poems and books on education. He also translated the poetry and fiction of Guillaume Apollinaire and the *Complete Poems of Blaise Cendrars*. Padgett's *New and Selected Poems* was published in 1995. A founding member of the Teachers and Writers Collaborative in New York City, Padgett has taught for thirty years in poetry-in-the-schools programs in many states. He is currently the director of publications for the Teachers and Writers Collaborative.

 Before You Read:

Do you have certain activities that seem to stimulate your imagination? Is writing one of them?

Advice to Young Writers

Ron Padgett

One of the things I've repeated to writing
students is that they should write when they don't
feel like writing, just sit down and start,
and when it doesn't go very well, to press on then,
to get to that one thing you'd otherwise
never find. What I forgot to mention was
that this is just a writing technique, that
you could also be out mowing the lawn, where
if you bring your mind to it, you'll also eventually
come to something unexpected ("The robin he
hunts and pecks"), or watching the FARM NEWS
on which a large man is referring to the "Greater
Massachusetts area." It's alright, students, not
to write. Do whatever you want. As long as you find
that unexpected something, or even if you don't.

 For Discussion:

1. Does Padgett deliver the advice he promises in his title? What is it?
2. How many writing techniques have you been taught that you can think of? How
    are they similar to or different from what is offered here?
3. The speaker here suggests that his "writing technique" can be applied to just about
    anything. How, in your experience, has that been true?
4. Do you think it's all right, as the speaker claims, if you don't find "that unexpected
    something"?

 For Fact-Finding, Research, and Writing:

1. What traits identify this piece of writing as a poem?
2. Padgett's biographical note indicates that he is also a translator. Can you find his
    translations under his name in the OSU library? How else would you search for
    these books?

3. Find the correct format in MLA and/or APA for citing a translated book.
4. Using a reliable online search engine, what can you find out about the Teachers and Writers Collaborative that Padgett founded?

Plato, "The Allegory of the Cave"

Plato (428–347 B.C.) lived in Athens and studied closely with Socrates. Much of Plato's writing is in the form of imagined dialogues between Socrates and Plato, with occasional questions from various students. After Socrates was sentenced to death in 399 B.C., Plato founded the Academy, an institution of learning that endured for almost a thousand years. Many of the practices and beliefs begun by Plato in the Academy are still visible in the basic organization and educational premises of most modern universities. "The Allegory of the Cave" models the belief that we cannot rely on our senses to tell us the truth about the world; it also suggests a relationship between our ability to understand what is outside ourselves and our ability to lead.

 Before You Read:

How do you know that what you perceive with your senses is real? Why might this be an important question? Or isn't it?

The Allegory of the Cave

And now, I said, let me show in a figure how far our nature is enlightened or unenlightened:—Behold! human beings living in an underground den, which has a mouth open towards the light and reaching all along the den; here they have been from their childhood, and have their legs and necks chained so that they cannot move, and can only see before them, being prevented by the chains from turning round their heads. Above and behind them a fire is blazing at a distance, and between the fire and the prisoners there is a raised way; and you will see, if you look, a low wall built along the way, like the screen which marionette players have in front of them, over which they show the puppets.

I see.

And do you see, I said, men passing along the wall carrying all sorts of vessels, and statues and figures of animals made of wood and stone and various materials, which appear over the wall? Some of them are talking, others silent.

You have shown me a strange image, and they are strange prisoners.

Like ourselves, I replied; and they see only their own shadows, or the shadows of one another, which the fire throws on the opposite wall of the cave?

True, he said; how could they see anything but the shadows if they were never allowed to move their heads?

And of the objects which are being carried in like manner they would only see the shadows?

Yes, he said.

And if they were able to converse with one another, would they not suppose that they were naming what was actually before them?

Very true.

And suppose further that the prison had an echo which came from the other side, would they not be sure to fancy when one of the passers-by spoke that the voice which they heard came from the passing shadow?

No question, he replied.

To them, I said, the truth would be literally nothing but the shadows of the images.

That is certain.

And now look again, and see what will naturally follow if the prisoners are released and disabused of their error. At first, when any of them is liberated and compelled suddenly to stand up and turn his neck round and walk and look towards the light, he will suffer sharp pains; the glare will distress him, and he will be unable to see the realities of which in his former state he had seen the shadows; and then conceive someone saying to him, that what he saw before was an illusion, but that now, when he is approaching nearer to being and his eye is turned towards more real existence, he has a clearer vision—what will be his reply? And you may further imagine that his instructor is pointing to the objects as they pass and requiring him to name them,—will he not be perplexed? Will he not fancy that the shadows which he formerly saw are truer than the objects which are now shown to him?

Far truer.

And if he is compelled to look straight at the light, will he not have a pain in his eyes which will make him turn away to take refuge in the objects of vision which he can see, and which he will conceive to be in reality clearer than the things which are now being shown to him?

True, he said.

And suppose once more, that he is reluctantly dragged up a steep and rugged ascent, and held fast until he is forced into the presence of the sun himself, is he not likely to be pained and irritated? When he approaches the light his eyes will be dazzled, and he will not be able to see anything at all of what are now called realities.

Not all in a moment, he said.

He will require to grow accustomed to the sight of the upper world. And first he will see the shadows best, next the reflections of men and other objects in the water, and then the objects themselves; then he will gaze upon the light of the moon and the stars and the spangled heaven; and he will see the sky and the stars by night better than the sun or the light of the sun by day?

Certainly.

Last of all he will be able to see the sun, and not mere reflections of him in the water, but he will see him in his own proper place, and not in another; and he will contemplate him as he is.

Certainly.

He will then proceed to argue that this is he who gives the season and the years, and is the guardian of all that is in the visible world, and in a certain way the cause of all things which he and his fellows have been accustomed to behold?

Clearly, he said, he would first see the sun and then reason about him.

And when he remembered his old habitation, and the wisdom of the den and his fellow prisoners, do you not suppose that he would felicitate himself on the change, and pity them?

Certainly, he would.

And if they were in the habit of conferring honors among themselves on those who were quickest to observe the passing shadows and to remark which of them went before, and which followed after, and which were together; and who were therefore best able to draw conclusions as to the future, do you think that he would care for such honors and glories, or envy the possessors of them? Would he not say with Homer,

Better to be the poor servant of a poor master,

and to endure anything, rather than think as they do and live after their manner?

Yes, he said, I think that he would rather suffer anything than entertain these false notions and live in this miserable manner.

Imagine once more, I said, such a one coming suddenly out of the sun to be replaced in his old situation; would he not be certain to have his eyes full of darkness?

To be sure, he said.

And if there were a contest, and he had to compete in measuring the shadows with the prisoners who had never moved out of the den, while his sight was still weak, and before his eyes had become steady (and the time which would be needed to acquire this new habit of sight might be very considerable), would he not be ridiculous? Men would say of him that up he went and down he came without his eyes; and that it was better not even to think of ascending; and if any one tried to loose another and lead him up to the light, let them only catch the offender, and they would put him to death.

No question, he said.

This entire allegory, I said, you may now append, dear Glaucon, to the previous argument; the prison house is the world of sight, the light of the fire is the sun, and you will not misapprehend me if you interpret the journey upwards to be the ascent of the soul into the intellectual world according to my poor belief, which, at your desire, I have expressed— whether rightly or wrongly God knows. But, whether true or false, my opinion is that in the world of knowledge the idea of good appears last of all, and is seen only with an effort; and, when seen, is also inferred to be the universal author of all things beautiful and right, parent of light and of the lord of light in this visible world, and the immediate source of reason and truth in the intellectual; and that this is the power upon which he who would act rationally either in public or private life must have his eye fixed.

I agree, he said, as far as I am able to understand you.

Moreover, I said, you must not wonder that those who attain to this beatific vision are unwilling to descend to human affairs; for their souls are ever hastening into the upper world where they desire to dwell; which desire of theirs is very natural, if our allegory may be trusted.

Yes, very natural.

And is there anything surprising in one who passes from divine contemplations to the evil state of man, misbehaving himself in a ridiculous manner; if, while his eyes are blinking and before he has become accustomed to the surrounding darkness, he is compelled to fight in courts of law, or in other places, about the images or the shadows of images of justice, and is endeavoring to meet the conceptions of those who have never yet seen absolute justice?

Anything but surprising, he replied.

Anyone who has common sense will remember that the bewilderments of the eyes are of two kinds, and arise from two causes, either from coming out of the light or from going into the light, which is true of the mind's eye, quite as much as of the bodily eye; and he who remembers this when he sees anyone whose vision is perplexed and weak, will not be too ready to laugh; he will first ask whether that soul of man has come out of the brighter life, and is unable to see because unaccustomed to the dark, or having turned from darkness to the day is dazzled by excess of light. And he will count the one happy in his condition and state of being, and he will pity the other; or, if he have a mind to laugh at the soul which comes from below into the light, there will be more reason in this than in the laugh which greets him who returns from above out of the light into the den.

That, he said, is a very just distinction.

But then, if I am right, certain professors of education must be wrong when they say that they can put a knowledge into the soul which was not there before, like sight into blind eyes.

They undoubtedly say this, he replied.

Whereas, our argument shows that the power and capacity of learning exists in the soul already; and that just as the eye was unable to turn from darkness to light without the whole body, so too the instrument of knowledge can only by the movement of the whole soul be turned from the world of becoming into that of being, and learn by degrees to endure the sight of being, and of the brightest and best of being, or in other words, of the good.

Very true.

And must there not be some art which will effect conversation in the easiest and quickest manner; not implanting the faculty of sight, for that exists already, but has been turned in the wrong direction, and is looking away from the truth?

Yes, he said, such an art may be presumed.

And whereas the other so-called virtues of the soul seem to be akin to bodily qualities, for even when they are not originally innate they can be implanted later by habit and exercise, the virtue of wisdom more than anything else contains a divine element which always remains, and by this conversion is rendered useful and profitable; or, on the other hand, hurtful and useless. Did you never observe the narrow intelligence flashing from the keen eye of a clever rogue—how eager he is, how clearly his paltry soul sees the way to his end; he is the reverse of blind, but his keen eyesight is forced into the service of evil, and he is mischievous in proportion to his cleverness?

Very true, he said.

But what if there had been a circumcision of such natures in the days of their youth; and they had been severed from those sensual pleasures, such as eating and drinking, which, like leaden weights, were attached to them at their birth, and which drag them down and turn the vision of their souls upon the things that are below—if, I say, they had been released from these impediments and turned in the opposite direction, the very same faculty in them would have seen the truth as keenly as they see what their eyes are turned to now.

Very likely.

Yes, I said; and there is another thing which is likely, or rather a necessary inference from what has preceded, that neither the uneducated and uninformed of the truth, nor yet those who never make an end of their education, will be able ministers of State; not the former, because they have no single aim of duty which is the rule of all their actions, private as well as public; nor the latter, because they will not act at all except upon compulsion, fancying that they are already dwelling apart in the islands of the blessed.

Very true, he replied.

Then, I said, the business of us who are the founders of the State will be to compel the best minds to attain that knowledge which we have already shown to be the greatest of all—they must continue to ascend until they arrive at the good; but when they have ascended and seen enough we must not allow them to do as they do now.

What do you mean?

I mean that they remain in the upper world: but this must not be allowed; they must be made to descend again among the prisoners in the den, and partake of their labors and honors, whether they are worth having or not.

But is not this unjust? he said; ought we to give them a worse life, when they might have a better?

You have again forgotten, my friend, I said, the intention of the legislator, who did not aim at making any one class in the State happy above the rest; the happiness was to be in the whole State, and he held the citizens together by persuasion and necessity, making them benefactors of the State, and therefore benefactors of one another; to this end he created them, not to please themselves, but to be his instruments in binding up the State.

True, he said, I had forgotten.

Observe, Glaucon, that there will be no injustice in compelling our philosophers to have a care and providence of others; we shall explain to them that in other States, men of their class are not obliged to share in the toils of politics: and this is reasonable, for they grow up at their own sweet will, and the government would rather not have them. Being self-taught, they cannot be expected to show any gratitude for a culture which they have never received. But we have brought you into the world to be rulers of the hive, kings of yourselves and of the other citizens, and have educated you far better and more perfectly than they have been educated, and you are better able to share in the double duty. Wherefore each of you, when his turn comes, must go down to the general underground abode, and get the habit of seeing in the dark. When you have acquired the habit, you will see ten thousand times better than the inhabitants of the den, and you will know what the several images are, and what they represent, because you have seen the beautiful and just and good in their truth. And thus our State, which is also yours, will be a reality, and not a dream only, and will be administered in a spirit unlike that of other States, in which men fight with one another about shadows only and are distracted in the struggle for power, which in their eyes is a great good. Whereas the truth is that the State in which the rulers are most reluctant to govern is always the best and most quietly governed, and the State in which they are most eager, the worst.

Quite true, he replied.

And will our pupils, when they hear this, refuse to take their turn at the toils of State, when they are allowed to spend the greater part of their time with one another in the heavenly light?

Impossible, he answered; for they are just men, and the commands which we impose upon them are just; there can be no doubt that every one of them will take office as a stern necessity, and not after the fashion of our present rulers of State.

Yes, my friend, I said; and there lies the point. You must contrive for your future rulers another and a better life than that of a ruler, and then you may have a well-ordered State; for only in the State which offers this, will they rule who are truly rich, not in silver and gold, but in virtue and wisdom, which are the true blessings of life. Whereas if they go to the administration of public affairs, poor and hungering after their own private advantage, thinking that hence they are to snatch the chief good, order there can never be; for they will be fighting about office, and the civil and domestic broils which thus arise will be the ruin of the rulers themselves and of the whole State.

Most true, he replied.

And the only life which looks down upon the life of political ambition is that of true philosophy. Do you know of any other?

Indeed, I do not, he said.

For Discussion:

1. Plato describes the process of education as similar to emerging from a cave. He considers the essential quality of an educated person to be tolerance of others. Consider your own education, both formal and informal. Does your own education agree with Plato's version of education?

2. Explain Plato's statement, "And surely it is those who are no lovers of governing who must govern." What in his argument leads him to this conclusion? Do you agree?

3. Where do modern means of communication like television and the Internet fit into Plato's cave metaphor? Do they help us to apprehend the world outside of the cave, or do they act as the shadows on the wall inside the cave, or both?

4. If the material world is an illusion, as Plato asserts, how would over-reliance on materialism affect a person's decision-making ability?

 For Fact-Finding, Research, and Writing:

1. Plato believes that educated people owe a debt to their communities that should be paid by useful service to that community. Identify and provide basic background on two educational programs that strongly emphasize this service ethic today.

2. Using appropriate reference materials, identify the allusion to Plato's allegory in the writing of St. Paul.

3. Compare Plato's ideas on education to those of Russell or Gardner.

Roger Schank, "Where Stories Come from and Why We Tell Them"

Roger Schank is the Director of the Institute for Learning Sciences and John Evans Professor of Electrical Engineering and Computer Science, Psychology, and Education at Northwestern University. His publications include *The Creative Attitude: Learning to Ask and Answer the Right Questions, Narrative and Freedom: The Shadows of Time,* and *Tell Me A Story: Narrative and Intelligence,* from which "Where Stories Come From and Why We Tell Them" is excerpted. An expert in both education and computers, Schank explains how narratology (the study of how the mind organizes reality into stories) can provide a model of human thought processes useful in the development of Artificial Intelligence. In "Where Stories Come From and Why We Tell Them" Schank categorizes stories according to their goals.

Before You Read:

What are urban legends? How many can you name? Where did you learn them?

Where Stories Come from and Why We Tell Them

I WAS SITTING in my office one day when three people came in, one at a time, to talk to me. The first was a foreign student who was about to become a graduate student. He told me the following story.

> In order to go to graduate school, I had to postpone going into the army. Ordinarily, three years of service are required, but my country decided that if I wanted to study for a Ph.D. now, I would owe them five years after I finish my studies. I agreed to this, but after I agreed, my country called and said I would owe six years of service. Again I agreed, and again I received a call saying that now they had decided seven years would be required. What should I do?

The second person who entered my office was someone who worked for me. This was his story:

> My ex-wife just called. She's moving back to town, and she's planning to put our child in public school here. She's had him in private school, but now she wants me to pay the tuition money to her instead. She isn't planning on working and is trying to get me to support her. I just called my lawyer to ask him what to do.

The third person was a friend. He had been looking to change jobs and had negotiated a fine deal for himself in another town. This was his story:

> I've been busy selling my house and otherwise preparing for the move. All of a sudden, my appointment has been stopped at the highest levels of the company. No one will tell me why, but I think someone who was my enemy in the past has a friend at the company. And I think she wrote a letter that prejudiced them against me. I'm very upset.

Schank, Roger C. "Where Stories Come from and Why We Tell Them," from *Tell Me A Story: Narrative and Intelligence*. Evanston: Northwestern University Press, 1990, pp. 28–55. Reprinted by permission.

Everyday human communication revolves around stories such as these. Where do we get stories to tell? Obviously, stories digest one's experiences. We tell what happened to us. But we also create stories. I, for example, had a story to tell at the end of that day about how people mistreat one another, and I needed to tell it.

When people talk to you, they can only tell you what they know. And the knowledge that people have about the world around them is really no more than the set of experiences that they have had. Now, of course, not every experience that someone has had is worth remembering, let alone telling to someone else. The experiences we do remember form the set of stories that constitute our view of the world and characterize our beliefs. In some sense, we may not even know what our own view of the world is until we are reminded of and tell stories that illustrate our opinion on some aspect of the world.

Types of Stories

With the exception of certain questions and some straightforward and factual answers, such as "What room is Jones in?" followed by "1244," everything people say regarding their opinions or experiences is a story of some sort. Some stories are too dull to worry about, but the process of search, retrieval, and adaptation of stories is the same whether the story is long or short. One question is where stories come from. We start life without stories, and we go through life acquiring them. Some are handed to us directly by others and some we invent for ourselves.

With respect to the issue of where stories come from, there are five basic types of stories:

1. official
2. invented (adapted)
3. firsthand experiential
4. secondhand
5. culturally common

Official Stories

Official stories are those we learn from an official place, such as school or church or a business or from the government. They are stories that have been told many times, and no one knows or cares who thought them up first. Governments and other official bodies have a kind of script for inventing them, and people in general know how much credence to give them. We know official stories about the creation of the universe, for example. Science has its versions, and religions have theirs. From time to time, we tell an official story because our job requires us to or because the official story is the only one we know.

Official stories are those that our boss, our government, our parents, or anyone in authority instructs us to tell. They are repeated as originally related. People can tell their own official stories. For example, Gary Hart in the 1987–1988 political campaign told an official story about his alleged lover Donna Rice that it seemed no one, not even he, could have believed. But it was the official story. One of my favorite official stories is about Sydney Biddle Barrows, the so-called Mayflower Madam. The following was taken from the *New York Post*:

MAYFLOWER MADAM SAILS INTO A NEW BUSINESS

The Mayflower Madam, a thirty-three-year-old blonde blueblood awaiting trial on charges of running a $1000-a-night prostitution ring, is back in business as the Makeover Madam. She has founded a house-call service for women who want to eat better, dress better, and look better, called We Can Work It Out. Sydney Biddle Barrows, the beautiful descendant of Mayflower pilgrims, will send training counselors to enforce tough diet and exercise regimens on middle-class women.

Her attorney and friend, Risa Dickstein, yesterday told of the project, still in its infancy. In a three-hundred-page motion filed in Manhattan Supreme Court, Mrs. Dickstein asked for a dismissal of the charges against Miss Barrows on grounds ranging from insufficient evidence to prosecutorial misconduct.

She painted a heartwarming picture of the woman accused of running a prostitution ring for high-class clients. She said Miss Barrows:

- *voluntarily reads to a blind college student and helps him with term papers in a program to aid the handicapped;*
- *instructed her employees to patronize an Upper West Side food store because it supplied free meals to the needy on Thanksgiving;*
- *doesn't drink, smoke, or take drugs—not even aspirin;*
- *has the support of her mother, stepfather, and siblings in her ordeal;*
- *lost the love of her natural father because of her arrest.*

Mrs. Dickstein said in her motion that Miss Barrows has a totally unblemished record. It is undisputed that she comes from a family which is well recognized not only as law-abiding but also for its commitment to public service. She is accurately viewed by those who know her well as a well-bred, well-educated, responsible citizen for her community.

The defense argues that the escort agencies run by Miss Barrows were legitimate businesses in which clients paid for companionship. Sex, when it took place, was indulged in freely by the escorts—and at no extra charge.

Official stories are ones that have been carefully constructed by one or more people to tell a version of events that is sanitized and presumed to be less likely to get anyone in trouble. Alternatively, official stories are often the position of a group that has a message to sell and treats that message independently of the facts. A rather grisly example of this was recently placed on a billboard overlooking I–95 in Bridgeport, Connecticut. The sign showed an iridescent skeleton crawling into a body bag. The legend over the picture said: "AIDS—It's a Hop in the Sack." Such epithets are quite typical of official stories. The facts are made simple, often to the point of being wrong, so that a message can be made public. Official stories often leave out details that would make things clearer in order to portray situations as being less complicated than they are.

The overall intention of an official story is to make complex issues seem clearer than they otherwise might appear. When we don't have answers, official stories give us those answers. We learn these stories when we have no stories of our own for those particular situations. As soon as we do have a story of our own that we believe more than the official version, we tend to ignore the official story.

Invented Stories

Obviously, people can make up stories, but the process of story creation and invention is one of adaptation rather than creation out of nothing. Official stories are made up by adapting real stories into appropriately sterilized stories. Invented stories can also, of course, be official stories. In any case, the processes behind the creation of these two story types are remarkably similar. Both of these story types tend to use a real story, that is, a firsthand experiential story, something that really happened to somebody, and then expand upon that story in some way.

The invented story expands upon an experience for the purpose of entertainment, sometimes leaving the original experience unrecognizable in the process. The official story is created in the same way, albeit for a different purpose. An official story tends to obscure the facts of the original experience for the purposes of eliminating culpability on the part of the actors in the story.

Invented stories are also created brand-new by authors, by parents, and often by people who pose a hypothetical case in order to make a point in an argument; however, even brand-new invented stories are usually adaptations of previous stories and frequently, but by no means always, have a point. They tend to be much less rich in detail at first, but their continued elaboration can make them very rich over time.

A good way to understand the story invention process is to observe it firsthand. Unfortunately, when people create a new story, we have difficulty knowing exactly how they found the various pieces of the story they are telling. We cannot easily know what has been invented out of thin air and what has been adapted from prior experiences or other stories. We can reasonably assume, however, that true creation can hardly exist with respect to stories. Every story we tell has to have its basis in something that we have already experienced. Of course, the better we are at telling stories, the better we are at giving them the appearance of being complete fiction. This can mean that even we as tellers see the story as fictional, not realizing the adaptation process that we ourselves have used. Even stories that are pure fantasy are adaptations of more realistic stories where certain constraints of the real world are relaxed. People can take past experiences, consciously or unconsciously, and modify them into stories where the original experience is completely hidden.

One way to see this is to observe a child who is learning to tell stories. When my daughter, Hana, was very little, I recorded some stories that she told at various ages. Here are some of them, taken from *Scripts, Plans, Goals and Understanding* (Roger Schank and Robert Abelson; Hillsdale, NJ: Lawrence Erlbaum Associates, 1977). Hana, age two years, eleven months:

PAPA: I met you in the plant store and then what happened?

HANA: I don't know.

PAPA: Oh, come on, I thought you were going to tell me a story.

HANA: I went on a bike and you drived, and you buckled me in and we went riding the park, and droved and went on one swing and then the other swing and two swings and then we, I went on two slides and then went in the sandbox and then I met somebody, and then I met, and then I went right on our bicycle, and took the thing off and and and we went on and you drived on and then you taked the one street and then you ride on the other side and then we were home and then we were opened, I opened, you opened, I opened the door and then I went right in and I take my jacket off and said hang up your coat and I hanged up my coat and said and went right in the kitchen and and was almost time to dinner.

PAPA: And then what happened?

HANA: I don't know.

PAPA: What happened after you took your coat off?

HANA: Then we went take a nap and you were and then we, you, we went to the plant store and then Nadine was at home and then at our home, and then she was clean, changed, cleared all the rugs, and then I wake woke up and then I I was . . . went into living room and there's something I didn't ask her and and then she I didn't want and watched and watched cartoons. I watched this, I watched, I did, when we got home I watched I watched TV um "Sesame Street." That's the end.

This is a story in the sense that it is what my daughter told when she was asked to tell a story. But obviously she has just recapped the day's experiences. By age four, Hana could really invent a new story. The story itself is invented in the sense that it didn't happen as such, but each individual event in the story did happen. Hana had experienced it all before; she just adapted the events for her use here. We lose coherence here because Hana hasn't yet learned standard coherent story forms that an adult might know. Other than that, though, the process of story creation is remarkably similar to the adult process.

PAPA: Tell me a story.

HANA: Once upon a time there was a little girl and she lived with her mother and father in a big house, not an apartment house, and she was born in California. She has her own passport, her brother has a passport, too. Everyone has a passport, you know that, 'cause they have to have passports for special reasons. They went out to London and they had a good time there. They went riding on horses and they had real good times. They played. They brang lots of toys to play with, even books. Well, books are not such things to play with, you read them. And so then they went out, and then they saw a rabbit and they said hi to the rabbit, and then they said would the rabbit be their pet. But the rabbit said it couldn't be their pet and then they came up to a kitten. They said to the kitten, "Could we have a kitten?" And then, after they had the kitten for their own, then they named it, Joan, Joe, and then they walked on. The kitten was almost in danger. It got struck by a big wolf came and almost tried to bite it and then eat it, but it finally chased the wolf out and Mama and Papa got danger, Hana helped, Joshua was too little, he just said "ah da" to the wolf. And then they came up to a great forest, they had lots of pine trees. And then they came up something shiny with bright eyes, another kitten, instead it was a mother. And so, they took good care of the two kittens and then rode back to where they were, and got, and then went to sleep, and often got dressed the next morning and went out to have their breakfast. They had Chinese breakfast, but Hana in case didn't bring the cat and left it outside by mistake, and Mama and Daddy, locked it in a cage. It was barking the next day, and meowing the next day, and then, away from danger, they saw balloons and then one bursted the balloon and then they got all the rest of the balloons. They had all the money that they needed for to buy a balloon. It was free. They didn't know that, so they paid some money. And then they got all the money that they paid. And then they went home to their own real house and wrote down that they had a good time and sended it to someone and everyone got a chance to read that. And then they had such good time, they had a jolly time here and from all you, this is telling the story. That's the end.

Story invention, for children or adults, is a process of the massaging of reality. How reality is massaged, how old stories are transformed into new ones, depends upon the goals of the teller. If the teller has something to hide, a fantasy to express, a political point to make, whatever, the original story can be changed in a variety of ways. Invention is not a process that comes from nowhere.

Firsthand Stories

People tell about their own experiences all the time, but they do not necessarily tell about the same experience in the same way every time. The telling process, even in the relating of a firsthand experience, can be a highly inventive process. That is, the art of storytelling involves finding good ways to express one's experiences in a way appropriate to the listener. A fine line exists, therefore, between invented stories and the relation of firsthand experiences. The entertainment factor exists in relating firsthand experiences just as it does in inventing stories. Nobody wants to listen to what happened to you today unless you can make what happened appear interesting. The process of livening up an experience can involve simply telling that experience in such a way as to eliminate the dullest parts, or it also can involve "jacking up" the dull parts by playing with the facts.

Firsthand experiential stories are the type of stories we talk about most. They represent our own personal experiences. Some of these experiences have been digested and analyzed so that we know their point or points and are reminded of them when those points come up. But many firsthand stories come up because of random associations, and many have no intended point; they are just stories about ourselves which have not necessarily been fully understood and from which no conclusions may have yet been drawn. Or more often firsthand stories are told because they relate information that is nonstandard in some way. We don't tell about experiences that we believe everyone else has also had. We tell about what we believe to be unusual. The more usual such an experience is, the less we want to tell about it. Good stories are about things that are unusual and could not have easily been predicted.

Secondhand Stories

Secondhand stories are acquired secondhand. We often tell the stories of others. Telling secondhand experiences tends to be a much more straightforward process than telling firsthand stories, because the task is mostly an attempt at proper recall of the facts as they were heard. The problem, of course, is that we can't recall all the facts, even when the event being related is firsthand, much less when it is secondhand. Here again, "facts" are made up as needed to preserve coherence, although tellers may not actually be aware that they are making up part of the story. The parlor game of telephone relies upon the inability of people to recall and to relate properly what they have just heard.

Secondhand experiential stories are simply the firsthand stories of others that we have heard and remembered. Usually the indices to them are much less rich, much more specific. These stories often have clear points and are frequently remembered in terms of the points that they are intended to illustrate.

Culturally Common Stories

The culturally common story is not as obvious a category as the other four. We get culturally common stories from our environment. No one person tells them, and no one person makes them up. They are pervasive nevertheless. Below are two examples of culturally common stories, again taken from a movie, this time *Casablanca*:

YVONNE:	Will I see you tonight?
RICK:	I never make plans that far ahead.

CAPTAIN RENAULT:	And what in heaven's name brought you to Casablanca?
RICK:	My health. I came to Casablanca for the waters.
RENAULT:	Waters? What waters? We're in the desert.
RICK:	I was misinformed.

Both of the above statements by Rick are stories. Obviously, they are not your usual kind of story and to all outward appearances seem to be merely tag lines that are meant to be funny. But the reason one can speak in such a shorthand and humorous way and be understood not only by one's listener but also by a movie audience is that both statements are simply cryptic ways of referring to well-known stories, stories that the movie writers, in this instance, are assuming their audience knows.

Culturally common stories are usually referred to rather than told. For example, the following one-liner from the Woody Allen movie *Love and Death* is a reference to stories that we all know about insurance salesmen:

> *There are worse things in life than death—If you have ever spent an evening with an insurance salesman, you know what I mean.*

The commonality of our culture's views of insurance salesmen allows us to communicate in this way about insurance salesmen. The culturally common story here is simply that insurance salesmen are boring and painful to listen to.

To a large extent, a story's usefulness depends upon how much of the original detail has remained over time. An ossified story is useful as a rule applicable to many specific situations but not to all the situations which in its original form it might have been. A story still present in its full form in memory can be applied to a variety of situations but not necessarily as widely as a distilled story. Memory richness versus memory succinctness is a trade-off between multiple labels, or ways of referring to a story, with general applicability and few labels with specific applicability.

On the other hand, distilling a story sufficiently gives back its general applicability. A proverb is an ossified distilled story, but it has lost so much of its original detail that it needs the hearer to supply some detail. Thus a proverb can be seen to carry with it great wisdom because the hearer has supplied the specific referents to the general frame which is the proverb. This is the case with the *I Ching,* a collection of ossified distilled stories that seem to contain great wisdom when one adds one's own details. The following, a comment on the Hsu hexagram, is a passage from the *I Ching:*

2. The second line, undivided, shows its subject waiting on the sand (of the mountain stream). He will (suffer) the small (injury of) being spoken (against), but in the end there will be good fortune.
3. The third line, undivided, shows its subject in mud (close by the stream). He thereby invites the approach of injury.
4. The fourth line, divided, shows its subject waiting in (the place of) blood. But he will get out of the cavern.

In some sense, much of what we consider to be creativity is no more than the adaptation of a story from one domain for use in another. Taking a neutral story and adding detail can also be considered to be creative; indeed, many new stories for television are written in precisely this way. We are also creative when we understand the stories of others by adding details of our own lives that allow us to read more into a story than may have been put there by the author. In each case, the story adapted from the original is now a story in its own right and can be stored in memory with new indices.

The opposite side of the coin is that some stories get told in their least detailed form, making them understandable only to those who already know them. Such stories can become so short that they do not in any way appear to be stories, and in some obvious sense, they are not stories. Maybe the best way to illustrate what I mean here is by a well-known joke.

> The prisoners in a maximum-security prison had little to entertain themselves with so they told jokes to each other. But they had long since run out of new jokes to tell, so they simply numbered the jokes and yelled out the numbers. A new prisoner hearing "forty-two," "sixty-four," "one hundred eight" being yelled down the hall with raucous laughter following each number asked about what was happening, and it was explained to him. He asked if he could try it, and his cellmate said sure. He hollered "thirty-six," and nothing happened. Next he tried "twenty-seven" and still nothing. The new prisoner finally asked his cellmate what was wrong, and he replied, "You didn't tell them so well."

Is "forty-two" a story? Of course it is, and it isn't. It doesn't sound like a story; it's more the name of a story, so to speak. In some sense, every story is simply the name of a longer story. No one tells all the details of any story, so each story is shortened. How much shortening has to take place until there is no story left? A story shortened so that it ceases to be understood is no longer a story, but what is understandable to one person may not be understandable to another, so it is clear that "story" is a relative term. In any case, as long as it *is* understood, it remains a story. For this reason, there are some very short stories.

One of my favorite short stories comes from the movie *Manhattan*:

YALE: She's gorgeous.

ISAAC: She's seventeen. I'm forty-two, and she's seventeen.

More needn't be said here because the point has been made without saying more. We all know stories or can imagine stories involving the complexity of a relationship between a forty-two-year-old man and a seventeen-year-old girl. Of course, the movie goes on to tell exactly that story. The referent here is to a story we all know which then serves as the basis for the new story we are about to hear.

Why We Tell Stories

People can be viewed in some sense as repositories of stories. Old people most obviously tell the same story again and again, but many people have a number of stories to tell and take the occasion to tell them whenever that opportunity arises. When we look at particular stories, we can think about the points that they express and attempt to understand why a given story may have come to mind at any specific point in a conversation, but particular stories don't really matter. The issue here is why do we tell stories at all? What is interesting about stories? What is the point of telling a story instead of just saying what we want to say directly? In order to understand why we tell stories, we must identify the goals that people have in a conversation. Because stories are usually told to someone and not to an empty room, no story commonly satisfies only one goal. Rather, tellers may have one goal for themselves and another goal for their listeners.

In broad terms, then, we usually have one of three basic reasons for telling stories. First, we may derive some satisfaction from telling a story. Second, we may derive satisfaction from the effect we believe, or convince ourselves to believe, that a story will have on our listener. Or third, we sometimes tell a story because of the effect we believe that the story will have on the conversation itself. We can categorize our intentions in storytelling as follows:

> **Category 1:** Me-goals (the intentions that storytellers have with respect to themselves)
> **Category 2:** You-goals (the intentions that storytellers have with respect to others)
> **Category 3:** Conversational goals (the intentions that storytellers have with respect to the conversation itself)

Me-goals

The first category, me-goals, includes our intentions in telling stories to satisfy our own personal goals. When we tell stories to others, we often do so entirely because of our own goals for ourselves that are satisfied by the listener paying attention in the desired way. Tellers can have five intentions with respect to themselves: to achieve catharsis, to get attention, to win approval, to seek advice, or to describe themselves. Several intentions are frequently present at once. For example, imagine a man at a party where he sees a woman he wants to meet. He begins to tell a story that is designed immediately to get the attention of the group he is talking to and ultimately to get the woman's approval for his being sensitive. The story he chooses is self-descriptive and tells about a horrible situation that allows him to become emotional in the telling. As a result of telling the story, he feels better, but, more important, the woman in the group notices him, likes his emotional qualities, and feels that she can tell him something that will help him in his predicament. We can see that the teller's intentions fall into all categories.

In the following scene from the movie *The Apartment*, a character tells a story to prevent herself from committing suicide on Christmas. Her intention, in other words, is cathartic:

> *I think I'm going to give it all up. Why do people have to love people, anyway? I don't want it. What do you call it when somebody keeps getting smashed up in automobile*

accidents? That's me with men. I've been jinxed from the word go—first time I was ever kissed was in a cemetery. I was fifteen—we used to go there to smoke. His name was George—he threw me over for a drum majorette. I just have this talent for falling in love with the wrong guy in the wrong place at the wrong time. The last one was manager of a finance company, back home in Pittsburgh—they found a little shortage in his accounts, but he asked me to wait for him—he'll be out in 1965. So I came to New York and moved in with my sister and her husband—he drives a cab. They sent me to secretarial school, and I applied for a job with Consolidated—but I flunked the typing test—oh, I can type up a storm, but I can't spell. So they gave me a pair of white gloves and stuck me in an elevator—that's how I met Jeff—Oh, God, I'm so fouled up. What am I going to do now? Maybe he does love me—only he doesn't have the nerve to tell his wife.

The teller of this story needs to explain why she has reached an emotional crisis and doesn't seem especially interested in how the listener feels about what she says. Of course, we can't know for sure what her attitude toward the listener is. She may intend to elicit an emotional response from him, and his reaction to her, if sympathetic, may affect how successfully cathartic the telling of her story is. But either way, telling her story attempts to accomplish the hoped-for catharsis.

In response to her story, the listener offers a story of his own which falls not into the me-goals but into the you-goals category, a story told to have an effect on someone else. He tells the story seemingly to display some kind of feeling—"We are in this together"— for the teller of the original story:

I know how you feel, Miss Kubelik. You think it's the end of the world—but it's not, really. I went through exactly the same thing myself. Well, maybe not exactly—I tried to do it with a gun. She was the wife of my best friend, and I was mad for her. But I knew it was hopeless—so I decided to end it all. I went to a pawnshop and bought a .45 automatic and drove up to Eden Park—do you know Cincinnati? Anyway, I parked the car and loaded the gun—well, you read in the papers all the time that people shoot themselves, but believe me, it's not that easy—I mean, how do you do it? Here or here or here [with cocked finger, he points to his temple, mouth, and chest]. You know where I finally shot myself? [Indicates knee.] Here. While I was sitting there, trying to make my mind up, a cop stuck his head in the car, because I was illegally parked—so I started to hide the gun under the seat, and it went off—pow! Took me a year before I could bend my knee—but I got over the girl in three weeks. She still lives in Cincinnati, has four kids, gained twenty pounds—she—Here's the fruitcake. [Shows it to her under Christmas tree.] And you want to see my knee?

Within the me-goal category, we also tell stories expressly to get attention. One way to grab attention is to tell stories that will interest the group one is involved with at the moment. The teller of attention-getting stories often wants to impress listeners as being very funny or sympathetic or honest or powerful, etc. The teller may have the allied intention of entertaining the listener so that the teller can continue telling stories and thus remain the center of attention. In the following story from Tennessee Williams's *The Glass Menagerie*, a woman tries to win the approval of a gentleman caller and in the process draw attention to the virtues of her exceedingly shy daughter:

> *It's rare for a girl as sweet an' pretty as Laura to be domestic! But Laura is, thank heavens, not only pretty but also very domestic. I'm not at all. I never was a bit. I never could make a thing but angel food cake. Well, in the South we had so many servants. Gone, gone, gone. All vestige of gracious living! Gone completely! I wasn't prepared for what the future brought me. All of my gentlemen callers were sons of planters and so of course I assumed that I would be married to one and raise my family on a large piece of land with plenty of servants. But man proposes—and woman accepts the proposal! To vary that old saying a little bit—I married no planter! I married a man who worked for the telephone company! That gallantly smiling gentleman over there! . . . A telephone man who fell in love with long-distance! Now he travels and I don't even know where!*

We tell stories to describe ourselves not only so others can understand who we are but also so we can understand ourselves. Telling our stories allows us to compile our personal mythology, and the collection of stories we have compiled is to some extent who we are, what we have to say about the world, and tells the world the state of our mental health.

To some extent, our stories, because they are shaped by memory processes that do not always have their basis in hard fact, are all fictions. But these fictions are based on real experiences and are our only avenue to those experiences. We interpret reality through our stories and open our realities up to others when we tell our stories. We can also tell stories to escape reality, to paint a picture that is more like what we would like to have happened than what actually happened. But, it should be understood, this is to some extent what we do all the time with stories. The extent to which we can stretch reality and still be considered mentally healthy is not all that clear.

Our intentions in telling self-descriptive stories are often complex. Our goals with respect to ourselves and to others are sometimes complementary and sometimes contradictory. One might, for example, tell a story hoping to rekindle a friendship in the eyes of another but in reality attempting to manipulate the other for personal gain.

Because telling a self-descriptive story often satisfies at least two goals, me-goals and you-goals, and often the conversational-goal as well, the self-descriptive prototype is both common and important. People have a great many things to say about themselves for a great many reasons and thus have many stories to illustrate various aspects of their personalities, their points of view, and their hopes and their problems. As we saw in the story sequence from *The Apartment*, the description of the woman's problem reminded her listener of a similar problem in his own life. His quickness in telling the story suggests that he has told the story before. People love to match stories, communicating by having similar experiences to relate. For this reason, we tend to tell the same stories over and over until we fashion a stock story which illustrates a point about ourselves effectively. The man, however, also intended to make a further point to the woman about the resilience of human beings and thus to prevent her suicide.

In the following story from *Long Day's Journey into Night*, a man tries to justify choosing a low-cost state sanitarium for his ill son by recounting events from his own childhood that shaped his character. Again, his story seems to be well rehearsed to illustrate a basic point about himself:

> *We never had clothes enough to wear, nor food enough to eat. Well, I remember one Thanksgiving, or maybe it was Christmas, when some Yank in whose house Mother had been scrubbing gave her a dollar extra for a present, and on the way home she spent it all on food. . . . It was in those days I learned to be a miser. A dollar was worth so much then. And once you've learned a lesson, it's hard to unlearn it. You have to look for bargains. If I took this state farm sanitarium for a good bargain, you'll have to forgive me. The doctors did tell me it's a good place.*

Another example, but much shorter, of telling a stock story to describe oneself occurs in the movie *A Thousand Clowns*:

MURRAY: You're going to have to stop crying.

SANDRA: I cry all the time, and I laugh at the wrong places in the movies.

The story—crying all the time, laughing at the wrong places in the movies—is an example of a personal myth derived from our experiences and confirmed again in the telling. Here, the story has been reduced again and again until only its essential message remains.

The next story from *All the President's Men* is another example of a self-descriptive narrative. Woodward and Bernstein are in their car, parked outside the house of yet another CREEP employee on their list. The frustrations of working for a newspaper are getting to Bernstein. He attempts to make sense of his present work by remembering an incident early on in his career:

> *My first day as a copyboy I was sixteen and wearing my only grown-up suit—it was cream colored. At two-thirty, the head copyboy comes running up to me and says, "My God, haven't you washed the carbon paper yet? If it's not washed by three, it'll never be dry for tomorrow." And I said, "Am I supposed to do that?" and he said, "Absolutely, it's crucial." So I run around and grab all the carbon paper from all the desks and take it to the men's room. I'm standing there washing it, and it's splashing all over me, and the editor comes in to take a leak, and he says, "What the fuck do you think you're doing?" And I said, "It's two-thirty. I'm washing the carbon paper."*
> *I'm beginning to feel like I never stopped.*

We also acquire personal myths from our parents, teachers, friends, enemies—in short, from anyone who tells us stories about ourselves. Listening to and telling these stories has an effect on memory which makes it almost impossible not to believe the stories that describe who we are. The following stories are examples of self-descriptive myths initiated by other family members; thus, the process of telling begins with a you-goal intention, and the retelling involves the me-goal intention. In the first example from Elizabeth Stone's *Black Sheep and Kissing Cousins*, Peter Mott, a nuclear physicist, attempts to explain why he and his sister defined themselves according to their mother's story.

> *My mother's father, whom she always saw as a comforter, had died. . . . Then her two sisters died—one of scarlet fever and the other of spilling boiling water on herself. Then my grandmother, my mother's mother, died of a heart attack. My mother was pregnant with my sister at this time, and so they named my sister Blanche, which had been my grandmother's name. In fact my grandmother's maiden name was Kane, and they named my sister Blanche Kane Mott. . . . My mother was in terrible shape. . . . She was hospitalized—she had a nervous breakdown—and there was a nursemaid to take care of my sister. . . . My mother could never bring herself to use the name Blanche with my sister, so she called her Missy. It was just too much, the death was too much and the daughter was too much. Perhaps my sister was just too much of a reminder. But anyhow, my sister was the one in the family who could do nothing right. As a consequence, she was raised as if she were dirt, or incompetent, or terrible. Growing up, I didn't consciously recognize how my sister was being devalued, but one of the most extraordinary aspects of all this family stuff is that for most of my adult life, I dealt with my sister as my mother had dealt with her. As for me . . . I was "the Golden Boy." The doctor told my mother to have another child to make her well. I was that child, and I could do no wrong.*

In the following passage from *The Pawnbroker*, the narrator tells a story about himself, but he also has a conversational goal in telling the story—to respond to a question. Sol Nazerman has been a survivor of the death camps for twenty years. His wife and children died at Auschwitz. Before the war, he was a professor at the University of Cracow, but now he runs a pawnshop in Spanish Harlem. One evening, his apprentice asks Sol, "How come you people come to business so naturally?" Sol responds:

> *You begin . . . you begin with several thousand years during which you have nothing except a great bearded legend. Nothing else. You have not land to grow food on. No land on which to hunt. Not enough time in one place to have a geography, or an army, or a land-myth. You have only a little brain in your head and this bearded legend to sustain you . . . convince you there is something special about you, even in your poverty. But this little brain . . . that is the real key. With it you obtain a small piece of cloth, wool, silk, cotton—it doesn't matter. You take this cloth, and you cut it in two and sell the two pieces for a penny or two more than you paid for the one. With this*

*money, then, you buy a slightly larger piece of cloth. Which perhaps may be cut into
three pieces. And sold for three pennies profit. You must never succumb to buying an
extra piece of bread at this point. Or a toy for your child. Immediately you must repeat the process. And so you continue until there is no longer any temptation to dig in
the earth and grow food. No longer any desire to gaze at limitless land which is in your
name. You repeat this process over and over for centuries. And then, all of a sudden,
you discover you have a mercantile heritage. You are known as a merchant. You're also
known as a man with secret resources, usurer, pawnbroker, a witch, or what have you.*

  But by then it is instinct. Do you understand?

We tell stories like this in order to express our feelings, to get out our anger, or to
explain ourselves in some fundamental way. These stories become who we are and telling
them allows us to feel these feelings that define us yet again. We avoid telling stories that
evoke feelings that we do not care to relive.

You-goals

Obviously, the above story contains many unspoken stories, but unspoken stories, as other
survivors of Auschwitz have testified, change substantively in memory or disappear altogether. The survivors of the Holocaust tell stories to preserve their memories for themselves
and for their listeners. Their intentions in recounting what happened to them at the hands
of the Nazis fall within both the me-goal and the you-goal categories.

  As we have already seen, when we tell stories about ourselves our goals are often internal and difficult to determine, but when we tell stories intended for other people our
goals tend to fall within five categories:

> to illustrate a point
> to make the listener feel some way or another
> to tell a story that transports the listener
> to transfer some piece of information in our head into the head of the listener
> to summarize significant events

Most stories have a point, or at least are supposed to have one. What exactly a point
is, is difficult to define, but we know when one is missing. In such cases, we ask *What's your
point?* We tell stories, then, to illustrate points we wish to make or to help listeners achieve
their goals. In an essay in which he reflects on the costs of personal success, Tennessee
Williams illustrates his point with a story.

*I lived on room service. But in this, too, there was disenchantment. Sometime between
the moment when I ordered dinner over the phone and when it was rolled into my living room like a corpse on a rubber-wheeled table, I lost all interest in it. Once I ordered a sirloin steak and a chocolate sundae, but everything was so cunningly disguised*

on the table that I mistook the chocolate sauce for gravy and poured it over the sirloin steak. . . .

I got so sick of hearing people say, "I loved your play!" that I could not say thank you anymore. I choked on the words and turned rudely away from the usually sincere person. I no longer felt any pride in the play itself but began to dislike it, probably because I felt too lifeless inside ever to create another. . . .

This curious condition persisted about three months, till late spring, when I decided to have another eye operation mainly because of the excuse it gave me to withdraw from the world behind a gauze mask. . . .

Well, the gauze mask served a purpose. While I was resting in the hospital the friends whom I had neglected or affronted in one way or another began to call on me and now that I was in pain and darkness, their voices seemed to have changed. . . .

When the gauze mask was removed, I found myself in a readjusted world. I checked out of the handsome suite at the first-class hotel, packed my papers and a few incidental belongings, and left for Mexico, an elemental country where you can quickly forget the false dignities and conceits imposed by success, a country where vagrants innocent as children curl up to sleep on the pavements and human voices, especially when their language is not familiar to the ear, are soft as birds'. My public self, that artifice of mirrors, did not exist here and so my natural being was resumed.

A second reason for telling stories with you-goals is to make the listener feel some way or other, in other words, to tell an affective story. Trying to get someone to fall in love with you or to make a special exception in your pathetic case or simply to feel better is typical of the affective intention. We can, of course, have goals for both ourselves and others in a story we tell; sometimes the distinction can be confusing. However, stories that are intended to make somebody feel something are very common and very important. They may also make the teller feel something as well, often unintentionally.

In a passage from *Below the Line*, the narrator recalls telling an affective story that failed to achieve the effect he wanted:

One day—this is how I got in the worst trouble—my baby was crying. We didn't have no money, no food, so I went to the grocery store. I told the owner—he knew that I had boughten there before—I told the owner, I was crying, I told him, "Please can you do me a favor, give me a dozen eggs, a loaf of bread, a gallon of milk, and I'll pay you back in the morning." He told me no. So I went back home and I took out my gun and I went back. I said, "Now give it to me." Then I went back home. Within fifteen minutes they locked me up, but I didn't care. I did it for my kids.

For reasons similar to telling affective stories, we tell transportive stories to make others experience certain sensations, feelings, or attitudes vicariously. One way to achieve this effect is to be clever enough in our descriptive capabilities in order to make listeners come to view the scene the way we want them to. Usually, we have some additional purpose in mind when we tell a transportive story; nevertheless, stories are so often heavily laden with description of a transportive nature, we should recognize the transportive intention independently of other motivations. In the play *That Championship Season*, a high school basketball team gets together for a reunion with their old coach. The coach reminisces:

> You were a rare and a beautiful thing, boys . . . a miracle to see people play beautifully together . . . like when I was a boy . . . long time past . . . the whole town would come together. We'd have these huge picnics, great feasts of picnics. My father ran the only bank in town. An elegant man. Bach was played in his house. He quoted Shakespeare, "To be or not to be, that's the question." Shoulders like a king . . . he carried me on his back into the freezing, God, yes, waters of the lake. So clear you could see the white pebbles on the bottom. Gone now, all gone, vanished. Lake, picnic grounds, gone now. All concrete and wires and glass now. Used car lots now. Phil's trucks came and took it away. . . . Jesus, I can still see buckets of ice cream . . . great red slabs of beef . . . kites, yes, the sky full of blue and red kites, men playing horseshoes, big silver pails of beer, in the late afternoon the men would dive from the high rocks, so high they made you dizzy to look down. I watched my father dive and turn and glisten in the sun, falling like a bird falls, and knife the water so clean as to leave only ripples.

We have similar intentions in telling stories that summarize significant events, i.e., historical synopses, and in telling stories that transfer information. Tellers want their listeners to know whatever it is they are telling them. Teachers want their students to know certain information; parents want children to know how to behave, how to play safely, etc.; and people who are talking to one another want their friends and associates to know about their lives or about various events in the world. All of them want to transfer some piece of knowledge in their heads into the heads of their listeners. Historical synopsis is a special case of transfer where the teller must reduce a tremendous amount of information into a form small enough to be absorbed.

Conversational Goals

The above stories have been relayed without the context of a surrounding conversation. When we tell stories within a conversation, the goals that need to be satisfied are more complex. The following set of intentions, unlike the others we have discussed, has nothing to do with the content of the conversation. People do not always speak to communicate some specific piece of information or remark. Sometimes we speak solely to keep on being able to speak or simply to get the general topic of the story on the floor for discussion. For example, we might tell a story about a problem in a particular relationship if we wanted to discuss relationships in general. Our intention, then, would be *topic opening*. On the other hand, we might open a new topic in order to close off or avoid another; in this case, our intention would be *topic changing*. We also tell stories to revive conversation. For example, in airplanes two people seated next to each other often tell stories for the sole purpose of having something to do during the flight. When the conversation bogs down, one of the speakers will tell a story to *continue* the conversation. So that the conversational partner won't go away or talk to someone else, often the speaker tells a story just to keep the conversation going.

A more significant but still in essence structural part of the story-telling process in a conversation involves the relationship that exists between the partners in a conversation. When someone tells a story, he or she expects conversational politeness, a response of some sort. Therefore, when you tell a story in turn, you may have no point in mind other than to be *responsive*.

One of the goals of history synopsis is often conversational as well. Above, we saw an example of history synopsis told to satisfy the you-goals, but often these stories are re- sponses to direct requests for stories, rather than spontaneous reminders. When we ask certain questions, we expect stories as answers. We associate stories with life events such as the story of our choosing a college, the story of our first job, the story of the birth of our child, the story of our first love, and the story of our marriage. Since these stories have usu- ally been told many times, they often have rehearsed and well-planned versions. Sometimes we get the whole story, and sometimes we get partial or cryptic stories. Below is an example from *Manhattan* of a cryptic yet revealing shorthand depiction of an obviously much larger history.

MARY: Why did you get divorced?

ISAAC: My wife left me for another woman.

Another category of responsive story is the argument. When you tell a story that implies something is wrong with yourself, you may hope for a story that disputes your point. Sometimes, you make an assertion, however, without intending to stir an *argumentative* response but do so anyway. Of course, not all arguments are unfriendly; mutual storytelling, even in the form of an argument, can make the storytellers feel closer to each other.

Stories can also be used as a defense. Sometimes we tell a story to *distract* our listen- ers from what they want to discuss. Many times we tell stories to avoid whatever it is we should be talking about, as a defense against what other people are liable to say. We dis- tract our conversational partners by giving them a range of other things to think about. Such stories are often made up on the fly, but sometimes they have been previously con- structed and are retrieved because they relate superficially to the question at hand. The goal of such a story is to avoid telling a different story. The reasons for distraction/obfuscation may be as simple as maintaining conversational sociability to avoid an argument or a pain- ful or perhaps embarrassing subject. Obversely, the reason may be psychologically complex. Someone with a checkered past might obfuscate when relating certain experiences if fear- ful of losing a friendship. Similarly, we may obfuscate to protect a family member or our- selves if we perceive a question as a threat. An example of this kind of story from *A Thou- sand Clowns* follows. In this story, Murray tells a joke to avoid being sad about something else, to avoid telling the story he should be telling:

SANDRA: Which job did you get?

MURRAY: I shall now leave you breathless with this strange and wondrous tale of this sturdy lad's adventures today in downtown Oz. Picture if you will, me. I am walking on East Fifty-first Street about an hour ago practicing how to say "I am sorry" with a little style.

SANDRA: Sorry about what?

MURRAY: Oh, not for anything—just rehearsing, you know how you are walking down the street talking to yourself, and suddenly you say something to yourself out loud? So I said: "I'm sorry"—and this fellow walking by, a complete stranger, said: "That's all right, Mac," and goes right on. He immediately forgave me. Now five o'clock rush hour in midtown, you could say "Sir, your hair is on fire," and they wouldn't even hear you. So I decided to test the whole thing out scientifically. I just stood there saying "I'm sorry" to everyone who came by. . . . Of course I got a few funny looks—but seventy-five percent of them forgave me. . . . I could run up on the roof right now, and I would say I'm sorry and a half a million people would say, "That's OK, just see that you don't do it again."

SANDRA: You didn't take any of the jobs.

MURRAY: I'm sorry. I'm very sorry. Damn it, lady, that was a beautiful apology. You got to love a guy who apologizes so well. I rehearsed it. Oh, Sandy, that's the most you should expect from life—a really good apology for all the things you won't get.

Conclusion

The various combinations of our intentions affect the processes that transform the gists of the stories that we have in our memories into the actual stories that we tell. We don't remember the stories that we tell or hear, in the sense that we cannot recall all the words. We extract gists when we listen to stories, and we recast gists when we transform them into actual stories. These memory processes—extraction of gists from stories for storage in memory and transformation of gists into stories that express an intention—are fundamental to the thinking process. How these processes work is the subject of later chapters.

I might add that the most you can expect from an intelligent being is a really good story. To get human beings to be intelligent means getting them to have stories to tell and having them hear and perhaps use the stories of others. Now, by stories here, recall that I mean having a set of interesting things that one has already thought up and stored, ready to say when necessary. There are other aspects to intelligence that come into play to finish the process to make something that is intelligent seem very intelligent. The first is storytelling ability. How a story is told greatly affects the receptivity of the listener. Good storytellers will make their stories seem interesting and that interestingness makes the stories more memorable and hence more useful to an understander. Good storytellers cause positive responses in their listeners. Thus, good storytellers seem very intelligent.

But intelligence is also manifest in the content of what one has to say. And new content, innovative ideas are seen by listeners as marking intelligence as well. We like inventive stories, even when told badly, because their new content excites us, and we deem the tellers of those stories to be intelligent as well.

Whatever the reason for telling a story, and whatever the origin of the content of the story, the concept here is a rather simple one. Intelligence means having stories to tell. If those stories are told well or are innovative in some way, so much the better, but a being must have a set of stories and tell them for the right reasons at the right time in order to be intelligent.

It would seem, then, that the cliché "Experience is the best teacher" is quite true. We learn from experience, or to put this more strongly, what we learn *are* experiences. The educational point that follows from this is that we must teach cases and the adaptation of cases by telling stories, not teach rules and the use of rules by citing rules. We may never find ourselves in a situation where the rules we were taught apply exactly. Ordinarily, we find answers for ourselves. Lots of stories and cases help, but methods of applying these stories and cases, especially in places where they weren't originally supposed to apply, help more.

 For Discussion:

1. What is a story? What isn't a story? What marks the boundary between a story and some other form of communicating information? Is there another form of communicating information?
2. What are some official stories you know? Do you remember learning them? How much of what you know about the world comes through official stories?
3. Is Schank right when he says, "Intelligence means having stories to tell"?

 For Fact-Finding, Research, and Writing:

1. Find two news stories on the same topic from opposing newspapers (for example, newspapers from different countries who oppose each other's policies). In what ways are stories used to support different interpretations of the event in question?
2. What does the progress between Hana's storytelling ability at age two and age four suggest about how we learn? Using an academic database, list two articles that deal with the importance of storytelling ability to cognitive development.
3. Research the differences and similarities between the use of storytelling in psychological therapy and storytelling as it is practiced on television talk shows.

Karen Brennan,
"Dream, Memory, Story, and the Recovery of Narrative"

Winner of the Associated Writing Programs 1990 short fiction award, Karen Brennan is author of *Here on Earth, Wild Desire,* and *The Garden in Which I Walk. Being with Rachel: A Personal Story of Memory and Survival,* from which the piece below is excerpted, was published in 2002. She teaches in the Warren Wilson Master of Fine Arts program for writers and is an Associate Professor at the University of Utah.

 Before You Read:

Do you remember your dreams? Do you think they ever tell you anything about yourself or your life that is significant or useful?

Dream, Memory, Story, and the Recovery of Narrative

Karen Brennan

I want to begin with a dream I had last summer in Mexico. Because it was a dream with two parts to it, I entitled it: Dead Girl in Two Parts. What follows is a direct transcription from my journal. Part I: A girl in a school uniform falls from a ledge, from between the arches of a wrought-iron railing, to her death. I am sitting on the ledge and my daughter Rachel may be there as well. The girl falls, I realize, because she is smaller than the arches, and (I think at the time) the wind blows her off. She is simply swept through the railing. When I look down I see her little pile of school clothes—it seems to be all that's left of her. I feel regretful but not horrified.

In the second part of this dream we—me, Rachel, and the little girl—are at the seashore, sitting on the beach, close to where the waves lap up. Suddenly a large wave washes over the little girl and kills her. Rachel and I look at her face staring up at us from beneath the water. It is a distinctive image, the face of the girl, eyes closed, under the shallow water, which moves softly over her. I feel more than regret now; I feel guilt. I feel that one of us (Rachel) should have been more attentive. There is a sense that Rachel had been in charge of this girl. I am therefore a little annoyed with Rachel's irresponsibility, but this isn't a major annoyance. It's more like the resigned feeling I get in real life when someone's done something wrong (as if, for example, Rachel wrecks the car I give her), and I realize, while it's futile to make a big deal over it, I'm nonetheless pissed.

Approximately a month after I transcribed this dream in my journal I received a phone call in my Mexico flat at 6 A.M. informing me that my twenty-five-year-old daughter Rachel had been in a motorcycle accident and that she was presently in a deep coma in Denver General Hospital's intensive care unit. Her friend, the driver, was fine, but Rachel's CAT scan, the informant, a neurosurgeon, told me, was very very ugly.

By 11 that morning I was on a first-class flight from Leon to Denver, sitting next to a woman who owned a travel agency in Guanajuato. She had been pretty, I remember, dark-haired, dressed in cream-colored slacks and a white blouse. She wore a tiny silver watch on her wrist, which, because I had misplaced my own somehow, I had recourse to consult now and again. She was on her way to Dallas for a romantic weekend with her husband. We had, what seems to me in retrospect, a pleasant conversation. I told her about Rachel's accident; she consoled me. I did not cry. I spoke reasonably, I thought at the time, having all the while that bizarre sensation that I was speaking someone else's words about someone else's daughter. I suppose I must have been in shock. I refused the first-class meal.

I remember that as we conversed my mind seemed to race along another track, somewhat at odds with our conversation. I imagined Rachel, even at that moment, woozily coming too, rubbing her eyes, her (perhaps) sore shoulders. I envisioned seeing her fully awake, out of the intensive care unit by the time I would arrive, and I planned her homecoming, her few weeks of rest. I even went so far as to imagine my sudden memory of this time—on the first-class flight to Denver next to the woman in the cream-colored slacks, when I was terrified out of my mind. How amusing it would be in retrospect! How unfounded this terror, this unreasonable refusal of first-class food!

As it turned out, what was unfounded were these wishful thoughts. And in the months that have followed that 18 August day I have come to have a terrible familiarity with the way the mind—my mind—makes up comforting stories, this narrative propensity akin to the instinct for survival and just as precarious.

Rachel continued in her coma for two months, more or less. I say more or less because, as it was explained to me, her injury was diffuse—literally, a diffuse axonal injury—and so her wake-up would be diffuse.

But when I arrived in Denver that first evening I knew nothing of brain injuries, of axons, of intercranial pressures, of ventilation or tracheotomies, of motor strips, frontal lobes, aphasic disorders, or unilateral neglects. I knew nothing of comas. What I knew was what I witnessed in the ICU unit, like a particularly grisly episode from "ER": bodies being whirled by on stretchers or corpselike in beds, hooked up to monitors, a nurse with a clipboard positioned at the end of each.

Rachel was one of these bodies. She had a tube running down one nostril (nagogastric) for feeding, another in her mouth (intubation) for breathing. A little semi-circle of her hair had been shaved, above the forehead on the left side, from which protruded a three-inch metal bolt. This was to measure her intercranial pressure. All the monitors flashed above the head of her bed on a large green screen: heart, respiration, blood oxygen, blood pressure, and intercranial pressure.

Rachel's eyes were closed. She had a small scrape on her cheek. The toes of her right foot were badly burned and grotesquely blistered. Occasionally, she moved, but these movements were not reassuring; rather, they were the unnatural movements of one who has severe brain damage called, in med-speak, posturing. At this stage Rachel's postures were the most severe variety—decerebrate—indicating damage at a deep level of the cortex. They consisted of Rachel flexing her body and limbs rigidly into an extended position, her hands and feet turned inward in a bizarre way. Every time she postured, her intercranial pressures rose, meaning that the fluid in her brain was increasing to a dangerous level. Eventually, another half-moon of hair would be shaved on the other side of her brow and a drainage tube inserted to draw off the excess fluid and blood.

But that evening, the evening I first saw her in her intensive care cubicle with the tubes and drains and breathing steadily through the ventilator, her intercranial pressures were holding their own. I held her hand for a long while, and then I went outside to smoke a cigarette.

Denver General Hospital is called, not so jokingly, the Gun and Knife Club. Some of its members—gangsters with cryptic faces and oversized jeans—smoked cigarettes nearby. In the orange lights I spotted and fixated on a little crop of dying zinnias. They seemed to be an important, if obvious, metaphor. Some had lost their petals; their color was drained in the artificial light. They were in concrete beds. A litter of cigarette butts surrounded their stalks. My thoughts were disorganized, I realized at the time—I had no story to tell myself, no future I could conceive of without horror. At which point a wheezing woman rolling an oxygen tank bummed a smoke from me. She was homeless, she explained; she had been evicted from her apartment. Now she was almost out of oxygen. I gave her a cigarette and twenty bucks. I sat in the grass.

My thoughts were disorganized, and so I needed an idea. I recalled the Buddhist wisdom, that impermanence is the true nature of things, the Hindu adage that everything is maya, illusion, that those who are enlightened can pass their hands through the fabric of the world. It was then that it occurred to me that Rachel would be OK. I had been looking at the sky, at a particular formation of gray cloud, and at the moon, which was clear rimmed and precise—and it came to me. She'll be fine. It will go on, and it will change, and it will be fine. She will. I stubbed my cigarette and went back to the ICU unit. Around the bed next to hers, a group of doctors were "harvesting" a body—one of the Gun and Knife Club. The monitors were flat above the head of that bed, but Rachel's were beeping along—pulse 82, blood pressure 118 over 70, ICUs about 12. I held her hand. I kissed her. I began to talk to her as if she could hear, to call her back from wherever she was.

After the journal account of my dream of last summer—Dead Girl Dream in Two Parts—I had appended a few notes. I noted that this was an important dream, having been recalled with that special lucidity one attributes to dreams of significance. I wondered about the two parts, the two scenes of the dream, wondered which came first in the actual dream and wondered why two parts. Were the two parts of my title, for example, a simple reference to the two parts of the dream, or were they, in a Freudian ambiguity, literally two parts of the girl—physical or mental?

Accompanying my dream account and dream notes were a series of sketches. I sketched the arches of the railing through which the girl fell to her death, and I sketched the girl herself standing under an arch, a stick figure with a skirt. Then I sketched the relative positions of Rachel and myself on the ledge, behind the railing, looking down on the little pile of school clothes, which I also sketched. After my account of part 2 of my dream, I made only one sketch, which I labeled "dead girl's face under a wave." The girl's eyes were closed, her hair snaked around her head, the wave replicated in a series of quivering lines, not unlike the surreal bars of some prison. Interesting, I noted, that in both dream scenes there was some reference to prison, both in the wrought-iron railing and in the lines I drew to suggest the wave over the dead girl's face. I wrote: Why a rooftop? Why a ledge? Why a threesome? Why two scenes? Why Rachel? Why guilty? Why pissed?

According to my notes, I had apparently figured that the dream had to do with me foisting off some little girl part of myself, that I had been neglecting some self-care, that I was shirking some responsibility. But I was not satisfied with this glib reading—I had written, "but the dream seems more complex than this."

Coming upon this account of my dream after Rachel's accident, of course, I read it in a new light. Now the dream seemed, absolutely, to be a portent of some sort. Indeed, the sketch of the dead girl's face under the wave struck me as bearing an uncanny resemblance to Rachel's face in her coma, a coma that lasted, by the way, for a grueling two months. And weren't the lines of water moving across her face, in fact, a brilliant figure for the hazy boundary that separated us at this time, she in her world, me in mine? Such an interpretation defied all that was reasonable and yet, oddly, was the most "reasonable" of any I could come up with: that is to say, it was able to connect most of the disparate elements into something that cohered. On the other hand, it was an entirely "unreasonable" account. What Aristotle would call the probable impossible, more the material of fiction than "reality."

For in Freud's schematics of dream interpretation, doesn't the dreamer participate in the dream interpretation precisely to discover the latent content of her unconscious? Certainly, a portent would refute all that. The significance of a portent exists outside the dreamer, in both space and time. A portent conflates time and space, conflates, in Yeats's formulation, the dreamer and the dreamed.

Still, as I sat at Rachel's bedside, looking at her perhaps dreaming face, the monitors measuring the steady waves of her vital functions, I recalled my dream of the dead girl in two parts and wondered which part was me and which part Rachel. Since that first evening I continued to speak to her as if she could hear me. I told her her life's story over and over. What I couldn't remember, I invented. I felt that it was more important to deliver a coherent narrative than to be faithful to a disjunctive truth. Even though I value fragmentation, in all its forms, I felt that had I been lying there in some kind of netherworld, I would want a story that made sense, whose points a and b and c were nicely connected.

But whose story was it? I became, more than occasionally, confused. Parts of my own life mingled weirdly with my story of hers just as, during that time, the outside world seemed to take on the sensual attributes of this inside, hospital one. I spent, on the average, eight hours a day by—or more usually in—her bed, and so I suppose it was reasonable that during my infrequent ventures to that other world expresso machines would sound like the suctioning apparatus for her trach, that someone's beeper would send a rush of alarm through me.

Finally, she began to really awaken, her left eye cracked open to reveal a tiny, beautiful chink of blue iris now roving back and forth, to sounds, to light; and she began to move her left thumb over the knuckles of my hand in an actual caress, a response; and on one joyous afternoon she reached and pushed a strand of my hair behind my ear, taking the initiative (a higher brain function) in an activity that I had neglected as a matter of course. Finally and suddenly, when all these things and more happened with a rapidity that stunned me, having become accustomed to the tabula rasa of her sleeping, motionless face, our merging, far from loosening, seemed to intensify, at least in the mind of this dreamer. At home, in front of my medicine cabinet mirror, for example, my hand through my hair felt oddly like her hand, and in my own bed before sleep I felt my body assuming her positions, right arm locked upward against my cheek, fingers rigid and clenched.

And when she began to speak—her first sentence on 15 November was, gratifyingly, "I want my Mom"—you'd think that hearing her voice would deliver me to myself, but it didn't. She spoke in breathy whispers at first, and so did I. We spoke endearments and bodily discomforts, having to pee and having to move the covers over our shoulders. Around this time I felt lightheaded as I walked through the hospital corridors; it seemed to me the ground was shifting under my feet. Rachel's head lolled to one side; at that point she was unable to hold it erect.

> I might say: I love my mama. She is the one. Next to her everyone pales. That's the truth of it. But I'm too old for these feelings. I tell her this. She says, Oh who cares? Or I think she does. She is wearing a green sweater covered with white vines that are of the same fabric of the sweater, which is wool. In the rectangle of the door, which is blue and rough, there is a toilet. There is a white towel on a floor of many small tiles of many hues of blue. The grouting is not clean. She is standing in her bare feet in front of the medicine cabinet mirror, and it is a sorrow to me that I cannot see her reflection, only her right-side-up face, which is to me quite beautiful. She says, Oh I'm a vain old woman. Vain perhaps, Mama, I say.
>
> Sometimes she asks, How are you doing? How are you doing, Lou? Are you feeling good? I say, Totally good, Madre. I call her all names for mother or, that is, as many as I can get a hold of. I remember words, this is true, language is my strongest point.
>
> Matcha, I say, Why does everyone have to watch me pee? No one does, she says, see? I'm not watching. I'm brushing my teeth, I'm watching the brushing of my teeth. It's OK, Matcha, I say, you can watch me pee. You can give me a shower. You can snuggle with me at night when we hear the floor creak and someone who may be opening the door, only you say no.

As of this writing Rachel, after five and a half months of hospitalization, has been home for two months. Her language is completely intact; indeed, it is eloquent. Her sense of humor is as sharp as ever. She is attentive; she is perceptive; she is occasionally philosophical and frequently wise. Her most severe deficit—aside from some paralysis that affects the right side of her body and keeps her confined, for the moment, to a wheelchair—is her short-term memory. Although memory deficit is common in traumatic brain injuries (TBIs), Rachel's seems especially severe. There have been some small improvements, but she frequently cannot remember from one five-minute segment to the next. If, for example, I ask her fifteen minutes after dinner what she ate, she'll shrug and say in her wry fashion, "Who can remember?"

> 14 March 1996: "Dear Sweet Diary: I feel as though I'm waking up from a bad dream because I mean I don't know the difference between right or left. I mean I do, but I'm trying to simplify everything. Today I have been learning about myself. That is to say I'm learning about the details of my accident. So granted I may never ever walk again. My memory sucks. But I'm beginning to understand what happened to me and such. Except I have very little to do with, well what will I do in the future? Perhaps I will become a famous shoe tyer. But maybe not; maybe I will be quite ambitious. Maybe I will become a teacher like my madre. So I hope I'm well enough to conquer the world again."

Memory, according to Bergson, occupies the space between mind and body. It conveys mind to body and body to mind. It gives us our quality of life—makes possible, in other words, the narratives that keep our lives going forward to the next thing. If the thing is not *next* it loses its richness—isolated and unlinked to a history, it becomes meaningless, even ridiculous. Biologically and neurologically, we are creatures of context, of narrative.

Consider, for example, the activity of the neurons or brain cells. Unlike the body's cells, which divide and multiply, microcosmically illustrating the propagation of the species, neurons are systems of communication. Their most salient features are a clutch of dendrites, which branch out to receive information across the synapses between cells, and a single, long axon, which reaches to the synapse—literally the space between neurons—through which chemical and electrical information are conveyed to the next cell.

By nature, then, the activity of the neuron is narrative, metonymic, associative. The information conveyed by each neuron accumulates along a complex circuitry of neurons and produces a thought, a corresponding action in the mind-body. If the information that passes from neuron to neuron is somehow tampered with—if the transmitters or receptors are artificially altered by drugs or disease, for example—memory, at its very biological foundation, will be altered or even incapacitated.

> Her feet are covered with blue veins. Blue veins on a blue tiled floor. So many blues. Which kind of vein are you? I ask her. She is brushing her hair, which is brown; which flies up into the brush like TV static.

I keep having the same dream. I do not remember details. Try to remember, she says. Was there a wave? Was there wind? I think, I say. Was there a girl? Perhaps, I say. Everything is skewed a little to the left: the table, the chair with its black-and-white pictures of parasols and ladies, the overhead fan with its wide white wings. All to the left. Where am I? I say.

You are here, she says. She leans over and puts her mouth to my ear. Here. Her breath is hot, like a mirror glare. Like a glint on tin. I say, If not her, then what? and this makes me worry. But she says, don't worry, just enjoy everything for the time being. Just look at that little fly on the kitchen table having a sip of orange juice or listen to the car roll by outside or brush your hair, here Lou, brush your hair.

She both understands everything and doesn't understand a thing. She goes on as if all were normal. She hands me the brush. Then she puts on lipstick. Next she will put lipstick on me. Why would I want lipstick? I am thinking, but I love my mama.

Memory is always configured on a gap—to *re-member* suggests the forgetfulness, the loss upon which it is founded. This forgetfulness, too, has its biological equivalents in the neurological activity of the brain. Indeed, in this most complicated of operations, the electrical impulses received by each neuron are converted to chemicals—packets of neurotransmitters—which are able to diffuse across the synaptic gap and activate the electrical signal in the next neuron. The process of conversion itself, as well as the infinite number of variables in each neuron, point to what has vanished as well as to what can be retrieved, point to the loss of the Real (in the absolute, psychoanalytic sense) and the construction of a representation.

Narrative has been the business of my life for many years now, both as a teacher and writer of fiction, but it was not until Rachel's brain injury that I realized these biological correlatives. We are hard-wired into narrative; it is, I would go so far to say, the purpose and not merely the effect of memory. The account of my dream of the dead girl, for example, is presumably based on my memory of it—but this memory is, at best, a shaky representation of a neurochemical process whose sparks and ebbings are irretrievable (if not nonsensical). What is important, we've learned from Freud, is the representation itself, assembled from whatever fragments, into a story that is the very material that divulges, if we are attentive, unconscious wishes.

Even our interpretation of dreams reveals a wish to make sense of the fragmentary, to weave into story, into history, an event that, unconnected to the life, may be troubling. Why else would I suspend my disbelief in portents than that I yearn for narrative continuity, even in retrospect, something to explain, however mystically, the strange and terrible turn of my daughter's and my life? The narrative inclination takes precedent, in this example, over reason itself, over what we know to be sensible and "true" about human experience. Which inclines me to believe that these fictions we call narrative and memory are at the foundation of our beings.

The days are a daze. I like that sentence because it is so truthful. I say it's the one true thing I am feeling. This feeling, which is the urge to push away some part of the air from in front of my face. It would be risky, I know. Because behind that part of air, there are things I actually want to forget. Now that I've said it and the minute I say it I think, no that's not true. Because why? Because it isn't.

Most of the time I just float in. I laugh quite a bit. Things strike me funny, and I can feel my lips go way up over my teeth in a manner that is not very attractive. The photo of my great-grandfather hanging on the wall in a brown frame is really quite funny to me, for example, though I couldn't tell you why exactly. He is very faded, and maybe it's the fadedness of him that is so like my own idea of things these days. That we all exist in a vault. That inside the vault are scraps with no meaning—torn photographs, letters from people we don't know, receipts, single words, like jewelry.

You *are* my memory, Rachel tells me, and it's true. I remember the actual as well as I can, and what I don't remember I shamelessly invent. You got up, you brushed your teeth, your therapists came over, and you stood up; you walked with your walker; you made everyone laugh when you asked for a big-assed cup of coffee. You admired my outfit and said, "You've got it going on, girlfriend."

What will we do tomorrow? she worries. She has less tolerance for the uncertainty of the future than the rest of us. What do I have to do? she says. We make lists of questions and answers; we record her voice and her day's activities as they occur into a palm-sized device called a voice organizer; we plan. We talk. Together we assemble an imperfect representation, a narrative we can rely on nonetheless, one that compels us forward to the next thing.

In brain injury literature there are several pathological behaviors associated with short-term memory loss, and these behaviors, I was stunned to discover, correspond to narrative pitfalls and graces, that is to say, to the way in which we all make narrative texts. Perseveration is the inclination of the brain-injured patient to get stuck obsessively on one track and to thus repeat over and over this one-tracked concern. Perseveration—a word I find especially illuminating, to persevere too much, as I take it—reflects a rigidity on the part of the perseverator. A failure of imagination, a failure of metonymy, of association, free or otherwise. The perseverator can only repeat, sometimes in different words—Rachel, for example, is quite eloquent in her perseverations—and this repetition, while in some cases may reinforce a narrative, cannot of itself deliver a narrative. The perseverator suffers from too much focus and a surfeit of schemes. He is the student of writing who can't seem to move beyond his one good idea, the student of fiction who gets stuck in a scene with a character who doesn't move or change. We all know these authors, these dull and doomed texts.

And while perseveration is this rigidity, this refusal or inability to change tracks, confabulation is exactly the opposite. To confabulate—literally to replace fact with fantasy in memory—is to wildly trope. The confabulator suffers from an unruly, unstoppable imagination, an inability to focus and develop a theme. The brain-injured confabulator concocts wild tales to compensate for his lack of memory—he fills in the gaps. Back when Rachel was confabulating, she thrilled (as well as alarmed) me with her imaginative richness, which seemed, for all its craziness, to make odd and accurate tropes for her situation.

Cinderella smashed all the windows, she announced one day, sadly. On another occasion she confided that she *knew* we were on a plane over Vietnam and that she had been shot. Then there was the time, during a particularly arduous session of stretching her spastic arm, that she joyfully proclaimed to her occupational therapist that she was giving birth to a baby. The confabulator is compelled by the absence of specific space/time representations. There is no focus to her story, no organizing principle, and, perhaps in extreme cases, a failure of mimesis.

Having made these links to all-too-common narrative pathologies, it occurs to me that without the compulsive activities of confabulation and perserveration a written narrative (much less a fiction) of any interest at all could not be made. The memoir I am at such pains to deliver, woven among bits of speculation not unrelated to my situation and your situation, perseverates in its relentless return to several subjects, not to say several perseverating rhetorical strategies. I suppose I confabulate. Had there really been decaying zinnias in a concrete bed in the Denver General smoking area? Had the moon really been as I described it, clear rimmed and precise? And my companion on flight 331 from Leon, Mexico, to Denver, Colorado, had she actually worn cream-colored slacks and not, say, a brown twill skirt? Had it been, in fact, flight 331? Or have I forgotten in the blur of anxiety and sorrow the details of my own experience? I confabulate to fill in the gaps. I perseverate to bide time. Both activities rely on, are compelled by, my forgetfulness; indeed, my narrative, I believe, benefits from this forgetfulness. I believe it brings me mysteriously closer to the truth.

> I think I am going somewhere. I think I must have been in an accident. I was not driving. I do not remember it.
>
> There was a piece of light that evaded me, then I was doomed. She wears red lipstick, as do I.
>
> When I woke up I was in a cloud, so really I have not woken up. You could say that. On the other hand, a building has a reality, and so does a banana. All things exist, therefore I do.
>
> Only I am looking at her string of pearls. Very pearly white. I finger them with my fingers and blow a bubble into my milk. Outside the world is covered up and cold.

Yet there is something in us—in me—that yearns for the seamless life, for a resolution (termination? thanatos?) of the chaotic or unbearable. Conventionally speaking, a memoir promises to deliver the kind of product that will pacify my anxieties. In its seamlessness—its artful seamlessness, I should say—the memoir seeks to fulfill a certain kind of desire for narrative "truth." It is nothing, I realize nervously, if not credible. Because a fiction is not concerned with credibility in the same way, it's able to represent the disjunctiveness of what's real. Stylistically, it can indulge and even parody its own compulsive operations. Consider this perseverative bit from Donald Barthelme's "The Falling Dog": "A dog jumped on me out of a high window. I think it was the third floor, or the fourth floor. Or the third floor." Or this confabulation from *Ulysses*: "Walk on roseleaves.

Imagine trying to eat tripe and cowheel. Where was that chap I saw in that picture some-where? Ah, in the dead sea, floating on his back, reading a book with a parasol open."

The perseverations and confabulations of Barthelme and Joyce—and every other writer we cherish—constitute what we value of their style. To rethink style in terms of compulsive pathological brain operations might recall Jacobsen's famous study of aphasics and the links to metaphor and metonymy he discovered in their flawed speech patterns. His point, like mine, is that these patterns persist in nonpathological brain states as effects of compulsive organic activities. Any good writer knows this, which is why we speak so lovingly of indulging our obsessions, of making use of our compulsions to confabulate and/or perseverate. There is no normal narrative making.

At some point I hit upon the idea that what I could do for Rachel that her therapists could not do, perhaps as feelingly, is offer her help with story making, with narrative. She has always been a talented storyteller, and her language abilities and imagination have endured despite severe brain trauma. So I've become her writing teacher. Tell me a story, Rachel, I urge. Make something up. At first her stories were nonnarrative confabulations. There is Justine with a bee on her head. What about Justine? I prompted. What about the bee? Rachel smiled, shrugged. That's it, she said. That's all. The end. Eventually, the sto-ries would acquire a narrative feel, but the narratives would be flat. Once upon a time, she might begin, but then the character Justine or a small, pale, weak girl or whoever would simply drift into some arena—the desert, the city, the mall—and stay there. These stories were shapeless, lacking destinies. Still, a sense of conflict was beginning; built into the notion of small, pale, and weak as the trajectory of its plot. Lately her stories attempt some kind of resolution: A very small weak girl struck out for the desert because she had been left alone and her father and mother had died and there was nothing she could think of to do but to go to the desert and weep under a mesquite. On the way there, however, she met a nice friend who happened to be called Charles. He had a bunch of chocolate with him, which he shared with the small, weak girl and which revitalized her. They had a great time, and eventually they went to Las Vegas. The end.

A sense, however tentative, of one idea proceeding from another, of a beginning and an ending, is not only indicative of Rachel's recovering memory but, it seems to me, is cru-cial in generating her memory along its circuitry of synapses. Narrative is the practice of memory and forgetfulness; it is how we accumulate experience and develop imaginative skills. Our stylistic compulsions make us utterly individual, or, to put it another way, our individuality is generated by our style. Which is to say the infinite variety of our neurons—we each have about two hundred billion—ensures our stylish individualities.

Having said all this, I confess that I'm working hard to keep this account from flying in all directions. Because these days I live in terror of the fragmentary—those blown-apart bits and pieces. I'm eschewing the loose end, the ragged transition, the unresolved thought—but, like every "unheimlich," they are poking through to haunt me. Just as in my life these days I am trying to keep everything together—Rachel, the five or six therapists who've become part of our weekdays, my students, my job, this piece of writing—and I sense from time to time a little tearing at the seams. I ignore those scratchy sounds. I proceed as if all will resolve itself. This is my assumption, my faith. In the space of a phone call my life went from a kind of random self-indulgence—I was melancholic, moody, bored—to a passionate necessary-ness. But I don't know the ending to this story, which is why the experience of writing it is so unsettling. I imagine the best because it's my only choice—it's the way I want to live.

Still, my head buzzes unpleasantly. There are worries. There are undecided questions and shaky transitions and thoughts right now that I have trouble completing. I'd like you to know that I'm writing this in my basement under these bare bulbs that hurt my eyes and that it's snowing outside and that I can hear the creak of Rachel's wheelchair overhead—she's put on rap again—and that I just quit smoking. I want to say this is not a memoir (too messy) and not a theory (too untheoretical) and not a fiction (too true); and that it occurs to me that the buzzing in my head is due to Radon, probably, and that it's cold in the basement and I detest snow and, like Rachel, I ask why why why? Why me?

Because it's unbelievable, isn't it? when life suddenly assumes the grotesque and overblown proportions of dreams. But which is the construction, the dream or the life? It occurs to me that we approach our dreams like "fiction," like impossibilities, that we've divided dream from life in order to preserve the smooth, untroubled narrative of our dailiness. Rachel, for example, frequently feels that she's in a dream or is waking from a dream. She asks: Is this reality? And I think that her reality is literally unbelievable to her—she cannot conceive of it.

> I say one thing then another. I say her skirt is unfathomably beautiful. I say the wind will tear at her hairnet. I say look closely, that's me feeding the fish. Leaning over and seeing my face superimposed on the faces of the fish.
>
> Here is my red jacket with the purple trim, my fake leopard hat, my woolen scarf, my mittens.
>
> Here is my bad arm, which I put in first, then my good arm. Here are my feet, which no longer move.
>
> Here is Matcha, my dear mother, hanging our clothes on the line, and here I am on a roof looking down. No wonder I feel off-balance. Such beautiful laundry! I yell. What? she says. You're not making sense.
>
> Then she throws me something. It is a red item with a hook. A bra? I say. Something to eat?

Recent brain-mind theory suggests that there is no division between the brain and the mind, between, that is, biology and what we call consciousness. What this means is that there are no qualitative boundaries separating dreaming and waking, in this paradigm, just a few chemical change-ups.

The new, hypertextual theories of dreams sound oddly like postmodern theories of literature. Dreams are no longer vehicles to texts of some occluded unconscious but are themselves, postmodernly, their own writerly pastiches of significance. Harvard psychiatrist Allen Hobson calls them "virtual representations" and "the fictions we live by." If there are purposes for dreams, argues Hobson, it is that the souped-up programs of REM sleep reinforce memories and rehearse plans of action, embedding these plans and memories in rich systems of neurocircuitry, which we could call meaning or even life. Our dreams are our testing grounds; we try new things, we readjust, we plan. They are the field upon which we invent the life.

No two brains are alike. For this reason brain theory has it that no two traumatic brain injuries are alike. But, despite the heartening open-endedness of this fact, the medical profession in its practice cleaves to its old self-protective generalizations: "she may never wake up," false; "she seems acutely aphasic," false; "she will never be able to lead an independent life," don't know.

What I have found is that, just as all good narratives defy teleological, economical, linear models in favor of messy, subversive, nonlinear ones, recoveries from brain injuries create their own disordered stories. Boundaries, such as those between fact and fiction, dreams and reality, and even, in our case, mother and daughter, are dissolved in order to make a place for something new, rich, and surprising to occur. This new "something" is identity—whatever transitory fiction we call self—and the project is not so different from what we, as feminist lit crit/creative writers, have been doing for the past ten years: dissolving/subverting/transgressing gender and genre boundaries in order to assemble new subjectivities.

Which brings me back (or forth) to my dream of the dead girl in two parts, the overdetermined feature of my own messy narrative. What does the dream mean for my life? What am I meant to draw from those strangely prophetic scenes of me and Rachel looking, in two ways, at a girl who died, tragically and almost, now that I think of it, comically? One minute a ledge. Then a fall. One minute a beach. Then a wave. A rehearsal, I think, for what will come inevitably in any life and from what perspectives we are able to witness. From above, looking down at that little pile of school clothes or eye level as the wave comes even before we knew it came, that quickly. And suddenly, as I write this down, I know what that dream is about and how I am bound to be in those two places—the ledge and the shore—even as this writing seeks to conflate and distinguish the memoir from the theory from the fiction and especially as I struggle to reimagine my daughter and myself.

The sun is melting the snow between my madre and me. When I touch her hair I can feel the feel of my hands running through. Who are you, Madre? I say. Are you on the inside or the outside, because, honestly, I can't tell.

 For Discussion:

1. Why do you think Brennan inserts passages written by her daughter? How do these passages strengthen her main point?
2. How do Brennan's observations about memory compare to Shachter's?

3. Compare Brennan's belief in the central role of storytelling to Schank and to Gardner. Do Schank and Brennan contradict Gardner, or do their ideas work within his framework?

4. What is the significance of Brennan's dream? Why do you think she returns to it at the end of the essay?

 For Fact-Finding, Research, and Writing:

1. According to de Zengotita's categories in "The Numbing of the American Mind," what kind of "real" category does this essay fall into? What about Rachel's journal entries?

2. This piece is creative non-fiction, sharing traits of fiction, autobiography, and the scholarly essay. How many similarities can you list between Brennan's essay and fiction? How many traits does it share with scholarly essays? What about more informal essays, like Schank or de Zengotita—could these be considered creative non-fiction?

3. Can you think of versions of "perseverators" and "confabulators" in your own life?

Daniel L. Schacter, "Building Memories: Encoding and Retrieving the Present and the Past"

Schacter is Chair of the Department of Psychology at Harvard University. His publications are concerned with the psychological and biological aspects of memory and amnesia. He has authored several books, including *Searching for Memory: The Brain, the Mind, and the Past,* from which this selection is taken.

 Before You Read:

Write down one or two metaphors that describe how memory works. Then make up one of your own.

"Building Memories: Encoding and Retrieving the Present and the Past"

Daniel L. Schacter

ONE OF MY favorite places is the Museum of Modern Art in midtown Manhattan. A native New Yorker, I have made regular pilgrimages to this mecca of art since high school days, and have come to regard many of the paintings there as wise and familiar old friends. Like close friends, however, they cannot always be there when you want them. More than once I have returned to a favorite spot, eagerly anticipating another look at an esteemed painting by de Chirico, Hopper, or Klee, only to learn that it was away on extended loan. Although the painting's absence is disappointing, I sometimes attempt to make up for it by conducting an informal study of my own memory for the piece: What objects and people does the painting include, and how are they located relative to one another? How big is the work? What are the dominant colors and important themes? I can check the accuracy of my answers by locating a reproduction in the museum shop.

The French artist Sophie Calle wondered what aspects of a painting linger in the memories of viewers who are familiar with it. To find out, she conducted a kind of naturalistic memory experiment with an artistic twist. Calle asked a cross section of museum personnel to describe their recollections of several paintings that had been removed from their usual locations at the Museum of Modern Art. She proceeded to create a "memory ghost" for each missing painting—exhibiting the exact words used by the museum workers to describe their recollections of the piece. The most striking outcome was the sheer variety of recollections that her inquiry elicited. Some people recalled only an isolated color or object; others remembered at length subtle nuances of form, space, people, and things.

Calle's observations imply that different people retain and recollect very different aspects of their everyday environments. Why would this be so? Scientists agree that the brain does not operate like a camera or a copying machine. Then what aspects of reality do remain in memory once an episode has concluded? These kinds of questions have dogged every philosopher, psychologist, and neuroscientist who has thought seriously about the nature of remembering and forgetting. Throughout much of the history of scholarly thinking about memory, dating back to the Greeks, people have approached these questions by adopting a spatial metaphor of the mind. The Greek philosophers held that memory is like a wax tablet on which experiences are imprinted, perhaps forever; centuries later, Sigmund Freud* and William James** both conjectured that memories are like

*Sigmund Freud: (1856–1939), Austrian neurologist and the founder of modern psychoanalysis.

**William James: (1842–1910), American psychologist and philosopher.

objects placed in rooms of a house. One pundit compared memory to a garbage can that contains a random assortment of objects.[1]

The cognitive psychologist Ulric Neisser called the idea that faithful copies of experience are kept in the mind, only to reappear again at some later time pretty much in their original form, the "reappearance hypothesis." Neisser proposed instead that only bits and pieces of incoming data are represented in memory. These retained fragments of experience in turn provide a basis for reconstructing a past event, much as a paleontologist is able to reconstruct a dinosaur from fragments of bone. "Out of a few stored bone chips," reflected Neisser, "we remember a dinosaur."[2]

A visual analogue of Neisser's reflections is found in the work of the Israeli artist Eran Shakine. Shakine has explored his personal past by making collaged paintings in which fragments of old photographs and text are submerged in layers of milky white paint as exemplified by his painting "Hadassah." Shakine struggles with the seeming paradox that our sense of self, the foundation of our psychological existence, depends crucially on these fragmentary and often elusive remnants of experience. What we believe about ourselves is determined by what we remember about our pasts. If memory worked like a video recorder, allowing us to replay the past in exact detail, we could check our beliefs about ourselves against an objective record of what happened in our lives. We must make do instead with the bits and pieces of the past that memory grants us.

The general idea that memories are built from fragments of experience can help us understand key aspects of the rememberer's recollective experience, as well as memory distortions and effects of implicit memory. . . . For now, it is important to understand something more about how the fragments are constructed and reconstructed.

Bubbles P. and the Nature of Encoding

Bubbles P., a professional gambler from Philadelphia, spends virtually all his time making bets: shooting craps at local gaming clubs, dealing cards in illegal poker games, attempting to come up with new systems to beat the numbers. He is not a highly educated man—Bubbles claims to have read only two books in his entire life—but he is capable of certain feats of memory that are well beyond the abilities of even the most erudite Ph.D.s. Most people have difficulty recalling in correct order a string of more than seven digits immediately after seeing or hearing them. When the task is to repeat them backward, most people remember even fewer digits. But Bubbles P.'s digit memory is usually spectacular in either direction.[3] To appreciate his ability, inspect each of the digits at the end of this sentence for one second each, then look away from the page and immediately try to recall them in reverse order: 43902641974935483256. I suspect that by the time you worked your way back to 8, 4, or 5, you were already having problems going any further, and I would be willing to place a bet that nobody made it to 0, much less all the way back to the beginning. Bubbles P., however, can rattle off in correct backward order every one of the twenty numbers in this sequence and similar ones. How does he do it? Has he simply been gifted with an extraordinary, perhaps photographic, memory?

The answer likely resides in the same process that contributes to constructing frag-ments of experience. Psychologists refer to it as an *encoding* process—a procedure for trans-forming something a person sees, hears, thinks, or feels into a memory. Encoding can be thought of as a special way of paying attention to ongoing events that has a major impact on subsequent memory for them.

Psychologists first recognized the importance of encoding processes during debates about short-term memory that raged in the 1960s. Short-term memories last for only sec-onds. Nowadays, researchers believe that such temporary records depend on a specialized system, called *working memory*, that holds small amounts of information for brief time pe-riods, as in the backward recall task you just performed. Everyone is familiar with the op-eration of working memory from experiences in day-to-day life. Imagine that you need to look up a friend's number in the phone book. You find the number, then walk across the room to make the call, all the while madly repeating the digits to yourself as rapidly as you can. If you are distracted for even a moment during your walk to the phone, you will need to consult the book again; if you punch in the number successfully, you will probably for-get it almost immediately. Why are such memories so fleeting?

Part of the answer is that working memory depends on a different network of brain structures than long-term memory systems do. Some patients with damage to the inner part of the temporal lobes in the center of the brain have little or no difficulty retaining a string of digits for several seconds, yet they have great difficulty forming and explicitly remem-bering more enduring memories. Other patients who have suffered damage to a specific part of the parietal lobe on the cortical surface can form long-term memories but cannot hold and repeat back a string of digits. They lack a specific part of working memory, known as the *phonological loop*, that most of us rely on when we need to hold a small amount of lin-guistic information in mind for several seconds.[4]

This is where the concept of encoding comes in. By relying on your phonological loop to repeat a phone number madly to yourself, you encode it only superficially. To establish a durable memory, incoming information must be encoded much more thoroughly, or deeply, by associating it meaningfully with knowledge that already exists in memory. You must do more than simply recycle the information in the phonological loop. Suppose that instead of just repeating the phone number—555-6024—to yourself over and over, you attempt to make the number meaningful in some way. For example, if you play golf (as I do), you might encode the number by thinking that 555 is the yardage of a par-5 hole and that 6024 is the length of a relatively short 18-hole course. You have now carried out a deep encoding and should be able to remember the information much longer and more accu-rately than if you merely repeat it. This is known in the psychological literature as a "depth of processing" effect.[5]

The same sort of effect is probably at work in cases like that of Bubbles P. Bubbles is knowledgeable about numbers and seems able to segregate effortlessly a long string of them into meaningful units or chunks. Rather than frantically recycling them, as most of us do, Bubbles uses the skill he has developed with numbers through years of gambling to link incoming digits to knowledge already in his memory. Bubbles does not have a generally extraordinary memory: his memory for words, faces, objects, and locations—anything other than numbers—is no better than average.

Elaborative Encoding

Memory researchers have tried to devise special techniques to gain control over the encoding operations that a person performs, and these operations have played a crucial role in the unfolding story of memory and amnesia research during the past twenty years.[6] Suppose I tell you that an hour from now, I will test your ability to recall the following words: floor, car, tree, cake, shirt, flower, cup, grass, dog, table. You might try to remember the words by conjuring up visual images, by simply repeating the words again and again, or by making up a story that connects the words to one another. As long as I leave you to your own devices, I cannot learn much about how encoding processes influence memory. I need to come up with some way of controlling how you think about the to-be-remembered items.

Memory researchers have solved this problem by using what is known as an orienting task. Instead of allowing people to memorize the target items in any manner they please, an orienting task guides encoding by requiring a person to answer a specific question about the target. For example, I could induce you to carry out a deep, semantic encoding of target words by asking for a yes or no answer to questions such as, "Is *shirt* a type of clothing?" You cannot answer this question accurately without thinking about the meaning of the word *shirt*. To induce you to engage in shallow, nonsemantic encoding of the word, I could ask you to answer a question such as, "Does *shirt* contain more vowels or more consonants?" You can answer this question easily without attending to the meaning of the word. If I later test your ability to recollect *shirt* and other words on the list, I can be fairly confident that you will be able to recall or recognize many of the words that you encoded semantically and few of the words that you encoded nonsemantically.

This finding may not seem particularly surprising; everyday experience suggests that something that is meaningful will be more easily remembered than something that is not. But it turns out that only a certain kind of semantic encoding promotes high levels of memory performance—an *elaborative* encoding operation that allows you to integrate new information with what you already know. For example, if I induce you to encode one of our study list words by posing the question, "Is *shirt* a type of insect?" you must pay attention to the meaning of the word in order to provide the correct answer. As you formulate a response to this question, however, you do not integrate the target word with your preexisting knowledge of shirts—that is, you do not carry out an effective elaboration of the word *shirt*. If I test you after you have answered this kind of orienting question, you will show surprisingly poor memory for whether the word *shirt* was on the list.[7]

In our everyday lives, memory is a natural, perhaps automatic, byproduct of the manner in which we think about an unfolding episode. If we want to improve our chances of remembering an incident or learning a fact, we need to make sure that we carry out elaborative encoding by reflecting on the information and relating it to other things we already know. Laboratory studies have shown that simply intending to remember something is unlikely to be helpful, unless we translate that intention into an effective elaborative encoding. For example, when preparing for an exam, a good student may make a special effort to form meaningful mental associations among the study materials, whereas the same student may not bother engaging in such elaborative encoding if she is not going to be tested. In my earlier example, carrying out the orienting task—answering the question, "Is *shirt* a type of clothing?"—ensures that you have already made effective use of elaborative encoding processes; "trying to remember" adds nothing beyond that.

The issue can be turned around, too: most experiences that we recall effortlessly from our day-to-day existence—yesterday's important lunch date, the big party last weekend, last year's summer vacation—are not initially encoded with any particular intention to remember them. Occasionally, the apparent significance of an event may prompt us to make a special effort to encode it deeply. However, day-to-day existence would be precarious and probably unmanageable if we had to make an intentional effort to encode each and every episode from our daily lives in order to be able to recollect it later. Instead, a kind of natural selection drives us. What we already know shapes what we select and encode; things that are meaningful to us spontaneously elicit the kind of elaborations that promote later recall. Our memory systems are built so that we are likely to remember what is most important to us.

Carrying out a deep, elaborative encoding influences not only the quantity of what can be remembered but also the quality of our recollective experience. . . . When we meet a new person and encode information elaboratively, we are more likely later to "remember" the episode; if we do not elaborate, we are more likely to "just know" that the person seems familiar. Elaborative encoding is a critical and perhaps necessary ingredient of our ability to remember in rich and vivid detail what has happened to us in the past.[8]

But the dependence of explicit memory on elaboration has a downside, too: if we do not carry out elaborative encoding, we will be left with impoverished recollections. Experiments have shown that people are surprisingly poor at remembering what is on the front and back of a penny, despite seeing and handling pennies all the time.[9] It is likely, however, that we encode the features of a penny quite superficially, because using pennies in everyday life requires only that we notice the general shape and color of the coin. The encoding process can halt once we have extracted the necessary information; there is no need to carry out a more elaborate analysis of the coin. In this example, we are behaving like experimental volunteers who perform shallow or superficial orienting tasks, and later recall little or nothing of what they have seen. If we operate on automatic pilot much of the time and do not reflect on our environment and our experiences, we may pay a price by retaining only sketchy memories of where we have been and what we have done.

Encoding and Mnemonic Devices

Elaborative encoding is a critical component of virtually all popular memory-improvement techniques. The oldest example of a memory-improvement strategy is visual imagery mnemonics, first developed by the Greek orator Simonides in 477 B.C. As the story goes, Simonides, a poet, was called to recite verse at a large banquet. During the course of the evening, he was unexpectedly summoned outside to meet two young men; the moment he left, the roof of the banquet hall collapsed, crushing and mutilating beyond recognition all the guests. Simonides became a hero because he was able to reconstruct the guest list by imagining each location around the table, which brought to mind the person who had been sitting there.

He accomplished this feat by using a system of mnemonics he had developed known as the method of *loci*, which became famous in ancient Greece after this incident. The method involves encoding information into memory by conjuring up vivid mental images and mentally placing them in familiar locations. Later, at the time of attempted recall, one consults the locations, just as Simonides did.[10] If, for example, you wanted to remember to buy beer, potato chips, and toothpaste, you could use rooms in your home as locations, and imagine your bedroom afloat in beer, your kitchen stuffed from top to bottom with bags of potato chips, and your living room slathered with toothpaste. Upon arriving at the store, you could then take a mental walk around your house and "see" what is in each room.

Modern practitioners use the method of loci and other related imagery techniques to perform such feats as remembering all the names and numbers listed in good-sized telephone books. These accomplishments are nothing new, however. Greek orators used mnemonics to memorize speeches of extraordinary length, and Roman generals used them to remember the names of tens of thousands of men in their command. During the Middle Ages, scholastics used mnemonics to aid in the learning of interminable religious tomes. In fact, throughout the Middle Ages, mnemonics played a major role in society, exerting a large influence on artistic and religious life.[11]

By the fifteenth and sixteenth centuries, Simonides' relatively simple method of loci had been superseded by increasingly baroque "memory theaters" that were conceived and drawn by some of Europe's most inventive minds. These intricate and sometimes beautiful structures consisted of hundreds of locations, each containing ideas and precepts that were frequently mystical. Learning all the locations and precepts in a memory theater—into which one could later mentally deposit new to-be-remembered information—was itself an arduous, sometimes impossible task. The excesses of mnemonic systems eventually created a backlash against them.[12]

My central point is that the core cognitive act of visual imagery mnemonics—creating an image and linking it to a mental location—is a form of deep, elaborate encoding. Mnemonic techniques produce rich and detailed encodings that are tightly linked to pre-existing knowledge, yet are distinctively different from other items in memory. It also seems likely, in light of my earlier discussion about the importance of visual reexperiencing in conscious recollection, that the visual format of imagery mnemonics enhances its usefulness as an aid to explicit remembering.[13] . . .

The Museum Test

The notion of elaboration also provides interesting perspectives on the recollections of the Museum of Modern Art personnel in the project I mentioned earlier. Several of them were asked to recall the Magritte painting, "The Menaced Assassin" (Fig. 1). Their memory reports are revealing:

1. There's a lot of pink flesh, red blood, guys in black. The background is blue with French ironwork on the balcony, the bedroom is beige, but the only striking color is that blood painted red that looks like ketchup.

2. It's a painting with a smooth surface, an easy one to spot check. It is approximately five feet high and seven feet long. It is framed in a plain, dark, walnut-stained molding, something austere. I never liked it. I don't like stories in painting. I don't like trying to figure them out. That's why I never gave it any time.

3. It has a film noir sort of feel, a mystery novel look to it. The puzzle is there. You have all those little clues that will probably lead you nowhere; there are men dressed in dark coats, and black bowler hats, the way Albert Finney was dressed in *Murder on the Orient Express*, placed in a room with a dead body. In the center, the one who seems to be the perpetrator is lifting the needle of a phonograph. Two weird-looking individuals are hiding to the side. There is a face looking from the balcony, almost like a sun on the horizon. And, when you look at her carefully, you realize that the towel probably conceals a decapitated head.

4. I think it's just a murder scene. Men in dark suits, a pale woman and dashes of red blood. That's all I remember.[14]

Based on what they recollected, I feel I can make reasonably confident guesses about their identities: Comment #4 probably belongs to a security guard or other nonprofessional staff, as does #1, which focuses solely on the physical features of the painting. Comment #2, which describes the work's exact measurements and properties of its frame, likely comes from someone charged with maintaining the painting. And the thematically rich set of memories in #3 no doubt belong to a curator or similar art professional. The rationale for these educated guesses is simple. What people remember about a painting is heavily influ-

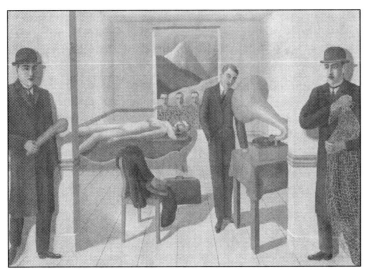

FIGURE 1 René Magritte, "The Menaced Assassin," 1926. 59¼" x 6' 4⅞". Oil on canvas. The Museum of Modern Art, New York. Kay Sage Tanguy Fund. Photograph © 1996 The Museum of Modern Art, New York.

Sophie Calle, an artist, queried museum personnel about their recollections of Magritte's painting, and elicited a wide variety of memories.

enced by how they think about or encode it, and exactly which aspects of a painting are elaborated depends on what kind of knowledge is already available in one's long-term memory.

Encoding and remembering are virtually inseparable. But the close relationship between the two can sometimes cause problems in our everyday lives. We remember only what we have encoded, and what we encode depends on who we are—our past experiences, knowledge, and needs all have a powerful influence on what we retain. This is one reason why two different people can sometimes have radically divergent recollections of the same event. . . .

Historical Interlude
The Story of Richard Semon

The study of memory, like that of any scientific endeavor, has a history full of pioneering figures whose achievements are recognized and honored by researchers active in the field today. As a graduate student, I became intrigued by Richard Semon, who played an unappreciated role in the history of memory research. My curiosity was sparked by tantalizing comments from some of the twentieth century's most towering intellects, such as the philosopher Bertrand Russell* and the physicist Erwin Schrödinger,** concerning the great value of his work. Hardly anyone working on memory in 1977 had heard of him, but I soon discovered that his ideas were both original and important.[15]

Semon was born in Berlin in 1859, the same year that Charles Darwin published *The Origin of Species*. As a young man, Semon fell under the spell of this innovative approach to understanding evolution, and he went off to study at the University of Jena with the most famous German proponent of the new theory, the controversial biologist Ernst Haeckel. Semon received his Ph.D. and became a rising young professor at the University of Jena, a major European center for evolutionary research. Then, in 1897, he fell in love with the wife of an eminent colleague, Maria Krehl, who eventually left her husband to live with Semon. The two were vilified, Semon resigned his professorship, and the pair moved to Munich, where they were married. Semon, working on his own as private scholar, developed a theory of memory.

In 1904, he published a monograph, *Die Mneme*, that attempted to unite the biological analysis of heredity with the psychological and physiological analysis of memory. Semon argued that heredity and reproduction could be thought of as memory that preserves the effects of experience across generations. *Mneme*, a term Semon created in allusion to the Greek goddess of memory, Mnemosyne, refers to a fundamental process that he believed sub-serves both heredity and everyday memory. He conceived it as an elemental elasticity of biological tissue that allows the effects of experience to be preserved over time.

---

*Bertrand Russell: Bertrand Arthur William Russell (1872–1970), English mathematician and philosopher.
**Erwin Schrödinger: (1887–1961), American physicist.

Semon distinguished three aspects or stages of Mneme that he deemed crucial to understanding both everyday memory and hereditary memory. Because he believed that ordinary language has too many potentially misleading connotations to be useful scientifically, Semon described the three stages with terms of his own invention: *engraphy* is Semon's term for encoding information into memory; *engram* refers to the enduring change in the nervous system (the "memory trace") that conserves the effects of experience across time; and *ecphory* is the process of activating or retrieving a memory.

Semon's unusual terminology and his emphasis on the memory/heredity analogy elicited a torrent of disapproval from prominent experts of the time. Yet precisely because of this controversy, his ideas about the operation of everyday memory tended to be overlooked. Only one reviewer of *Die Mneme*, the American psychologist Henry J. Watt, looked beyond the issues of heredity that so mesmerized biologists and picked out the single most important aspect of Semon's theory. "The most valuable part of the book is the concept of the ecphoric stimulus," reflected Watt. "However, Semon in his attempt to find something common in the reproduction of the organism and in the reproduction in the sense of memory, has lost sight of his own objective (the discovery of the nature of the ecphoric stimulus) and has gone astray."[16]

What exactly was Watt driving at? Psychologists at the time showed scant interest in memory-retrieval processes. Most of them believed that the likelihood of remembering an experience is determined entirely by the strength of associations that are formed when the information is initially encoded into memory. According to this view, if strong associations are formed—because the information is particularly vivid, or is repeated frequently enough—memory will later be good; if weak associations are formed, memory will later be poor. Semon, in contrast, argued that memory does not depend solely on the strength of associations. He contended that the likelihood of remembering also hinges on the ecphoric stimulus—the hint or cue that triggers recall—and how it is related to the engram, or memory trace, that was encoded initially. Watt realized that Semon had pinpointed a key aspect of memory that had been given short shrift, and wished that Semon had focused more extensively on it.

In 1909, Semon published a book that must have made Watt exceedingly happy. Entitled *Die Mnemischen Empfindungen* (*Mnemic Psychology*), it was entirely about everyday memory, leaving aside the contentious issues of heredity in *Die Mneme*. Semon elaborated his theory of ecphory (retrieval processes) and applied it to a host of critical issues. Sadly for Semon, however, the new book aroused slight interest among researchers and had no detectable impact on the study of memory. Psychologists had little use for Semon's iconoclastic views on retrieval processes; in fact, they misunderstood his ideas. In addition, Semon's status as a scientific isolate, without prestigious institutional affiliations, did not enhance his cause. He was accorded the same kind of treatment given to flat-earth theorists, believers in perpetual-motion machines, and other cranks who exist at the fringes of science: he was ignored.

In 1918, Semon's wife died of cancer. Later that year, he placed a German flag on his wife's bed and shot himself through the heart.

Despite his nagging despair over the neglect of his work, Semon believed that his ideas would soon achieve widespread recognition among researchers. His hopes went largely unrealized, with the exception of one of his terminological inventions: the engram. The great neuroscientist Karl Lashley wrote a paper in 1950 entitled "In Search of the Engram," which summarizes Lashley's unsuccessful attempts to find the engram (the representation of a memory in the brain) in any single, restricted location. Because the paper became a classic in the field and contains the first prominent invocation of the term *engram*, most scientists have assumed that Lashley invented the word—and he did not even cite, much less discuss, Semon's prior use of the term.

Engrams are the transient or enduring changes in our brains that result from encoding an experience. Neuroscientists believe that the brain records an event by strengthening the connections between groups of neurons that participate in encoding the experience. A typical incident in our everyday lives consists of numerous sights, sounds, actions, and words. Different areas of the brain analyze these varied aspects of an event. As a result, neurons in the different regions become more strongly connected to one another. The new pattern of connections constitutes the brain's record of the event: the engram. This idea was first suggested by the Canadian psychologist Donald Hebb, and has since been worked out in considerable detail.[17]

Engrams are important contributors to what we subjectively experience as a memory of something that has happened to us. But, as we have seen, they are not the only source of the subjective experience of remembering. As you read these words, there are thousands, maybe millions, of engrams in some form in your brain. These patterns of connections have the potential to enter awareness, to contribute to explicit remembering under the right circumstances, but at any one instant most of them lie dormant. If I cue you by asking you to remember the most exciting high school sports event you ever attended, a variety of engrams that only seconds ago were in a quiescent state become active as you sift through candidate experiences; if I ask you to remember what you ate the last time you had dinner at an Italian restaurant, a very different set of engrams enters into awareness. Had I not just posed these queries to you, the relevant engrams might have remained dormant for years.

Semon appreciated that, engrams being merely potential contributors to recollection, an adequate account of memory depends on understanding the influences that allow engrams to become manifest in conscious awareness: What properties of a cue allow it to "awaken" a dormant engram? Why are some cues effective in eliciting recollection whereas others are not? Semon argued that any given memory could be elicited by just a few select cues—parts of the original experience that a person focused on at the time the experience occurred. Thus, only a fraction of the original event need be present in order to trigger recall of the entire episode.

To recollect the most exciting high school sports event you ever attended, you need not reinstate all the cues that were present initially. Only a subset must be available, those that are closely related to your encoding of the event. Your original encoding and elaboration of the event—say, a football game in which the quarterback made a series of miraculous plays to pull off an unexpected victory—focused heavily on the role of the quarterback.

Years later, the mere mention of the quarterback's name, or even a glance at his face, may bring to your mind the game, the participants, and how your team won. But if you do not encounter the critical cues, you will not recall the experience. A friend may ask if you re-call the time your team beat the school with the young coach who went on to a career with a professional team. You may be puzzled about what game he is referring to, and have only a fuzzy recollection of the coach. But as soon as he says that it was the game in which your quarterback threw two long touchdown passes in the final minutes, you can retrieve the memory easily. Thus, if encoding conditions are not adequately reinstated at the time of attempted recall, retrieval will fail—even if an event has received extensive elaborative encoding. . . .

Because our understanding of ourselves is so dependent on what we can remember of the past, it is troubling to realize that successful recall depends heavily on the availability of appropriate retrieval cues. Such dependence implies that we may be oblivious to parts of our pasts because we fail to encounter hints or cues that trigger dormant memories. This may be one reason why encountering acquaintances we have not seen for years is often such an affecting experience: our old friends provide us with cues and reminders that are diffi-cult to generate on our own, and that allow us to recollect incidents we would ordinarily fail to remember. . . .

We must not, however, confuse these ideas with the notion that all experiences are recorded somewhere in our brains, only awaiting the appropriate retrieval cue to be brought into awareness. While controlled research has demonstrated over and over that cues and reminders can lead to recall of experiences that have seemingly disappeared, it does not necessarily follow that all experiences are preserved and potentially recallable. Sometimes we forget because the right cues are not available, but it is also likely that sometimes we forget because the relevant engrams have weakened or become blurred.[18]

Retrieval cues are a bit like the portable metal detectors that scavengers sometimes use to try to recover coins on a beach. If coins are hidden somewhere beneath the sands, then the scavenger needs the detector to find them. But if no coins remain in the sand, then even the most powerful detector will turn up nothing. Our brains include some beaches with hidden coins and others that are barren. Like the scavenger seeking money, we do not know before searching which are which.

Neil

Retrieval Processes and the Brain

In 1988, a fourteen-year-old English boy named Neil began radiation treatment for a tu-mor hidden deep within the recesses of his brain. Neil had been a normal child until the expanding tumor began to interfere with his vision and memory and to create a host of other medical problems. Chemotherapy was eventually successful, but Neil suffered heavy cognitive losses. He was virtually unable to read and could no longer name common ob-jects on sight. Neil was able to recount most of his life prior to the operation, but he had great difficulty remembering his ongoing, day-to-day experiences.

Curiously, however, Neil performed reasonably well at school, especially in English and mathematics. The psychologists who tested his memory wondered how he managed to do so well. To find out, they asked him some questions about an audiotaped book he had been studying, *Cider with Rosie*, by Laurie Lee. He remembered nothing. Noting Neil's frustration, and realizing that his class performance was based on written responses, the examiner asked Neil to write down his answers, beginning with anything that he could recall from the book. After a while he wrote: "Bloodshot Geranium windows Cider with Rosie Dranium smell of damp pepper and mushroom-growth." "What have I written?" he then asked, unable to read his own handwriting but able to speak normally. The examiner, who was familiar with the book, immediately recognized that the phrases came directly from its pages.

Intrigued by Neil's ability to write down information that he could not express orally, the examiner asked whether Neil could write anything about incidents related to his hospitalization some two years earlier, which he had been unable to remember when asked to talk about them. "A man had Gangrene," he wrote, correctly recalling the ailment of another man in the ambulance that brought Neil to the hospital.

Neil's parents asked him to write down the names of the children in his class. He produced a long list, which turned out to be accurate. When his mother asked him what had happened at school that day, Neil wrote, "Mum I saw tulips on the way home." This was the first time in two years that Neil had been able to relate to his mother a memory of something that had happened to him in her absence.

Neil's parents equipped him with a small notebook, and he began to communicate regularly about incidents in his everyday life. Yet he remained unable to recount these episodes orally. When he wrote them down, Neil was unable to read them, and often expressed surprise when someone told him what he had written. After an afternoon's excursion to several familiar locations, Neil was unable to remember anything when asked. But when told to write down what had happened, he provided a succinct, and accurate, summary of the afternoon's activities: "We went to the museum, and we had some pizza. Then we came back, we went onto the Beach and we looked at the sea. Then we came home."

This case is unprecedented in the annals of psychology, psychiatry, or neurology.[19] Neil's tumor did damage his brain, including some structures that are known to be important for memory. But nothing about the condition of his brain provides specific clues to how or why he could retrieve recent episodic memories through writing but not speaking.

There are other indications that the brain uses different systems for retrieving written and spoken information. The neuropsychologist Alfonso Caramazza has described two patients who suffered strokes in different regions of the left hemisphere that are usually associated with language impairments. Both patients subsequently had special problems producing English verbs (they could produce nouns normally). One patient had problems writing verbs but not saying them, whereas the other had problems saying verbs but not writing them.[20]

Caramazza's findings still leave us a long way from understanding how Neil could recall his recent experiences through writing but not speaking. But these strange cases of disruptions of retrieval raise questions that are essential to understanding memory: Exactly how does the retrieval process work? What goes on in my mind/brain that allows the cue "What did you do during your summer vacation?" to evoke in me the subjective experience of remembering beautiful sunlit days of hiking and swimming at Lake Tahoe? We do not understand precisely how the retrieval process works, but some clues are beginning to emerge.[21]. . .

Constructing Memories
The Role of the Retrieval Environment

Findings and ideas concerning brain mechanisms of retrieval are absolutely crucial to understanding memory's fragile power. But it is still important to develop an adequate conceptualization of retrieval at the psychological level. How are we to think about what is retrieved when we recall a past experience? Does the act of retrieval simply serve to activate, or bring into conscious awareness, a dormant memory?

Suppose, for example, that I provide a retrieval cue such as "tell me about last year's Thanksgiving dinner." It may take you a few seconds to recollect where it occurred and who was there, but by the time you reach the end of this sentence there is a good chance that you will recall some of the basic information. How did this subjective experience of remembering come about? The simplest account is that the cue somehow activated a dormant engram of the event, and that your subjective experience of remembering the event, however incomplete, is a straightforward reflection of the information that had been quiescent in your mind: a lightbulb that had been turned off is suddenly turned on.

But memory retrieval is not so simple. I have already suggested an alternative possibility, rooted in Neisser's analogy that retrieving a memory is like reconstructing a dinosaur from fragments of bone. For the paleontologist, the bone chips that are recovered on an archaeological dig and the dinosaur that is ultimately reconstructed from them are not the same thing; the full-blown dinosaur is constructed by combining the bone chips with other available fragments, in accordance with general knowledge of how the complete dinosaur should appear. Similarly, for the rememberer, the engram (the stored fragments of an episode) and the memory (the subjective experience of recollecting a past event) are not the same thing. The stored fragments contribute to the conscious experience of remembering, but they are only part of it. Another important component is the retrieval cue itself. Although it is often assumed that a retrieval cue merely arouses or activates a memory that is slumbering in the recesses of the brain, I have hinted at an alternative: the cue combines with the engram to yield a new, emergent entity—the recollective experience of the remember—that differs from either of its constituents. This idea was intimated in some of Proust's writings, in which memories emerge from comparing and combining a present sensation with a past one, much as stereoscopic vision emerges from combining information from the two eyes. . . .

Marcel Proust: Involuntary Memory

No single work of literature is more closely associated with human memory than Marcel Proust's *À la recherche du temps perdu (In Search of Lost Time)*.[22] The depth of Proust's obsession with recapturing the past is difficult to over-state. The eight volumes that constitute À *la recherche* were written over a period of nearly fifteen years, beginning around 1908 and concluding several months before his death in November 1922. The entire treatise exceeds three thousand pages, most concerned in one way or another with personal recollections or meditations on the nature of memory. Proust may have become so single-minded because he had largely withdrawn from society by the time he began writing his opus. He confined himself to his room throughout much of the writing, suffering from illness and exhaustion, and in so doing substituted a world of time for the world of space. But his obsession with the past also reflects Proust's passionate conviction that the truth of human experience could be grasped only through an understanding of memory and time.

In the most dramatic memory-related incident of the novel, the narrator, Marcel, is visiting his mother, who serves him tea and pastries known as *petites madeleines*. After dipping a madeleine into the tea and imbibing the mixture, he is overcome by an unexpected, overwhelming, and entirely mysterious sense of well-being. "Whence could it have come to me, this all-powerful joy?" he asks. "I sensed that it was connected with the taste of the tea and the cake, but that it infinitely transcended those savours, could not, indeed, be of the same nature. Whence did it come from? What did it mean? How could I seize and apprehend it?"[23] He tries to induce the experience again by tasting several more mouthfuls of the potent mixture, but each experience is weaker than the previous one, leading him to conclude that the basis of the effect "lies not in the cup but in myself." He surmises that the tea and cake have somehow activated a past experience, and wonders whether he will be able to recall it consciously.

Then comes the extraordinary instant when the mystery is resolved: "And suddenly the memory revealed itself. The taste was that of the little crumb of madeleine which on Sunday mornings at Combray [the fictional name of Proust's childhood town] when I went to say good morning to her in her bedroom, my aunt Leonie used to give me, dipping it first in her own cup of tea." Marcel notes that he had never elsewhere encountered the combination of smells and tastes that characterized the episode at his aunt's house, thus making them uniquely effective cues for an elusive but powerful memory: "But when from a long-distant past nothing subsists, after the people are dead, after the things are broken and scattered, taste and smell alone, more fragile but more enduring, more immaterial, more persistent, more faithful, remain poised for a long time, like souls, remembering, waiting and hoping, amid the ruins of all the rest; and bear unflinchingly, in the tiny and almost impalpable drop of their essence, the vast structure of recollection."

The moment when the madeleine memory revealed itself was the moment when the narrator saw that memory could be both fragile and powerful. Memories that can be elicited only by specific tastes and smells are fragile: they can easily disappear because there are few opportunities for them to surface. But those that survive are also exceptionally powerful: having remained dormant for long periods of time, the sudden appearance of seemingly lost experiences cued by tastes or smells is a startling event.

The madeleine episode also highlights that reexperiencing one's personal past sometimes depends on chance encounters with objects that contain the keys to unlocking memories that might otherwise be hidden forever. But Marcel's recognition that *involuntary* recollections are fleeting, lasting only several seconds, and depend on rare confrontations with particular smells or sights, leads him to alter the focus of his quest for the past. As the novel progresses, his quest for self-understanding depends increasingly on the active, *voluntary* retrieval of his past.[24] He explores the self-defining role of voluntary recollection in one of the key scenes from the final novel in the series, *Time Regained*. At a gathering of old friends whom Marcel has not seen for many years, he strains to recall their identities and to place them in the context of his remembered experiences. In so doing he achieves a synthesis of past and present that heightens his appreciation of his own identity.

Proust also draws on concepts and analogies from the science of optics to develop an analogy of time and memory, which he made explicit in a 1922 letter. "The image (imperfect as it is) which seems to me best suited to convey the nature of that special tense," Proust wrote, "is that of a telescope, a telescope pointed at time, for a telescope renders visible for us stars invisible to the naked eye, and I have tried to render visible to the consciousness unconscious phenomena, some of which, having been entirely forgotten, are situated in the past."[25]

Proust further develops his optical analogy. The experience of remembering a past episode, Proust contends, is not based merely on calling to mind a stored memory image. Instead, a feeling of remembering emerges from the comparison of two images: one in the present and one in the past. Just as visual perception of the three-dimensional world depends on combining information from the two eyes, perception in time—remembering—depends on combining information from the present and the past. The renowned Proust scholar Roger Shattuck explains: "Proust set about to make us *see time*. . . . Merely to remember something is meaningless unless the remembered image is combined with a moment in the present affording a view of the same object or objects. Like our eyes, our memories must see double; these two images then converge in our minds into a single heightened reality."[26] Foreshadowing scientific research by more than a half-century, Proust achieved the penetrating insight that feelings of remembering result from a subtle interplay between past and present.

Notes

1. Roediger (1980) reviews spatial metaphors of memory, and Landauer (1975) describes the "garbage can" analogy. Koriat and Goldsmith (in press) contrast the storehouse metaphor of memory to an alternative metaphor that emphasizes how well remembered events correspond to the original experiences.
2. Neisser (1967), p. 285.
3. Ceci, DeSimone, and Johnson (1992) describe the case of Bubbles P. and report a series of experiments concerning his memory abilities. The importance of the "magic number" seven was described by Miller (1956).
4. Research concerning working memory has been pioneered by Baddeley (1986) and colleagues. Baddeley fractionates working memory into several subsystems: a central executive or limited capacity workspace and two "slave" subsystems, the phonological loop and a visuospatial sketch pad that temporarily holds nonverbal information. For studies of patients with damage to the phonological loop, see Vallar and Shallice (1990).
5. The term *depth of processing*, synonymous with *levels of processing*, was introduced to the psychological literature in a classic paper by Craik and Lockhart (1972).

6. For a discussion of these special techniques, known as *orienting tasks*, see Craik and Tulving (1975).

7. This finding was first reported by Craik and Tulving (1975). Other early experiments documenting the importance of elaborative encoding included those by Stein and Bransford (1979), which revealed that even subtle differences in the exact kind of elaboration that people perform can have a major impact on subsequent memory performance.

8. See Gardiner and Java (1993) for elaborative encoding and experiences of remembering and knowing.

9. See Nickerson and Adams (1979).

10. This rendition of the story of Simonides is based on Yates (1966), who provides a definitive history of the origins of mnemonics.

11. The story of mnemonics and the Middle Ages is beautifully told by Carruthers (1990). Scholarly discussions of visual imagery mnemonics and memory improvement can be found in Bellezza (1981) and Bower (1972). A popular treatment of how to use mnemonics to enhance memory function has been provided by Lorayne and Lucas (1974), among many others. Herrmann, Raybeck, and Gutman (1993) focus specifically on improving memory performance in students.

12. For the backlash against mnemonics, see J. Spence (1984), pp. 4 and 12.

13. For wide-ranging discussions of imagery, mind, and brain, see Kosslyn (1981, 1994).

14. The quoted texts are from Storr (1992), p. 6.

15. For an overview of Semon's theory of memory, see Schacter, Eich, and Tulving (1978); for a broader treatment that delves into Semon's life and ideas in the context of the history and sociology of science, see Schacter (1982). For English translations of his work on memory, see Semon (1921, 1923).

16. Watt (1905), p. 130.

17. See Hebb (1949) for the original statement of what has come to be known as "Hebbian learning." For a modern treatment, see McNaughton and Nadel (1989), and for a review of recent evidence, see Merzenich and Sameshima (1993).

18. For a review of evidence from people and animals on retrieval of seemingly forgotten memories in response to cues and reminders, see Capaldi and Neath (1995).

19. Neil's case is described in detail by Vargha-Khadem, Isaacs, and Mishkin (1994). Quotes are from pp. 692–693 of that article. The tumor was in the pineal region of the third ventricle. Although it was treated successfully, MRI scans after treatment revealed abnormalities in structures thought to be important for memory, including the left hippocampal formation, parts of the diencephalon, and the fornix, which connects the hippocampus and diencephalon.

20. Caramazza and Hillis (1991).

21. For a readable discussion of possible cellular bases of memory retrieval, see Johnson (1991). For psychological and computational theories of retrieval, see McClelland (1995) and Metcalfe (1993).

22. Proust's collection of novels is best known in English as *Remembrance of Things Past*. My reading and all quotes are based on D. J. Enright's recent revision of earlier translations by C. K. Scott Moncrief and then Terence Kilmartin. In the Enright translation (Proust, 1992), the series is titled *In Search of Lost Time*.

23. This quote and the following ones are from the most recently revised translation of *Swann's Way* (Proust, 1992, pp. 60–63).

24. This point is made eloquently in Shattuck's (1983) superb analysis of the role played by memory and time in Proust's work.

25. The letter is quoted in ibid., p. 46.

26. Ibid., pp. 46–47.

Selected Bibliography

Baddeley, A. (1986). *Working memory*. Oxford: Clarendon.

Bellezza, F. S. (1981). Mnemonic devices: Classification, characteristics, and criteria. *Review of Educational Research, 51*, 247–275.

Bower, G. H. (1972). Mental imagery and associative learning. In L. Gregg (Ed.) Cognition and learning and memory. New York: Wiley.

Capaldi, E. J., & Neath, I. (1995). Remembering and forgetting as context discrimination. *Learning and Memory, 2,* 107–132.

Caramazza, A., & Hillis, A. E. (1991). Lexical organization of nouns and verbs in the brain. *Nature, 349,* 788–790.

Carruthers, M. J. (1990). *The book of memory: A study of memory in medieval culture.* New York: Cambridge University Press.

Ceci, S. J., DeSimone, M., & Johnson, S. (1992). Memory in context: A case study of "Bubbles P.," a gifted but uneven memorizer. In D. J. Herrmann, H. Weingartner, A. Searleman, & C. McEvoy (Eds.), *Memory improvement: Implications for memory theory* (pp. 169–186). New York: Springer-Verlag.

Craik, F. I. M., & Lockhart, R. S. (1972). Levels of processing: A framework for memory research. *Journal of Verbal Learning and Verbal Behavior, 11,* 671–684.

Craik, F. I. M., & Tulving, E. (1975). Depth of processing and the retention of words in episodic memory. *Journal of Experimental Psychology: General, 104,* 268–294.

Freud, S. (1899). Screen Memories. In J. Strachey (Ed. and Trans.), *The standard edition of the complete psychological works of Sigmund Freud* (Vol. 3). London: Hogarth Press.

Freud, S. (1926/1959). Inhibitions, symptoms, and anxiety. In J. Strachey (Ed. and Trans.), *The standard edition of the complete psychological works of Sigmund Freud* (Vol. 20). London: Hogarth Press.

Freud, S., & Breuer, J. (1966). *Studies on hysteria.* (J. Strachey, Trans.). New York: Avon.

Gardiner, J. M., & Java, R. I. (1993). Recognising and remembering. In A. F. Collins, S. E. Gathercole, M. A. Conway, & P. E. Morris (Eds.), *Theories of memory* (pp. 163–188). Hove, United Kingdom: Erlbaum.

Hebb, D. O. (1949). *The organization of behavior.* New York: Wiley.

Hermann, D., Raybeck, D., & Gutman, D. (1993). *Improving student memory.* Seattle, WA: Hogrefe & Huber.

James, W. (1890). *The principles of psychology.* New York: Holt.

Johnson, G. (1991). *In the palaces of memory: How we build the worlds inside our heads.* New York: Knopf.

Koriat, A., & Goldsmith, M. (in press). Memory metaphors and the everyday-laboratory controversy: The correspondence versus the storehouse conceptions of memory. *Behavioral and Brain Sciences.*

Landauer, T. K. (1975). Memory without organization: Properties of a model with random storage and undirected retrieval. *Cognitive Psychology, 7,* 495–531.

Lorayne, H., & Lucas, J. (1974). *The memory book.* New York: Ballantine.

McClelland, J. L. (1995). Constructive memory and memory distortions: A parallel-distributed processing approach. In D. L. Schacter, J. T. Coyle, G. D. Fischbach, M.-M. Mesulam, & L. E. Sullivan (Eds.), *Memory distortion: How minds, brains and societies reconstruct the past* (pp. 69–90). Cambridge, MA: Harvard University Press.

Metcalfe, J. (1993). Novelty monitoring, metacognition and control in a composite holographic associative recall model: Implications for Korsakoff amnesia. *Psychological Review, 100,* 3–22.

Miller, G. A. (1956). The magical number seven, plus or minus two: Some limits on our capacity for processing information. *Psychological Review, 63,* 81–96.

Neisser, U. (1967). *Cognitive psychology.* New York: Appleton-Century-Crofts.

Neisser, U., & Harsch, N. (1992). Phantom flashbulbs: False recollections of hearing the news about *Challenger.* In E. Winograd & U. Neisser (Eds.), *Affect and accuracy in recall: Studies of "flashbulb memories"* (pp. 9–31). Cambridge: Cambridge University Press.

Neisser, U., Winograd, E., Bergman, E. T., Schreiber, C. A., Palmer, S. E., & Weldon, M. S. (in press). Remembering the earthquake: Direct experience vs. hearing the news. *Memory.*

Nickerson, R. S., & Adams, M. J. (1970). Long-term memory for a common object. *Cognitive Psychology, 11,* 287–307.

Proust, M. (1992). *In search of lost time: Swann's way* (Moncrieff, C. K. S., Kilmartin, T., & Enright, D. J., Trans.). New York: The Modern Library.

Roediger, H. L., III (1980). Memory metaphors in cognitive psychology. *Memory & Cognition, 8,* 231–246.

Schacter, D. L. (1982). *Stranger behind the engram: Theories of memory and the psychology of science*. Hillsdale, NJ: Erlbaum.

Schacter, D. L., Eich, J. E., & Tulving, E. (1978). Richard Semon's theory of memory. *Journal of Verbal Learning and Verbal Behavior, 17*, 721–743.

Semon, R. (1904/1921). *The mneme*. London: George Allen & Unwin.

Semon, R. (1909/1923). *Mnemic psychology*. London: George Allen & Unwin.

Shattuck, R. (1983). *Proust's binoculars: A study of memory, time, and recognition in "A La Recherche du Temps Perdu."* Princeton: Princeton University Press.

Spence, J. (1984). *The memory palace of Matteo Ricci*. New York: Viking.

Stein, B. A., & Bransford, J. D. (1979). Constraints on effective elaboration: Effects of precision and subject generation. *Journal of Verbal Learning and Verbal Behavior, 18*, 769–777.

Storr, R. (1992). *Dislocations*. New York: The Museum of Modern Art.

Vallar, G., & Shallice, T. (1990). *Neuropsychological impairments of short-term memory*. Cambridge: Cambridge University Press.

Vargha-Khadem, F., Isaacs, E., & Mishkin, M. (1994). Agnosia, alexia and a remarkable form of amnesia in an adolescent boy. *Brain, 117*, 683–703.

Watt, H. J. (1905). Review of *Die Mneme*. *Archiv für die Gesamte Psychologie, 5*, 127–130.

Yates, F. A. (1966). *The art of memory*. Chicago: University of Chicago Press.

For Discussion:

1. Explain the difference between working memory and long-term memory. Why does some information become encoded in long-term memory while other information is forgotten?

2. How does Schacter explain why some people remember the same event differently than others do? What does this theory suggest about the possibility of recovering a "true" past?

3. What role do the stories of Bubbles P., Neil, and Richard Semon play in Schacter's argument? How does the function of each story differ?

4. What are some ordinary, everyday objects that we see every day but do not notice? List a few. Why, according to Schacter, do we fail to notice them?

For Fact-Finding, Research, and Writing:

1. What are mnemonics? What is Simonides's method of loci? Explain how you came up with the answers.

2. Locate Eran Shakine's painting "Hadassah." After examining the painting, add your ideas to Schacter's analysis of how Shakine represents the past.

3. Schacter argues that "our understanding of ourselves is . . . dependent on what we can remember of the past." Investigate the legal controversy surrounding "recovered memory."

4. Introductory science education used to depend on rote memory. How does the new trend toward inquiry-based science education reflect Schacter's argument about memory?

Howard Gardner, "A Rounded Version: The Theory of Multiple Intelligences"

Howard Gardner is the John H. and Elisabeth A. Hobbs Professor in Cognition and Education at the Harvard Graduate School of Education. Gardner has received numerous awards, including a MacArthur Prize Fellowship in 1981, the Grawemeyer Award in Education in 1990, and a Guggenheim Fellowship in 2000. The author of numerous books and articles, Gardner is best known for his theory of multiple intelligences. This theory, first published in *Frames of Mind* (1983), critiques the notion of a single intelligence that is measurable through standard testing, such as the intelligence quotient (IQ) test. This selection is excerpted from *Multiple Intelligences* (1993).

 Before You Read:

How do you define intelligence? How many different kinds of intelligences or ways of knowing can you categorize?

A Rounded Version: The Theory of Multiple Intelligences

Howard Gardner

TWO ELEVEN-YEAR-OLD children are taking a test of "intelligence." They sit at their desks laboring over the meanings of different words, the interpretation of graphs, and the solutions to arithmetic problems. They record their answers by filling in small circles on a single piece of paper. Later these completed answer sheets are scored objectively: the number of right answers is converted into a standardized score that compares the individual child with a population of children of similar age.

The teachers of these children review the different scores. They notice that one of the children has performed at a superior level; on all sections of the test, she answered more questions correctly than did her peers. In fact, her score is similar to that of children three to four years older. The other child's performance is average—his scores reflect those of other children his age.

A subtle change in expectations surrounds the review of these test scores. Teachers begin to expect the first child to do quite well during her formal schooling, whereas the second should have only moderate success. Indeed these predictions come true. In other words, the test taken by the eleven-year-olds serves as a reliable predictor of their later performance in school.

How does this happen? One explanation involves our free use of the word "intelligence": the child with the greater "intelligence" has the ability to solve problems, to find the answers to specific questions, and to learn new material quickly and efficiently. These skills in turn play a central role in school success. In this view, "intelligence" is a singular faculty that is brought to bear in any problem-solving situation. Since schooling deals largely with solving problems of various sorts, predicting this capacity in young children predicts their future success in school.

"Intelligence," from this point of view, is a general ability that is found in varying degrees in all individuals. It is the key to success in solving problems. This ability can be measured reliably with standardized pencil-and-paper tests that, in turn, predict future success in school.

What happens after school is completed? Consider the two individuals in the example. Looking further down the road, we find that the "average" student has become a highly successful mechanical engineer who has risen to a position of prominence in both the professional community of engineers as well as in civic groups in his community. His success is no fluke—he is considered by all to be a talented individual. The "superior" student, on the other hand, has had little success in her chosen career as a writer; after repeated rejections by publishers, she has taken up a middle management position in a bank. While certainly not a "failure," she is considered by her peers to be quite "ordinary" in her adult accomplishments. So what happened?

This fabricated example is based on the facts of intelligence testing. IQ tests predict school performance with considerable accuracy, but they are only an indifferent predictor of performance in a profession after formal schooling.[1] Furthermore, even as IQ tests measure only logical or logical-linguistic capacities, in this society we are nearly "brain-washed" to restrict the notion of intelligence to the capacities used in solving logical and linguistic problems.

To introduce an alternative point of view, undertake the following "thought experiment." Suspend the usual judgment of what constitutes intelligence and let your thoughts run freely over the capabilities of humans—perhaps those that would be picked out by the proverbial Martian visitor. In this exercise, you are drawn to the brilliant chess player, the world-class violinist, and the champion athlete; such outstanding performers deserve special consideration. Under this experiment, a quite different view of *intelligence* emerges. Are the chess player, violinist, and athlete "intelligent" in these pursuits? If they are, then why do our tests of "intelligence" fail to identify them? If they are not "intelligent," what allows them to achieve such astounding feats? In general, why does the contemporary construct "intelligence" fail to explain large areas of human endeavor?

In this chapter we approach these problems through the theory of multiple intelligences (MI). As the name indicates, we believe that human cognitive competence is better described in terms of a set of abilities, talents, or mental skills, which we call "intelligences." All normal individuals possess each of these skills to some extent; individuals differ in the degree of skill and in the nature of their combination. We believe this theory of intelligence may be more humane and more veridical than alternative views of intelligence and that it more adequately reflects the data of human "intelligent" behavior. Such a theory has important educational implications, including ones for curriculum development.

What Constitutes an Intelligence?

The question of the optimal definition of intelligence looms large in our inquiry. Indeed, it is at the level of this definition that the theory of multiple intelligences diverges from traditional points of view. In a traditional view, intelligence is defined operationally as the ability to answer items on tests of intelligence. The inference from the test scores to some underlying ability is supported by statistical techniques that compare responses of subjects at different ages; the apparent correlation of these test scores across ages and across different tests corroborates the notion that the general faculty of intelligence, does not change much with age or with training or experience. It is an inborn attribute or faculty of the individual.

Multiple intelligences theory, on the other hand, pluralizes the traditional concept. An intelligence entails the ability to solve problems or fashion products that are of consequence in a particular cultural setting or community. The problem-solving skill allows one to approach a situation in which a goal is to be obtained and to locate the appropriate route to that goal. The creation of a *cultural* product is crucial to such functions as capturing and transmitting knowledge or expressing one's views or feelings. The problems to be solved range from creating an end for a story to anticipating a mating move in chess to repairing a quilt. Products range from scientific theories to musical compositions to successful political campaigns.

MI theory is framed in light of the biological origins of each problem-solving skill. Only those skills that are universal to the human species are treated. Even so, the biological proclivity to participate in a particular form of problem solving must also be coupled with the cultural nurturing of that domain. For example, language, a universal skill, may manifest itself particularly as writing in one culture, as oratory in another culture, and as the secret language of anagrams in a third.

Given the desire of selecting intelligences that are rooted in biology, and that are valued in one or more cultural settings, how does one actually identify an "intelligence"? In coming up with our list, we consulted evidence from several different sources: knowledge about normal development and development in gifted individuals; information about the breakdown of cognitive skills under conditions of brain damage; studies of exceptional populations, including prodigies, idiots savants, and autistic children; data about the evolution of cognition over the millennia; cross-cultural accounts of cognition; psychometric studies, including examinations of correlations among tests; and psychological training studies, particularly measures of transfer and generalization across tasks. Only those candidate intelligences that satisfied all or a majority of the criteria were selected as bona fide intelligences. A more complete discussion of each of these criteria for an "intelligence" and the seven intelligences that have been proposed so far, is found in *Frames of Mind*.[2] This book also considers how the theory might be disproven and compares it to competing theories of intelligence.

In addition to satisfying the aforementioned criteria, each intelligence must have an identifiable core operation or set of operations. As a neutrally based computational system, each intelligence is activated or "triggered" by certain kinds of internally or externally presented information. For example, one core of musical intelligence is the sensitivity to pitch relations, whereas one core of linguistic intelligence is the sensitivity to phonological features.

An intelligence must also be susceptible to encoding in a symbol system—a culturally contrived system of meaning, which captures and conveys important forms of information. Language, picturing, and mathematics are but three nearly worldwide symbol systems that are necessary for human survival and productivity. The relationship of a candidate intelligence to a human symbol system is no accident. In fact, the existence of a core computational capacity anticipates the existence of a symbol system that exploits that capacity. While it may be possible for an intelligence to proceed without an accompanying symbol system, a primary characteristic of human intelligence may well be its gravitation toward such an embodiment.

The Seven Intelligences

Having sketched the characteristics and criteria of an intelligence, we turn now to a brief consideration of each of the seven intelligences. We begin each sketch with a thumbnail biography of a person who demonstrates an unusual facility with that intelligence. These biographies illustrate some of the abilities that are central to the fluent operation of a given intelligence. Although each biography illustrates a particular intelligence, we do not wish to imply that in adulthood intelligences operate in isolation. Indeed, except for abnormal individuals, intelligences always work in concert, and any sophisticated adult role will involve a melding of several of them. Following each biography we survey the various sources of data that support each candidate as an "intelligence."

Musical Intelligence

When he was three years old, Yehudi Menuhin was smuggled into the San Francisco Orchestra concerts by his parents. The sound of Louis Persinger's violin so entranced the youngster that he insisted on a violin for his birthday and Louis Persinger as his teacher. He got both. By the time he was ten years old, Menuhin was an international performer.[3]

Violinist Yehudi Menuhin's musical intelligence manifested itself even before he had touched a violin or received any musical training. His powerful reaction to that particular sound and his rapid progress on the instrument suggest that he was biologically prepared in some way for that endeavor. In this way evidence from child prodigies supports our claim that there is a biological link to a particular intelligence. Other special populations, such as autistic children who can play a musical instrument beautifully but who cannot speak, underscore the independence of musical intelligence.

A brief consideration of the evidence suggests that musical skill passes the other tests for an intelligence. For example, certain parts of the brain play important roles in perception and production of music. These areas are characteristically located in the right hemisphere, although musical skill is not as clearly "localized," or located in a specifiable area, as language. Although the particular susceptibility of musical ability to brain damage depends on the degree of training and other individual differences, there is clear evidence for "amusia" or loss of musical ability.

Music apparently played an important unifying role in Stone Age (Paleolithic) societies. Birdsong provides a link to other species. Evidence from various cultures supports the notion that music is a universal faculty. Studies of infant development suggest that there is a "raw" computational ability in early childhood. Finally, musical notation provides an accessible and lucid symbol system.

In short, evidence to support the interpretation of musical ability as an "intelligence" comes from many different sources. Even though musical skill is not typically considered an intellectual skill like mathematics, it qualifies under our criteria. By definition it deserves consideration; and in view of the data, its inclusion is empirically justified.

Bodily-Kinesthetic Intelligence

Fifteen-year-old Babe Ruth played third base. During one game his team's pitcher was doing very poorly and Babe loudly criticized him from third base. Brother Mathias, the coach, called out, "Ruth, if you know so much about it, YOU pitch!" Babe was surprised and embarrassed because he had never pitched before, but Brother Mathias insisted. Ruth said later that at the very moment he took the pitcher's mound, he KNEW he was supposed to be a pitcher and that it was "natural" for him to strike people out. Indeed, he went on to become a great major league pitcher (and, of course, attained legendary status as a hitter).[4]

Like Menuhin, Babe Ruth was a child prodigy who recognized his "instrument" immediately upon his first exposure to it. This recognition occurred in advance of formal training.

Control of bodily movement is, of course, localized in the motor cortex, with each hemisphere dominant or controlling bodily movements on the contra-lateral side. In right-handers, the dominance for such movement is ordinarily found in the left hemisphere. The ability to perform movements when directed to do so can be impaired even in individuals who can perform the same movements reflexively or on a nonvoluntary basis. The existence of specific *apraxia* constitutes one line of evidence for a bodily-kinesthetic intelligence.

The evolution of specialized body movements is of obvious advantage to the species, and in humans this adaptation is extended through the use of tools. Body movement undergoes a clearly defined developmental schedule in children. And there is little question of its universality across cultures. Thus it appears that bodily-kinesthetic "knowledge" satisfies many of the criteria for an intelligence.

The consideration of bodily-kinesthetic knowledge as "problem solving" may be less intuitive. Certainly carrying out a mime sequence or hitting a tennis ball is not solving a mathematical equation. And yet, the ability to use one's body to express an emotion (as in a dance), to play a game (as in a sport), or to create a new product (as in devising an invention) is evidence of the cognitive features of body usage. The specific computations required to solve a particular bodily-kinesthetic *problem*, hitting a tennis ball, are summarized by Tim Gallwey:

> At the moment the ball leaves the server's racket, the brain calculates approximately where it will land and where the racket will intercept it. This calculation includes the initial velocity of the ball, combined with an input for the progressive decrease in velocity and the effect of wind and after the bounce of the ball. Simultaneously, muscle orders are given: not just once, but constantly with refined and updated information. The muscles must cooperate. A movement of the feet occurs, the racket is taken back, the face of the racket kept at a constant angle. Contact is made at a precise point that depends on whether the order was given to hit down the line or cross-court, an order not given until after a split-second analysis of the movement and balance of the opponent.
>
> To return an average serve, you have about one second to do this. To hit the ball at all is remarkable and yet not uncommon. The truth is that everyone who inhabits a human body possesses a remarkable creation.[5]

Logical-Mathematical Intelligence

In 1983 Barbara McClintock won the Nobel Prize in medicine or physiology for her work in microbiology. Her intellectual powers of deduction and observation illustrate one form of logical-mathematical intelligence that is often labeled "scientific thinking." One incident is particularly illuminating. While a researcher at Cornell in the 1920s McClintock was faced one day with a problem: while *theory* predicted 50-percent pollen sterility in corn, her research assistant (in the "field") was finding plants that were only 25- to 30-percent sterile. Disturbed by this discrepancy, McClintock left the cornfield and returned to her office where she sat for half an hour, thinking:

> Suddenly I jumped up and ran back to the (corn) field. At the top of the field (the others were still at the bottom) I shouted "Eureka, I have it! I know what the 30% sterility is!" . . . They asked me to prove it. I sat down with a paper bag and a pencil and I started from scratch, which I had not done at all in my laboratory. It had all been done so fast; the answer came and I ran. Now I worked it out step by step—it was an intricate series of steps—and I came out with [the same result]. [They] looked at the material and it was exactly as I'd said it was; it worked out exactly as I had diagrammed it. Now, why did I know, without having done it on paper? Why was I so sure?[6]

This anecdote illustrates two essential facts of the logical-mathematical intelligence. First, in the gifted individual, the process of problem solving is often remarkably rapid—the successful scientist copes with many variables at once and creates numerous hypotheses that are each evaluated and then accepted or rejected in turn.

The anecdote also underscores the *nonverbal* nature of the intelligence. A solution to a problem can be constructed *before* it is articulated. In fact, the solution process may be totally invisible, even to the problem solver. This need not imply, however, that discoveries of this sort—the familiar "Aha!" phenomenon—are mysterious, intuitive, or unpredictable. The fact that it happens more frequently to some people (perhaps Nobel Prize winners) suggests the opposite. We interpret this as the work of theological-mathematical intelligence.

Along with the companion skill of language, logical-mathematical reasoning provides the principal basis for IQ tests. This form of intelligence has been heavily investigated by traditional psychologists, and it is the archetype of "raw intelligence" or the problem-solving faculty that purportedly cuts across domains. It is perhaps ironic, then, that the actual mechanism by which one arrives at a solution to a logical-mathematical problem is not as yet properly understood.

This intelligence is supported by our empirical criteria as well. Certain areas of the brain are more prominent in mathematical calculation than others. There are idiots savants who perform great feats of calculation even though they remain tragically deficient in most other areas. Child prodigies in mathematics abound. The development of this intelligence in children has been carefully documented by Jean Piaget and other psychologists.

Linguistic Intelligence

At the age of ten, T. S. Eliot created a magazine called "Fireside" to which he was the sole contributor. In a three-day period during his winter vacation, he created eight complete issues. Each one included poems, adventure stories, a gossip column, and humor. Some of this material survives and it displays the talent of the poet.[7]

As with the logical intelligence, calling linguistic skill an "intelligence" is consistent with the stance of traditional psychology. Linguistic intelligence also passes our empirical tests. For instance, a specific area of the brain, called "Broca's Area," is responsible for the production of grammatical sentences. A person with damage to this area can understand words and sentences quite well but has difficulty putting words together in anything other than the simplest of sentences. At the same time, other thought processes may be entirely unaffected.

The gift of language is universal, and its development in children is strikingly constant across cultures. Even in deaf populations where a manual sign language is not explicitly taught, children will often "invent" their own manual language and use it surreptitiously! We thus see how an intelligence may operate independently of a specific input modality or output channel.

Spatial Intelligence

Navigation around the Caroline Islands in the South Seas is accomplished without instruments. The position of the stars, as viewed from various islands, the weather patterns, and water color are the only sign posts. Each journey is broken into a series of segments; and the navigator learns the position of the stars within each of these segments. During the actual trip the navigator must envision mentally a reference island as it passes under a particular star and from that he computes the number of segments completed, the proportion of the trip remaining, and any corrections in heading that are required. The navigator cannot see the islands as he sails along; instead he maps their locations in his mental "picture" of the journey.[8]

Spatial problem solving is required for navigation and in the use of the notational system of maps. Other kinds of spatial problem solving are brought to bear in visualizing an object seen from a different angle and in playing chess. The visual arts also employ this intelligence in the use of space.

Evidence from brain research is clear and persuasive. Just as the left hemisphere has, over the course of evolution, been selected as the site of linguistic processing in right-handed persons, the right hemisphere proves to be the site most crucial for spatial processing. Damage to the right posterior regions causes impairment of the ability to find one's way around a site, to recognize faces or scenes, or to notice fine details.

Patients with damage specific to regions of the right hemisphere will attempt to compensate for their spacial deficits with linguistic strategies. They will try to reason aloud, to challenge the task, or even make up answers. But such nonspatial strategies are rarely successful.

Blind populations provide an illustration of the distinction between the spatial intelligence and visual perception. A blind person can recognize shapes by an indirect method: running a hand along the object translates into length of time of movement, which in turn is translated into the size of the object. For the blind person, the perceptual system of the tactile modality parallels the visual modality in the seeing person. The analogy between the spatial reasoning of the blind and the linguistic reasoning of the deaf is notable.

There are few child prodigies among visual artists, but there are idiots savants such as Nadia.[9] Despite a condition of severe autism, this preschool child made drawings of the most remarkable representational accuracy and finesse.

Interpersonal Intelligence

With little formal training in special education and nearly blind herself, Anne Sullivan began the intimidating task of instructing a blind and deaf seven-year-old Helen Keller. Sullivan's efforts at communication were complicated by the child's emotional struggle with the world around her. At their first meal together, this scene occurred:

> Annie did not allow Helen to put her hand into Annie's plate and take what she wanted, as she had been accustomed to do with her family. It became a test of wills— hand thrust into plate, hand firmly put aside. The family, much upset, left the dining room. Annie locked the door and proceeded to eat her breakfast while Helen lay on the floor kicking and screaming, pushing and pulling at Annie's chair. [After half an hour] Helen went around the table looking for her family. She discovered no one else

was there and that bewildered her. Finally, she sat down and began to eat her break-
fast, but with her hands. Annie gave her a spoon. Down on the floor it clattered, and
the contest of wills began anew.[10]

Anne Sullivan sensitively responded to the child's behavior. She wrote home: "The greatest problem I shall have to solve is how to discipline and control her without break-ing her spirit. I shall go rather slowly at first and try to win her love."

In fact, the first "miracle" occurred two weeks later, well before the famous incident at the pumphouse. Annie had taken Helen to a small cottage near the family's house, where they could live alone. After seven days together, Helen's personality suddenly underwent a profound change—the therapy had worked:

My heart is singing with joy this morning. A miracle has happened! The wild little crea-
ture of two weeks ago has been transformed into a gentle child.[11]

It was just two weeks after this that the first breakthrough in Helen's grasp of language occurred; and from that point on, she progressed with incredible speed. The key to the miracle of language was Anne Sullivan's insight into the *person* of Helen Keller.

Interpersonal intelligence builds on a core capacity to notice distinctions among oth-ers; in particular, contrasts in their moods, temperaments, motivations, and intentions. In more advanced forms, this intelligence permits a skilled adult to read the intentions and desires of others, even when these have been hidden. This skill appears in a highly sophis-ticated form in religious or political leaders, teachers, therapists, and parents. The Helen Keller–Anne Sullivan story suggests that this interpersonal intelligence does not depend on language.

All indices in brain research suggest that the frontal lobes play a prominent role in interpersonal knowledge. Damage in this area can cause profound personality changes while leaving other forms of problem solving unharmed—a person is often "not the same person" after such an injury.

Alzheimer's disease, a form of presenile dementia, appears to attack posterior brain zones with a special ferocity, leaving spatial, logical, and linguistic computations severely impaired. Yet, Alzheimer's patients will often remain well groomed, socially proper, and continually apologetic for their errors. In contrast, Pick's disease, another variety of pre-senile dementia that is more frontally oriented, entails a rapid loss of social graces.

Biological evidence for interpersonal intelligence encompasses two additional factors often cited as unique to humans. One factor is the prolonged childhood of primates, in-cluding the close attachment to the mother. In those cases where the mother is removed from early development, normal interpersonal development is in serious jeopardy. The sec-ond factor is the relative importance in humans of social interaction. Skills such as hunt-ing, tracking, and killing in prehistoric societies required participation and cooperation of large numbers of people. The need for group cohesion, leadership, organization, and soli-darity follows naturally from this.

Intrapersonal Intelligence

In an essay called "A Sketch of the Past," written almost as a diary entry, Virginia Woolf discusses the "cotton wool of existence"—the various mundane events of life. She contrasts this "cotton wool" with three specific and poignant memories from her childhood: a fight with her brother, seeing a particular flower in the garden, and hearing of the suicide of a past visitor:

> These are three instances of exceptional moments. I often tell them over, or rather they come to the surface unexpectedly. But now for the first time I have written them down, and I realize something that I have never realized before. Two of these moments ended in a state of despair. The other ended, on the contrary, in a state of satisfaction.
>
> The sense of horror (in hearing of the suicide) held me powerless. But in the case of the flower, I found a reason; and was thus able to deal with the sensation. I was not powerless.
>
> Though I still have the peculiarity that I receive these sudden shocks, they are now always welcome; after the first surprise, I always feel instantly that they are particularly valuable. And so I go on to suppose that the shock-receiving capacity is what makes me a writer. I hazard the explanation that a shock is at once in my case followed by the desire to explain it. I feel that I have had a blow; but it is not, as I thought as a child, simply a blow from an enemy hidden behind the cotton wool of daily life; it is or will become a revelation of some order; it is a token of some real thing behind appearances; and I make it real by putting it into words. [12]

This quotation vividly illustrates the intrapersonal intelligence—knowledge of the internal aspects of a person: access to one's own feeling life, one's range of emotions, the capacity to effect discriminations among these emotions and eventually to label them and to draw upon them as a means of understanding and guiding one's own behavior. A person with good intrapersonal intelligence has a viable and effective model of himself or herself. Since this intelligence is the most private, it requires evidence from language, music, or some other more expressive form of intelligence if the observer is to detect it at work. In the above quotation, for example, linguistic intelligence is drawn upon to convey intrapersonal knowledge; it embodies the interaction of intelligences, a common phenomenon to which we will return later.

We see the familiar criteria at work in the intrapersonal intelligence. As with the interpersonal intelligence, the frontal lobes play a central role in personality change. Injury to the lower area of the frontal lobes is likely to produce irritability or euphoria; while injury to the higher regions is more likely to produce indifference, listlessness, slowness, and apathy—a kind of depressive personality. In such "frontal-lobe" individuals, the other cognitive functions often remain preserved. In contrast, among aphasics who have recovered sufficiently to describe their experiences, we find consistent testimony; while there may have been a diminution of general alertness and considerable depression about the condition, the individual in no way felt himself to be a different person. He recognized his own needs, wants, and desires and tried as best he could to achieve them.

The autistic child is a prototypical example of an individual with impaired intrapersonal intelligence; indeed, the child may not even be able to refer to himself. At the same time, such children often exhibit remarkable abilities in the musical, computational, spatial, or mechanical realms.

Evolutionary evidence for an intrapersonal faculty is more difficult to come by, but we might speculate that the capacity to transcend the satisfaction of instinctual drives is relevant. This becomes increasingly important in a species not perennially involved in the struggle for survival.

In sum, then, both interpersonal and intrapersonal faculties pass the tests of an intelligence. They both feature problem-solving endeavors with significance for the individual and the species. Interpersonal intelligence allows one to understand and work with others; intrapersonal intelligence allows one to understand and work with oneself. In the individual's sense of self, one encounters a melding of inter- and intrapersonal components. Indeed, the sense of self emerges as one of the most marvelous of human inventions—a symbol that represents all kinds of information about a person and that is at the same time an invention that all individuals construct for themselves.

Summary: The Unique Contributions of the Theory

As human beings, we all have a repertoire of skills for solving different kinds of problems. Our investigation has begun, therefore, with a consideration of these problems, the contexts they are found in, and the culturally significant products that are the outcome. We have not approached "intelligence" as a reified human faculty that is brought to bear in literally any problem setting; rather, we have begun with the problems that humans *solve* and worked back to the "intelligences" that must be responsible.

Evidence from brain research, human development, evolution, and cross-cultural comparisons was brought to bear in our search for the relevant human intelligences: a candidate was included only if reasonable evidence to support its membership was found across these diverse fields. Again, this tack differs from the traditional one: since no candidate faculty is *necessarily* an intelligence, we could choose on a motivated basis. In the traditional approach to "intelligence," there is no opportunity for this type of empirical decision.

We have also determined that these multiple human faculties, the intelligences, are to a significant extent *independent*. For example, research with brain-damaged adults repeatedly demonstrates that particular faculties can be lost while others are spared. This independence of intelligences implies that a particularly high level of ability in one intelligence, say mathematics, does not require a similarly high level in another intelligence, like language or music. This independence of intelligences contrasts sharply with traditional measures of IQ that find high correlations among test scores. We speculate that the usual correlations among subtests of IQ tests come about because all of these tasks in fact measure the ability to respond rapidly to items of a logical-mathematical or linguistic sort; we believe that these correlations would be substantially reduced if one were to survey in a contextually appropriate way the full range of human problem-solving skills.

Until now, we have supported the fiction that adult roles depend largely on the flowering of a single intelligence. In fact, however, nearly every cultural role of any degree of sophistication requires a combination of intelligences. Thus, even an apparently straightforward role, like playing the violin, transcends a reliance on simple musical intelligence. To become a successful violinist requires bodily-kinesthetic dexterity and the interpersonal skills of relating to an audience and, in a different way, choosing a manager; quite possibly it involves an intrapersonal intelligence as well. Dance requires skills in bodily-kinesthetic, musical, interpersonal, and spatial intelligences in varying degrees. Politics requires an interpersonal skill, a linguistic facility, and perhaps some logical aptitude. Inasmuch as nearly every cultural role requires several intelligences, it becomes important to consider individuals as a collection of aptitudes rather than as having a singular problem-solving faculty that can be measured directly through pencil-and-paper tests. Even given a relatively small number of such intelligences, the diversity of human ability is created through the differences in these profiles. In fact, it may well be that the "total is greater than the sum of the parts." An individual may not be particularly gifted in any intelligence; and yet, because of a particular combination or blend of skills, he or she may be able to fill some niche uniquely well. Thus it is of paramount importance to assess the particular combination of skills that may earmark an individual for a certain vocational or avocational niche.

Notes

1. Jencks, C. (1972). *Inequality*. New York: Basic Books. [Gardner's note]
2. Gardner, H. (1983). *Frames of mind: The theory of multiple intelligences*. New York: Basic Books. [Gardner's note]
3. Menuhin, Y. (1977). *Unfinished journey*. New York: Knopf. [Gardner's note]
4. Connor, A. (1982). *Voices from Cooperstown*. New York: Collier. (Based on a quotation taken from *The Babe Ruth story*, Babe Ruth & Bob Considine. New York: Dutton, 1948.) [Gardner's note]
5. Gallwey, T. (1976). *Inner tennis*. New York: Random House. [Gardner's note]
6. Keller, E. (1983). *A feeling for the organism* (p. 104). Salt Lake City: W. H. Freeman. [Gardner's note]
7. Soldo, J. (1982). Jovial juvenilia: T. S. Eliot's first magazine. *Biography*, 5. 25–37. [Gardner's note]
8. Gardner, H. (1983). *Frames of mind: The theory of multiple intelligences*. New York: Basic Books. [Gardner's note]
9. Selfe, L. (1977). *Nadia: A case of extraordinary drawing in an autistic child*. New York: Academic Press. [Gardner's note]
10. Lash, J. (1980). *Helen and teacher: The story of Helen Keller and Anne Sullivan Macy* (p. 52). New York: Delacorte. [Gardner's note]
11. Lash (p. 54). [Gardner's note]
12. Woolf, V. (1976). *Moments of being* (pp. 69–70). Sussex: The University Press. [Gardner's note]

For Discussion:

1. How would you define intelligence, and why? Does Gardner's theory of multiple intelligences resemble or contrast to your own definition?
2. What is the relationship, for Gardner, between culturally constructed and biologically determined (innate) qualities? How do these two types of qualities help to define intelligence?
3. What is the difference between interpersonal and intrapersonal intelligence?
4. List Gardner's types of intelligence. How is each intelligence independent? In what ways do these intelligences work together?

 For Fact-Finding, Research, and Writing:

1. The word "creative" is now frequently added to the names of programs formerly titled "Gifted and Talented." Why and why did this change occur?
2. Many universities (including the prestigious University of California) are abandoning standardized testing as an important criterion for admission. Find information about the controversy surrounding this decision. How does Gardner's thinking appear to have been influential in the reasoning offered for using and disregarding such tests?
3. Compare Gardner's theory of multiple intelligences with Plato's conception of knowledge or Hofstadter's concept of the intellectual. Are Plato's or Hofstadter's ideas "traditions"? In what ways does either Plato's or Hofstadter's theory extend beyond "logical-mathematical" intelligence?

Ron Carlson, "The Ordinary Son"

Long regarded as one of America's finest short story writers, Ron Carlson is Professor of English at Arizona State University in Scottsdale, Arizona. He has published five books of fiction. His short stories are regularly anthologized in *Best American Short Stories* and *The O. Henry Prize Stories*, and his work has appeared in *The New Yorker, Esquire, Harper's Gentlemen's Quarterly*, and *Tin House*. "The Ordinary Son" is taken from Carlson's latest short story collection *At the Jim Bridger*, published in 2002. It can also be found in *The Best American Short Stories 2000* and *The Pushcart Prize Anthology 2001*.

Before You Read:

Using any source that comes to mind (movies, television, sports) come up with as many examples of "genius" as you can and try to arrive at a working definition of the term.

The Ordinary Son

Ron Carlson

THE STORY OF my famous family is a story of genius and its consequences, I suppose, and I am uniquely and particularly suited to tell the story since genius avoided me—and I it—and I remain an ordinary man, if there is such a thing, calm in all weathers, aware of event, but uninterested and generally incapable of deciphering implication. As my genius brother Garrett used to say, "Reed, you're not screwed too tight like the rest of us, but you're still screwed." Now, there's a definition of the common man you can trust, and further, you can trust me. There's no irony in that or deep inner meaning or Freudian slips, any kind of slips really, simply what it says. My mother told me many times I have a good heart, and of course, she was a genius, and that heart should help with this story, but a heart, as she said so often, good as it may be, is always trouble.

Part of the reason this story hasn't come together before, the story of my famous family, is that no one remembers they were related. They all had their own names. My father was Duncan Landers, the noted NASA physicist, the man responsible for every facet of the photography of the first moon landing. There is still camera gear on the moon inscribed with this name. That is, Landers. He was born Duncan Lrsdyksz, which was changed when NASA began their public-relations campaigns in the mid-sixties; the space agency suggested that physicists who worked for NASA should have more vowels in their names. They didn't want their press releases to seem full of typographical errors or foreigners. Congress was reading this stuff. So Lrsdyksz became Landers. (My father's close associate Igor Oeuroi didn't get just vowels; his name became LeRoy Rodgers. After le Cowboy Star, my mother quipped.)

My mother was Gloria Rainstrap, the poet who spent twenty years fighting for workers' rights from Texas to Alaska; in one string she gave four thousand consecutive lectures in her travels, not missing a night as she drove from village to village throughout the country. It still stands as some kind of record.

Wherever she went, she stirred up the best kind of trouble, reading her work and then spending hours in whatever guest house or spare bedroom she was given, reading the poems and essays of the people who had come to see her. She was tireless, driven by her over-whelming sense of fairness, and she was certainly the primary idealist to come out of twen-tieth-century Texas. When she started leaving home for months, years at a time, I was just a lad, but I remember her telling my father, Duncan, one night, "Texas is too small for what I have to do."

This was not around the dinner table. We were a family of geniuses and did not have a dinner table. In fact, the only table we did have was my father's drafting table, which was in the entry so that you had to squeeze sideways to even get into our house. "It sets the tone," Duncan used to say. "I want anyone coming into our home to see my work. That work is the reason we have a roof, anyway." He said that one day after my friend Jeff Shreckenbah and I inched past him on the way to my room. "And who are these people coming in the door?"

"It is your son and his friend," I told him.

"Good," he said, his benediction, but he said it deeply into his drawing, which is where he spent his time at home. He wouldn't have known if the Houston Oilers had ar-rived, because he was about to invent the modern gravity-free vacuum hinge that is still used today.

Most of my father, Duncan Landers's, work was classified, top-secret, eyes-only, but it didn't matter. No one except Jeff Shreckenbah came to our house. People didn't come over.

We were geniuses. We had no television, and we had no telephone. "What should I do," my father would say from where he sat in the entry, drawing, "answer some little buzz-ing device? Say hello to it?" NASA tried to install phones for us. Duncan took them out. It was a genius household and not to be diminished by primitive electronic foo-fahs.

My older sister was named Christina by my father and given the last name Rossetti by my mother. When she finally fled from M.I.T. at nineteen, she gave herself a new sur-name: Isotope. There had been some trouble, she told me, personal trouble, and she needed the new name to remind herself she wouldn't last long—and then she asked me how I liked my half-life. I was twelve then, and she laughed and said, "I'm kidding, Reed. You're not a genius; you're going to live forever." I was talking to her on the "hot line," the secret phone our housekeeper, Clovis Armandy, kept in a kitchen cupboard.

"Where are you going?" I asked her.

"West with Mother," she said. Evidently, Gloria Rainstrap had driven up to Boston to rescue Christina from some sort of meltdown. "A juncture of some kind," my father told me. "Not to worry."

Christina said, "I'm through with theoretical chemistry, but chemistry isn't through with me. Take care of Dad. See you later."

We three children were eight years apart; that's how geniuses plan their families. Christina had been gone for years, it seemed, from our genius household; she barely knew our baby brother, Garrett.

Garrett and I took everything in stride. We accepted that we were a family of geniuses and that we had no telephone or refrigerator or proper beds. We thought it was natural to eat crackers and sardines months on end. We thought the front yard was supposed to be a jungle of overgrown grass, weeds, and whatever reptiles would volunteer to live there.

Twice a year the City of Houston street crew came by and mowed it all down, and daylight would pour in for a month or two. We had no cars. My father was always climbing into white Chevrolet station wagons, unmarked, and going off to the NASA Space Center south of town. My mother was always stepping up into orange VW buses driven by other people and driving off to tour. My sister had been the youngest student at M.I.T. My brother and I did our own laundry for years and walked to school, where by about seventh grade, we began to see the differences between the way ordinary people lived and the way geniuses lived. Other people's lives, we learned, centered fundamentally on two things: television and soft foods rich with all the versions of sugar.

By the time I entered junior high school, my mother's travels had kicked into high gear, and she hired a woman we came to know well, Clovis Armandy, to live in and to assist with our corporeal care. Gloria Rainstrap's parental theory and practice could be summed up by the verse I heard her say a thousand times before I reached the age of six: "Feed the soul, the body finds a way." And she fed our souls with a groaning banquet of iron ethics at every opportunity. She wasn't interested in sandwiches or casseroles. She was the kind of person who had a moral motive for her every move. We had no refrigerator because it was simply the wrong way to prolong the value of food, which had little value in the first place. We had no real furniture because furniture became the numbing insulation of drones for the economy, an evil in itself. If religion was the opiate of the masses, then home furnishings were the Novocain of the middle class. Any small surfeit of comfort undermined our moral fabric. *We live for the work we can do, not for things,* she told us. I've met and heard lots of folks who shared Gloria's posture toward life on this earth, but I've never found anyone who put it so well, presented her ideas so convincingly, beautifully, and so insistently. They effectively seduced you into wanting to go without. I won't put any of her poems in this story, but they were transcendent. The *Times* called her "Buddha's angry daughter." My mother's response to people who were somewhat shocked at our empty house and its unkempt quality was, "We're ego distant. These little things," she'd say, waving her hand over the litter of the laundry, discarded draft paper, piles of top-secret documents in the hallway, various toys, the odd empty tin of sardines, "don't bother us in the least. We aren't even here for them." I always loved that last and still use it when a nuisance arises: I'm not even here for it. "Ego distant," my friend Jeff Shreckeubah used to say; standing in our empty house, "which means your ma doesn't sweat the small stuff."

My mother's quirk, and one she fostered, was writing on the bottom of things. She started it because she was always gone, away for months at a time, and she wanted us to get her messages throughout her absence and thereby be reminded again of making correct decisions and ethical choices. It was not unusual to find ballpoint-pen lettering on the bottom of our shoes, and little marker messages on the bottom of plates (where she wrote in a tiny script), and anywhere that you could lift up and look under, she would have left her mark. These notes primarily confused us. There I'd be in math class and cross my legs and see something on the edge of my sneaker and read, "Your troubles, if you stay alert, will pass very quickly away."

I'm not complaining. I never, except once or twice, felt deprived. I like sardines, still. It was a bit of a pinch when we got to high school, and I noted with new poignancy that I didn't quite have the wardrobe to keep up. Geniuses dress plain but clean, and not always as clean as their ordinary counterparts, who have nothing better to do with their lives than buy and sort and wash clothes.

Things were fine. I turned seventeen. I was hanging out sitting around my bare room, reading books, the History of This, the History of That, dry stuff, waiting for my genius to kick in. This is what had happened to Christina. One day when she was ten, she was having a tea party with her dolls, which were two rolled pink towels, the next day she cataloged and diagrammed the amino acids, laying the groundwork for two artificial sweeteners and a mood elevator. By the time my mother, Gloria Rainstrap, returned from the Northwest and my father looked up from his table, the State Department "mentors" had been by and my sister, Christina, was on her way to the inner sanctums of the Massachusetts Institute of Technology. I remember my mother standing against my father's drafting table, her hands along the top. Her jaw was set and she said, "This is meaningful work for Christina, her special doorway."

My father dragged his eyes up from his drawings and said, "Where's Christina now?"

So the day I went into Garrett's room and found him writing equations on a huge scroll of butcher paper, which he had used until that day to draw battle re-creations of the French and Indian War, was a big day for me. I stood there in the gloom, watching him crawl along the paper, reeling out figures of which very few were numbers I recognized, most of the symbols being X's and Y's and the little twisted members of the Greek alphabet, and I knew that it had skipped me. Genius had cast its powerful, clear eye on me and said, "No thanks." At least I was that smart. I realized that I was not going to get to be a genius.

The message took my body a piece at a time, loosening each joint and muscle on the way up and then filling my face with a strange warmth, which I knew immediately was relief.

I was free.

I immediately took a job doing landscaping and general cleanup and maintenance at the San Jacinto Resort Motel on the old Hempstead Highway. My friend Jeff Shreckenbah worked next door at Alfredo's American Cafe, and he had told me that the last guy doing handiwork at the motel had been fired for making a holy mess of the parking lot with a paintbrush, and when I applied, Mr. Rakkerts, the short little guy who owned the place, took me on. These were the days of big changes for me. I bought a car, an act that would have at one time been as alien for me as intergalactic travel or applying to barber college. I bought a car. It was a four-door lime-green Plymouth Fury III, low miles. I bought a pair of chinos. These things gave me exquisite pleasure. I was seventeen and I had not known the tangible pleasure of having things. I bought three new shirts and a wristwatch with a leather strap, and I went driving in the evenings, alone south from our subdivision of Spring Woods with my arm on the green sill of my lime-green Plymouth Fury III through the vast spaghetti bowl of freeways and into the mysterious network of towers that was downtown Houston. It was my dawning.

Late at night, my blood rich with wonder at the possibilities of such a vast material planet, I would return to our tumbledown genius ranch house, my sister off putting new legs on the periodic table at M.I.T., my mother away in Shreveport showing the seaport workers there the way to political and personal power, my brother in his room edging closer to new theories of rocket reaction and thrust, my father sitting by the entry, rapt in his schematics. As I came in and sidled by his table and the one real light in the whole front part of the house, his pencilings on the space station hinge looking as beautiful and inscrutable to me as a sheet of music, he'd say my name as simple greeting. "Reed."

"Duncan," I'd say in return.

"How goes the metropolis?" he'd add, not looking up. His breath was faintly reminiscent of sardines; in fact, I still associate that smell, which is not as unpleasant as it might seem, with brilliance. I know he said *metropolis* because he didn't know for a moment which city we were in.

"It teems with industrious citizenry well into the night," I'd answer.

Then he'd say it, "Good," his benediction, as he'd carefully trace his lead-holder and its steel-like wafer of 5H pencil-lead along a precise new line deep into the vast white space. "That's good."

The San Jacinto Resort Motel along the Hempstead Highway was exactly what you might expect a twenty-unit motel to be in the year 1966. The many bright new interstates had come racing to Houston and collided downtown in a maze, and the old Hempstead Highway had been supplanted as a major artery into town. There was still a good deal of traffic on the four-lane, and the motel was always about half full, and as you would expect, never the same half. There were three permanent occupants, including a withered old man named Newcombe Shinetower, who was a hundred years old that summer and who had no car, just a room full of magazines with red and yellow covers, stacks of these things with titles like *Too Young for Comfort* and *Treasure Chest*. There were other titles. I was in Mr. Shinetower's room only on two occasions. He wore the same flannel shirt every day of his life and was heavily gone to seed. Once or twice a day I would see him shuffling out toward Alfredo's American Cafe, where Jeff told me he always ate the catfish. "You want to live to be a hundred," Jeff said, "eat the catfish." I told him I didn't know about a hundred and that I generally preferred smaller fish. I was never sure if Mr. Shinetower saw me or not as I moved through his line of sight. He might have nodded; it was hard to tell. What I felt was that he might exist on another plane, the way rocks are said to; they're in there but in a rhythm too slow for humans to perceive.

It was in his room, rife with the flaking detritus of the ages, that Jeff tried to help me reckon with the new world. "You're interested in sex, right?" he asked me one day as I took my break at the counter of Alfredo's. I told him I was, but that wasn't exactly the truth. I was indifferent. I understood how it was being packaged and sold to the American people, but it did not stir me, nor did any of the girls we went to school with, many of whom were outright beauties and not bashful about it. This was Texas in the sixties. Some of these buxom girls would grow up and try to assassinate their daughters' rivals on the cheerleading squad. If sex was the game, some seemed to say, deal me in. And I guess I felt it was a game, too, one I could sit out. I had begun to look a little closer at the ways I was different from my peers, worrying about anything that might be a genius tendency. And I took great comfort in the unmistakable affection I felt for my Plymouth Fury III.

"Good," he said. "If you're interested, then you're safe; you're not a genius. Geniuses"—here he leaned closer to me and squinted his eyes up to let me know this was a ground-breaking postulate—"have a little trouble in the sex department."

I liked Jeff; he was my first "buddy." I sat on the round red Naugahyde stool at Alfredo's long Formica counter and listened to his speech, including, "sex department," and I don't know, it kind of made sense to me. There must have been something on my face, which is a way of saying there must have been nothing on my face, absolutely nothing, a blank blank, because Jeff pulled his apron off his head and said, "Meet me out back in two minutes." He looked down the counter to where old Mr. Shinetower sucked on his soup. "We got to get you some useful information."

Out back, of course, Jeff led me directly around to the motel and Mr. Shinetower's room, which was not unlocked, but opened when Jeff gave the doorknob a healthy rattle. Inside in the sour dark, Jeff lit the lamp and picked up one of the old man's periodicals.

Jeff held the magazine and thumbed it like a deck of cards, stopping finally at a full-page photograph that he presented to me with an odd kind of certainty. "There," he said. "This is what everybody is trying for. This is the goal." It was a glossy color photograph, and I knew what it was right away, even in the poor light, a shiny shaved pubis, seven or eight times larger than life size. "This makes the world go round."

I was going along with Jeff all the way on this, but that comment begged for a remark, which I restrained. I could feel my father in me responding about the forces that actually caused and maintained the angular momentum of the earth. Instead I looked at the picture, which had its own lurid beauty. Of course, what it looked like was a landscape, a barren but promising promontory in not this but another world, the seam too perfect a fold for anything but ceremony. I imagined landing a small aircraft on the tawny slopes and approaching the entry, stepping lightly with a small party of explorers, alert for the meaning of such a place. The air would be devoid of the usual climatic markers (no clouds or air pressure), and in the stillness we would be silent and reverential. The light in the photograph captivated me in that it seemed to come from everywhere, a flat, even twilight that would indicate a world with one or maybe two distant polar suns. There was an alluring blue shadow that ran along the cleft the way a footprint in snow holds its own blue glow, and that aberration affected and intrigued me.

Jeff had left my side and was at the window, on guard, pleased that I was involved in my studies. "So," he said. "It's really something, isn't it?" He came to me, took the magazine and took one long look at the page the way a thirsty man drinks from a jug, and he set it back on the stack of Old Man Shinetower's magazines.

"Yes," I said. "It certainly is." Now that it was gone, I realized I had memorized the photograph, that place.

"Come on. Let's get out of here before he gets back." Jeff cracked the door and looked out, both ways. "Whoa," he said, setting the door closed again. "He's coming back. He's on the walk down about three rooms." Jeff then did an amazing thing: he dropped like a rock to all fours and then onto his stomach and slid under the bed. I'd never seen anyone do that; I've never seen it since. I heard him hiss: "Do something. Hide."

Again I saw myself arriving in the photograph. Now I was alone. I landed carefully and the entire venture was full of care, as if I didn't want to wake something. I had a case of instruments and I wanted to know about that light, that shadow. I could feel my legs burn as I climbed toward it step by step.

What I did in the room was take two steps back into the corner and stand behind the lamp. I put my hands at my side and my chin up. I stood still. At that moment we heard a key in the lock and daylight spilled across the ratty shag carpet. Mr. Shinetower came in. He was wearing the red-and-black plaid shirt that he wore every day. It was like a living thing; someday it would go to lunch at Alfredo's without him.

He walked by me and stopped for a moment in front of the television to drop a handful of change from his pocket into a mason jar on top, turn on the television until it lit and focused, and then he continued into the little green bathroom, and I saw the door swing halfway closed behind him.

Jeff slid out from the bed, stood hastily, his eyes whirling, and opened the door and went out. He was closing it behind him when I caught the edge and followed him into the spinning daylight. When I pulled the door, he gasped, so I shut it and we heard it register closed, and then we slipped quickly through the arbor to the alley behind the units and then ran along the overgrown trail back to the bayou and sat on the weedy slope. Jeff was covered with clots of dust and hairy white goo-gah. It was thick in his hair and I moved away from him while he swatted at it for a while. Here we could smell the sewer working at the bayou, an odd, rich industrial silage, and the sky was gray, but too bright to look at, and I went back to the other world for a moment, the cool perfect place I'd been touring in Mr. Shinetower's magazine, quiet and still, and offering that light. Jeff was spitting and pulling feathers of dust from his collar and sleeves. I wanted so much to be stirred by what I had seen; I had stared at it and I wanted it to stir me, and it had done something. I felt something. I wanted to see that terrain, chart it, understand where the blue glow arose and how it lay along the juncture, and how that light, I was certain, interfered with the ordinary passage of time. Time? I had a faint headache.

"That was close," Jeff said finally. He was still cloaked with flotsam from under Mr. Shinetower's bed. "But it was worth it. Did you get a good look? See what I'm talking about?"

"It was a remarkable photograph," I said.

"Now you know. You've seen it, you know. I've got to get back to work. Let's go fishing this weekend, eh?" He rose and, still whacking soot and ashes and wicked whatevers from his person, ran off toward Alfredo's.

"I've seen it," I said, and I sat there as the sadness bled through me. Duncan would have appreciated the moment and corrected Jeff the way he corrected me all those years. "Seeing isn't knowing," he would say. "To see something is only to establish the first terms of your misunderstanding." That I remembered him at such a time above the rife bayou moments after my flight over the naked photograph made me sad. I was not a genius, but I would be advised by one forevermore.

Happily, my work at the motel was straightforward and I enjoyed it very much. I could do most of it with my shirt off, cutting away the tenacious vines from behind each of the rooms so that the air-conditioning units would not get strangled, and I sweated profusely in the sweet humid air. I painted the pool fence and enameled the three metal tables a kind of turquoise blue, a fifties turquoise that has become tony again just this year, a color that calls to the passerby: Holiday! We're on holiday!

Once a week I poured a pernicious quantity of lime into the two manholes above the storm sewer, and it fell like snow on the teeming backs of thousands of albino water-bugs and roaches that lived there. This did not daunt them in the least. I am no expert on any of the insect tribes nor do I fully understand their customs, but my association with those subterranean multitudes showed me that they looked forward to this weekly toxic snowfall.

Twice a week I pressed the enormous push broom from one end of the driveway to the other until I had a wheelbarrow full of gravel and the million crushed tickets of litter people threw from their moving vehicles along the Hempstead Highway. It was wonderful work. The broom alone weighed twenty pounds. The sweeping, the painting, the trimming braced me; work that required simply my back, both my arms and both my legs, but neither side of my brain.

Mr. Leeland Rakkerts lived in a small apartment behind the office and could be summoned by a bell during the night hours. He was just sixty that June. His wife had passed away years before and he'd become a reclusive little gun nut, and had a growing gallery of hardware on a pegboard in his apartment featuring long-barreled automatic weaponry and at least two dozen huge handguns. But he was fine to me, and he paid me cash every Friday afternoon. When he opened the cash drawer, he always made sure that be you friend or foe, you saw the .45 pistol that rested there, too. My mother would have abhorred me working for him, a man she would have considered the enemy, and she would have said as much, but I wasn't taking the high road, nor the low road, just a road. That summer, the upkeep of the motel was my job, and I did it as well as I could. I'd taken a summer job and was making money. I didn't weigh things on my scale of ethics every ten minutes, because I wasn't entirely sure I had such a scale. I certainly didn't have one as fully evolved as my mother's.

It was a bit like being in the army: when in doubt, paint something. I remeasured and overpainted the parking lot where the last guy had drunkenly painted a wacky series of parentheses where people were supposed to park, and I did a good job with a big brush and five gallons of high mustard yellow, and when I finished I took the feeling of satisfaction in my chest to be simply that: satisfaction. Even if I was working for the devil, the people who put their cars in his parking lot would be squared away.

Getting in my Plymouth Fury III those days with a sweaty back and a pocketful of cash, I knew I was no genius, but I felt—is this close?—like a great guy, a person of some command.

That fall my brother, Garrett Lrsdyksz (he'd changed his name back with a legal kit that Baxter, our Secret Service guy, had got him through the mail), became the youngest student to matriculate at Rice University. He was almost eleven. And he didn't enter as a freshman; he entered as a junior. In physics, of course. There was a little article about it on the wire services, noting that he had, without any assistance, set forward the complete set of equations explaining the relationship between the rotation of the earth and "special atmospheric aberrations most hospitable to exit trajectories of ground-fired propulsion devices." You can look it up and all you'll find is the title because the rest, like all the work he did his cataclysmic year at Rice, is classified, top-secret, eyes-only. Later he explained his research this way to me: "There are storms and then there are storms, Reed. A high-pressure area is only a high-pressure area down here on earth; it has a different pressure on the other side."

I looked at my little brother, a person forever in need of a haircut, and I thought: He's mastered the other side, and I can just barely cope with this one.

That wasn't exactly true, of course, because my Plymouth Fury III and my weekly wages from the San Jacinto Resort Motel allowed me to start having a little life, earthbound as it may have been. I started hanging out a little at Jeff Shreckenbah's place, a rambling hacienda out of town with two out-buildings where his dad worked on stock cars. Jeff's mother called me Ladykiller, which I liked, but which I couldn't hear without imagining my mother's response; my mother who told me a million times, "Morality commences in the words we use to speak of our next act."

"Hey, Ladykiller," Mrs. Shreckenbah would say to me as we pried open the fridge looking for whatever we could find. Mr. Shreckenbah made me call him Jake, saying we'd save the last names for the use of the law-enforcement officials and members of the Supreme Court. They'd let us have Lone Star long-necks if we were staying, or Coca-Cola if we were hitting the road. Some nights we'd go out with Jake and hand him wrenches while he worked on his cars. He was always asking me, "What's the plan?" an opening my mother would have approved of.

"We're going fishing," I told him, because that's what Jeff and I started doing. I'd greet his parents, pick him up, and then Jeff and I would cruise hard down Interstate 45 fifty miles to Galveston and the coast of the warm Gulf of Mexico, where we'd drink Lone Star and surf-cast all night long, hauling in all sorts of mysteries of the deep. I loved it.

Jeff would bring along a pack of Dutch Masters cigars and I'd stand waist deep in the warm water, puffing on the cheap cigar, throwing a live shrimp on a hook as far as I could toward the equator, the only light being the stars above us, the gapped two-story skyline of Galveston behind us, and our bonfire on the beach, tearing a bright hole in the world.

When fish struck, they struck hard, waking me from vivid daydreams of Mr. Leeland Rakkerts giving me a bonus for sweeping the driveway so thoroughly, a twenty so crisp it hurt to fold it into my pocket. My dreams were full of crisp twenties. I could see Jeff over there, fifty yards from me, the little orange tip of his cigar glowing, starlight on the flash of his line as he cast. I liked having my feet firmly on the bottom of the ocean standing in the night. My brother and sister and my mother and father could shine their lights into the elemental mysteries of the world; I could stand in the dark and fish. I could feel the muscles in my arm as I cast again; I was stronger than I'd been two months ago, and then I felt the fish strike and begin to run south.

Having relinquished the cerebral, not that I ever had it in my grasp, I was immersing myself in the real world the same way I was stepping deeper and deeper into the Gulf, following the frenzied fish as he tried to take my line. I worked him back, gave him some, worked him back. Though I had no idea what I would do with it, I had decided to make a lot of money, and as the fish drew me up to my armpits and the bottom grew irregular, I thought about the ways it might be achieved. Being no genius, I had few ideas.

I spit out my cigar after the first wavelet broke over my face, and I called to Jeff, "I got one."

He was behind me now, backing toward the fire, and he called, "Bring him up here and let's see."

The top half of my head, including my nose, and my two hands and the fishing pole were all that were above sea level when the fish relented and I began to haul him back. He broke the surface several times as I backed out of the ocean, reeling as I went. Knee deep, I stopped and lifted the line until a dark form lifted into the air. I ran him up to Jeff by the fire and showed him there, a two-pound catfish. When I held him, I felt the sudden shock of his gaffs going into my finger and palm.

"Ow!" Jeff said. "Who has got whom?" He took the fish from me on a gill stick.

I shook my stinging hand.

"It's all right," he assured me, throwing another elbow of driftwood onto the fire and handing me an icy Lone Star. "Let's fry this guy up and eat him right now. I'm serious. This is going to be worth it. We're going to live to be one hundred years old, guaranteed."

We'd sit, eat, fish some more, talk, and late late we'd drive back, the dawn light gray across the huge tidal plain, smoking Dutch Masters until I was queasy and quiet, dreaming about my money, however I would make it.

Usually this dream was interrupted by my actual boss, Mr. Leeland Rakkerts, shaking my shoulder as I stood sleeping on my broom in the parking lot of the hot and bothered San Jacinto Resort Motel, saying, "Boy! Hey! Boy! You can take your zombie fits home or get on the stick here." I'd give him the wide-eyed nod and continue sweeping, pushing a thousand pounds of scraggly gravel into a conical pile and hauling it in my wheelbarrow way out back into the thick tropical weeds at the edge of the bayou and dumping it there like a body. It wasn't a crisp twenty-dollar bill he'd given me, but it was a valuable bit of advice for a seventeen-year-old, and I tried to take it as such.

Those Saturdays after we'd been to the Gulf beat in my skull like a drum, the Texas sun a thick pressure on my bare back as I moved through the heavy humid air skimming and vacuuming the pool, rearranging the pool furniture though it was never, ever moved because no one ever used the pool. People hadn't come to the San Jacinto Resort Motel to swim. Then standing in the slim shade behind the office, trembling under a sheen of sweat, I would suck on a tall bottle of Coca-Cola as if on the very nectar of life, and by midafternoon as I trimmed the hedges along the walks and raked and swept, the day would come back to me, a pure pleasure, my lime-green Plymouth Fury III parked in the shady side of Alfredo's American Cafe, standing like a promise of every sweet thing life could offer.

These were the days when my brother, Garrett, was coming home on weekends, dropped at our curb by the maroon Rice University van after a week in the research dorms, where young geniuses from all over the world lived in bare little cubicles, the kind of thing somebody with an I.Q. of 250 apparently loves. I had been to Garrett's room on campus and it was perfect for him. There was a kind of pad in one corner surrounded by a little bank of his clothing and the strip of butcher paper running the length of the floor, covered with numbers and letters and tracked thoroughly with the faint gray intersecting grid of sneaker prints. His window looked out onto the pretty green grass quad.

It was the quietest building I have ever been in, and I was almost convinced that Garrett might be the only inmate, but when we left to go down to the cafeteria for a sandwich, I saw the other geniuses in their rooms, lying on their stomachs like kids drawing with crayons on a rainy day. Then I realized that they were kids and it was a rainy day and they were working with crayons; the only difference was that they were drawing formulas for how many muons could dance on a quark.

Downstairs there were a whole slug of the little people in the dining hall sitting around in the plastic chairs, swinging their feet back and forth six inches off the floor, ignoring their trays of tuna-fish sandwiches and tomato soup, staring this way and then that as the idea storms in their brains swept through. You could almost see they were thinking by how their hair stood in fierce clusters.

There was one adult present, a guy in a blue sweater vest who went from table to table urging the children to eat: Finish that sandwich, drink your milk, go ahead, use your spoon, try the soup, it's good for you. I noticed he was careful to register and gather any of the random jottings the children committed while they sat around doodling in spilled milk. I guess he was a member of the faculty. It would be a shame for some nine-year-old to write the key to universal field theory in peanut butter and jelly and then eat the thing.

"So," I said as we sat down, "Garrett. How's it going?"

Garrett looked at me, his trance interrupted, and as it melted away and he saw me and the platters of cafeteria food before us, he smiled. There he was, my little brother, a sleepy-looking kid with a spray of freckles up and over his nose like the crab nebula, and two enthusiastic front teeth that would be keeping his mouth open for decades. "Reed," he said. "*How's it going?* I love that. I've always liked your acute sense of narrative. So linear and right for you." His smile, which took a moment and some force to assemble, was ancient, beneficent, as if he both envied and pitied me for something, and he shook his head softly. "But things here aren't *going*, kid." He poked a finger into the white bread of his tuna sandwich and studied the indentation like a man finding a footprint on the moon. "Things here *are*. This is it. Things . . ." He started again. "Things aren't bad, really. It's kind of a floating circle. That's close. Things aren't going; they float in the circle. Right?"

We were both staring at the sandwich; I think I might have been waiting for it to float, but only for a second. I understood what he was saying. Things existed. I'm not that dumb. Things, whatever they might be, and that was a topic I didn't even want to open, had essence, not process. That's simple; that doesn't take a genius to decipher. "Great," I said. And then I said what you say to your little brother when he sits there pale and distracted and four years ahead of you in school, "Why don't you eat some of that, and I'll take you out and show you my car."

It wasn't as bad a visit as I'm making it sound. We were brothers; we loved each other. We didn't have to say it. The dining room got me a little until I realized I should stop worrying about these children and whether or not they were happy. Happiness wasn't an issue. The place was clean; the food was fresh. Happiness, in that cafeteria, was simply beside the point.

On the way out, Garrett introduced me to his friend Donna Li, a ten-year-old from New Orleans, whom he said was into programming. She was a tall girl with shiny hair and a ready smile, eating alone by the window. This was 1966 and I was certain she was involved somehow in television. You didn't hear the word *computer* every other sentence back then. When she stood to shake my hand, I had no idea of what to say to her and it came out, "I hope your programming is floating in the circle."

"It is," she said.

"She's written her own language," Garrett assured me, "and now she's on the applications."

It was my turn to speak again and already I couldn't touch bottom, so I said, "We're going out to see my car. Do you want to see my car?"

Imagine me in the parking lot then with these two little kids. On the way out I'd told Garrett about my job at the motel and that Jeff Shreckenbah and I had been hanging out and fishing on the weekends and that Jeff's dad raced stock cars, and for the first time all day Garrett's face filled with a kind of wonder, as if this were news from another world, which I guess it was. There was a misty rain with a faint petrochemical smell in it, and we approached my car as if it were a sleeping Brontosaurus. They were both entranced and moved toward it carefully, finally putting their little hands on the wet fender in unison. "This is your car," Garrett said, and I wasn't sure if it was the *your* or the *car* that had him in awe.

I couldn't figure out what floats in the circle or even where the circle was, but I could rattle my keys and start that Plymouth Fury III and listen to the steady sound of the engine, which I did for them now. They both backed away appreciatively.

"It's a large car," Donna Li said.

"Reed," Garrett said to me. "This is really something. And what's that smell?"

I cocked my head, smelling it, too, a big smell, budging the petrocarbons away, a live, salty smell, and then I remembered: I'd left half a bucket of bait shrimp in the trunk, where they'd been ripening for three days since my last trip to Galveston with Jeff.

"That's rain in the bayou, Garrett."

"Something organic," Donna Li said, moving toward the rear of the vehicle.

"Here, guys," I said, handing Garrett the bag of candy, sardine tins, and peanut-butter-and-cheese packs I'd brought him. I considered for half a second showing him the pile of rotting crustaceans; it would have been cool and he was my brother. But I didn't want to give the geniuses the wrong first impression of the Plymouth.

"Good luck with your programming," I told Donna Li, shaking her hand. "And Garrett, be kind to your rocketry."

Garrett smiled at that again and said to Donna, "He's my brother."

And she added, "And he owns the largest car in Texas."

I felt bad driving my stinking car away from the two young people, but it was that or fess up. I could see them standing in my rearview mirror for a long time. First they watched me, then they looked up, both of them for a long time. They were geniuses looking into the rain; I counted on their being able to find a way out of it.

 For Discussion:

1. Identify a few of the recurring images or phrases found in the story. How do these contribute to the story?
2. Do you believe Reed, the narrator, when he says he is not a genius? Does Gardner's "Linguistic Intelligence" category explain Reed? Examine the story for cues as to whether we are to believe or doubt the narrative voice.
3. What do you think Garrett means when he says to Reed, "*How's it going? I love that. I've always loved your acute sense of narrative.*"

 For Fact-Finding, Research, and Writing:

1. Are there any governmental or educational institutions that define genius? Find at least two and evaluate the credibility of the definition.
2. How is funding for Gifted and Talented programs in the state of Oklahoma established? By the state? Local school districts? Go to government websites to uncover this information. Will it be cut in this current year? Who makes such decisions?
3. Consider "The Ordinary Son" in light of Schank's theory of narrative. How might Schank assess its goals and its place within the categories he establishes?
4. How do the stages of education described by Plato in "The Allegory of the Cave" help to explain Reed's experiences through the course of the story?

CHAPTER TWO

Who Controls Knowledge?

Introduction

Do you know which foods you eat contain harmful additives, or even ingredients made from insects? How can apparently normal people allow, and even serve as accomplices for, the torture of innocents? How does group psychology encourage people to think and act in ways they would otherwise condemn? How do the conventions of our language influence the transmission of knowledge? Which writers have plagiarized portions of their books? Which researchers faked their data? Which journalists are making up tonight's news? Which students have robbed others, and perhaps even you, by cheating their way through school?

Over the last few decades we have witnessed unprecedented technological and scientific advancements. We have mapped the human genome, and can now manipulate the human body at the genetic level. The explosive growth of the Internet has made available to virtually anyone an immense store of information on seemingly every topic imaginable. But with these advancements come a series of difficult questions about the control of information. Should people of all ages have access to the same kind of information? Should governments be able to sequester controversial information as "classified" documents? Should you obey the wishes of authority figures who demand the unethical, the immoral— or even the sadistic?

Those who control information influence virtually every aspect of our existence. Knowing how and why knowledge is collected, shared, or even concealed allows us to make thoughtful decisions about how to live our lives. How should we regulate the exchange of information? How can we protect ourselves against the misuse of information? What is the best way to act on the information we have? Such questions about the control of knowledge are the crucial issues of this century. How we answer them determines both the face of our world today, and of the world to come.

Dave Barry, "English, as It Were"

Dave Barry is a Pulitzer Prize winning humor columnist for the *Miami Herald*. Some of Barry's many books include *Stay Fit and Healthy Until You're Dead* (1985), *Dave Barry's Complete Guide to Guys* (1996), and *Dave Barry: Boogers Are My Beat* (2003).

 Before You Read:

What aspects of English make absolutely no sense to you? Have you ever judged anyone by how well he or she speaks English?

English, as It Were

Dave Barry

Once again we are pleased to present Mister Language Person, the internationally recognized expert and author of the authoritative *Oxford Cambridge Big Book o' Grammar*.

Q. What is the difference between "criteria" and "criterion"?

A. These often-confused words belong to a family that grammarians call "metronomes," meaning "words that have the same beginning but lay eggs underwater." The simplest way to tell them apart is to remember that "criteria" is used in the following type of sentence: "When choosing a candidate for the United States Congress, the main criteria is, hair." Whereas "Criterion" is a kind of car.

Q. What is the correct way to spell words?

A. English spelling is unusual because our language is a rich verbal tapestry woven together from the tongues of the Greeks, the Latins, the Angles, the Klaxtons, the Celtics, the 76ers, and many other ancient peoples, all of whom had severe drinking problems. Look at the spelling they came up with for "colonel" (which is actually pronounced "lieutenant"); or "hors d'oeuvres" or "Cyndi Lauper." It is no wonder that young people today have so much trouble learning to spell: Study after study shows that young people today have the intelligence of Brillo. This is why it's so important that we old folks teach them the old reliable spelling rule that we learned as children, namely:

"I" before "C,"
Or when followed by "T,"
O'er the ramparts we watched,
Not excluding joint taxpayers filing singly.
EXCEPTION: "Suzi's All-Nite E-Z Drive-Thru Donut Shoppe."

Q. What the heck are "ramparts," anyway?

A. They are parts of a ram, and they were considered a great delicacy in those days. People used to watch o'er them.

Q. How do you speak French?

A. French is very easy to speak. The secret is, no matter what anybody says to you, you answer, "You're wrong," but you say it with your tongue way back in gargle position and your lips pouted way out like you're sucking grits through a hose, so it sounds like this: "Urrrrooonnngggg." Example:

FRENCH PERSON: *Où est la poisson de mon harmonica?* ("How about them Toronto Blue Jays?")

YOU: Urrrrooonnngggg.

FRENCH PERSON: *Quel moron!* ("Good point!")

Q. I know there's a difference in proper usage between "compared with" and "compared to," but I don't care.

A. It depends on the context.

Q. Please explain punctuation?

A. It would be "my pleasure." The main punctuation marks are the period, the coma, the colonel, the semi-colonel, the probation mark, the catastrophe, the eclipse, the Happy Face, and the box where the person checks "yes" to receive more information. You should place these marks in your sentences at regular intervals to indicate to your reader that some kind of punctuation is occurring. Consider these examples:

WRONG: O Romeo, Romeo, wherefore art thou Romeo?

RIGHT: O Romeo! Yo! *Romeo!!* Wherethehellfore ART thou? Huh??

ROMEO: I art down here! Throw me the car keys!

Q. Does anybody besides total jerks ever use the phrase "as it were"?

A. No.

Q. What is the correct form of encouraging "chatter" that baseball infielders should yell to the pitcher?

A. They should yell: "Hum babe hum babe hum babe HUM BABE HUM BABE."

Q. May they also yell: "Shoot that ball in there shoot it shoot it SHOOT SHOOT SHOOT WAY TO SHOOT BABE GOOD HOSE ON THAT SHOOTER"?

A. They most certainly may.

Q. What is the difference between "take" and "bring"?

A. "Take" is a transitory verb that is used in statements such as "He up and took off." "Bring" is a consumptive injunction and must be used as follows: "We brung some stewed ramparts to Aunt Vespa but she was already dead so we ate them ourselfs."

Q. What is President Bush's native language?

A. He doesn't have one

Today's Language Tip: A good way to impress people such as your boss is to develop a "Power Vocabulary" by using big words. Consider this example:

YOU: Good morning, Mr. Johnson.

YOUR BOSS: Good morning, Ted. (Obviously you're not making much of an impression here. Your name isn't even "Ted." Now watch the difference that a couple of Power Vocabulary words can make:)

YOU: Good morning, Mr. Johnson, you hemorrhoidal infrastructure.

YOUR BOSS: What?

You Got a Question for Mister Language Person? We are not surprised.

 For Discussion:

1.   Barry's piece is humorous, but he is also making a point. What is his thesis? How does he support it?
2.   What are some oddities about English that Barry leaves out?
3.   What in Barry's essay makes it funny?

 For Fact-Finding, Research, and Writing:

1.   Barry parodies academic books when he mentions the fictional "*Oxford Cambridge Big Book o' Grammar.*" Using a library database, find a real book that might fit this stuffy stereotype.

2. Using Barry's style as inspiration, write your own short article about something that confuses most people.
3. Barry is a member of The Rock Bottom Remainders, a literary rock band that includes Stephen King, Amy Tan, Matt Groening, Barbara Kingsolver, and several others. Using the library catalog, locate (and write down the call numbers for) books by at least six different members of the band.
4. Locate and photocopy the original source of Barry's essay.

Brian Hansen, "Combating Plagiarism"

Brian Hansen, formerly a staff writer for the *Colorado Daily* and the *CQ Researcher*, is now a freelance writer specializing in social and environmental issues. *The CQ Researcher* is published on-line 44 times per year, and each issue addresses a different topic from multiple perspectives. It is aimed at the general public, university faculty and students, and media journalists seeking information.

 Before You Read:

How do you define plagiarism? Do you view yourself as a person of high academic integrity?

Combating Plagiarism

Brian Hansen

The Issues

Susan Maximon, a social-studies teacher at Fairview High School in Boulder, Colo., knows teenage writing when she sees it. So a bright red flag went up last year when one of her 11th-grade students turned in a research paper teeming with $10 words.

"I knew he didn't write it," Maximon says. "It was filled with big words and expressions that he never used and probably didn't even understand."

Robert Rivard, editor of the *San Antonio Express-News*, had a similar revelation last April as he was reading a *New York Times* article about the mother of an American soldier missing in Iraq. "I was bewildered," Rivard recalls. "I thought I'd read it before." He had—in his own paper—eight days earlier. That's why *The Times'* story by Jayson Blair sounded so familiar.

"It suddenly dawned on me that it was an act of plagiarism," Rivard says. "It was subtly changed and manipulated, but it was clearly" by *Express-News* reporter Macarena Hernandez.

In the Fairview High case, the student confessed after Maximon confronted him with evidence his paper was nearly identical to one available on the Internet. Maximon gave him a zero for the assignment.

Blair's case was not resolved so quietly. The 27-year-old resigned on May 1, shortly after Rivard alerted *Times* editors. They soon discovered that Blair had plagiarized, fabricated or otherwise falsified parts of at least three-dozen articles. "He fabricated comments. He concocted scenes. He lifted material from other newspapers and wire services," *The Times* said in a front-page, 14,000-word mea culpa published on May 11.[1]

The much-publicized scandal dealt a devastating blow to the 152-year-old *Times*, widely considered the greatest newspaper in the world. Some experts worried that Blair had tarnished the reputations of all news organizations. "In a lot of people's minds, *The Times* is the bell cow of American journalism," said Don Wycliff, public editor of the *Chicago Tribune*. "They'll think, 'Well, if it's done there, you know it's done everywhere.'"[2]

Derived from the Latin word *plagiarius* ("kidnapper"), plagiarism can range from purloining someone else's reportage or buying a prewritten term paper and turning it in as one's own to copying a few sentences from a book or Web site without citing the source.[3] According to the authoritative Modern Language Association, plagiarism is "a form of cheating that has been defined as the false assumption of authorship: the wrongful act of taking the product of another person's mind, and presenting it as one's own."[4] (*See box; p. 95.*)

Although plagiarism among high school and college students is not new, some educators say students today are more likely to plagiarize because of the Internet. "Kids have always plagiarized, but the Web has made it a lot easier," says Joyce Valenza, a librarian at Springfield Township High School in Erdenheim, Pa. "It's given them an enormous resource for finding materials that they don't think their teachers can verify as not their own."

"Academic honesty is the cornerstone of college learning and liberal education and, indeed, is a continuing problem that colleges face," says Debra Humphreys, vice president of communications and public affairs at the Association of American Colleges and Universities. "Our members are facing different challenges than in the past as a result of the Internet. Problems related to plagiarism on campus parallel problems in the larger society, such as newspaper plagiarism scandals and illegal file sharing of music and movies."

Moreover, Internet resources are widely considered to be free for the taking. "There's a belief among young people that materials found online are free, or are somehow inherently different from something you buy at a record store or get out of a book or magazine,"

MOST STUDENTS SAY PLAGIARISM IS WRONG

Many educators say today's students don't understand what plagiarism is or don't consider it as serious cheating. But according to a recent survey, nearly 90 percent of college students strongly view major acts of plagiarism as unethical.

Students' Ethical Views on Acts of Plagiarism

	Strongly Agree or Somewhat Agree	Neither Agree nor Disagree	Somewhat Disagree or Strongly Disagree
Is It Wrong To:			
Hand in Someone Else's Writing as One's Own	89.1%	7.0%	3.9%
Use the Internet to Copy Text to Hand in as One's Own	89.3%	7.7%	3.1%
Purchase Papers From Print Term-Paper Mills	89.1%	6.8%	4.1%
Purchase Papers From Online Term-Paper Mills	89.8%	6.1%	4.1%

Source: Patrick M. Scanlon and David R. Newmann, "Internet Plagiarism Among College Students," *Journal of College Student Development*, May/June 2002.

says John Barrie, president of TurnItIn.com, an Oakland, Calif., firm that sells software that helps thousands of schools detect plagiarism. "Kids download music from the Internet even though it's a form of intellectual-property theft. It's naïve to think that attitude is not going to have a large impact on plagiarism at educational institutions."

"On a given day, we process between 10,000 and 15,000 student papers, and about 30 percent are less than original," Barrie says.

Recent studies indicate that 40 percent of college students have plagiarized material at least once. (*See graph, p. 97.*) Although plagiarism is not a crime, authors and musicians who think they have been plagiarized can sue for copyright infringement. To win damages, a plaintiff must typically prove that the plagiarism harmed "the potential market for, or value of," their copyrighted work.[5]

Last April, French jazz pianist Jacques Loussier sued the rapper Eminem for $10 million, claiming his hit song, "Kill You" borrowed heavily from Loussier's 20-year-old song "Pulsion." The suit is pending. Even former Beatle George Harrison was successfully sued for plagiarism.

In addition to musicians, several best-selling historians have run into plagiarism problems, including Doris Kearns Goodwin and Stephen Ambrose. Goodwin acknowledged in January her publisher had paid an undisclosed sum in 1987 to settle allegations that Goodwin's *The Fitzgeralds and the Kennedys* contained plagiarized text from Lynne McTaggart's *Kathleen Kennedy: Her Life and Times.*

Ambrose was criticized for not putting quotation marks around passages in his celebrated World War II book *The Wild Blue* that were identical to passages in *Wings of Morning*, an earlier chronicle by University of Pennsylvania history Professor Thomas Childers. Ambrose had cited Childers' book in his footnotes and claimed the mistake was inadvertent. Journalists later found unquoted passages from other authors in at least six of Ambrose's other books, but he vigorously denied he was a plagiarist. "I stand on the originality of my work," he wrote last May, just before his death. "The reading public will decide whether my books are fraudulent and react accordingly."[6]

Punishments for students who plagiarize range from failing grades on individual assignments to flunking an entire course—or worse. Some schools have revoked degrees from people whose plagiarism came to light months or years after they graduated. At other schools—especially those with strict honor codes—plagiarism can be grounds for suspension or expulsion.

For example, at the University of Virginia—famous for its tough honor code—48 students quit or were expelled for plagiarism between April 2001 and November 2002. The university revoked the degrees of three of the plagiarists who had graduated before their cases were adjudicated by the student-run Honor Committee. "The cases ranged from the wholesale copying of entire papers to copying a few sentences here and there," says Nicole Eramo, special assistant to the committee. "Most of our students are fairly intolerant of that type of cheating."

However, some experts say educators are going overboard in trying to root out plagiarism. Rebecca Moore Howard, an associate professor of writing and rhetoric at Syracuse University, blames the crackdown more on "hysteria" than real understanding of the issues. She says plagiarism is frequently the result of students not knowing—or never having been taught—how to properly cite sources.

"All writers appropriate language from other sources and reshape it as their own, but inexperienced writers don't do that very well," Howard says. "They don't realize that what they're doing is plagiarism."

According to University of Colorado freshman Liz Newton, "It was kind of unclear at my high school what plagiarism really was. You were just kind of expected to know what it was and not do it."

"The perception [among college professors] is that students are no longer learning about plagiarism adequately at the high-school level so there's an education and re-education process that needs to take place," says renowned academic-integrity researcher Donald McCabe. Some high-school teachers themselves "don't even understand" what constitutes plagiarism in the digital age, adds the Rutgers University professor and founder of the Center for Academic Integrity at Duke University. "They're still catching up, particularly with regard to plagiarism using the Internet."

Because students are arriving at college without a sound understanding of what plagiarism is, some colleges and universities are spending more time than they used to teaching newly arriving students how to avoid it. "There's a concerted effort across campus for courses that require any kind of writing to really work with students so they understand what plagiarism is," says Fran Ebbers, librarian at St. Edward's University, in Austin, Texas. "We've had university-wide discussions about this."

As plagiarism scandals plague campuses and newsrooms across the country, here is a closer look at some of the questions being debated:

Has the Internet increased the incidence of student plagiarism?

In the past, students who plagiarized first had to spend hours poring over dusty library books to find material to copy, then retype it. If they bought material from a term-paper mill, they had to wait for it to arrive through the mail.

Today, students surfing the Web can access millions of documents on every subject imaginable—without leaving their desks. With the click of a mouse, they can electronically "cut and paste" text—a few sentences or entire documents—into their "own" work.

HOW MUCH PLAGIARISM?

High-school students plagiarize significantly more than college students, according to several studies in which students are asked to "self-report" copying. Although plagiarism appears to have remained relatively stable during the past 40 years, Donald McCabe of Rutgers University thinks it is actually far more prevalent today because many students don't consider cut-and-paste Internet copying as cheating. In addition, McCabe notes other types of dishonesty—such as cheating on exams—have skyrocketed.

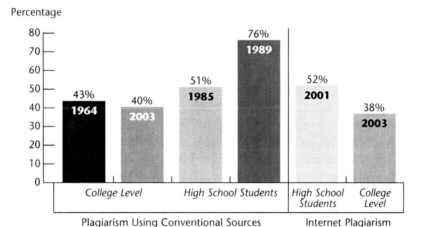

Percentage of Students Admitting to One or More Acts of Plagiarism

Sources: W.J. Bowers, "Student Dishonesty and Its Control in College," Columbia University, 1964; Donald McCabe, unpublished study, Rutgers University, 2003; Donald McCabe, "Cheating: Why Students Do It and How We Can Help Them Stop," *American Educator*, winter 2001; B. Brandes, "Academic Honesty: A Special Study of California Students," 1986; Fred Schub, "Schooling Without Learning: Thirty Years of Cheating in High School," *Adolescence*, Vol. 23, 1991.

Experts generally agree that the Internet and other modern technologies have made plagiarism easier. They disagree, however, about whether the new technologies encourage more students to plagiarize. Louis Bloomfield, a University of Virginia physics professor who two years ago accused 158 students of submitting plagiarized term papers, says technology is partly to blame. "Plagiarism has become so easy," he says, "It's everywhere, and if you think you don't have it going on in your institution, you're naïve."

But Jim Purdy, assistant director of the Center for Writing Studies at the University of Illinois, Urbana-Champaign, says the Internet is simply not creating vast numbers of new student plagiarizers. "Based on my personal experiences," he says, "this fear is being blown somewhat out of proportion."

Over the years, researchers have tried to quantify the incidence of plagiarism and other forms of academic cheating.[7] Most of the studies are based on surveys in which students "self-report" their behaviors. Taken at face value, the studies generally belie the notion that the advent of the Internet has led to an increase in academic plagiarism.

Professor W.J. Bowers of Columbia University documented the incidence of plagiarism and academic cheating among college students 40 years ago—long before the advent of the Internet. In a 1964 survey, Bowers found that 43 percent of the respondents acknowledged plagiarizing at least once.[8] In a recent survey of 18,000 U.S. college students by Rutgers University's McCabe, 38 percent of respondents acknowledged engaging in one or more instances of Internet-facilitated "cut-and-paste" plagiarism. But notably, a slightly bigger group—40 percent—said they had plagiarized using conventional books, journals and other sources.

In another recent study, Rochester Institute of Technology (RIT) professors Patrick Scanlon and David Neumann found that the number of students who admitted to Internet plagiarism was about the same as during the pre-Internet era.[9] "Our study indicates that some of the estimates of Internet-facilitated plagiarism are overblown," Scanlon says. "We didn't find evidence of the epidemic of Internet plagiarism that's been touted in the popular press. If anything, the numbers for plagiarism have actually gone down [from the pre-Internet era], or it's a wash."

According to Scanlon and Neumann, nearly 25 percent of the students admitted to plagiarizing from the Internet: 16.5 percent "sometimes" cut and paste text from an Internet source without citation, 8 percent do so "often." The study found that 6 percent "sometimes" buy papers from online term-paper mills and 2.3 percent do so "often."

Notably, the respondents thought other students plagiarized much more frequently than they did. For example, while only 8 percent "often" took text from Internet sources without citation, 54.4 percent believed their peers often did so. "That's consistent with studies of other kinds of things," Scanlon says. "People will overestimate behaviors in others that they themselves are not taking part in."

Significantly more plagiarism is self-reported by high-school students. Of the 2,294 juniors surveyed by McCabe in 2000–2001, for example, 52 percent said they had "copied a few sentences from a Web site without footnoting them," and 16 percent acknowledged turning in papers "obtained in large part from a term-paper mill or Web site."[10] McCabe contends that many high-school students plagiarize more than their college counterparts because they don't fully understand what plagiarism is or how to avoid it. But others do it because they believe they won't get caught, he says.

However, pre-Internet era studies also found high incidences of high-school plagiarism. In a 1985 California survey, 51 percent of the students admitted plagiarizing.[11] And 76 percent of the high-schoolers surveyed by a University of Georgia researcher in 1989 admitted to copying "word for word" out of a book.[12]

Critics maintain there is much more Internet-facilitated plagiarism occurring today than self-reporting studies indicate, because many students—at both the high-school and college levels—either don't understand or refuse to admit that copying from the Web is wrong.

"A lot of kids don't understand that they can't cut and paste text from the Internet into their own papers [without citing the source]," says Leigh Campbell-Hale, a social-studies teacher at Boulder's Fairview High School. "I even had one kid say to me, 'If I pay for a paper I bought online, it's mine.'"

McCabe found similar attitudes in his recent college survey: 44 percent of the students considered minor, cut-and-paste Internet plagiarism as "trivial" cheating or not cheating at all.

Kids dismiss Internet plagiarism as trivial because they have bought into the "techie" culture, which holds that anything found on the Web is "free"—that copyright laws do not apply on the Internet, according to some experts. Students regard Internet plagiarism much like downloading music files, they say. But as the music industry's recent copyright-infringement suit indicates, such piracy is considered intellectual-property theft.[13]

"A lot of high-school and college students don't see that as a problem at all," says librarian Ebbers, at St. Edward's University.

Jill Vassilakos-Long, a librarian at California State University, San Bernardino, has a slightly different view. "A lot of students would agree that plagiarism and downloading music are theft, but they see them as victimless crimes."

But the music industry blames online music-sharing and downloading in part for a 26 percent drop in CD sales and a 14 percent drop in revenues. "Our industry is being ravaged by piracy," said Zack Horowitz, president and chief operating officer of Universal Music Group.[14]

There are non-economic repercussions as well, says Barrie, of TurnItIn.com. "A lot of students bust their derrières to get into the best university or medical school or law school, but some get out-competed by students who cheat," he says. "I have zero sympathy for that. Students should be held accountable for what they do."

Moreover, if plagiarism were allowed to go unchecked, the impact on society could be catastrophic, according to Lawrence M. Hinman, director of the Values Institute at the University of San Diego. Hinman says trust is fundamental to the social, political and economic fabric of any successful society. "Without trust in public and business institutions outside the family, an economy stops developing after a certain point," he says.

Researchers, for their part, acknowledge that self-reporting studies may underrepresent the true size of the plagiarism problem, given students' wide-ranging views on the morality of the activity.

CONFRONTING PLAGIARISM CAN POSE RISK

Punishments for plagiarism usually are meted out without incident. But occasionally, things get ugly—for the accusers. Teachers and professors who impose harsh consequences on plagiarizing students sometimes face unpleasant consequences from their students, parents and unsupportive colleagues and administrators.

Law Professor John L. Hill, for example, was sued, verbally harassed and had his house vandalized after he filed plagiarism complaints against five law students at St. Thomas University in Miami, Fla., in 1995. But "the worst part" of the ordeal was the lack of support from colleagues and school officials, recalls Hill, who now teaches law at Indiana University in Indianapolis.

Hill says the five students incorporated materials from the *Stanford Law Review* and other publications into their own papers without attribution. One student copied "about 30 pages" of text—original footnotes and all. "It was pretty clear-cut," Hill recalls. "It was verbatim plagiarism."

Thus Hill was shocked when his own colleagues and the student-run honor committee did not support him. "A number of faculty just refused to accept that [plagiarism] was a significant problem," Hill says. "One colleague insisted I was on a 'witch hunt.' And the president of the university ordered the dean to punt—to basically do nothing—because he didn't want to deal with any possible legal implications."

When the students refused to admit wrongdoing, Hill referred them to the honor committee. Shortly thereafter, Hill says he started getting harassing phone calls, his house was egged and his front door was twice ripped from its hinges. During the trial proceedings, students booed and hissed at him. One of the defendants even tried to taint Hill as a plagiarist. "They tore apart everything I'd ever written in the hope of finding some plagiarism, which they didn't," Hill says. "I was really portrayed as the bad guy."

Ultimately, two of the cases were dismissed and a third student was acquitted. A fourth student pleaded guilty, and the final defendant was convicted on a split vote. For punishments, the two guilty students were ordered to write five-page papers on plagiarism.

Later, one of the convicted plagiarists sued Hill and the university for "loss of ability to obtain a job as an attorney."[1]

Some educators refrain from pursuing student plagiarizers because they fear either litigation or lack of support from administrators wishing to avoid negative publicity.[2] But Hill says he'd do the same thing again. "It was an unpleasant experience, to say the least," Hill says, "but I just wouldn't feel good about letting something like [plagiarism] ride."

Christine Pelton, a biology teacher at Piper High School in Piper, Kan., had a similar experience in 2001 after assigning her 10th-graders to write scientific reports about leaves. The project represented half of the semester's grade, so students had to do well to pass the course. Pelton spelled that out in a contract she had her students and their parents sign. Section No. 7 warned, "Cheating and plagiarism will result in the failure of the assignment."

After checking her students' reports with TurnItIn.com, a plagiarism-detection service, Pelton concluded that 28 of her 118 students—one-quarter of the entire sophomore class—had plagiarized from Internet sites, books or each other. Pelton flunked them all.

Outraged parents demanded that Pelton change the grades, arguing she hadn't adequately explained what constitutes plagiarism. Pelton, noting the contract, adamantly denied the charge. "I made a big point of telling them [that plagiarism] would cause them to fail," she said. "I gave them ample warning."[3]

When Pelton refused to change the grades, the parents went to the school board. On Dec. 11, 2001, the board and District Superintendent Michael Rooney decreed that the project would count for only 30 percent of the students' semester grades. All the students who would have failed due to plagiarism would now pass.

Rooney announced the policy change the following morning. Pelton was furious that her authority had been stripped away. "I went to my class and tried to teach the kids, but they were whooping and hollering and saying, 'We don't have to listen to you anymore,'" she said.[4]

Pelton immediately resigned, telling Rooney that she couldn't work in a district that didn't support her. "I knew I couldn't teach," she later recalled. "I left at noon and didn't come back."[5]

At least nine other Piper teachers quit in protest. The town's residents, many of whom had supported Pelton throughout the ordeal, ousted one school board member in a special recall election. Another board member resigned and a third did not seek re-election. Rooney also resigned under pressure last year.

Pelton, who opened a home day-care center after the plagiarism imbroglio, was honored last year with a certificate of appreciation from Kansas lawmakers. "I knew what I did that day would have an impact on my future," she said of her decision to resign. "Students not only need the building blocks of learning, but [also] morals and values."[6]

1. For background, see Carolyn Kleiner and Mary Lord, "The Cheating Game," *U.S. News & World Report*, Nov. 22, 1999, p. 55.
2. For background, see Kathy Koch, "Cheating in Schools," *The CQ Researcher*, Sept. 22, 2000, pp. 745–768.
3. Quoted in Richard Jerome and Pam Grout, "Cheat Wave: School Officials Let Plagiarists Off Easy, So Teacher Christine Pelton Quit—Sending Her Town into a Tizzy," *Time*, June 17, 2002, p. 83.
4. Quoted in Diane Carroll, "Plagiarism Dispute Divides a School District," *The Kansas City Star*, Jan. 29, 2002, p. A1.
5. Quoted in Bill Lagamata, "Paying the Piper," CBS News' "48 Hours," May 31, 2002.
6. Quoted in "House Honors Teacher Who Resigned in Plagiarism Incident," The Associated Press, May 6, 2002.

"It's a moving target as far as students are concerned as to what actually constitutes plagiarism," says Rutgers' McCabe. "When I debrief a small percentage of them [after a survey], some of them say, 'Yeah, I did that, but I don't consider it cheating, so I didn't check it off.'"

Should teachers use plagiarism-detection services?

Many schools use private companies to ferret out student plagiarism. Chicago-based Glatt Plagiarism Services—whose clients include DePaul University and the U.S. Naval Academy—operates on the premise that students should be able to reproduce any document they actually wrote. After the company's software eliminates every fifth word of a suspected plagiarist's paper, the student is then asked to fill in the blanks to prove authorship. The program calculates a "plagiarism probability score" based on the number of correct responses, the time it took a student to complete the task and other factors.

"We authenticate authorship using techniques of cognitive science," said company founder Barbara Glatt. "It's easy and accurate."[15]

The system developed by TurnItIn.com functions like a supercharged search engine, comparing students' papers to documents residing in three places: public portions of the Internet; a proprietary database of books, journals and newspapers; and a proprietary database of all the student-authored papers ever submitted to it by all its clients. An "originality report" prepared for every paper checked by TurnItIn.com tells instructors what percent of the paper, if any, matches text ("strings" of approximately eight words or more) in other documents.

"An instructor can sit down with a student and say, 'Please explain to me why 82 percent of your paper came from this book or Web site,'" Barrie says. "Instructors no longer have to rely on gut feelings when they suspect plagiarism. There is just no way to sneak plagiarized material through our system—no way."

But some educators consider detection services as superficial "quick fixes" that allow teachers to sidestep the issues that caused their students to plagiarize in the first place. "Teachers who get too caught up acting like detectives ignore what they really ought to be doing as teachers, which is talking to students about things like originality and using sources correctly," says RIT's Scanlon. "Using a plagiarism checker gives you a reason to avoid having those conversations."

Syracuse's Howard agrees, adding that lazy teachers are also partly to blame for the plagiarism problem. "Giving students canned, mindless assignments that have no meaning for them just invites plagiarism," Howard says. "Those assignments are so mind-deadening that students who have not managed their time well may look for papers online, because they're not getting anything out of the experience anyway."

Howard says teachers who use plagiarism-detection services risk alienating their students—especially the honest ones—by sending the message that everyone is a potential plagiarist. She likens teachers who use the services to employers who subject their employees to mandatory drug testing.

"Using [detection services] to certify students' honesty, paper by paper, what that does to pedagogy is, to me, just horrific," Howard says.

Howard and other critics also contend that copying students' papers into TurnItIn.com's "proprietary" database and providing them to clients violates students' privacy rights and amounts to unauthorized copying and distribution of their intellectual property.

But many teachers say they inform their students at the start of a course that their work will be copied, retained and perhaps used as "evidence" by the detection service. However, some schools, including the University of California, Berkeley, have refused to use TurnItIn due to concerns about privacy and copyright violations.

"There probably were ways we could have done it legally, but given all the questions, the administration here just felt that it really didn't want to go in that direction," says Mike Smith, Berkeley's assistant chancellor for legal affairs.

Barrie maintains that his company is on "very solid legal ground" and uses students' papers only in ways authorized by the U.S. Copyright Act.[16] "The thousands of institutions that are currently our clients all sign an agreement with us, and we wouldn't have one client if what we were doing was illegal," Barrie says.

Are news organizations doing enough to guard against plagiarism and other types of journalistic fraud?

The Jayson Blair scandal has prompted news organizations everywhere to re-examine their ethics policies.

The Miami Herald, for example, was one of many newspapers that revamped its policy regarding the use of wire-service copy in articles written by staff reporters. *The Herald's* new policy requires reporters to more clearly distinguish the wire copy from their own text and tell readers specifically where it came from. Executive Editor Tom Fiedler says he was surprised that some of his reporters didn't think such attribution was necessary.

"They thought if it was on the wires, it was fair game" for them to use without attribution, Fiedler says.

Other news organizations clarified or changed their policies regarding the use of datelines, which traditionally indicate where the reporter actually worked on the story. New York-based Bloomberg News had bucked convention and used datelines to reflect where a story's action occurred, regardless of the reporter's physical location. But Bloomberg changed its policy after *The Times* revealed Blair had falsified datelines to conceal the fact that he hadn't traveled to the scene. Bloomberg Editor-in-chief Matthew Winkler said his organization had decided the old policy "could be misleading."[17]

Still other organizations revamped their policies regarding the use of unnamed or "anonymous" sources. Quotes that Blair fabricated and attributed to law-enforcement officials while covering the sniper case prompted a prosecutor in the case to call a news conference to deny the made-up assertions. Many experts were shocked when *The Times* conceded this spring that Blair's editors never asked him to identify his anonymous sources.

"That's just unbelievable," says Thomas Kunkel, dean of Blair's alma mater, the University of Maryland School of Journalism. "If I've got a reporter making accusations [like Blair did] on the front page of *The New York Times*, if I'm the editor, I'm going to want to know where they're coming from."

Rivard discourages the use of anonymous sources at the *San Antonio Express-News*. But if they are used, their identities must be revealed to senior editors. "If a reporter came in and said, 'I've got something but I can't tell you who the source is,' we wouldn't publish it," Rivard says.

At the *Seattle Times*, the Blair affair prompted editors to revive the paper's old system of newsroom "accuracy checks," in which news sources are contacted and asked about the accuracy, fairness and completeness of the paper's coverage.

"Accuracy is our prime directive," Executive Editor Michael Fancher wrote in a June 15 column announcing he was resurrecting the old policy. "Each of us in the newsroom has a personal responsibility to the highest standards of integrity and honesty, starting with devotion to accuracy in all our work."[18]

But no news organization did more to shore up its ethical standards than *The New York Times*. Shortly after the Blair scandal broke, Assistant Managing Editor Allan Siegal was asked to form a committee to determine why Blair hadn't been stopped sooner. The so-called Siegal Committee of 25 *Times* staffers and three distinguished outside journalists began its work in mid-May.

Heads also rolled at *The Times*. On June 5, Executive Editor Howell Raines and Managing Editor Gerald Boyd both resigned under pressure from Publisher Arthur Sulzberger Jr. On July 14, op-ed columnist Bill Keller, a former *Times* managing editor, became executive editor. On June 30, his first day on the job, Keller unveiled the committee's report and announced that he would accept its major recommendations, which he said would "improve the way we run the newsroom" and "protect our precious credibility."[19]

Among its many recommendations, the report suggested the appointment of a "public editor"—a position known at other newspapers as an ombudsman—to deal with reader complaints and write periodic columns about the *Times'* "journalistic practices." Keller said the public editor "can make us more sensitive on matters of fairness and accuracy, and enhance our credibility."[20] Keller also tapped Siegal as the paper's new "standards editor," who will establish journalistic standards and educate staffers on accuracy and ethics.

Geneva Overholser, a former editor of the *Des Moines Register* and a one-time ombudsman at *The Washington Post*, calls the *Times'* decision to appoint a public editor "a terrific first step. [It's] something that could have been helpful to them in the difficulties of the last few months."[21]

But *Washington Post* columnist Robert J. Samuelson thinks the *Times* still doesn't get it. "No place in American journalism is so smug and superior as *The New York Times*," he wrote on Aug. 13. "It [is] this conceit—the belief that *The Times* must be right because it is *The Times* and sets the rules—that ultimately caused the Jayson Blair debacle. Until that conceit is purged, *The Times* will remain vulnerable to similar blunders."[22]

In addition, Samuelson groused, "The public editor's appointment will last for a year and be reviewed; the editor's independence is compromised by being responsible to the executive editor; and it's unclear how often the public editor will write."

Rivard and other experts say news organizations are not doing enough to guard against plagiarizing reporters. "I think plagiarism is a bigger problem in American journalism today than many of us [in the media] have understood or acknowledged," he says. "The development of the Web may be the single, most important factor in both spawning an environment where plagiarism is committed more and where people succumb to that weakness more."

Kelly McBride, an ethics instructor at the St. Petersburg, Fla.-based Poynter Institute for journalism, says few news organizations devote much time to training their reporters to recognize and avoid plagiarism. "I don't think there's much conversation about plagiarism in most newsrooms, other than 'don't do it,'" McBride says.

Trudy Lieberman, a contributing editor at the *Columbia Journalism Review* and a media ethics instructor at New York University, agrees. Lieberman says journalistic plagiarism persists, in part, because news organizations don't deal with plagiarizing reporters in a consistent manner. "Plagiarism is acceptable at some organizations but not at others," Lieberman says. "Somebody can plagiarize and still be 'king of the hill' if they're a good columnist or someone the organization wants to keep. But more marginal employees [who get caught plagiarizing] may be asked to leave. There doesn't seem to be a standard punishment for journalistic plagiarism at all."

Michael Richards and Clay Calvert, professors of journalism and law at Pennsylvania State University, argue in a forthcoming article that rogue journalists—and their employers—should be legally liable for plagiarism and other journalistic fraud.[23]

In the Blair case, according to Richards, *The Times* acted negligently and perpetrated fraud on its readers because it "ignored the warning signs" that Blair was filing demonstrably false stories. "*The Times*' top editors knew they had a problem, but they chose to ignore it," he says. "They abrogated their responsibility by ignoring the warning signs."[24]

But the University of Maryland's Kunkel and other experts point out that no news organization is safe from a rogue reporter. "Somebody who wants to undermine the system can do it very easily," Kunkel says. "You can say what you want and put in all kinds of safeguards, but basically, it's a system that depends on the trustworthiness of the reporters."

Background
Imitation Encouraged

Plagiarism has not always been regarded as unethical. In fact, for most of recorded history, drawing from other writers' works was encouraged. This view was grounded in the belief that knowledge of the human condition should be shared by everyone, not owned or hoarded. The notion of individual authorship was much less important than it is today.

"Writers strove, even consciously, to imitate earlier great works," wrote authors Peter Morgan and Glenn Reynolds in their 1997 book *The Appearance of Impropriety*. "That a work had obvious parallels with an early work—even similar passages or phrases—was a mark of pride, not plagiarism. Imitation was bad only when it was disguised or a symptom of laziness. It was not denounced simply on the grounds of being 'unoriginal.' "[25]

Examples of this tradition abound in literature. In ancient Greece, for example, writers such as Homer, Plato, Socrates and Aristotle borrowed heavily from earlier works. "Aristotle lifted whole pages from Democritus," wrote Alexander Lindey in his 1952 book *Plagiarism and Originality*.

Novelist and former Vassar College English Professor Thomas Mallon agrees that the concept of originality was radically different centuries ago. "Jokes about out-and-out literary theft go back all the way to Aristophanes and "The Frogs" [a play written in 405 B.C.], but what we call plagiarism was more a matter for laughter than litigation," Mallon wrote in his 1989 book *Stolen Words: Forays into the Origins and Ravages of Plagiarism*. "The Romans rewrote the Greeks. Virgil is, in a broadly imitative way, Homer, and for that matter, typologists can find most of the Old Testament in the New."

The Greek concept of imitation—known as *mimesis*—continued to influence writers during the Middle Ages. According to Syracuse's Howard, the Catholic Church promoted the medieval emphasis on mimesis because it was concerned with spreading the message of God. "The individual writer in this economy of authorship is beside the point, even a hindrance," Howard writes in her 1999 book *Standing in the Shadow of Giants: Plagiarists, Authors, Collaborators.* "Instead, the writer voices God's truth . . . and participates in the tradition of that truth-telling. Even in patron-sponsored writing for the purpose of entertainment, the writer's identity and originality are only tangentially at issue. Plagiarism was a concern that seldom arose."

Rise of Copyright

Attitudes about plagiarism began to change in the 16th century, as the Protestant Reformation swept across Western Europe. The notion that salvation could be attained without adhering to strict Catholic sacraments gave new importance to the concepts of originality and individual thought. These ideals were spread far and wide through the use of the printing press—invented in 1440—and new copyright laws, which advanced the notion that individual authorship was good and that mimesis was bad.

Notably, religious reformers like Martin Luther were among the staunchest opponents of the new copyright laws—first proposed in the late 1400s—because they believed human learning should circulate unrestricted for the common good and betterment of mankind.

"Much like defenders of Internet freedoms of access and speech today, Luther and others objected that copyright laws would limit the free circulation of ideas and knowledge that had been made so widely and instantly available . . . [by] the printing press," scholar C. Jan Swearingen wrote in a 1999 essay.[26]

Passage of the first copyright laws—in England in 1710 and in the United States in 1790—transformed writing into a viable economic pursuit. Mimesis was no longer tolerated or encouraged—in fact it was illegal. "No longer was a writer supposed to build on top of the structures left by earlier figures; now one was supposed to sweep the ground clear and build from scratch," Morgan and Reynolds write. "Once money was involved, people became more vigilant for copying, whether real or imagined."[27]

Mallon agrees. "Plagiarism didn't become a truly sore point with writers until they thought of writing as their trade," he writes in *Stolen Words*. "The writer, a new professional, was invented by a machine [the printing press]. Suddenly, his capital and identity were at stake. Things were now competitive and personal, and when writers thought they'd been plundered they fought back."[28]

'Fertile Ground'

Meanwhile, other forces were creating "fertile ground for plagiarism" at America's colleges and universities, explains Sue Carter, an associate professor of English at Ohio's Bowling

Green State University. Admissions started rising dramatically in the mid-1800s, in part because schools began accepting women for the first time. As enrollments increased, schools began requiring students to present more of their work in writing, rather than orally, as they had in the past, Carter says.

"At Harvard . . . by the 1890s, first-year students wrote a new paper every two weeks as well as one short paper six days a week for the entire academic year," Carter wrote in a 1999 article on the history of plagiarism. "In such a climate . . . students may have felt plagiarism to be a viable option."[29]

Aside from the sheer volume of writing, students also may have felt pushed toward plagiarism because many schools assigned unimaginative, "canned topics" for those papers, Carter says. "Some students believed it was OK to cheat because the teachers weren't doing their jobs. For them, it made sense to plagiarize."

To be sure, not all the student plagiarism of the mid-19th century was intentional. There were no universally agreed-upon guidelines for using sources properly. Writer's manuals didn't appear until the late 19th or early 20th centuries. "It's not like there was an *MLA Handbook* or a *Chicago Manual of Style*," Carter says. "Students knew they couldn't claim another person's words as their own, but there was nothing to give them specific, concrete guidelines about avoiding plagiarism, such as using quotation marks or footnotes."

Still, students who were so inclined in the mid-1800s could easily obtain completed papers from fraternity houses or "term-paper mills" that set up shop near many universities. A graduate student who taught writing at Harvard in the 1890s even sold term papers himself, Carter says.

Inadvertent academic plagiarism began to level off in the 1920s, as specialized handbooks began to appear providing guidelines on the correct use of sources. Even so, the number of students who patronized term-paper mills continued to grow. Calling themselves academic "research" companies, they advertised in campus newspapers and "alternative" publications and often employed graduate students to do the writing.

In Boston in the 1960s and '70s, for example, term papers were hawked on street corners and from Volkswagen buses, says Kevin Carleton, assistant vice president for public relations at Boston University (BU). "You could find them in Kenmore Square and Harvard Square and at Boston College and Northeastern University," Carleton says.

In 1972, BU sued several local term-paper mills for fraud and won an injunction prohibiting them from operating. The following year, the Massachusetts legislature banned the sale of term papers. Today, 16 states ban term-paper mills, according to the Denver-based National Conference of State Legislatures.

But BU wasn't so successful in 1997 when it tried to use federal anti-racketeering laws to prohibit all term-paper mills from using the fledgling Internet. A federal court dismissed the university's suit on the grounds that the Internet-based mills could not be prosecuted under the racketeering law. The judge also ruled that the university could not prove that it had been substantially harmed by the mills, since it could name only one student who tried to pass off an Internet-purchased paper as his own.

The mills named in the suit had planned to mount a free-speech defense, but they didn't have to use it. "We prepared a very strong First Amendment stance," said Boston lawyer Harvey Schwartz, who represented two of the operations. "This case was about academic freedom on the Internet."[30]

Second Chances

As in the literary and academic worlds, attitudes toward plagiarism also have changed over time in the realm of journalism. "Twenty or 30 years ago, there was plenty of plagiarism, embellishment and other ethical shortcuts," said Howard Kurtz, media critic for *The Washington Post*. "But they didn't always come to light, in part because journalists were reluctant to expose one another."[31]

The University of Maryland's Kunkel agrees. "When I first broke into the business 30 years ago, I worked with a guy who once in a while made up quotes and things," Kunkel recalls. "It was in high-school sports, and he sort of viewed it as saving everybody's time because the quotes were so predictable and innocuous. I don't think his editors knew, but it was pretty common knowledge in newsrooms around the county that there were people who did stuff like that."

In 1972, for example, the now-defunct *National Observer* fired journalist Nina Totenberg for lifting without attribution several paragraphs from a *Washington Post* profile of Rep. Thomas P. "Tip" O'Neill, D-Mass., who was about to become House majority leader. "I was in a hurry. I used terrible judgment," Totenberg said in a 1995 interview. "I should have been punished. I have a strong feeling that a young reporter is entitled to one mistake and to have the holy bejeezus scared out of her to never do it again."[32]

Totenberg got a second chance and today is a well-regarded legal-affairs correspondent for National Public Radio.

Other high-profile cases in which admitted or alleged plagiarists returned to journalism after their work was questioned include:

● **Mike Barnicle**—the legendary *Boston Globe* columnist resigned in 1998 amid allegations of plagiarism and fabricating articles. Today he writes a column for the *New York Daily News* and frequently appears on MSNBC's "Hardball" and other television programs.

● **Elizabeth Wurtzel**—was fired by *The Dallas Morning News* in 1988 for plagiarism. Wurtzel went on to write for prestigious magazines such as *New York* and *The New Yorker*. She has also written two best-selling books, *Prozac Nation: Young and Depressed in America* (1994) and *Bitch: In Praise of Difficult Women* (1999).

● **Marcia Stepanek**—who was fired by *Business Week* magazine in January 2001 for plagiarizing a *Washington Post* article on computer privacy. Stepanek said she did not intend to plagiarize. "I was sloppy with my notes but nothing more," she said.[33] Today, she is the executive editor of *CIO Insight*, a magazine for information-technology professionals.

Stephen Glass, who was fired by *The New Republic* in 1998 for plagiarizing and fabricating articles, also has cashed in on his wrongdoing. His "novel" about his exploits, *The Fabulist*, was published in May. It recounts the misadventures of a young writer named Stephen Glass who gets fired from a Washington, D.C.-based magazine for making up news stories and features. The protagonist—like the real Glass—even creates bogus voicemail recordings and Web sites to conceal his deceit. A movie about the young reporter's deceptions, "Shattered Glass," is slated to open next month.

Charles Lane, the editor who fired Glass from *The New Republic* in 1998, said he was stunned "that someone could do what Steve did and cash in on it."[34]

"Being disgraced is not so bad these days," said McBride, at the Poynter Institute. "In our society . . . people can capitalize on values [such as] cleverness, creativity, glibness, sharp-tongued wit and cynicism. It really says something about the entertainment society we live in—in that world, we don't really care how smarmy you are."[35]

Current Situation

Plagiarism and Politics

From time to time, plagiarism ensnares politicians as well. Sen. Joseph Biden Jr., D-Del., for example, was forced to abandon his quest to become his party's 1988 presidential nominee when sleuthing reporters caught him delivering campaign speeches containing phrases plagiarized from other American and British politicians. The senator also faced allegations he had plagiarized a paper during law school. In dropping out of the race, Biden acknowledged that he "made some mistakes," but claimed the media "exaggerated" his missteps.[36]

In recent months, critics have assailed President Bush and British Prime Minister Tony Blair over revelations that they touted two bogus reports about Iraq's alleged weapons of mass destruction (WMD)—one found to contain plagiarized materials and the other based on forged documents—to win support for attacking Iraq.

The report containing plagiarized materials was posted on Blair's official Web site on Feb. 3, 2003.[37] Among other things, it claimed to provide "up-to-date details" of Iraq's efforts to conceal its alleged weapons of mass destruction from U.N. weapons inspectors. Secretary of State Colin Powell cited the report in his Feb. 5, 2003, address to the U.N. Security Council, saying "I would call my colleagues' attention to the fine paper that the United Kingdom distributed yesterday which describes in exquisite detail Iraqi deception activities."[38]

Within hours, news organizations discovered that the report that Powell had cited was based largely on out-of-date magazine articles from the *Middle East Review* and other journals that had been plagiarized—typographical errors and all—from the Internet.[39]

In an interview with *The New York Times*, a spokesman for Blair acknowledged that the report was, indeed, a "pull-together of a variety of sources." The spokesman added that "we should . . . have acknowledged which bits came from public sources and which bits came from other sources."[40]

Reporters quickly tracked down the author of one of the plagiarized articles, Ibrahim al-Marashi, who said British officials had not asked permission to incorporate his work into their intelligence dossier. Al-Marashi, who had written the article as a postgraduate student at the Monterey Institute of International Studies in Monterey, Calif., said he believed his work was accurate, but he told a *New York Times* reporter, "Had they [British officials] consulted me, I could have provided them with more updated information."[41]

In a later interview, al-Marashi said British officials distorted his work to make the Iraqi threat appear more serious than he believed it to be. "It connected me with the . . . case for going to war," al-Marashi said this summer. "It was never my intention to have it support such an argument to provide evidence to go to war."[42]

To date, none of the WMD described by President Bush and Prime Minister Blair have been found in Iraq.

'Poisonous Atmosphere'

Some journalists say news organizations have gone overboard in their effort to enforce tougher, new ethical standards in the wake of the Jayson Blair scandal.

Many point to the trouble that befell Rick Bragg, a Pulitzer Prize-winning *New York Times* reporter. Bragg angrily resigned from the paper on May 28, five days after *The Times* published an editor's note saying an article he had written the previous June had relied too heavily on the work of an uncredited freelance journalist, J. Wesley Yoder. *The Times* stated in its editor's note that the article, which described the lives of oystermen on Florida's Gulf Coast, should have carried Yoder's byline as well as Bragg's. *The Times* suspended Bragg for two weeks as a result of the incident.

Bragg readily admitted that he had done little firsthand reporting on the story, and said he didn't tell his editors about Yoder's contribution to the story because it was *The Times*' practice not to credit freelancers. "It would have been nice for [Yoder] to share a byline, or at least a tagline, but that's not the policy," he told the *Columbia Journalism Review* on May 23. "I don't make the policies."[43]

Yoder saw it that way as well. "This is what stringers do—the legwork," he said. "I did most of the reporting and Rick wrote it. Rick tried to bring the piece alive, to take the reader there, and he did a darn good job of it."[44]

In an interview a few days later, Bragg blamed his suspension on the "poisonous atmosphere" that he said had developed at *The Times* following the Jayson Blair incident. "Obviously, I'm taking a bullet here; anyone with half a brain can see that," he told *The Washington Post*'s Kurtz. "Reporters are being bad-mouthed daily. I hate it. It makes me sick."[45]

Bragg quit the paper. But his defense—that it was a common and accepted practice at *The Times* for correspondents to rely on the work of unattributed freelancers, stringers and interns—didn't sit well with some of his colleagues. Peter Kilborn, a reporter in *The Times*' Washington bureau, chastised Bragg in an e-mail to the newspaper's national desk. "Bragg's comments in defense of his reportorial routines are outrageous," Kilborn wrote. "I hope there is some way that we as correspondents . . . can get the word out . . . that we do not operate that way. Bragg says he works in a poisonous atmosphere. He's the poison."[46]

Despite his rocky departure from *The Times*, Bragg landed on his feet. He has negotiated a $1 million deal to write a book about Pvt. Jessica Lynch—about whom Jayson Blair had falsified one of his reports.

Action in Schools

Teachers and schools across the country are taking a variety of steps to combat plagiarism. Some school districts have policies for dealing with plagiarism at the elementary, middle school and secondary school levels. The Springfield Township School District in Erdenheim, Pa., for example, defines plagiarism as "Direct copying of the work of another submitted as the student's own." Under the district's policy, plagiarism includes "Lack of in-text or in-project documentation; Documentation that does not check out or does not match Works Cited/Works Consulted;" and "Work that suddenly appears on final due date without a clear provenance."

"We believe that we must not only teach the ethics and mechanics of documentation, but we must also hold students accountable for the ethical use of the ideas and words of others," the district's policy states. "Plagiarism, in any form, is unethical and unacceptable."

Lawrence High School in Fairfield, Maine, requires students and parents to sign a plagiarism policy every year that defines plagiarism and lays out the consequences for violators. First-time offenders get three options: rewrite the plagiarized paper within a week; write an entirely different paper within a week; or receive a zero on the rejected paper. Subsequent offenses receive automatic zeros. The policy also outlines procedures in which students can challenge plagiarism allegations.

"School faculty members and administrators should take special care to define [plagiarism] and explain how to avoid it," Kelley R. Taylor, general counsel of the National Association of Secondary School Principals (NASSP), wrote in a recent issue of *Principal Leadership*, the NASSP's journal. "Teach your faculty members to teach students what plagiarism is and how to avoid it with proper references and source citations."[47]

Taylor says teachers can do a number of things in their classrooms to combat plagiarism, such as structuring writing assignments so students have to revise their work and requiring students to turn in annotated bibliographies, to show they are familiar with their sources.

Many college professors and administrators, though, complain that high schools aren't doing enough to teach students about plagiarism. "I don't know what's going on in high schools. Some students don't seem to be prepared to do proper citation and research" at the college level, says Ronald Stump, vice chancellor of student affairs at the University of Colorado at Boulder. "I don't want to paint every high school in the same way, but a lot of students do seem to be surprised" when they get accused of plagiarism.

Most Colorado professors talk to their classes about plagiarism or include warnings about it on their course syllabi, Stump says. Like many schools, the university has a student-run honor committee that disseminates information about plagiarism and adjudicates plagiarism cases referred to it by school faculty. Penalties for plagiarism range from a letter saying a student broke the honor code to expulsion. In addition, plagiarists frequently are

AT ISSUE

Should educators use commercial services to combat plagiarism?

JOHN BARRIE
President, TurnItIn.com
Written for the CQ Researcher, September 2003

I spent more than 10 years researching how our brains create a conscious representation of the world, and the take-home message is that we draw from the past to create the present. Academic endeavors work in a similar manner. Students from elementary school to postgraduate are constantly learning from and building upon the corpus of prior work from their peers, authors of books or journal articles, lectures from faculty or from information found on the Internet. One of the best methods for learning involves collaboration or peer review among groups of students in order to share ideas and criticism regarding course material.

Subsequent intellectual accomplishments of students—or academics—are sometimes measured by their ability to distill weeks, months or years of hard work into a manuscript of original thought. For example, a high-school student might compose a book report about Othello while a college undergrad might write a manuscript regarding the sublime philosophy of Nietzsche. In either case, the faculty is attempting to ascertain whether that student has understood the course material. The problem begins when faculty cannot determine whether a student wrote a term paper or plagiarized it from other sources. But is that a problem?

TurnItIn receives about 15,000 papers *per day* from students in 51 countries writing across the curriculum, and about 30 percent of those papers are less than original. This is supported by the largest-ever study of plagiarism involving more than 18,000 students on 23 campuses. The study (released this month by Rutgers University Professor Donald McCabe) concluded that nearly 40 percent of college undergraduates admitted to plagiarizing term papers using information cut-and-pasted from the Internet.

This raises the obvious question: "Why is Internet plagiarism growing exponentially in the face of honor codes, vigilant faculty and severe punishments ranging all the way to expulsion?" The answer: The status quo doesn't work, and our society's future leaders are rapidly building a foundation of shaky ethics while cheating their way to a degree.

The real shame is that while some administrators shirk their responsibility to face the problem or are in complete dereliction of their duty as educators by not demanding original work from all students, ethical, hard-working students are being out-competed by their cheating peers—and it's an outrage.

Digital plagiarism is a digital problem and demands a digital solution, whether it's TurnItIn or otherwise. No one wants to live in a society populated by Enron executives.

REBECCA MOORE HOWARD
Associate Professor of Writing and Rhetoric, Syracuse University
Written for the CQ Researcher, September 2003

Teaching, not software, is the key to preventing plagiarism. Today's students can access an array of electronic texts and images unimaginable just 20 years ago, and students' relationship to the practice of information-sharing has changed along with the technology.

But today's students lack extensive training and experience in working carefully from print sources, and they may not understand that they need to learn this skill. They may also find it difficult to differentiate between kinds of sources on the Internet. With information arriving as a cacophony of electronic voices, even well-intentioned students have difficulty keeping track of—much less citing—who said what.

Moreover, the sheer volume of available information frequently leaves student writers feeling that they have nothing new to say about an issue. Hence too many students—one in three, according to a recent survey conducted by Rutgers University Professor Donald McCabe—may fulfill assignments by submitting work they have not written.

Were we in the throes of widespread moral decay, capture-and-punishment might provide an appropriate deterrent. We are, however, in the midst of a revolution in literacy, and teachers' responses must be more complex. They must address the underlying issues: students' ability to conduct research, comprehend extended written arguments, evaluate sources and produce their own persuasive written texts, in explicit dialogue with their sources.

Classrooms must engage students in text and in learning—communicating a value to these activities that extends beyond grades earned and credentials accrued. McCabe, who is a founder of the renowned Center for Academic Integrity at Duke University, recommends pedagogy and policies that speak to the causes of plagiarism, rather than buying software for detection and punishment. In a 2003 position statement, the Council of Writing Program Administrators urges, "Students should understand research assignments as opportunities for genuine and rigorous inquiry and learning." The statement offers extensive classroom suggestions for teachers and cautions that using plagiarism-catching software may "justify the avoidance of responsible teaching methods."

Buying software instead of revitalizing one's teaching means that teachers, like students, have allowed the electronic environment to encourage a reductive, automated vision of the educational experience. As one of my colleagues recently remarked, "The 'world's leading plagiarism-prevention system' is not TurnItIn.com—it's careful pedagogy."

HOW TO AVOID PLAGIARISM

"Plagiarism involves two kinds of wrong," according to the Modern Language Association (MLA). "Using another person's ideas, information, or expressions without [acknowledgment] constitutes intellectual theft. Passing off another person's ideas, information, or expressions as your own . . . constitutes fraud." Here are the MLA's plagiarism guidelines for writers:

You have plagiarized if you:

● Took notes without differentiating summaries, paraphrases or quotations from others' work or ideas and then presented wording from the notes as if they were your own.
● Copied text from the Web and pasted it into your paper without quotation marks or citation.
● Presented facts without saying where you found them.
● Repeated or paraphrased wording without acknowledgment.
● Took someone's unique or particularly apt phrase without acknowledgment.
● Paraphrased someone's argument or presented someone's line of thought without acknowledgment.
● Bought or otherwise acquired a research paper and handed in part or all of it as your own.

To avoid plagiarism:

● List the writers and viewpoints discovered in your research and use the list to double-check the material in your report before turning it in.
● While taking notes, keep separate and distinct your own ideas, summaries of others' ideas or exact wording from other people's work.
● Identify the sources of all exact wording, paraphrases, ideas, arguments and facts that you borrow.
● Ask your instructor if you are uncertain about your use of sources.

Source: Joseph Gibaldi, *The MLA Handbook for Writers of Research Papers*, Sixth Edition, Modern Language Association of America, 2003.

required to attend academic-integrity classes, says Allison Jennings, 21, a political science major and the director of adjudication for the university's honor code council. "It really discusses how not to plagiarize," Jennings says of the class. "It's really about education."

The University of Virginia also goes to great lengths to educate students about plagiarism, says Eramo, of the school's Honor Committee. While most professors educate and warn their students about plagiarism, the specifics of the warnings vary. "They often will put statements on their syllabi about what plagiarism is and what they will and will not accept, and what kinds of citation requirements they have," Eramo says. "But it definitely varies from faculty member to faculty member."

Eramo says the Honor Committee is trying to get faculty members to understand that not every student has the same understanding of what plagiarism is and how to avoid it. "So many students are coming here without that knowledge, and the faculty are sort of expecting them to have it, and they don't," Eramo says.

The Honor Committee has its own plagiarism-education program, Eramo says. Students who attend the summer orientation session, for example, get a 20-minute presentation about the honor system that includes information on plagiarism. Each fall, Honor Committee staff visit every dormitory and speak to students about the consequences for plagiarism and other forms of cheating. The committee also hosts voluntary round-table discussions about the honor code during the year.

Outlook

Internet Blamed

Although the Jayson Blair scandal sent a loud wake-up call to all reporters and editors, academics and working journalists alike say journalism will continue, nonetheless, to be occasionally tainted by plagiarizing reporters. Many blame the ease of plagiarizing from the Internet and the demands of online journalism's round-the-clock deadline pressure.

Before the Internet, reporters' deadlines typically fell only once a day, notes the University of Maryland's Kunkel. Today, however, reporters for both print and electronic news outlets are often expected to break stories on their employers' Web sites as soon as possible, and update them whenever the circumstances change. The pressure-packed environment tempts some reporters to plagiarize, he says. "Some plagiarizing is certainly driven by [deadline] pressure," says Kunkel, who adds that "computers and electronic databases have made it easy—maybe too easy—to co-opt other people's work."

The San Antonio Express-News's Rivard agrees. "People who might not have copied something out of another newspaper in the pre-electronic era can now get an extraordinary amount of information about any topic, anytime, using the Internet," Rivard says. "It's easy to abuse that kind of access."

Others downplay the connection between plagiarism and online journalism. "We do operate under more pressure than in the past, but that's no excuse for failing to follow the protections and guidelines that should be in place for ensuring the integrity of a story," says *The Miami Herald's* Fiedler. "We would never tell our reporters to cut corners or not verify something in order to get it online quickly—we just don't do that."

Fiedler does not believe the Blair scandal will permanently alter the public's perception of the media. "Most readers who followed it did not leap to some drastically dark conclusion that the credibility of the media is now gone," he says. "If they were skeptical of what they saw in the media [before the scandal] they just added a count to their indictment. But if they tended to give the media generally good marks for credibility, I think they will continue to do so."

Kunkel, ultimately, also is optimistic. "American journalism has never been more professional than it is today, and the instances of plagiarism are probably rarer than ever," he says. "But when somebody like Jayson Blair gets exposed, there's such an uproar that everybody believes the industry is going to hell in a handbasket. That's not so."

A similar debate promises to continue raging over plagiarism in education. Some experts say the problem is only going to get worse until students change their perception of the Internet. Rutgers' McCabe says many feel that material found on the Internet is in the public domain and that they may freely "cut and paste" it into their own papers.

"A large number of students understand that adults—teachers and others—think that [cut-and-paste plagiarism] is wrong, but they don't think it is," McCabe says. "Whether they believe it's wrong or not, they're trying to make the argument that it's not cheating."

Other experts say schools should combat plagiarism—not by focusing on detection and interdiction—but by better clarifying what plagiarism is in a digital age. "As teachers, we really own the problem," says Springfield Township High School librarian Valenza. "At our school, we're really trying to develop a culture where kids understand what plagiarism is and how to avoid it."

The Rochester Institute's Scanlon agrees. "We seem to be turning over to computers a problem that's supposedly caused by computers and the Internet, and I'm not so sure that's wise," he says. "Plagiarism is not a technological problem—it's a problem that has to do with ethical behavior and the correct use of sources. And it existed long before the advent of the Internet."

Notes

1. Quoted in Dan Barry *et al.*, "Correcting the Record: Times Reporter Who Resigned Leaves Long Trail of Deception," *The New York Times*, May 11, 2003, p. A1.
2. Quoted in Peter Johnson, "Media Weigh In On 'Journalistic Fraud,'" *USA Today*, May 12, 2003, p. A1.
3. The *Oxford English Dictionary* defines plagiarism as "the wrongful appropriation or purloining, and publication as one's own, of the ideas, or the expression of the ideas (literary, artistic, musical, mechanical, etc.) of another.
4. Alexander Lindey, *Plagiarism and Originality* (1952), in Joseph Gibaldi, *MLA Handbook for Writers of Research Papers*, 6th ed. (2003), p. 66.
5. The effect that a plagiarized work has on the market value of a copyrighted work in a key provision of the Copyright Act of 1976. For background, see Kenneth Jost, "Copyright and the Internet," *The CQ Researcher*, Sept. 29, 2000, pp. 769–792.
6. Quoted in Stephen Ambrose, "Accusations of Plagiarism Deserve an Honest Reply," Newhouse News Service, May 2, 2002.
7. For background, see Kathy Koch, "Cheating in Schools," *The CQ Researcher*, Sept. 22, 2000, pp. 745–768.
8. Donald McCabe and Linda Trevino, "What We Know About Cheating in College: Longitudinal Trends and Recent Developments," *Change*, January/February 1996, pp. 29–33.
9. See Patrick M. Scanlon and David R. Neumann, "Internet Plagiarism Among College Students," *Journal of College Student Development*, May/June 2002, pp. 375–384.
10. See Donald McCabe, "Cheating: Why Students Do It and How We Can Help them Stop," *American Educator*, winter 2001, pp. 38–43.
11. See B. Brandes, "Academic Honesty: A Special Study of California Students," California State Department of Education, 1986.

12. See Fred Schab, "Schooling Without Learning: Thirty Years of Cheating in High School," *Adolescence*, Vol. 23 (1991), pp. 681–687.
13. Amy Harmon, "261 Lawsuits Filed on Music Sharing," *The New York Times*, Sept. 9, 2003, p. A1. See also John Leland, "Beyond File-Sharing, A Nation of Copiers," *The New York Times*, Sept. 14, 2003, Sec. 9, p. 1.
14. Bruce Orwall, *et al.*, "Music Industry Presses 'Play' on Plan to Save Its Business," *The Wall Street Journal*, Sept. 9, 2003, p. A1.
15. Quoted in Tom Anderson, "Software Tattles on Academic Plagiarists," *The Oakland* [California]*Tribune*, Feb. 4, 2002.
16. For more information on U.S. copyright law, see Jost, *op. cit.* A detailed legal brief addressing copyright-related questions directed against TurnItIn.com is at www.turnitin.com/static/legal/legal_documents.html.
17. Quoted in Howard Kurtz, "Rick Bragg Quits at New York Times," *The Washington Post*, May 29, 2003, p. C1.
18. Quoted in Micheal R. Fancher, "Newspaper Bringing Back System of Accuracy Checks," *The Seattle Times*, June 15, 2003, p. A2.
19. Keller's memo and the Siegal report are available at www.nytco.com.
20. *Ibid.*
21. Quoted in Howard Kurtz, "N.Y. Times to Appoint Ombudsman," *The Washington Post*, July 31, 2003, p. C1.
22. Robert J. Samuelson, "Smug Journalism," *The Washington Post*, Aug. 13, 2003, p. A27.
23. The article will be published this fall in the *Fordham Intellectual Property, Media and Entertainment Law Journal*.
24. Quoted in Cynthia Cotts, "Can The Times be Sued?" *The Village Voice*, Sept. 10, 2003.
25. Quoted in Peter W. Morgan and Glenn H. Reynolds, *The Appearance of Impropriety: How the Ethics Wars Have Undermined American Government, Business, and Society* (1997).
26. See C. Jan Swearingen, "Originality, Authenticity, Imitation and Plagiarism: Augustine's Chinese Cousins," in Lise Buranen and Alice M. Roy (eds.), *Perspectives on Plagiarism and Intellectual Prosperity in a Postmodern World* (1999), pp. 19–30.
27. Morgan and Reynolds, *op. cit.*
28. Quoted in Thomas Mallon, *Stolen Word: Forays into the Origins and Ravages of Plagiarism* (1989), pp. 3–4.
29. Quoted in Sue Carter Simmons, "Compelling Notions of Authorship: A Historical Look at Students and Textbooks on Plagiarism and Cheating," in Lise Buranen and Alice M. Roy (eds.), *Perspectives on Plagiarism and Intellectual Property in a Postmodern World* (1999), pp. 41–51.
30. Quoted in Ralph Ranalli, "Judge Drops BU Lawsuit Against Web 'Paper Mills,'" *The Boston Herald*, Dec. 8, 1998, p. A14.
31. Quoted in Kathy Koch, "Journalism Under Fire," *The CQ Researcher*, Dec. 25, 1998, pp. 1121–1144.
32. Quoted in Trudy Lieberman, "Plagiarize, Plagiarize, Plagiarize . . . Only Be Sure To Call It Research," *Columbia Journalism Review*, July/August 1995, p. 21.
33. Quoted in Howard Kurtz, "Stephen Glass Waits for Prime Time to Say 'I Lied,'" *The Washington Post*, May 7, 2003, p. C1.
34. Quoted in Howard Kurtz, "Business Week Fires Writer for Plagiarism; Story on Computer Privacy Was Similar to Post Article," *The Washington Post*, Feb. 10, 2001, p. C3.
35. Quoted in Maria Puente, "Disgrace, Dishonor, Infamy: They're Not So Bad Anymore," *USA Today*, May 22, 2003, p. D1.
36. Quoted in David Espo, "Biden Quits Races, Cites 'Exaggerated Shadow' of Mistakes," The Associated Press, Sept. 23, 1987.
37. The report can be viewed online at www.number-10.gov.uk/files/pdf/Iraq/pdf.
38. A transcript is available at: www.state.gov/secretary/rm/2003/17300.htm.
39. For background, see Sarah Lyall, "Britain Admits That Much of Its Report on Iraq Came From Magazines," *The New York Times*, Feb. 8, 2003, p. A9.

40. *Ibid.*
41. *Ibid.*
42. Quoted in Ben Russell, "Government Risked My Life by Copying Iraq Study," *The* [London] *Independent,* June 20, 2003, p. 10.
43. Quoted in Geoffrey Gray, "More Trouble at The Times: Rick Bragg Suspended," *Columbia Journalism Review* (online version), May 23, 2003.
44. *Ibid.*
45. Quoted in Howard Kurtz, "Suspended N.Y. Times Reporter Says He'll Quit," *The Washington Post,* May 27, 2003, p. C1.
46. Kilborn's e-mail was quoted in Seth Mnookin, "Firestorm in the Newsroom: The Times' National Staff Defends Their Reporting Methods," *Newsweek* (online version), May 28, 2003.
47. Kelley R. Taylor, "Cheater, cheater . . ." *Principal Leadership*, April 2003, pp. 74–78.

Bibliography

Selected Sources

Books

Buranen, Lise, and Alice M. Roy (eds.), *Perspectives on Plagiarism and Intellectual Property in a Postmodern World,* State University of New York Press, 1999.
> Essays by scholars and copyright attorneys on copyright law, changing attitudes toward plagiarism and strategies for dealing with academic plagiarism.

Glass, Stephen, *The Fabulist,* Simon & Schuster, 2003.
> A fictionalized account of the author's infamous career at *The New Republic*, where he was exposed as a plagiarist and journalistic fraud in 1998.

Howard, Rebecca Moore, *Standing in the Shadow of Giants: Plagiarists, Authors, Collaborators,* Ablex, 1999.
> A professor of writing and rhetoric at Syracuse University chronicles attitudes toward plagiarism since ancient times, maintaining academic plagiarism is frequently inadvertent.

Lathrop, Ann, and Kathleen Foss, *Student Cheating and Plagiarism in the Internet Era: A Wake-Up Call,* Libraries Unlimited, 2000.
> This discussion deals with how students use the Internet to download term papers and purloin text from online sources. Lathrop is a professor emeritus at California State University, Long Beach; Foss is a librarian at the Los Alamitos Unified School District.

Mallon, Thomas, *Stolen Words: Forays into the Origins and Ravages of Plagiarism,* Ticknor & Fields, 1989.
> A novelist and a former English professor discusses plagiarism in literature and popular culture, maintaining society is generally too lax in prosecuting plagiarists.

Articles

Ambrose, Stephen, "Accusations of Plagiarism Deserve an Honest Reply," Newhouse News Service, May 2, 2002.
> The best-selling historian defends himself against the plagiarism allegations that dogged him in the final months of his life.

Barry, Dan, *et. al,* "Correcting the Record: Times Reporter Who Resigned Leaves Long Trail of Deception," *The New York Times,* May 11, 2003, p. A1.
> This is *The Times'* internal account of Jayson Blair, the rogue reporter who plagiarized and fabricated dozens of articles. A companion piece documents problems *The Times* found in 39 articles by Blair.

Edmundson, Mark, "How Teachers Can Stop Cheaters," *The New York Times*, Sept. 9, 2003, p. A29.

> Some professors think teachers need to stop looking exclusively for technological solutions to the problem of plagiarism in schools.

Kumar, Anita, "High-Tech Sleuthing Catches College Cheats," *The St. Petersburg Times*, Aug. 31, 2003, p. A1.

> A journalist interviews educators who say plagiarism-detection services are desperately needed and those who argue they are the wrong way to deal with plagiarism.

Kurtz, Howard, "To the Editors: How Could This Happen? N.Y. Times Staff, Execs in 'Painful and Honest' Meeting Over Plagiarism Fiasco," *The Washington Post*, May 15, 2003, p. C1.

> *The Washington Post's* media critic chronicles how *New York Times* staffers reacted with shock and anger after Jayson Blair was exposed as a fraud.

Lyall, Sarah, "Britain Admits That Much of Its Report on Iraq Came From Magazines," *The New York Times*, Feb. 8, 2003, p. A9.

> Reporter Lyall documents how the British government plagiarized articles for its official report about Iraq's efforts to hide its weapons of mass destruction.

Puente, Maria, "Disgrace, Dishonor, Infamy: They're Not So Bad Anymore," *USA Today*, May 22, 2003, p. D1.

> Reporter Puente writes about disgraced journalists who wrote books and articles after committing journalistic fraud.

Studies and Reports

McCabe, Donald, "Cheating: Why Students Do It and How We Can Help them Stop," *American Educator*, winter 2001.

> A management professor at Rutgers University and an expert on academic cheating documents how and why high-school students engage in plagiarism.

Scanlon, Patrick M., and David R. Neumann, "Internet Plagiarism Among College Students," *Journal of College Student Development*, May/June 2002, pp. 375–384.

> Professors of communication at the Rochester Institute of Technology conclude that the Internet has not caused a dramatic increase in plagiarism.

Siegal, Allan M. (ed.), "Report of the Committee on Safeguarding the Integrity of Our Journalism," *The New York Times*, July 28, 2003; www.nytco.com.

> *Times* staffers and outside journalists recommend a number of changes following the Jayson Blair scandal; the report is available at www.nytco.com.

Academic Honor Codes/Plagiarism

Bartlett, Thomas, "Historical Association Will No Longer Investigate Allegations of Wrongdoing," *The Chronicle of Higher Education*, May 23, 2003, p. 12.

> The American Historical Association announced it would no longer investigate complaints alleging plagiarism or other forms of professional misconduct by historians.

Boorstein, Michelle, "U-Va. Expels 48 Students After Plagiarism Probe," *The Washington Post*, Nov. 26, 2002, p. B1.

> Forty-eight students were dismissed from the University of Virginia (UVA) after a massive plagiarism investigation uncovered widespread cheating in some classes.

Hoover, Eric, "Honor for Honor's Sake?" *The Chronicle of Higher Education*, May 3, 2002, p. 35.

> Some educators and students are very critical of UVA's strict honor code, and others have accused the system of racial bias.

Zernike, Kate, "With Student Cheating on the Rise, More Colleges Are Turning to Honor Codes," *The New York Times*, Nov. 2, 2002, p. A10.

> Some colleges and universities have turned to low-tech solutions for cheating: their honor codes.

Anti-Plagiarism Programs/Companies

"Let No One Else's Work Evade Your Eyes," *The Economist*, March 16, 2002.

A recent upsurge in cheating and plagiarism at schools has seen a rapid increase in interest in software designed to catch the cheats, like TurnItIn.com.

Banks, Ann, "Web Can Thwart Word Thieves," *USA Today*, April 18, 2002, p. A11.

With its anonymity, the Internet would seem to promise student cheaters endless bounty, but some students are finding the Internet can track their word-pilfering as well.

Eakin, Emily, "Stop, Historians! Don't Copy That Passage! Computers Are Watching," *The New York Times*, Jan. 26, 2002, p. B9.

Over the last decade, plagiarism detection has gone high-tech, and today's software market is flooded with programs designed to rout out copycats.

Foster, Andrea L., "Plagiarism-Detection Tool Creates Legal Quandary," *The Chronicle of Higher Education*, May 17, 2002, p. 37.

Some college lawyers and professors are warning that one of the most widely used plagiarism-detection services may be trampling on students' copyrights and privacy.

Hastings, Michael, and Sonia Kolesnikov-Jessop, "Cheater Beaters," *Newsweek*, Sept. 8, 2003, p. 32.

The Internet is as useful for cheating as it is for learning, and several new software companies are taking aim at plagiarists.

McCarroll, Christina, "Beating Web Cheaters at Their Own Game," *The Christian Science Monitor*, Aug. 28, 2001, p. 16.

Cheating on schoolwork has simmered on as long as there have been students averse to studying, but the Internet has woven new twists into the problem of plagiarism.

Internet Plagiarism

Kellogg, Alex P., "Students Plagiarize Online Less Than Many Think, a New Study Finds," *The Chronicle of Higher Education*, Feb. 15, 2002, p. 44.

A new study by two professors at the Rochester Institute of Technology concludes that online plagiarism is not nearly as widespread as has frequently been suggested.

Rimer, Sara, "A Campus Fad That's Being Copied: Internet Plagiarism Seems on the Rise," *The New York Times*, Sept. 3, 2003, p. B7.

A study conducted among more than 15,000 students on 23 college campuses has found that Internet plagiarism is rising among students.

Schulte, Brigid, "Cheatin', Writin' & 'Rithmetic," *The Washington Post Magazine*, Sept. 15, 2002, p. 16.

Many teachers and parents are increasingly worried about the ease with which many students are including plagiarized material from the Internet in their work.

Sessions Stepp, Laura, "Point. Click. Think?" *The Washington Post*, July 16, 2002, p. C1.

As students increasingly use the Internet for legitimate research and learning, teachers are trying to warn them away from Internet-abetted cheating and plagiarism.

Wilogren, Jodi, "School Cheating Scandal Tests a Town's Values," *The New York Times*, Feb. 14, 2002, p. A1.

Even small-town America isn't immune to Internet cheating scandals, as recent events in Piper, Kan., exposed a wide ring of computer-based cheating.

Journalistic Plagiarism

Caldwell, Christopher, "The New York Times's Meltdown," *The Weekly Standard*, May 26, 2003.

Media pundits argue that the Jayson Blair scandal at *The New York Times* is just one manifestation of a continuing crisis in American journalism.

Hernandez, Macarena, "What Jayson Blair Stole From Me, and Why I Couldn't Ignore It," *The Washington Post*, June 1, 2003, p. B5.

> Some journalists say Jayson Blair's misdeeds are not, despite what the some critics say, about affirmative action.

Kurtz, Howard, "N.Y. Times Uncovers Dozens of Faked Stories by Reporter," *The Washington Post*, May 11, 2003, p. A1.

> The failure of the *New York Times* staff to catch Jayson Blair's deceit is more than just an editorial scandal, it's also a portrait of a wide-ranging newspaper management failure.

Mnookin, Seth, "Total Fiction," *Newsweek*, May 19, 2003, p. 70.

> Five years ago, a hot young writer for *The New Republic* got fired for making up outrageous yarns.

Paulson, Amanda, "Beyond Jayson," *The Christian Science Monitor*, May 16, 2003, p. 1.

> More than the Blair scandal, a much less sinister occurrence undermines the credibility of most newspapers every day: the unintentional errors, that make their way into each issue.

Plagiarism and Copyright

Eunjung Cha, Ariana, "Harry Potter and the Copyright Lawyer," *The Washington Post*, June 18, 2003, p. A1.

> Some book, music and movie houses argue that so-called fan fiction is more plagiarism than art and have demanded that operators of Web sites remove the offending material.

Leland, John, "Beyond File-Sharing, A Nation of Copiers," *The New York Times*, Sept. 14, 2003, Sec. 9, p. 1.

> Citing the work of Rutgers University ethics researcher Donald L. McCabe. Leland suggests that the growing incidence of copying from the Internet is "just one part of a broader shift toward all copying, all the time."

McTaggart, Lynne, "Fame Can't Excuse a Plagiarist," *The New York Times*, March 16, 2002, p. A15.

> In cases where plagiarized words are protected by copyright, copying in more than minimal amounts is illegal, regardless of whether the copying was unintentional.

Vincent, Norah, "Publishing, Pressure, Profits and Plagiarism," *Los Angeles Times*, Feb. 28, 2002, p. B15.

> Recent instances of plagiarism reveal a rash of mendacity in history and a serious betrayal of public trust, not to mention an egregious breach of intellectual copyright.

Plagiarism by Leaders

Broadway, Bill, "Borrowed Sermons Roil Downtown Congregation," *The Washington Post*, Aug. 16, 2003, p. A1.

> A preacher in New York City has become embroiled in a plagiarism controversy, after Web-savvy congregation members spotted lifted passages in his sermons.

Cockburn, Alexander, "The Great 'Intelligence' Fraud," *The Nation*, March 3, 2003, p. 8.

> A recent British intelligence report turned out to be a series of plagiarisms from news articles and a paper on Iraqi politics written by a student at the Monterey Institute of International Studies.

Hakim, Danny, "Clergyman Is Accused of Plagiarism," *The New York Times*, March 13, 2002, p. A18.

> The rector of a Detroit church has been suspended while church officials investigate charges that he plagiarized some of his sermons from Internet sites and mailing lists.

Pareles, Jon, "Plagiarism in Dylan, Or a Cultural Collage?" *The New York Times*, July 12, 2003, p. B7.

> After recent uproars over historians and journalists who used other researchers' material without attribution, could it be that Bob Dylan is one more plagiarist?

For More Information

American Library Association, 50 E. Huron St., Chicago, IL 60611; (800) 545-2433; www.ala.org. Publishes articles about how educators can detect and prevent plagiarism.

Berkman Center for Internet and Society at Harvard Law School, 511 Pound Hall, 1563 Massachusetts Ave., Cambridge, MA 02138; (617) 495-7547; http://cyber.law.harvard.edu. The center's Web site contains numerous articles about plagiarism in the Internet age.

Center for Academic Integrity, Duke University, Box 90434, Durham, NC 27708; (919) 660-3045; www.academicintegrity.org. A consortium of 200 colleges and universities concerned about academic plagiarism.

Center for Excellence in Teaching and Learning, University of Albany, 1400 Washington Ave., Albany, NY 12222; (518) 437-3920; www.albany.edu/cetl. The center's Web site discusses avoiding plagiarism and has plagiarism-detection software available for downloading.

Center for the Study of College Student Values, Florida State University, 113 Stone Building, Tallahassee, FL 32306-4452; (850) 644-3691; www.collegevalues.org. Publishes the *Journal of College and Character* and studies ethical issues.

Council of Writing Program Administrators, P.O. Box 8101, North Carolina State University, Raleigh, NC 27695-8105; (919) 513-4080; www.ilstu.edu/~ddhesse/wpa. This national association provides Web resources for preventing plagiarism.

Poynter Institute for Media Studies, 801 Third St. South, St. Petersburg, FL 33701-4920; (727) 821-9494; www.poynter.org. Conducts classes for journalism students, teachers and professionals. Poynter columnist Jim Romenesko tracks plagiarism in journalism. The nonprofit institute owns Congressional Quarterly Inc.

TurnItIn.com, 1624 Franklin St., Suite 818, Oakland, CA 94612; (510) 287-9720; www.turnitin.com. A leading provider of plagiarism-detection services.

 For Discussion:

1. How should plagiarists be penalized? Should the penalty vary depending upon the circumstances?

2. According to one study Hansen cites, "40 percent of college students have plagiarized material at least once." Do you think this number is accurate? Why do you think college students cheat?

3. One study cited in Hansen's article claims that "high school students plagiarize significantly more than college students." Do you agree with this assessment? Is cheating in high school different from cheating in college or in the workplace?

4. If you had to educate the entire campus—including the faculty, staff, and administrators—about the principles of academic integrity, how would you do it?

For Fact-Finding, Research, and Writing:

1. Using a library database, find information about a prominent case of plagiarism. What were the circumstances of the case, and how was the plagiarist or plagiarists penalized?
2. Find two recently published sources that deal with the issue of plagiarism detection services. Where do these two articles stand on the use of such services?
3. Hansen points out that Mike Barnicle, Stephen Glass, Marcia Stepanek, Nina Totenberg, and Elizabeth Wurtzel were each fired from their journalism jobs for plagiarism. Pick one of these people and find one of their plagiarized articles, then locate the original source of that information.
4. Hansen's article mentions Donald McCabe who founded Duke University's Center for Academic Integrity. Use the library databases to find two of McCabe's recent publications concerning academic integrity. Write a paragraph explaining some of the McCabe's findings.

Lawrence Lessig, "Privacy as Property"

Lawrence Lessig is currently Professor of Law at Stanford Law School, where he founded Stanford's Center for Internet and Society. Prior to joining the faculty at Stanford, he was Professor of Law at the Harvard Law School, a fellow at Wissenschaftskolleg zu Berlin, and Professor at the University of Chicago Law School. In addition to his law degree from Yale, Lessig also holds an MA in Philosophy from Cambridge University in England. Adding to his distinguished legal career (he was called as an expert witness in the government's anti-trust case against Microsoft), he is the author of several books on the relationship between the Internet, intellectual property, and the "real world," most notably *Code And Other Laws of Cyberspace* (1999) and *The Future of Ideas* (2001). Most recently, Lessig has founded the Creative Commons Project, which is devoted to simplifying the process by which creators of original online content can license their work and protect it from misuse. This essay originally appeared in the journal *Social Research* in 2002.

 Before You Read:

What is privacy? How do you define it? Why is it important to you? How do you define property, and in what ways is it important or irrelevant?

Privacy as Property*

Lawrence Lessig

A SOCIETY PROTECTS its values in different and overlapping ways. The values of free speech in America are protected by a constitution that guards against speech abridging regulation (U.S. Constitution, First Amendment). They are supported by copyright regulation intended as an "engine of free expression" to fuel a market of creativity (*Harper & Row Publishers, Inc. v. Nation Enterprises*, 471 U.S. 539 (1985)). They are supported by technologies such as the Internet that assure easy access to content (Lessig, 1999: 164–185). And they are supported by norms that encourage, or at least allow, dissenting views to be expressed (Lessig, 1999: 164–185; 235–239). These modalities together establish cultural resources that to some degree support the right to speak freely within American society.

This is an essay about the cultural resources that support the values of privacy. My aim is to promote one such cultural resource—the norms associated with property talk—as a means of reinforcing privacy generally. In my view, we would better support privacy within American society if we spoke of privacy as a kind of property. Property talk, in other words, would strengthen the rhetorical force behind privacy.[1]

Such a view is not popular among privacy advocates and experts in the field of privacy law. It has been expressly rejected by some of the best in the field.[2] Thus it is my burden to demonstrate the value in this alternative conception.

This essay alone will not carry that burden. But my hope is that it will at least evince a benefit from our reconceiving privacy talk. I will address some of the objections to this form of speaking, but only after advancing the arguments in its favor.

The essay moves in six parts. I first introduce two stories that will frame my argument (parts I and II). I then consider one account by Professor Jonathan Zittrain that might explain the tension that is revealed between these two stories (part III). Part IV offers a different account from the one proposed by Professor Zittrain. In the final part, I offer a brief response to some of the criticisms that have been made of the privacy as property model. I then conclude.

I

At a public debate about the increasing scope of patent protection granted by U.S. law to software and business method inventors, Jay Walker, the president of Priceline.com and

---

*I am grateful to Jason Catlett for correction of and advice about parts of this essay. That is not to say he agrees.

Walker Digital and a holder of many of these new, and controversial, patents, was asked to justify them. Did we know, Walker was asked, whether increasing the scope of these new forms of regulation would actually increase innovation? Or would they, by requiring every developer to add to its team covens of lawyers, increase the costs so much as to chill or stifle innovation? ("Internet Society," 2000).

Walker did not have a strong answer. In the face of evidence that these patents harm innovation, he could cite no firm evidence to the contrary. Would it not make sense then, Walker was asked, to have a moratorium on this new form of patent protection until we learn something about its economic effects? Why not study the effect, and if it is not clear that they do any good, then why not halt this explosion of regulation?

Walker exploded in anger at the very suggestion. Grabbing the mic, he said to the questioner: "Does that mean if Microsoft takes *my property*, I can't bring a suit against them, is that what you're suggesting?" ("Internet Society," 2000; emphasis added).

II

Amazon.com is a collector of data. It sells books to collect that data. These data help it do an extraordinary job understanding its customers' wants. By monitoring their behavior, Amazon can build large and accurate profiles about its customers. And using powerful data-matching techniques, it can predict what books they are likely to want to buy.

Amazon had a privacy policy. The data it was collecting, Amazon said, would not be sold to others, at least if a customer sent Amazon an email asking that such data never be sold. The data was therefore collected only for Amazon's use. And for anyone who had used Amazon frequently, much of that use was obvious and familiar. Amazon watched its customers, and used the data from that watching to better serve its customers; relying on this policy, people gave Amazon years' worth of data from this watching.

At the end of 2000, however, Amazon announced a new policy.[3] From that point on, data from Amazon could be sold to or shared with people outside Amazon, regardless of a consumer's request that it not. The privacy policy would therefore no longer assure users that only Amazon would know what books they bought. Amazon, and anyone Amazon decided, could know their consumers' buying patterns.

The extraordinary feature of this announcement—and the one on which I want to focus here—was its retroactive effect.[4] Not only was Amazon announcing that from then on, data collected could be subject to sale. It also made that policy retroactive. Customers who had relied on Amazon's promise in the past and had indicated that they "never" wanted their information sold were now told their data could be sold. Amazon refused requests to delete earlier data; the consumers who had relied on its policy were told they had no right to remove the data they had given. Their data was now subject to sale.[5]

Amazon justified this change, and this retroactive effect, based on an escape clause built into the company's privacy policy. This policy, the clause explained, was always subject to change. Consumers were therefore on notice, Amazon explained, that the rules could change. They knew the risks they were taking.

III

In a recent essay, Harvard professor Jonathan Zittrain argued that there is no conceptual difference between the "privacy problem" and the "copyright problem" (Zittrain, 2000). Both, he argued, are examples of data getting out of control. In the context of privacy, it is personal data over which the individual loses control—medical records, for example, that find their way to a drug company's marketing department; or lists of videos rented, that before the protections granted by Congress, found their way to a Senate confirmation hearing. The problem with privacy is that private data flows too easily—that it too easily falls out of the control of the individual.

So understood, Zittrain argued, the problem of copyright is precisely the same. It too is a problem of data getting out of control. Music is recorded on a digital CD; that CD is "ripped" (that is, the audio extracted), and the contents are placed on a computer server; that content is then duplicated and placed on a thousand servers around the world. The data has thus gotten out of control. Copyright holders who would otherwise want to condition access to their data find the ability to condition access upon payment gone. Just as the individual concerned about privacy wants to control who gets access to what and when, the copyright holder wants to control who gets access to what and when. In both cases the presence of ubiquitous computing and saturating networks means that the control is increasingly lost.

Zittrain then considered the steps that have been taken to deal with each of these problems. These, not surprisingly, turn out to be quite different. In the context of copyright, technologists are developing many new technologies to re-empower the copyright holder—to assure that the use of his data is precisely as he wishes. Trusted systems, for example, will give the copyright holder the power to decide who can listen to what. A digital object with music inside can be released on the Internet, but it will only play if the possessor has a permitting key. It will then play just as the copyright holder wants—once, or ten times, or forever, depending on how the object is coded. Trusted systems promise to rebuild into the code an extraordinary system of control. It promises to use *code* to solve this problem of data getting out of control.

Changes in technology, however, are not the only changes that copyright owners have sought, and secured, to remedy the problem of data getting out of control. Copyright holders have also benefited from significant changes in law. In a series of significant acts of legislation, the U.S. Congress has increased the penalty for using copyrighted material without the permission of the copyright holder. It is now a felony to publish more than $1,000 of copyrights without the copyright holder's permission.[6] Congress has also added important rights and protections for copyrighted work online with the Digital Millennium Copyright Act (DMCA).[7] If a copyright holder uses technology to protect his copyright, then the DMCA protects that software with law by making it an offense to develop and distribute tools that circumvent that software. Software code thus increasingly protects copyrighted material. Legal code increasingly protects copyrighted material more strongly. And with the DMCA, law now protects code that protects copyright. These changes will thus balance the risk that copyrighted "data" will get out of control.

What about the response to the problem of privacy? Here the story is very different. We do not have a collection of new federal laws restoring control over their data to individuals. Law has been successfully resisted with a familiar rhetoric—that "we should let the market take care of itself." So far, these opponents have been quite successful. Congress has yet to pass an Internet privacy regulation, although it has passed regulation to protect financial privacy.[8]

Technology, too, has been slow to emerge. Not that there are not a host of creative technologies out there—technologies to anonymize transactions and presence, and technologies to facilitate control over the use of personal data.[9] But these technologies have not quite had the financial backing that copyright control technology has had. Germany, for example, requires that Internet service providers (ISPs) offer anonymous accounts.[10] That has spurred a market for providing such anonymity in Germany. But we have no such requirement in America, and hence we have not sufficiently spurred a market to provide this technology.

Zittrain puts these two stories together, and asks, What explains the difference? The same problem—losing control over our data—is raised in two very different contexts. In the one context, copyright, both law and technology (or we might say, "East Coast code" and "West Coast code") rally to defend the copyright holder against the users who would use it without control; in the context of privacy, both law and technology have been slow to respond. Same problem, two radically different responses. What explains the difference?

Zittrain offers a dark explanation: follow the money (Zittrain, 2000). If you want to understand why all controlled creativity in the world is allied on one side of this problem and only the public spirited, Marc Rotenberg-like are allied on the other, follow the money. When it pays to protect privacy—when it pays to build tools to protect privacy—you will see lots more privacy. But just now, it is Hollywood that pays, so it is copyright that gets protected.

IV

My aim in this essay is to explore a different account of why these two similar problems get fundamentally different treatment in Washington. This account focuses less on the dark motivations of dollars chasing policy. Instead, the difference I want to focus on is a difference in norms, or a difference in the ordinary understanding, or construction, or *social meaning* of the problem (see, e.g., Lessig, 1995: 943). This difference is seen in the two stories I began with at the start: the story of Jay Walker and Amazon.com.

Recall Walker's response to the suggestion that we investigate a bit more whether patents do any good before we issue more patents to protect software or business methods. And allow Microsoft, he asked, to steal "*my property?*" Focus on this term, "property." Jay Walker framed the question of proper patent policy within a familiar, and deeply American, discourse about property. The issue, so framed, is whether one is for property or not; the punishment for those who would question patents is thus the same as the punishment for questioning property: Are you or have you ever been a communist?

This move—as a matter of rhetoric—is brilliant, although the idea that "patents" should be spoken of as this sort of property would be strange to anyone with a sense of history. The framers of our constitution did not speak of patents as "property." Patents were understood as exclusive rights granted by the government for a public purpose, not natural rights recognized by the government as an aspect of natural justice. This was the import of Jefferson's famous description of patents,[11] and it explains in part why the term "intellectual property" did not enter our legal vocabulary until late into the nineteenth century.[12]

But ordinary people are not constrained by any sense of history. They instead are open to this more familiar way of speaking about patents. And Walker's use of the term "property" is an increasingly familiar way in which "intellectual property" is discussed. Thus, despite the dissonance with Jefferson, Walker can talk about "stealing" his "property" without anyone noticing anything funny in his speech. The debate then focuses on why people should be allowed to "steal" rather than on why a "patent" is "property."[13]

Yet had Walker been forced to use the language of the framers, his rhetorically powerful rhetorical question—"you want Microsoft to steal my property while you conduct your studies about what does what good?"—would have been the extremely weak rhetoric—"you want Microsoft to invade my monopoly while you conduct studies to determine whether the monopoly does any good?" In their language, the idea that Walker, or anyone, has a moral claim to a government-backed monopoly would seem odd. Had he been forced to express himself in just these terms, his question would have answered itself quite differently.

There is something in this story that we who would like stronger protection for privacy might learn. The story shows the different social resources that are available within our culture to claims that are grounded in property.

To see the point a bit more directly, think about the Amazon story with one fundamental change. Imagine that people spoke about their privacy as if privacy were a form of property. What constraints—social constraints—on what people can do to private data would exist then?

I know many want to resist this idea of speaking about privacy as property, and I certainly know that one must justify the usage if it is to be accepted (though I really do not recall reading the justification that transformed monopoly-speak in the context of patents and copyright into property-speak, but let us put that aside for a second). Before we get to justification, or even possibility, just imagine if we thought about our personal data the way we think about a car. And then think about this analogous case about a contract governing a car.

You drive into a parking lot, and the attendant hands you a ticket. The ticket lists a number of rules and promises on the back of the ticket. The lot is not responsible for damage to the car; the car must be picked up by midnight, etc. And then imagine, as with Amazon, that at the bottom of the ticket, the last condition is that this license can be modified at anytime by the management.

Imagine you walk up to the parking lot, hand him the ticket, and say, "I would like my car." And the attendant says to you, "Well, as you'll see at the bottom of your ticket, we reserved the right to change the conditions at any time. And in fact, I'm afraid we have changed the conditions. From here on out, we've decided to sell the cars we take in. And so we've decided to sell your very nice car. We therefore cannot return your car; the car is probably in New Jersey by now. We're sorry, but that's our policy."

Obviously, in ordinary property thought, this is an absurd idea. It would be crazy to interpret a condition in a license stating that the license could be changed to mean that the license might be changed to allow the parking lot to sell your car. One might well imagine a Jay Walker moment—"Hey, that's my property. You can't steal my property. You can't change the license and then run away with my car."

And yet, notice that these same intuitions are not excited when people hear the story about Amazon. I do not mean that there are not people who think what Amazon has done is awful—clearly there are such people, and perhaps most think what Amazon has done is awful. My claim is not that people agree with Amazon; my point is that because we do not think of privacy the way Hollywood has convinced us to think about copyright, we cannot easily invoke the rhetoric of property to defend incursions into privacy. If it were taken for granted that privacy was a form of property, then Amazon simply could not get away with announcing that this personal information was now theirs. That would be "theft," and this is my point: "theft" is positively un-American.

Property talk would give privacy rhetoric added support within American culture. If you could get people (in America, at this point in history) to see a certain resource as property, then you are 90 percent to your protective goal. If people see a resource as property, it will take a great deal of converting to convince them that companies like Amazon should be free to take it. Likewise, it will be hard for companies like Amazon to escape the label of thief. Just think about the rhetoric that surrounds Napster—where thousands are sharing music for no commercial gain. This practice is comfortably described by many—not me, but many others—as "theft." And more important, it is hard for the defendants to defend against this label of theft. The issue becomes whether the user has a right to steal—not the kind of case you would want to have to prove.

We could strengthen the cultural resources supporting the protection of privacy if we could come to think of privacy as property, just as the cultural resources available to Jay Walker have been strengthened by the happenstance of a legal culture that has come to refer to "patents" as intellectual property. Norms about property would support restrictions on privacy, just as norms about property resist limitations on Walker's "property."

That is the affirmative claim, but before I address objections, there are some qualifications I must offer to assure that certain confusions do not detain the debate.

1. To promote property talk is not to promote anarchism, or even libertarianism. "Property" is always and everywhere a creation of the state. It always requires regulation to secure it, and regulation requires state action. The DMCA is a law designed to protect what most think of as "property." That is regulation. Police are deployed to protect property. That too is regulation. Zoning laws regulate and control property. Rules regulating the market control how property is exchanged. And rules establishing privacy as property would govern when and how a privacy right can be traded. Property is inher-

ently the construction of the state; and to confuse the promotion of property with the promotion of laissez-faire is to fall into the vision of the world that libertarians delude themselves with. There is no such thing as property without the state; and we live in a state where property and regulation are deeply and fundamentally intertwined.

2.   Although property is often resisted by liberals because of the inequality that property systems produce, privacy as property could create less extreme inequality. If the privacy as property system were properly constructed, it would be less troubling from this perspective than, say, copyright or ordinary property. For if the law limited the ability to alienate such property completely—by permitting contracts about, for example, secondary uses but not tertiary uses—the owner of this property would be less likely to vest it in others in ways that would exacerbate inequalities.

3.   Property talk is often resisted because it is thought to isolate individuals. It may well. But in the context of privacy, isolation is the aim. Privacy is all about empowering individuals to choose to be isolated. One might be against the choice to be isolated; but then one is against privacy. And we can argue long and hard about whether privacy is good or not, but we should not confuse that argument with the argument that property would better protect any privacy we have agreed should be protected.

4.   To view privacy as property is not to argue that one's rights to use that property should be absolute or unregulated. All property law limits, in certain contexts, the right to alienate; contract law restricts the contexts in which one can make enforceable contacts. The state has a valid and important role in deciding which kinds of exchanges should be permitted. And especially given the ignorance about the Internet that pervades the ordinary user's experience, I would be wildly in favor of regulation of what people were allowed to do with "their property." Indeed, I imagine there is no legislative recommendation of the Electronic Privacy Information Center (EPIC), for example, for regulating privacy that I would oppose (see <http://www.epic.org>).

Thus, to promote property talk is not to demote the role of regulation, or to believe that the "market will take care of itself," or to question the strong role the government should have to assure privacy. It is simply to recognize that the government is not the only, or often, most important protector of human rights. And that where norms can carry some of the water, my argument is that we should not be so quick to condemn these norms.

V

Privacy and property talk is resisted, however, by many in the privacy community. Their resistance is strong, and their arguments are good. I will not in this short essay be able to rebut these arguments in opposition. But I do hope to suggest how they might be resisted.

To make the criticism clearer and, obviously, to aid in the resistance of these criticisms, consider first a picture of what I imagine a property system protecting privacy to be.

In the world that I imagine, individuals interact online through machines that connect to other machines. My computer is a machine; it links across the Internet to a machine at Amazon.com. In this interaction, the machine could reveal to the other machine that a machine with a certain ID—for example, that a machine with an ID with characteristics A, B, and C purchased goods, X, Y, and Z after looking at pages k, l, m. This ID need not be linked back to a particular person, although it could be. The property right that I am imagining governs the terms under which one machine can access certain data from the other machine. It says that the party who would collect these facts cannot do so without permission from the ID. The default is that the facts cannot be collected, but that default can be negotiated around.

The negotiation occurs through technology that sets the terms under which facts A, B, and C may be collected. These facts then get wrapped in a digital envelope that in turn carries the terms with them. At this stage the problem is directly the problem of trusted systems in copyright law. And as with trusted systems, a system that trades these facts can only do so when dealing with a secure system that trades the facts according to the rules in the wrappers.

The terms on the wrapper could be many. I do not know which would be critical. Perhaps it is a permission for primary and secondary use, but not tertiary use. If so, after the secondary use, the fact would digitally "disappear." But access might also be granted on very different terms—conditioned on the promise that the fact will not be related back to the human who has control over the ID. Whatever the term, I assume the trusted system could implement it through secure trading technologies.

What are the problems with a regime so constituted?

"It would be unconstitutional." The strongest argument against the privacy as property position—if true—is that it would be unconstitutional for the government to grant property rights in privacy. This, the argument goes, would be just like granting property rights in facts, and facts, the Supreme Court has come very close to holding, cannot be secured by at least one particular form of property right—namely copyright (*Feist Publications v. Rural Telephone Service Co.*, 499 U.S. 340 (1991)). Thus, because copyright cannot protect facts, Congress cannot protect facts, and a property regime for privacy would therefore be unconstitutional.

But although I am a very strong believer in constitutional limitations on the intellectual property power, this argument moves too quickly. No doubt you could not grant an *intellectual property right* in private facts. It does not follow, however, that you cannot, through law, control the right to use or disseminate facts. Trade secret law protects certain "facts" from disclosure (Merges, Menell, and Lemley, 2000). Contract law can punish individuals for disclosing facts they have promised to keep secret (*Cohen v. Cowles Media Co.*, 501 U.S. 663 (1991)). These limitations on the right to distribute facts stem from regimes that are grounded on a constitutional authority other than the Copyright and Patent Clause.

For this privacy as property claim to be constitutional, it would require a constitutional source of authority other than the Copyright and Patent Clause. The most natural alternative source would be the Commerce Clause (U.S. Constitution, Art. 1, Sec. 8, Clause 3). There is a substantial body of evidence to suggest that fear about privacy inhibits online commerce. The same fear was said to undermine the use of wireless communications generally. Congress was able to regulate that communication under the Electronic Communications Privacy Act and the Wiretapping and Electronic Surveillance Act.[14] The same authority should support the construction of a stronger right through property.

No doubt there are limits on the ability to protect facts through property, especially in light of the important First Amendment interests that are involved. Those limits were well described in the most recent case considering the intersection between privacy and the First Amendment: *Bartnicki v. Vopper*.[15] But *Bartnicki* does not establish that private facts cannot be protected through law. It establishes only that the use of those facts illegally obtained cannot, in certain circumstances, be constitutionally restrained. The same limits would restrict privacy as property. They would not, however, render it unconstitutional per se.

Of course, other constitutional powers cannot, or should not, be relied on to support a privacy as property right if that right is of the kind that the Copyright and Patent Clause protects. But if trademarks are not the sort of right that the Copyright and Patent Clause protects (see, e.g., *Trade-Mark Cases*, 100 U.S. 82 (1879)), I do not believe privacy would be either. Thus, whether or not privacy as property is a good idea, it would not, I believe, be unconstitutional because of the Copyright and Patent Clause.

"It would queer intellectual property law." A second criticism is related to the first. Some fear that thinking of privacy as property would further strengthen property talk about intellectual property. Thus, increasing protection for privacy would perversely increase the already too expansive (in my view and the view of these critics) protection for intellectual property (see, e.g., Samuelson, 2000: 1140).

I share the concern about overprotecting intellectual property, so here again I think that if the criticism were correct, it would be strong. But I think the fear is overstated. Given the plethora of property talk that shoots through our society, it is fanciful at best to imagine that one more dimension of rights talk would tip any fundamental balance with intellectual property. If the power itself were grounded in the Copyright and Patent Clause, I would agree that it would create dangerous pressure on intellectual property law. I do not think that would be the source of any such power, and I therefore do not think that would be its effect.

"It would tend to promote the alienation of privacy, by encouraging a better, or more efficient, market in its trading." A third criticism is more pragmatic than the previous two. Its concern is with consequences. The fear is that increasing property talk would tend to increase the alienation of privacy. Property is associated with markets; markets associated with trade; trade is the alienation of this for the acquisition of that.[16]

It is certainly true that by thinking of privacy as property, one makes it easier to think about trading privacy within a market. But equally, if the essence of a "property right" is that the person who wants it must negotiate with its holder before he can take it, propertizing privacy would also reinforce the power of an individual to *refuse* to trade or alienate his privacy. Whether he or she alienates the property depends on what he or she wants. And while people who have pork bellies may well prefer cash for their property (and hence property facilitates the trade in pork bellies), it would not follow that family heir-looms would be better protected if we denied the current owner a "property right" in those heirlooms. Property defends the right of the farmer to alienate pork bellies as much as it defends my right to keep you from getting a mirror my grandmother gave me.

What property does do affirmatively is to allow individuals to differently value their privacy. It is the consequence of a property system that by protecting the right of an individual to hold his property until he or she chooses to alienate it, different individuals get to value different bits of privacy differently. I may be a freak about people knowing my birthday, and so would never "sell" access to that fact for any price, but someone else might be willing to sell access in exchange for 100 frequent flyer miles. The advantage of a property system is that both of our wishes get respected, even though the wishers are so different.

There is nonetheless a legitimate and residual concern that propertizing privacy will tend to facilitate "too much" alienation of privacy, and that we should therefore resist the move to propertize.

This criticism, however, must be divided into two distinct parts. For the criticism begs the question of how much alienation is too much? And also, from what perspective is the judgment of "too much" made?

For some critics, the only legitimate perspective is the individual. Under this view, the criticism must be that propertizing privacy would create market pressures for people to alienate privacy beyond what they otherwise would individually prefer. Or they may be pressured into alienating a kind of privacy they would not otherwise prefer. But if this is the complaint, then there is no reason it could not be met by specific, or targeted legisla-tion. If there is some indignity in alienating a particular bit of privacy, then a law could make trading in that privacy illegal (as it does, for example, with facts about children).[17]

For others, the concern about "over alienation" is a kind of paternalism, though by "paternalism" I do not mean anything derogatory. I am all for paternalism in its proper place. It would be the proper place here if we could rightly conclude that people would, if given the chance, alienate more privacy than they should.

The problem is knowing whether the amount they would alienate is more than they "should." I am skeptical about whether we can know that yet. If we narrow the focus of the privacy that we are concerned about to the "stuff" revealed between machines in the ex-changes with others online, then at this stage in the life of the Internet, I believe we know very little about the harms or dangers this exchange will create. And in a context where we know little, my bias is for a technology that would encourage diversity.

That is precisely the aim of a market. A market would help us find a mix that reflected people's wants, and if, as I believe, people's wants were very different, then the range of different wants could be respected.

It may be that people have a very similar set of wants, and that the property system is an unnecessary expense in finding this common set of privacy preferences. This relates to the final criticism that I will survey here, but if true, then once we discover it is true, we may well choose to substitute a rule for a market. I am just not as convinced we know enough now to know what that rule would be.

"A property system for privacy would be difficult to implement." Property systems are not costless. They require real resources to make them work. A final line of criticism objects that the costs of making privacy property outweigh any benefit.

This last criticism may well be true, but we should be clear about the costs. The cost of a property system depends on the architecture that implements it. My assumptions about the value of a property system assume that the negotiations and preferences about privacy would be expressed and negotiated in the background automatically. This was the aspiration of the technology Platform for Privacy Protection (P3P) in its first description. It is a fair criticism of my position that the technology it depends on has yet to be developed.[18]

Yet technologies do not get invented in a vacuum. It was only after pollution regulations were adopted that innovative technologies for abating pollution were developed. And likewise here: establishing a strong property right in privacy and punishing the taking of that right without proper consent would induce technologies designed to lower the costs of that consent.

It may again in the end not lower the costs enough. The costs of a property rule may well exceed any benefits. And if that were so, then the alternative of a liability rule, which is pushed by privacy advocates who oppose privacy as property, would make most sense. But this, too, is not something we can know in the abstract.

I do not expect these responses to the criticism about privacy as property will convince. To answer the substantial criticism would require much more attention than I am permitted in these pages. But I do hope this is enough to identify the contours of a reply. My claim is not that the property view is right; it is the much less bold (much more balanced) claim that it could do some good, and that there is no obvious reason it is wrong.

VI

The law of privacy in America was born in a debate about property. In their seminal article giving birth to a "right to privacy," Brandeis and Warren related the need for that right to a change in how property was distributed (Brandeis and Warren, 1890: 193, 198–199). They described an earlier time when property functioned as the protector of privacy: since one could not trespass, one could not invade the sanctity of the right to be left alone. That world had changed, Warren and Brandeis argued. Because property had become so unequal, protecting privacy through protecting property would no longer equally protect privacy. The landed may have had privacy; the person living in a tenement did not. Privacy should therefore be separated from property, they argued, so that privacy could be better protected.

Privacy advocates embrace this argument as a way of resisting the argument in favor of propertizing privacy. But notice an important conflation. The complaints Brandeis and Warren made about *physical property* would not necessarily apply to the *intangible property* I am describing here. Indeed, given the difference in the nature of such "property," very different conclusions should follow.

In my view, we should be as pragmatic about property as Brandeis and Warren were. But such pragmatism will sometimes mean that we embrace property to protect privacy, just as it sometimes means that we should resist property to protect privacy. Whether we should depends on the contingencies of the technologies for establishing and protecting property. And those, I suggest, cannot be known in the abstract.

Put another way, when invoking Brandeis and Warren's argument, it is important not to make Jay Walker's mistake. Real property is different from intangible property. Facts about real property do not necessarily carry over into the realm of intangible property. The physics of intangible property are different, and hence, so should be our analysis.

My claim is that in addition to the resources of law that Rotenberg and Catlett rightly advance (see <http://www.junkbusters.com>), and the resources of technology that Zeroknowledge et al. provide, and the mix of law and technology that Zittrain describes, we need to think, in a less politically charged and politically correct way, about adding to the arsenal in support of privacy the favored weapon of Disney and Jay Walker: the ability to rely on the rhetorical force of—"you mean you want to steal my property?"

Notes

1. There are many others who have pushed the view that privacy be seen as a kind of property. Paul Sholtz (2001) has offered a transaction costs justification that closely tracks my own. His work, like mine, trades fundamentally on the distinction drawn in Guido Calabresi and Douglas Melamed's foundational work between property rules and liability rules (1972: 1089). See also Safier (2000: 6); Schwartz (2000: 743, 771–776). Other property-based arguments about privacy include "Developments in the Law" (1999); Kang (1998: 1193, 1246–94); Shapiro and Varian (1997).

    The view that law should push to property over liability rules is not limited to privacy (whether or not it should be). For a strong push, see Epstein (1997: 2091).
2. *Stanford Law Review*'s recent "Symposium on Privacy" has a strong collection of property's opponents. See, for example, Cohen (2000: 1373); Lemley (2000: 1545); Litman (2000: 1283); Samuelson (2000: 1125–1126) (there are "some reasons to doubt that a property rights approach to protecting personal data would actually achieve the desired effect of achieving more information privacy"). See also Rotenberg (2001).
3. For a summary of the facts surrounding these events, see <http://www.junkbusters.com/amazon.html>.
4. I do not mean it changed the rules that existed before. My claim is about expectations.
5. Under the policy before the change, Amazon permitted customers to send a message to an Amazon email address and be automatically removed from the list of customers who would permit their personal data to be disclosed.
6. *No Electronic Theft Act*, Public Law 105–147, 105th Cong., 1st sess. (16 December 1997): 111, 2678. This law, also known as the "NET Act," amended 17 U.S.C. § 506(a).
7. The anticircumvention provision of the DMCA was recently upheld in the Second Circuit. *See The Digital Millennium Copyright Act*, 17 U.S.C.S. § 1201; *Universal City Studios, Inc. v. Corley*, 2001 WL 1505495 (2nd Cir. 2001).
8. *Gramm-Leach-Bliley Act*, Public Law 106–102, 15 U.S.C. § 6801–6810 (1999).
9. See, for example, <http://www.zeroknowledge.com>.
10. See <http://www.iid.de/rahmen/iukdgebt.html#a2>.
11. As Jefferson wrote:

    If nature has made any one thing less susceptible than all others of exclusive property, it is the action of the thinking power called an idea, which an individual may exclusively possess as long as he keeps it to himself; but the moment it is divulged, it forces itself into the possession of everyone, and the receiver cannot dispossess himself of it. Its peculiar character, too, is that no one possesses the less, because every other possess the whole of it. He who receives an idea from me, receives instruction himself without lessening mine; as he who lites his taper at mine, receives light without darkening me. That ideas should freely spread from one to another over the globe, for the moral and mutual instruction of man, and improvement of his condition, seems to have been peculiarly and benevolently designed by nature, when she made them, like fire, expansible over all space, without lessening their density at any point, and like the air in which we breathe, move, and have our physical being, incapable of confinement, or exclusive appropriation. Inventions then cannot, in nature, be a subject of property.

Letter from Thomas Jefferson to Isaac McPherson, 13 August 1813 (Jefferson, 1861: 175, 180).

12. Professor Fisher traces its origins to the late nineteenth century; see Fisher (1999: 2, 8).

13. But among lawyers, however, this does not mean patents cannot be considered "property." All property is held subject to public necessity; any property right is defined in relation to conceptions of the public good. What makes a right a "property right" is that the holder has the right to alienate that right, and the person wanting the right must negotiate with the holder before he or she can use that right. Among lawyers, what defines a right as a property right is that the law protects an individual's right to dispose of that right as he or she chooses.

14. *Electronic Communications Privacy Act*, 100 Stat. 1848 (1986), 108 Stat. 4279 (1994). See reference in *Bartnicki v. Vopper*, 121 S. Ct. 1753 (2001).

15. See *Omnibus Crime Control and Safe Streets Act*, Title III, 82 Stat. 211 (1968); *Bartnicki v. Vopper, supra*. See also *U.S. West v. FCC*, 182 F.3d 1224 (10th Cir. 1999) (striking certain privacy regulations of businesses on First Amendment grounds). *Bartnicki* is a centrally important case defining the future balance between privacy and First Amendment interests. In my view, the key distinction that would enable privacy regulations to survive is that they regulate a kind of access, and not the use of the facts accessed. I believe a property right could be so structured. For a careful and balanced (if skeptical) view toward the other side, see Singleton (2000: 97).

16. This view is well developed in Rotenberg (2001, ¶92).

17. Rotenberg rightly criticized my overly condensed treatment of his position in *Code* (Lessig, 1999: 161). His and EPIC's view is a far more subtle mix of policies that builds directly and strongly on an important tradition in privacy law that balances privacy interests that are to be kept out of the market with interests that can, properly, be within the market. I have little to criticize about that balance in the context of these traditional, and critical, privacy concerns. My focus here is on the emerging issue of informational privacy, and the particular issues the expanded capacity to manipulate those data creates.

18. For an extraordinary website that summarizes the debate on P3P exceptionally well, see "P3P Viewpoints" <http://www.stanford.edu/~ruchika/P3P/>. See also the World Wide Web Consortium <http://www.w3.org/>.

References

Brandeis, Louis, and Samuel Warren. "The Right to Privacy." *Harvard Law Review* 4 (1890).

Calabresi, Guido, and A. Douglas Melamed. "Property Rules, Liability Rules and Inalienability: One View of the Cathedral." *Harvard Law Review* 85 (1972).

Cohen, Julie. "Examined Lives: Informational Privacy and the Subject as Object." *Stanford Law Review* 52 (May 2000).

"Developments in the Law—The Law of Cyberspace." *Harvard Law Review* 112 (May 1999): 1647–48.

Epstein, Richard A. "A Clear View of the Cathedral: The Dominance of Property Rules." *Yale Law Journal* 106 (1997): 2091.

Fisher III, William W. *The Growth of Intellectual Property: A History of the Ownership of Ideas in the United States* (1999) <http://cyber.law.harvard.edu/ipcoop/97fish.1.html>.

Internet Society Panel on Business Method Patents <http://www.oreillynet.com/lpt/a/434>.

Jefferson, Thomas. *The Writings of Thomas Jefferson*. Vol. 6. Ed. H. A. Washington. 1861.

Kang, Jerry. "Information Privacy in Cyberspace Transactions." *Stanford Law Review* 50 (1998): 1193, 1246–94.

Lemley, Mark A. "Private Property." *Stanford Law Review* 52 (May 2000).

Lessig, Lawrence. "The Regulation of Social Meaning." *University of Chicago Law Review* 62 (1995).

———. *Code and Other Laws of Cyberspace*. New York: Basic Books, 1999.

Litman, Jessica. "Information Privacy/Information Property." *Stanford Law Review* 52 (May 2000).

Merges, Robert P., Peter S. Menell, and Mark A. Lemley. *Intellectual Property in the New Technological Age*. New York: Aspen Law and Business, 2000: 557–794.

Rotenberg, Marc. "Fair Information Practices and the Architecture of Privacy: (What Larry Doesn't Get)." *Stanford Technology Law Review* 1 (2001) <http://stlr.stanford.edu/STLR/Articles/01_STLR_1/>.

Safier, Seth. "Between Big Brother and the Bottom Line: Privacy in Cyberspace." *Virginia Journal of Law and Technology* 5 (Spring 2000).

Samuelson, Pamela. "Privacy as Intellectual Property?" *Stanford Law Review* 52 (May 2000).

Schwartz, Paul. "Beyond Lessig's *Code* for Internet Privacy: Cyberspace Filters, Privacy Control, and Fair Information Practices." *Wisconsin Law Review* (2000).

Shapiro, Carl, and Hal R. Varian. "U.S. Government Information Policy." School of Information Management and Systems, University of California, Berkeley. 30 July 1997 <http://www.sims.Berkeley.edu/~hal/Papers/policy/policy.html>.

Sholtz, Paul. "Transaction Costs and the Social Costs of Online Privacy." *First Monday* 6:5 (May 2001) <http://www.firstmonday.org/issues/issue6_5/sholtz/index.html>.

Singleton, Solveig. "Privacy Versus the First Amendment: A Skeptical Approach." *Fordham Intellectual Property, Media and Entertainment Law Journal* 11 (2000).

Zittrain, Jonathan. "What the Publisher Can Teach the Patient: Intellectual Property and Privacy in an Era of Trusted Privication." *Stanford Law Review* 52 (May 2000): 1201–1250.

 ## For Discussion:

1. Do you agree with Jonathan Zittrain's argument that privacy and copyright are both essentially about the control of data?

2. Lessig argues that privacy and property are treated very differently by the law. What is his evidence? Do you agree with him that they are essentially the same?

3. Is Lessig correct in saying that "if you could get people . . . to see a certain resource as property, then you are 90 percent to your prospective goal"? What does that imply about our values and us?

 ## For Fact-Finding, Research, and Writing:

1. Lawrence Lessig has published on a similar topic in the magazine, *American Spectator*. Find information that would lead you to identify the ideological perspective from which this magazine is published.

2. Is your body your own property to do with as you wish? Is it "private"? What does the law say?

Lucas D. Introna, "Workplace Surveillance, Privacy, and Distributive Justice"

Lucas Introna is currently Visiting Professor of Information Systems at the University of Pretoria. He is Associate Editor of *Information Technology & People*, and Co-Editor of *Ethics and Information Technology*. Introna is interested in the social dimension of information technology and its consequences for society, and in the way information technology mediates social interaction. His publications and academic papers cover topics such as virtual organizations, theories of information, and information technology.

 Before You Read:

What do you think about work surveillance? Does it impede on one's privacy?

Workplace Surveillance, Privacy, and Distributive Justice

Lucas D. Introna

Introduction

Surveillance has become a central issue in our late modern society. The surveillance of public spaces by closed circuit television, the surveillance of consumers through consumer surveys and point of sale technology, and workplace surveillance, to name but a few. As surveillance increases, more and more questions are being raised about its legitimacy. In this paper I want to focus on one of the more problematic areas of surveillance, namely workplace surveillance. There is no doubt that the extensive use of information technology in all organisational processes has created enormous potential for cheap, implicit, and diffused surveillance, surveillance that is even more 'close' and continuous than any human supervisor could be. The extent of current surveillance practices are reflected in the following indicators:

● Forty-five percent of major U.S. firms record and review employee communications and activities on the job, including their phone calls, e-mail, and computer files. Additional forms of monitoring and surveillance, such as review of phone logs or videotaping for security purposes, bring the overall figure on electronic oversight to 67.3% (American Management Association 1999).

● Piller (1993) reported in a *MacWorld* survey of 301 business that 22% of the business have searched employee computer files, voice mail, e-mail, or other networking communications. The percentage jumped to 30% for business with 1000 or more employees.

● The International Labour Office (1993) estimates that some 20 million Americans may be subject to electronic monitoring on the job, *not including telephone monitoring*.

● In 1990 it was reported that up to one million jobs in Britain are subject to security checks (Lyon 1994, p. 131).

It would be reasonable to say that these formal surveys do not reflect the actual practice. It would also be reasonable to assume that organisations would not tend to publicise the degree to which they engage in systematic monitoring. Surveillance often functions as a resource for the execution of power, and power is most effective when it hides itself. One can imagine that the vast majority of organisations engage in anything from isolated incidents of specific monitoring to large-scale systematic monitoring.

The purpose of this paper is not to bemoan surveillance as such. I believe it is rather more important to understand the context and logic of surveillance in the workplace. In this paper I will argue that the real issue of workplace surveillance is justice as fairness. I will argue that it is the inherent political possibilities of surveillance that concerns employees, that they simply do not trust the interested gaze of management, and they have very good reason for such mistrust. Finally I will discuss the possibility of using Rawls' theory of justice to establish a framework for distributing the rights of privacy and transparency between the individual (employee) and the institution (the employer).

Resisting Workplace Surveillance

In the second half of the twentieth century, two major trends seem to create the background for our contemporary discussion of workplace surveillance. The first of these are the increasing challenges by the employees of their conditions of work, especially the normalising practices of discipline. The social revolution of Marxism and later of liberal democracy trickled into the production floor. Initially as labour became increasingly unionised, the debate about surveillance became articulated as a conflict between labour and capital in the Marxist idiom. Later workers demanded rights in the workplace they were already accorded elsewhere. Modern management increasingly needed to justify its surveillance practices. A second trend that intensified the debate was the rapid development of surveillance technology that created unprecedented possibilities for comprehensive surveillance. With the new technology, surveillance became less overt and more diffused. In fact, it became built into the very machinery and processes of production (workflow systems, keystroke monitoring, telephone accounting, etc.). This increasingly 'silent' and diffused potential of surveillance technology also started to concern policy makers, unions, social activists, and the like. However, in spite of their best efforts, and considerable progress in the establishment of liberal democracy in Western society, the balance of power is still firmly in the hands of the employer. The United States Congress' Office of Technology Assessment report (U.S. Congress 1987) into employee monitoring concludes that *"employers have considerable latitude in making use of new monitoring technologies; they have generally been considered merely extensions of traditional management prerogatives"* (p. 6). Even today there exists very little enacted legislation in Western democracies that articulate the fair use of workplace monitoring[1] (U.S. Congress 1987, Appendix A). I would argue that that one of the reasons for this lack of adequate protection may be the inappropriate way in which the workplace monitoring debate has developed (I will address this in detail in the next section).

In the United States, the right of the employer to conduct workplace surveillance as a means to protect the employer's interest to organise work, select technology, set production standards, and manage the use of facilities and other resources is recognised by the law. This means that there is no legal obligation on employees to ensure that "monitoring be 'fair', that jobs be well designed or that employees be consulted about work standards, except insofar as these points are addressed in union contracts . . ." (U.S. Congress 1987, p. 2). As less than 20% of office work in the US is unionised, it seems that decisions about work monitoring are made solely at the discretion of employers.

Recent legal developments seem to confirm this asymmetry of power. For example, in the area of e-mail monitoring, the right to use surveillance of communications technology supplied for business purposes has been confirmed in the Electronic Communications Privacy Act of 1986 ("ECPA"). Essentially the ECPA expanded preexisting prohibitions on the unauthorised interception of wire and oral communications to encompass other forms of electronic communications. However, the ECPA does not guarantee a right to e-mail privacy in the workplace because of three very important exceptions. I will just focus on two here. The first is the *business extension* or ordinary course of business exception. This exception allows the employer to monitor any communications that use communications technology supplied to the employee in the ordinary course of business for use in conducting the ordinary course of business. This means that the telephone or the e-mail account supplied to an employee to conduct their work can legally be monitored as long as the monitoring can be justified as having a valid business purpose (Dichter and Burkhardt 1996, p. 14). The second is the *consent exception*. This exception allows monitoring in those cases where prior consent has been obtained. It is important to note that implied consent is also recognised by the law. Employers who notify employees that their telephone conversations or e-mail is likely to be monitored will have the implied consent of their employees (Santarelli 1997). It also seems as if common law does not provide any correction in the balance of power. In common law the decision of permissibility hinges on the notion of a "reasonable expectation of privacy." This may mean, for example, that if an employee is provided with a space to store personal belongings, or a particular phone line for personal calls, it would be reasonable for them to expect it not to be monitored. Johnson (1995) and others have remarked that this expectation of privacy can easily be removed by an explicit policy that all communication using company equipment can and will be subjected to monitoring.

From this brief discussion it is clear that it would be fairly easy for employers to monitor all aspects of work and communications (on equipment made available for ordinary business use) as long as the employer explicitly communicates policy that monitoring can take place, and that the employer can justify it for a valid business purpose. It is hard to imagine what sort of monitoring—excluding some extreme cases—can not be defended as being for a valid business purpose (productivity, company moral, safety, etc). It is also hard to imagine what sort of resources an individual employee can use to generate a 'reasonable expectation of privacy' in a context where accepting an employment contract also means accepting the policies of the organisation and thereby relinquishing the right to a "reasonable expectation of privacy"—assuming there is an explicit monitoring policy. In the context of the typical asymmetry of power present in such employment situations, it is hardly a matter of choice. It is clear, and acknowledged by many, that the current US climate is heavily biased in favour of the employer.[2] The lack of legislation in other countries would also indicate that it would be reasonable to conclude that workplace monitoring is still largely viewed as a right of employers with the burden of proof on the employee to show that it is invasive, unfair, or stressful. It would seem that a legal correction in the imbalance of power is not likely to be forthcoming in the near future.

In spite of this imbalance of power, surveillance has not become a widespread practice, as one would assume (U.S. Congress 1987, p. 31). In addition, it seems that where surveillance is operating, it is not always challenged to the degree that one would assume (U.S. Congress 1987, p. 31). Why is this so? It seems that there is not sufficient evidence to suggest surveillance of *individuals* would lead to *long term* productivity improvements. To use Denning's well known quality dictum (revised accordingly): productivity is not merely a matter of surveillance, but is rather an emerging element of a system designed for productivity as a whole. There is also accumulating evidence that surveillance of *individuals* lead to stress, a lost of sense of dignity, and a general environment of mistrust. In this environment of mistrust employees tend to act out their employer's expectations of them—thereby eradicating any benefit that the surveillance may have had (Marx 1986; U.S. Congress 1987). Furthermore, I believe surveillance is not always challenged because we all at times benefit from its fruits. For example, the use of surveillance data for performance assessment can result in a more equitable treatment of employees. Such data can provide evidence to prevent unfair allocation of blame. It would be possible to think of many ways in which employees may use surveillance for their own benefit, such as "the boss can see on the CCTV that I do actually work many hours overtime," and the like.

Like power, surveillance "passes through the hands of the mastered no less than through the hands of the masters" (Foucault 1977). It does not only bear down upon us as a burden but also produces possibilities and resources for action that can serve multiple interests. Surveillance is no longer an unambiguous tool for control and social certainty, nor is it merely a weight that weighs down on the employee—rather its logic and its effects has become increasingly difficult to see clearly and distinctly. Surveillance, with modernity, has lost its shine.

In the next section, I want to consider the relationship between surveillance and autonomy and indicate its link with justice. This will provide the background for the following section where I will develop a framework for distributing the rights of privacy and transparency between the individual and the collective.

Privacy as a Matter of Justice

Privacy is by no means an uncontroversial issue. Some, like Posner (1978), tend to see the need for privacy as a way of hiding or covering up what ought to be exposed for scrutiny. He argues that exposure through surveillance would provide a more solid basis for social interaction because the participants will be able to discern all the facts of the matter for themselves. Privacy, for him, creates opportunities for hiding information that could render many social interactions "fraudulent." To interact with someone without providing that person with all information would be to socially defraud that person, or so he argues. This is a very compelling argument, which has made Posner's paper one of the canons in the privacy literature. As such, it provides a good starting point for our discussion.

At the root of Posner's argument—and the argument for surveillance in general—is the fundamental flaw of the modernity's belief in surveillance as a neutral gaze, as a sound basis for certainty—for knowing that we know. Surveillance can only fulfill its role as guarantor of certainty if it is complete and comprehensive—in short, omnipresent—and if it can be done from a vantage point where all things are of equal or no value—which is impossible. If these conditions can be fulfilled, then Posner's argument will be valid. However, once surveillance looses its omnipresent and value free status—which it never had in the first place—it no longer deals with facts but rather with values and interests. Science becomes politics—as it has been from the beginning (Latour 1987; Latour and Woolgar 1986 [1979]). Knowing is replaced by choosing. We have to select what to survey, and most importantly, we have to select how to value what we find in our surveillance.

Employees do not fear the transparency of surveillance, as such, in the way argued by Posner. It is rather the choices, both explicit and implicit, that the employers will by necessity be making that employees mistrust. They are concerned that these choices may only reflect the interests of the employer. They are rightly concerned that the employer will only have 'part of the picture', and that they may be reduced, in subsequent judgements, to that 'part of the picture' alone. They are also concerned that employers will apply inappropriate values when judging this 'part of the picture.' More than this, they will also be concerned by the fact that employers may implicitly and unbeknowingly bring into play a whole lot of other 'parts' of pictures that ought not be considered in that *particular context*—for example, judging a particular employee candidate for promotion or not because it is also known that the employee is a Muslim. They are concerned because we can not, contrary to the modern mind, separate out what 'pictures' we take into account or not when making judgements, *in the act of judging itself* (Merleau-Ponty 1962).

We are entangled and immersed in our values and beliefs to the point that they are merely there, available for use, part of the background that we do not explicitly attend to in making actual judgements (Heidegger 1962 [1937]). It is part of our thrownness (*Befindlichkeit*). It is therefore fruitless to posit that we should or should not apply particular data or particular values in making a particular judgment. We can simply not say to what degree we did or did not allow our judgement to become influenced by certain facts and certain value dispositions in making a particular judgement. The facts and values are not like fruits in a basket before us from which we can select, by rational choice, to take some and not others. We are immersed, engrossed, and entangled in our world in ways that would not normally make us explicitly attend to the particular facts, values, and interests that we draw upon in making particular judgements. We can of course attempt to make them explicit as bureaucracies and scientific management tried to do. However, Dreyfus (1992; 1986) has shown that skilled actors do not normally draw upon these explicit representations *in action*. Foucault (Foucault 1977) has also shown that these explicit representations are more important as resources for the play of power than resources for 'objective' judgements, which is exactly why employees mistrust them.

To conclude: It is the very political possibilities of surveillance, in the data selected, the values applied, the interest served, and the implicit and entangled nature of the judgement process, which makes employees—and persons in general—have a default position of mistrust rather than trust in 'exposing' themselves. It is this untrustworthy nature of judgements—of the products of surveillance—that moved Johnson (Johnson 1989) to define privacy as the right to the "freedom from the judgement of others." It is also this untrustworthy nature of judgements that made the OTA report argue that they view the issue of fairness as the most central issue of workplace monitoring. Fairness, as the levelling of the playing field, as serving all interests, not only the few.

Thus, the issue of workplace privacy is not merely a matter of 'bad' employees wanting to hide their unscrupulous behaviour behind a call for privacy (undoubtedly this is the case in some instances); it is rather a legitimate concern for justice in a context in which the employees are, for the most part, in a relationship of severe power asymmetry. I would therefore argue that the development of the workplace privacy debate will be best served if it is developed along the lines of *fairness and organisational justice* rather than along the lines of a general notion of privacy as a matter of some personal space. The personal dignity and autonomy argument can so easily be seen as personal lifestyle choices that have no place in the public workplace as expressed by Cozzetto and Pedeliski (1999) in their paper on workplace monitoring: "*Autonomy embraces areas of central life choice and lifestyle that are important in terms of individual expression, but irrelevant to an employer and of no public concern.*" I believe many employers and authors in the field find the concept of workplace privacy problematic because they link it to the general debates on privacy that are often cast exclusively in the mould of personal dignity and autonomy. This leads to claims of irrelevance. As one employer expressed it in the Canadian Information and Privacy Commissioner's (IPC) report (1993) on workplace privacy. "*The paper overstates this issue as a problem of pressing concern for employees and employers and the general public . . . the IPC is making more of an issue out of this, and looking for problems where none need exist*" (p. 9).

If we accept the general idea that workplace privacy and surveillance is a matter of justice, how should one go about structuring the debate? In the next section I will discuss the distribution of privacy and transparency as an issue of distributive justice using the work of Rawls (1972).

Privacy, Surveillance, and Distributive Justice

For the individual, privacy secures autonomy, creates social capital for intimacy, and forms the basis of structuring many diverse social relations (Introna 1997; Westin 1967). It is generally accepted that it is in the interest of the individual to have maximum control over her privacy—here taken to be the *freedom from the inappropriate judgement of others*. For the collective or institution, transparency secures control and thereby efficiency of resource allocation and utilisation, as well as creating mechanisms for disciplinary intervention (Foucault and Sheridan 1979). It is generally accepted that it is in the interest of the collective or institution to have maximum control over surveillance—here taken to mean *subjecting all individuals in the institution to reasonable scrutiny and judgement*. If the individuals are given an absolute right to privacy, they may act only in their own interest and may thereby defraud the institution. If the institution is given a complete right to transparency, it may strip the individual of autonomy and self-determination by making inappropriate judgements that only serve its own interest.

Thus, from a justice perspective we need a framework that would distribute the rights to privacy—of the individual (the employee in this case)—and right of transparency—of the collective (the employer in this case)—in a way that would be seen to be fair to all concerned. I would argue that wherever individuals and institutions face each other, the distribution of privacy and transparency rights will become an issue to be resolved. In this regard the institution can be as diverse as the family, the workplace, the community, the state, and so forth. At this stage I will exclude from my discussion the conflict of privacy and transparency rights between different institutions such as between the corporation and the state. Given this conflict between the individual employee and the institutionalised workplace, how can we decide on a fair distribution of privacy and transparency rights? I will propose that we may use the Rawlsian theory of justice as a starting point. Obviously one could use other frameworks. I am not arguing that Rawls is the only or even vastly superior perspective. Nevertheless, it does seem as if the Rawlsian framework is useful in this regard.

Rawls (in his seminal work A *Theory of Justice* of 1971) proposes a framework of justice as fairness in opposition to the leading theory of the day, viz. utilitarianism. For Rawls, utilitarianism puts no restrictions upon the subordination of some people's interests to those of others, except that the net outcome should be good. This would allow for any degree of subordination, provided the benefit to those advantaged was great enough. Rawls argues that a theory of justice cannot allow disadvantages to some to be justified by advantages to others. In our case this would imply a view that may posit the limited cost of the loss of individual privacy against the enormous economic benefit to the collective of securing effective control over productive resources. Such utilitarian arguments can easily make the individual's claim to privacy look trivial in the face of the economic prosperity of the whole. I would claim that it is exactly this utilitarian type of logic that continues to limit the legitimacy of the individual employee's claim to privacy in the workplace.

If this is so, how can we establish as set of rules that would ensure a fair distribution of privacy and transparency rights? Rawls (1972) argues that this can only happen behind a 'veil of ignorance' in the so-called original position. According to this formulation, a fair set of rules for this distribution would be a set of rules that *self-interested* participants would choose if they were completely ignorant about their own status in the subsequent contexts where these rules will be applied. What would be the rules for distributing privacy and transparency rights that may be selected from behind such a veil of ignorance?

As a starting point we need to outline the facts—about interests and positions— which we may assume to be available to those in the original position. This information will provide the force that may shape their choices. Obviously these need to be debated, but I would propose the following facts are known—first from the perspective of the individual, then from the perspective of the collective.

From the individual perspective:

- That there are no such things as neutral or objective judgements. Every judgement implies interests. Once data is recorded, it can in principle become incorporated into a judgement process that may not serve the individual's interests. It would therefore seem reasonable that the self-interested individual would try to limit all forms of capturing of data about themselves and their activities.
- In the context of typical organisational settings, the employee is normally in a disadvantaged position—in a relation of severe power asymmetry. Thus, it is not possible for the individual, as an individual, to bargain for and ensure the fair use of data once it is captured. It would therefore be in the interest of the individual to limit all forms of capturing of data about themselves and their activities.
- If data about themselves and their activities are captured, it is in their interest to have maximum control over it—what is captured, who sees it, for what purposes, and so forth.

From the perspective of the collective:

- Without the capturing of complete and comprehensive information about the relevant activities of the individual, resources can not be efficiently and effectively allocated and control over the use of these resources can not be maintained. Without such control the collective would suffer. It would therefore seem reasonable to monitor all relevant activities of the individual. Relevant here would be understood to be those activities that imply the allocation and utilisation of collective resources.
- Self-interested individuals would not always tend to use resources—allocated by the collective—for the sole purposes of furthering the aims and objectives of the collective. In fact they may use it completely for their own purposes. It would therefore

seem reasonable to monitor all individual activities that allocate and utilise collective resources.

- The collective needs to use data collected to coordinate and control the activities of the individuals for the good of the collective. It would be in the interest of the collective to have maximum control over the capturing and utilisation of relevant data about the individuals.

Given these facts—and other similar ones we may enumerate—what rules would those behind the veil of ignorance choose in distributing individual privacy and collective transparency rights? Before attempting to suggest some rules, it may be important to highlight Rawls' 'difference principle'—which he argues those behind the veil of ignorance would tend to choose. This principle states that an inequality is unjust except insofar as it is a necessary means to improving the position of the worst-off members of society. Without this principle it would be difficult for those behind the veil of ignorance to establish rules for distributing privacy and transparency rights, as its seems equally reasonable to grant and limit these rights both to the individual and the collective. However, we know, as indicated above, that in the context of the modern organisation the individual is in a position of severe power asymmetry. In the prevailing climate it would be difficult to argue that the individual employee is not 'the worst-off' with respect of securing a fair and reasonable level of privacy rights in the workplace. This would seem to indicate that most individuals behind the veil of ignorance would tend to want to argue for some bias towards securing the rights of the individual over and against that of the institution. With this in mind I will suggest—mostly for illustrative purpose—a set of fair 'rules' or guidelines that may be put forward by those behind the veil of ignorance. I would contend that they would acknowledge the following:

- That the collective (employer) does indeed have a right to monitor individuals' activities with respect to the allocation and utilisation of collective resources. The collective also has a right to use the data collected in a fair and reasonable way for the overall good of the collective as a whole.
- That the individual (employee) does have a legitimate claim to limit the surveillance of their activities in the workplace. The individual also has a right to secure a regime of control that will justify all monitoring and that will ensure that the data collected will be used in a fair and reasonable way.
- Based on the 'difference principle', it will be up to the collective (employer) to justify the collection of particular data in particular contexts. Furthermore, the regimes for controlling the collected data should be biased towards the individual.

Obviously one could develop these rules in much more detail. However, even this very limited, initial reflection would seem to suggest that the prevailing organisational practices that favour the collective (both in capturing and control) would seem to be unfair.

Obviously this analysis is still too crude and unsophisticated. However, it does illustrate that one may arrive at very different conclusions if one takes the issue of workplace privacy to be one of fairness rather than as a matter of working out the private/public distinction in the workplace—since it will always be relatively easy to argue that the workplace is a de facto public space, devoid of almost any privacy rights.

Conclusion and Some Implications

The potential for workplace surveillance is rapidly increasing. Surveillance technology is becoming cheap, silent, and diffused. Surveillance technology has created the potential to build surveillance into the very fabric of organisational processes. How should we concern ourselves with these facts? Clearly each workplace will be different. Some will be more bureaucratic, some more democratic. Nevertheless, the conflict between the individual right to privacy and the institutional right to transparency will always be there. In each individual case, different tactics will be used by the different parties to secure their interests.

In the case of workplace privacy, the prevailing legal and institutional infrastructure makes it difficult for the individuals to secure their interests, leaving them power-less, but by no means powerless. One of the major reasons for the unsuccessful challenge of modern workplace surveillance is the inappropriate manner in which the workplace privacy debate has evolved. In my opinion it incorrectly attached itself to the public/private distinction, which leaves the employee in a position of severe power asymmetry. In opposition to this debate I have argued that if one articulates the issue of workplace surveillance along the lines of competing, but equally legitimate claims (for privacy and transparency), needs to fairly distribute the possibilities for the individual to resist inappropriate workplace surveillance increases dramatically. Using the Rawlsian theory of justice I argued that those behind the veil of ignorance would tend to adopt a position that biases the right of the employee—the worst off—over that of the employer. This would suggest that a fair regime of workplace surveillance would tend to avoid monitoring unless explicitly justified by the employer. It will also provide mechanisms for the employee to have maximum control over the use of monitoring data. Both of these rules seem to suggest that most of the prevailing organisational surveillance practices are unfair. This, I believe, is the challenge to us: To set up the intellectual and organisational resources to ensure that workplace surveillance becomes and stays fair.

References

(ILO), International Labour Organisation. 1993. *Conditions of work digest: Monitoring and surveillance in the workplace*. Geneva: International Labour Office.

Association, American Management. 1999. *Workplace monitoring and surveillance*: American Management Association.

Commissioner/Ontario, Information and Privacy. 1993. *Workplace Privacy: The need for a Safety-Net*, http://www.ipc.on.ca/web_site.ups/matters/sum_pap/papers/safnet-e.htm: Information and Privacy Commissioner/Ontario.

Cozzetto, D and T.B. Pedeliski. 1999. *Privacy and the Workplace: Technology and Public Employement*, http://www.ipma-hr.org/pubs/cozzfull.html: International Personnel Association.

Dichter, MS and MS Burkhardt. 1996. Electronic Interaction in the Workplace: Monitoring, Retrieving, and Storing Employee Communications in the Internet Age. In *The American Employment Law Council: Fourth Annual Conference*. Asheville, North Carolina.

Dreyfus, Hubert L. 1992. *What computers still can't do: A critique of artificial reason*. Cambridge, MA: The MIT Press.

Dreyfus, Hubert L and Stuart E Dreyfus. 1986. *Mind over machine: The power of human intuition and expertise in the era of the computer*. New York: The Free Press.

Foucault, M. 1977. Truth and Power. In *Power/Knowledge: Selected Interviews & Other Writings 1972–1977*, ed. C. Gordon. New York: Pantheon Books.

Foucault, Michel and Alan Sheridan. 1979. *Discipline and punish: the birth of the prison*. Harmondsworth: Penguin.

Heidegger, Martin. 1962 {1937}. *Being and time*. Translated by John Macquarrie.
Edward Robinson. Oxford: Basil Blackwell.

Introna, L.D. 1997. Privacy and the Computer: Why We Need Privacy in the Information Society. *Metaphilosophy* 28, no. 3: 259–275.

Johnson, BT. 1995. *Technological Surveillance in the Workplace*, http://www.fwlaw.com/techserv.html: Fairfield and Woods P.C.

Johnson, J.L. 1989. Privacy and the Judgement of Others. *The Journal of Value Inquiry* 23: 157–168.

Latour, Bruno. 1987. *Science in action: How to follow scientists and engineers through society*. Cambridge, MA: Harvard University Press.

Latour, Bruno and Steve Woolgar. 1986 {1979}. *Laboratory life: The construction of scientific facts*. Princeton: Princeton University Press.

Lyon, David. 1994. *The Electronic Eye: the rise of the surveillance society*. Cambridge: Polity Press.

Marx, G.T. 1986. Monitoring on the Job: How to Protect Privacy as well as Property. *Technology Review*.

Merleau-Ponty, M. 1962. *Phenomenology of Perception*. Translated by Colin Smith. London: Routledge.

Piller. 1993. Bosses with x-ray eyes. *MacWorld*, no. July: 118–123.

Posner, R. 1978. The Right to Privacy. *Georgia Law Review* 12: 383–422.

Rawls, J. 1972. *A Theory of Justice*. Cambridge, Mass: Harvard University Press.

Santarelli, N. 1997. *E-mail Monitoring in the Work Place: Preventing Employer Liability*, http://wings.buffalo.edu/complaw/complawpapers/santarelli/html: Computers and Law Internet site.

U.S. Congress, Office of Technology Assessment (OTA Report). 1987. *The Electronic Supervisor: New Technology, New Tensions*. Washington DC: US Congress.

Westin, A. 1967. *Privacy and Freedom*. New York: Ateneum.

Notes

1. Sweden is the exception here. The Swedish Codetermination Act of 1976 require employers and employees to participate in decisions about electronic monitoring (U.S. Congress 1987, Appendix A).
2. There has been an attempt to change this in the unsuccessful Privacy of Consumers and Workers Act (PCWA) of 1993.

 For Discussion:

1. Do you see work surveillance as the right of the employer?
2. Although work surveillance is accepted by the law, privacy is considered by many to be a fundamental right. Where do you stand in this debate?

3.   Do you agree with Introna's statement, "If the individuals are given an absolute right to privacy, they may act only in their interest and may thereby defraud the institution"? Why or why not?

 For Fact-Finding, Research, and Writing:

1.   Introna's article revolves around privacy vs. transparency in the workplace. Compare and contrast his article with other articles that address the issue of privacy. Based on all these articles, formulate a definition of privacy.
2.   Find three government documents on privacy in America. What main ideas do these documents cover?
3.   Where does the Constitution actually affirm a right to privacy?
4.   What Supreme Court decision first treated the issue of personal privacy?
5.   In what specific ways have issues of privacy been affected by the 2002 Homeland Security Act?

Doris Lessing, "Group Minds"

Born to British parents in Persia (now Iran) in 1919, Doris Lessing attended school in what is present-day Zimbabwe. At the age of thirteen she dropped out of school and never again pursued a formal education. Lessing published her first book, *The Grass is Singing*, in 1949, and she has subsequently published more than twenty-five novels. Though Lessing also writes short stories, poetry, plays, essays, and non-fiction, she is probably best known for her novels *The Golden Notebook* (1962) and *Briefing for a Descent into Hell* (1971).

 Before You Read:

How many different groups do you belong to? Do you think or act differently depending upon the group you are in at the time? Have you ever gone along with a group decision you did not agree with?

Group Minds

Doris Lessing

People living in the West, in societies that we describe as Western, or as the free world, may be educated in many different ways, but they will all emerge with an idea about themselves that goes something like this: I am a citizen of a free society, and that means I am an individual, making individual choices. My mind is my own, my opinions are chosen by me, I am free to do as I will, and at the worst the pressures on me are economic, that is, I may be too poor to do as I want.

This set of ideas may sound something like a caricature, but it is not so far off how we see ourselves. It is a portrait that may not have been acquired consciously, but is part of a general atmosphere or set of assumptions that influence our ideas about ourselves.

People in the West therefore may go through their entire lives never thinking to analyze this very flattering picture, and as a result are helpless against all kinds of pressures on them to conform in many kinds of ways.

The fact is that we all live our lives in groups—the family, work groups, social, religious, and political groups. Very few people indeed are happy as solitaries, and they tend to be seen by their neighbors as peculiar or selfish or worse. Most people cannot stand being alone for long. They are always seeking groups to belong to, and if one group dissolves, they look for another. We are group animals still, and there is nothing wrong with that. But what is dangerous is not the belonging to a group, or groups, but not understanding the social laws that govern groups and govern us.

When we're in a group, we tend to think as that group does: we may even have joined the group to find "like-minded" people. But we also find our thinking changing because we belong to a group. It is the hardest thing in the world to maintain an individual dissident opinion, as a member of a group.

It seems to me that this is something we have all experienced—something we take for granted, may never have thought about it. But a great deal of experiment has gone on among psychologists and sociologists on this very theme. If I describe an experiment or two, then anyone listening who may be a sociologist or psychologist will groan, oh God not again—for they will have heard of these classic experiments far too often. My guess is that the rest of the people will never have heard of these experiments, never have had these ideas presented to them. If my guess is true, then it aptly illustrates my general thesis, and the general idea behind these talks, that we (the human race) are now in possession of a great deal of hard information about ourselves, but we do not use it to improve our institutions and therefore our lives.

A typical test, or experiment, on this theme goes like this. A group of people are taken into the researcher's confidence. A minority of one or two are left in the dark. Some situation demanding measurement or assessment is chosen. For instance, comparing lengths of wood that differ only a little from each other, but enough to be perceptible, or shapes that are almost the same size. The majority in the group—according to instruction—will assert stubbornly that these two shapes or lengths are the same length, or size, while the solitary individual, or the couple, who have not been so instructed will assert that the pieces of wood or whatever are different. But the majority will continue to insist—speaking metaphorically—that black is white, and after a period of exasperation, irritation, even anger, certainly incomprehension, the minority will fall into line. Not always, but nearly always. There are indeed glorious individuals who stubbornly insist on telling the truth as they see it, but most give in to the majority opinion, obey the atmosphere.

When put as badly, as unflatteringly, as this, reactions tend to be incredulous: "I certainly wouldn't give in, I speak my mind. . . ." But would you?

People who have experienced a lot of groups, who perhaps have observed their own behavior, may agree that the hardest thing in the world is to stand out against one's group, a group of one's peers. Many agree that among our most shameful memories is this, how often we said black was white because other people were saying it.

In other words, we know that this is true of human behavior, but how do we know it? It is one thing to admit it, in a vague uncomfortable sort of way (which probably includes the hope that one will never again be in such a testing situation) but quite another to make that cool step into a kind of objectivity, where one may say, "Right, if that's what human beings are like, myself included, then let's admit it, examine and organize our attitudes accordingly."

This mechanism, of obedience to the group, does not only mean obedience or submission to a small group, or one that is sharply determined, like a religion or political party. It means, too, conforming to those large, vague, ill-defined collections of people who may never think of themselves as having a collective mind because they are aware of differences of opinion—but which, to people from outside, from another culture, seem very minor. The underlying assumptions and assertions that govern the group are never discussed, never challenged, probably never noticed, the main one being precisely this: that it *is* a group mind, intensely resistant to change, equipped with sacred assumptions about which there can be no discussion.

But suppose this kind of thing were taught in schools?

Let us just suppose it, for a moment. . . . But at once the nub of the problem is laid bare.

Imagine us saying to children, "In the last fifty or so years, the human race has become aware of a great deal of information about its mechanisms; how it behaves, how it must behave under certain circumstances. If this is to be useful, you must learn to contemplate these rules calmly, dispassionately, disinterestedly, without emotion. It is information that will set people free from blind loyalties, obedience to slogans, rhetoric, leaders, group emotions." Well, there it is.

For Discussion:

1. Do you agree with Lessing's description of Western people? Is this description a "caricature" or a "portrait" of the Western person?
2. Does our thinking change depending upon the groups we join? In what ways might these changes become evident? How much power does an individual have over the group's decisions?
3. Lessing argues that some groups are "large, vague, ill-defined collections of people who may never think of themselves as having a collective mind." What groups might these be? Do you belong to any?

 For Fact-Finding, Research, and Writing:

1. Lessing herself has belonged to some controversial groups. Find one journal article and one book that addresses Lessing's participation in various groups.
2. Discuss what Lessing means when she writes, "what is dangerous is not the belonging to a group, or groups, but not understanding the social laws that govern groups and govern us."
3. Lessing describes a psychological experiment used to analyze how people react in groups. Using a library database, find an article about a similar experiment.

Philip G. Zimbardo, "The Stanford Prison Experiment"

Born in the South Bronx to an impoverished Italian immigrant family, Philip G. Zimbardo went on to have a distinguished career as Professor of Psychology at Stanford University. Author of over three hundred publications on various aspects of psychology and an internationally recognized expert on the psychology of aggression, Zimbardo also has his own PBS television show, *Discovering Psychology*.

 Before You Read:

Do certain occupations or social roles encourage sadistic behavior?

The Stanford Prison Experiment

Philip G. Zimbardo

As well known—and as controversial—as the Milgram obedience experiments, the Stanford Prison Experiment (1973) raises troubling questions about the ability of individuals to resist authoritarian or obedient roles, if the social setting requires these roles. Philip G. Zimbardo, professor of psychology at Stanford University, set out to study the process by which prisoners and guards "learn" to become compliant and authoritarian, respectively. To find subjects for the experiment, Zimbardo placed an advertisement in a local newspaper:

Male college students needed for psychological study of prison life. $15 per day for 1–2 weeks beginning Aug. 14. For further information & applications, come to Room 248, Jordan Hall, Stanford U.

The ad drew 75 responses. From these Zimbardo and his colleagues selected 21 college-age men, half of whom would become "prisoners" in the experiment, the other half "guards." The elaborate role-playing scenario, planned for two weeks, had to be cut short due to the intensity of subjects' responses. This article first appeared in the *New York Times Magazine* (April 8, 1973).

In prison, those things withheld from and denied to the prisoner become precisely what he wants most of all.
—Eldridge Cleaver, *"Soul on Ice"*

Our sense of power is more vivid when we break a man's spirit than when we win his heart.
—Eric Hoffer, *"The Passionate State of Mind"*

Every prison that men build is built with bricks of shame, and bound with bars lest Christ should see how men their brothers maim.
—Oscar Wilde, *"The Ballad of Reading Gaol"*

Wherever anyone is against his will that is to him a prison.
—Epictetus, *"Discourses"*

The quiet of a summer morning in Palo Alto, Calif., was shattered by a screeching squad car siren as police swept through the city picking up college students in a surprise mass arrest. Each suspect was charged with a felony, warned of his constitutional rights, spread-eagled against the car, searched, handcuffed, and carted off in the back seat of the squad car to the police station for booking.

After fingerprinting and the preparation of identification forms for his "jacket" (central information file), each prisoner was left isolated in a detention cell to wonder what he had done to get himself into this mess. After a while, he was blindfolded and transported to the "Stanford County Prison." Here he began the process of becoming a prisoner—stripped naked, skin-searched, deloused, and issued a uniform, bedding, soup, and towel.

The warden offered an impromptu welcome:

"As you probably know, I'm your warden. All of you have shown that you are unable to function outside in the real world for one reason or another—that somehow you lack the responsibility of good citizens of this great country. We of this prison, your correctional staff, are going to help you learn what your responsibilities as citizens of this country are. Here are the rules. Sometime in the near future there will be a copy of the rules posted in each of the cells. We expect you to know them and to be able to recite them by number. If you follow all of these rules and keep your hands clean, repent for your misdeeds, and show a proper attitude of penitence, you and I will get along just fine."

There followed a reading of the 16 basic rules of prisoner conduct, "Rule Number One: Prisoners must remain silent during rest periods, after lights are out, during meals, and whenever they are outside the prison yard. Two: Prisoners must eat at mealtimes and only at mealtimes. Three: Prisoners must not move, tamper, deface, or damage walls, ceilings, windows, doors, or other prison property. . . . Seven: Prisoners must address each other by their ID number only. Eight: Prisoners must address the guards as 'Mr. Correctional Officer'. . . . Sixteen: Failure to obey any of the above rules may result in punishment."

By late afternoon these youthful "first offenders" sat in dazed silence on the cots in their barren cells trying to make sense of the events that had transformed their lives so dramatically.

If the police arrests and processing were executed with customary detachment, however, there were some things that didn't fit. For these men were now part of a very unusual kind of prison, an experimental mock prison, created by social psychologists to study the effects of imprisonment upon volunteer research subjects. When we planned our two-week-long simulation of prison life, we sought to understand more about the process by which people called "prisoners" lose their liberty, civil rights, independence, and privacy, while those called "guards" gain social power by accepting the responsibility for controlling and managing the lives of their dependent charges.

Why didn't we pursue this research in a real prison? First, prison systems are fortresses of secrecy, closed to impartial observation, and thereby immune to critical analysis from anyone not already part of the correctional authority. Second, in any real prison, it is impossible to separate what each individual brings into the prison from what the prison brings out in each person.

We populated our mock prison with a homogeneous group of people who could be considered "normal-average" on the basis of clinical interviews and personality tests. Our participants (10 prisoners and 11 guards) were selected from more than 75 volunteers recruited through ads in the city and campus newspapers. The applicants were mostly college students from all over the United States and Canada who happened to be in the Stanford area during the summer and were attracted by the lure of earning $15 a day for participating in a study of prison life. We selected only those judged to be emotionally stable, physically healthy, mature, law-abiding citizens.

The sample of average, middle-class, Caucasian, college-age males (plus one Oriental student) was arbitrarily divided by the flop of a coin. Half were randomly assigned to play the role of guards, the others of prisoners. There were no measurable differences between the guards and the prisoners at the start of the experiment. Although initially warned that as prisoners their privacy and other civil rights would be violated and that they might be subjected to harassment, every subject was completely confident of his ability to endure whatever the prison had to offer for the full two-week experimental period. Each subject unhesitatingly agreed to give his "informed consent" to participate.

The prison was constructed in the basement of Stanford University's psychology building, which was deserted after the end of the summer-school session. A long corridor was converted into the prison "yard" by partitioning off both ends. Three small laboratory rooms opening onto this corridor were made into cells by installing metal barred doors and replacing existing furniture with cots, three to a cell. Adjacent offices were refurnished as guards' quarters, interview-testing rooms, and bedrooms for the "warden" (Jaffe) and the "superintendent" (Zimbardo). A concealed video camera and hidden microphones recorded much of the activity and conversation of guards and prisoners. The physical environment was one in which prisoners could always be observed by the staff, the only exception being when they were secluded in solitary confinement (a small, dark storage closet, labeled "The Hole").

Our mock prison represented an attempt to simulate the psychological state of imprisonment in certain ways. We based our experiment on an in-depth analysis of the prison situation, developed after hundreds of hours of discussion with Carlo Prescott (our ex-con consultant), parole officers, and correctional personnel, and after reviewing much of the existing literature on prisons and concentration camps.

"Real" prisoners typically report feeling powerless, arbitrarily controlled, dependent, frustrated, hopeless, anonymous, dehumanized, and emasculated. It was not possible, pragmatically or ethically, to create such chronic states in volunteer subjects who realize that they are in an experiment for only a short time. Racism, physical brutality, indefinite confinement, and enforced homosexuality were not features of our mock prison. But we did try to reproduce those elements of the prison experience that seemed most fundamental.

We promoted anonymity by seeking to minimize each prisoner's sense of uniqueness and prior identity. The prisoners wore smocks and nylon stocking caps; they had to use their ID numbers; their personal effects were removed and they were housed in barren cells. All of this made them appear similar to each other and indistinguishable to observers. Their smocks, which were like dresses, were worn without undergarments, causing the prisoners to be restrained in their physical actions and to move in ways that were more feminine than masculine. The prisoners were forced to obtain permission from the guard for routine and simple activities such as writing letters, smoking a cigarette, or even going to the toilet; this elicited from them a childlike dependency.

Their quarters, though clean and neat, were small, stark, and without esthetic appeal. The lack of windows resulted in poor air circulation, and persistent odors arose from the unwashed bodies of the prisoners. After 10 P.M. lockup, toilet privileges were denied, so prisoners who had to relieve themselves would have to urinate and defecate in buckets provided by the guards. Sometimes the guards refused permission to have them cleaned out, and this made the prison smell.

Above all, "real" prisons are machines for playing tricks with the human conception of time. In our windowless prison, the prisoners often did not even know whether it was day or night. A few hours after falling asleep, they were roused by shrill whistles for their "count." The ostensible purpose of the count was to provide a public test of the prisoners' knowledge of the rules and of their ID numbers. But more important, the count, which occurred at least once on each of the three different guard shifts, provided a regular occasion for the guards to relate to the prisoners. Over the course of the study, the duration of the counts was spontaneously increased by the guards from their initial perfunctory 10 minutes to a seemingly interminable several hours. During these confrontations, guards who were bored could find ways to amuse themselves, ridiculing recalcitrant prisoners, enforcing arbitrary rules, and openly exaggerating any dissension among the prisoners.

The guards were also "deindividualized": They wore identical khaki uniforms and silver reflector sunglasses that made eye contact with them impossible. Their symbols of power were billy clubs, whistles, handcuffs, and the keys to the cells and the "main gate." Although our guards received no formal training from us in how to be guards, for the most part they moved with apparent ease into their roles. The media had already provided them with ample models of prison guards to emulate.

Because we were as interested in the guards' behavior as in the prisoners', they were given considerable latitude to improvise and to develop strategies and tactics of prisoner management. Our guards were told that they must maintain "law and order" in this prison, that they were responsible for handling any trouble that might break out, and they were cautioned about the seriousness and potential dangers of the situation they were about to enter. Surprisingly, in most prison systems, "real" guards are not given much more psychological preparation or adequate training than this for what is one of the most complex, demanding, and dangerous jobs our society has to offer. They are expected to learn how to adjust to their new employment mostly from on-the-job experience, and from contacts with the "old bulls" during a survival-of-the-fittest orientation period. According to an orientation manual for correctional officers at San Quentin, "the only way you really get to know San Quentin is through experience and time. Some of us take more time and must go through more experiences than others to accomplish this; some really never do get there."

You cannot be a prisoner if no one will be your guard, and you cannot be a prison guard if no one takes you or your prison seriously. Therefore, over time a perverted symbiotic relationship developed. As the guards became more aggressive, prisoners became more passive; assertion by the guards led to dependency in the prisoners; self-aggrandizement was met with self-deprecation, authority with helplessness, and the counterpart of the guards' sense of mastery and control was the depression and hopelessness witnessed in the prisoners. As these differences in behavior, mood, and perception became more evident to all, the need for the now "righteously" powerful guards to rule the obviously inferior and powerless inmates became a sufficient reason to support almost any further indignity of man against man:

GUARD K: "During the inspection, I went to cell 2 to mess up a bed which the prisoner had made and he grabbed me, screaming that he had just made it, and he wasn't going to let me mess it up. He grabbed my throat, and although he was laughing I was pretty scared. . . . I lashed out with my stick and hit him in the chin (although not very hard), and when I freed myself I became angry. I wanted to get back in the cell and have a go with him, since he attacked me when I was not ready."

GUARD M: "I was surprised at myself . . . I made them call each other names and clean the toilets out with their bare hands. I practically considered the prisoners cattle, and I kept thinking: 'I have to watch out for them in case they try something.'"

GUARD A: "I was tired of seeing the prisoners in their rags and smelling the strong odors of their bodies that filled the cells. I watched them tear at each other on orders given by us. They didn't see it as an experiment. It was real and they were fighting to keep their identity. But we were always there to show them who was boss."

Because the first day passed without incident, we were surprised and totally unprepared for the rebellion that broke out on the morning of the second day. The prisoners removed their stocking caps, ripped off their numbers, and barricaded themselves inside the cells by putting their beds against the doors. What should we do? The guards were very much upset because the prisoners also began to taunt and curse them to their faces. When the morning shift of guards came on, they were upset at the night shift who, they felt, must have been too permissive and too lenient. The guards had to handle the rebellion themselves, and what they did was startling to behold.

At first they insisted that reinforcements be called in. The two guards who were waiting on stand-by call at home came in, and the night shift of guards voluntarily remained on duty (without extra pay) to bolster the morning shift. The guards met and decided to treat force with force. They got a fire extinguisher that shot a stream of skin-chilling carbon dioxide and forced the prisoners away from the doors; they broke into each cell, stripped the prisoners naked, took the beds out, forced the prisoners who were the ringleaders into solitary confinement, and generally began to harass and intimidate the prisoners.

After crushing the riot, the guards decided to head off further unrest by creating a privileged cell for those who were "good prisoners" and then, without explanation, switching some of the troublemakers into it and some of the good prisoners out into the other cells. The prisoner ringleaders could not trust these new cellmates because they had not joined in the riot and might even be "snitches." The prisoners never again acted in unity against the system. One of the leaders of the prisoner revolt later confided:

"If we had gotten together then, I think we could have taken over the place. But when I saw the revolt wasn't working, I decided to toe the line. Everyone settled into the same pattern. From then on, we were really controlled by the guards."

It was after this episode that the guards really began to demonstrate their inventiveness in the application of arbitrary power. They made the prisoners obey petty, meaningless, and often inconsistent rules, forced them to engage in tedious, useless work, such as moving cartons back and forth between closets and picking thorns out of their blankets for hours on end. (The guards had previously dragged the blankets through thorny bushes to create this disagreeable task.) Not only did the prisoners have to sing songs or laugh or refrain from smiling on command; they were also encouraged to curse and vilify each other publicly during some of the counts. They sounded off their numbers endlessly and were repeatedly made to do pushups, on occasion with a guard stepping on them or a prisoner sitting on them.

Slowly the prisoners became resigned to their fate and even behaved in ways that actually helped to justify their dehumanizing treatment at the hands of the guards. Analysis of the tape-recorded private conversations between prisoners and of remarks made by them to interviewers revealed that fully half could be classified as nonsupportive of other prisoners. More dramatic, 85 percent of the evaluative statements by prisoners about their fellow prisoners were uncomplimentary and deprecating.

This should be taken in the context of an even more surprising result. What do you imagine the prisoners talked about when they were alone in their cells with each other, given a temporary respite from the continual harassment and surveillance by the guards? Girl friends, career plans, hobbies or politics?

No, their concerns were almost exclusively riveted to prison topics. Their monitored conversations revealed that only 10 percent of the time was devoted to "outside" topics, while 90 percent of the time they discussed escape plans, the awful food, grievances or ingratiating tactics to use with specific guards in order to get a cigarette, permission to go to the toilet, or some other favor. Their obsession with these immediate survival concerns made talk about the past and future an idle luxury.

And this was not a minor point. So long as the prisoners did not get to know each other as people, they only extended the oppressiveness and reality of their life as prisoners. For the most part, each prisoner observed his fellow prisoners allowing the guards to humiliate them, acting like compliant sheep, carrying out mindless orders with total obedience, and even being cursed by fellow prisoners (at a guard's command). Under such circumstances, how could a prisoner have respect for his fellows, or any self-respect for what *he* obviously was becoming in the eyes of all those evaluating him?

The combination of realism and symbolism in this experiment had fused to create a vivid illusion of imprisonment. The illusion merged inextricably with reality for at least some of the time for every individual in the situation. It was remarkable how readily we all slipped into our roles, temporarily gave up our identities, and allowed these assigned roles and the social forces in the situation to guide, shape, and eventually to control our freedom of thought and action.

But precisely where does one's "identity" end and the one's "role" begin? When the private self and the public role behavior clash, what direction will attempts to impose consistency take? Consider the reactions of the parents, relatives, and friends of the prisoners who visited their forlorn sons, brothers, and lovers during two scheduled visitors' hours. They were taught in short order that they were our guests, allowed the privilege of visiting only by complying with the regulations of the institution. They had to register, were made to wait half an hour, were told that only two visitors could see any one prisoner; the total visiting time was cut from an hour to only 10 minutes, they had to be under the surveillance of a guard, and before any parents could enter the visiting area, they had to discuss their son's case with the warden. Of course they complained about these arbitrary rules, but their conditioned, middle-class reaction was to work within the system to appeal privately to the superintendent to make conditions better for their prisoners.

In less than 36 hours, we were forced to release prisoner 8612 because of extreme depression, disorganized thinking, uncontrollable crying, and fits of rage. We did so reluctantly because we believed he was trying to "con" us—it was unimaginable that a volunteer prisoner in a mock prison could legitimately be suffering and disturbed to that extent. But then on each of the next three days another prisoner reacted with similar anxiety symptoms, and we were forced to terminate them, too. In a fifth case, a prisoner was released after developing a psychosomatic rash over his entire body (triggered by rejection of his parole appeal by the mock parole board). These men were simply unable to make an adequate adjustment to prison life. Those who endured the prison experience to the end could be distinguished from those who broke down and were released early in only one dimension—authoritarianism. On a psychological test designed to reveal a person's authoritarianism, those prisoners who had the highest scores were best able to function in this authoritarian prison environment.

If the authoritarian situation became a serious matter for the prisoners, it became even more serious—and sinister—for the guards. Typically, the guards insulted the prisoners, threatened them, were physically aggressive, used instruments (night sticks, fire extinguishers, etc.) to keep the prisoners in line, and referred to them in impersonal, anonymous, deprecating ways: "Hey, you," or "You [obscenity], 5401, come here." From the first to the last day, there was a significant increase in the guards' use of most of these domineering, abusive tactics.

Everyone and everything in the prison was defined by power. To be a guard who did not take advantage of this institutionally sanctioned use of power was to appear "weak," "out of it," "wired up by the prisoners," or simply a deviant from the established norms of appropriate guard behavior. Using Erich Fromm's definition of sadism, as "the wish for absolute control over another living being," all of the mock guards at one time or another during this study behaved sadistically toward the prisoners. Many of them reported—in their diaries, on critical-incident report forms, and during post-experimental interviews—being delighted in the new-found power and control they exercised and sorry to see it relinquished at the end of the study.

Some of the guards reacted to the situation in the extreme and behaved with great hostility and cruelty in the forms of degradation they invented for the prisoners. But oth-

ers were kinder; they occasionally did little favors for the prisoners, were reluctant to punish them, and avoided situations where prisoners were being harassed. The torment experienced by one of these good guards is obvious in his perceptive analysis of what it felt like
to be responded to as a "guard":

"What made the experience most depressing for me was the fact that we were continually called upon to act in a way that just was contrary to what I really feel inside. I don't
feel like I'm the type of person that would be a guard, just constantly giving out [orders] . . .
and forcing people to do things, and pushing and lying—it just didn't seem like me, and to
continually keep up and put on a face like that is just really one of the most oppressive
things you can do. It's almost like a prison that you create yourself—you get into it, and it
becomes almost the definition you make of yourself, it almost becomes like walls, and you
want to break out and you want just to be able to tell everyone that 'this isn't really me at
all, and I'm not the person that's confined in there—I'm a person who wants to get out and
show you that I am free, and I do have my own will, and I'm not the sadistic type of person that enjoys this kind of thing."

Still, the behavior of these good guards seemed more motivated by a desire to be liked
by everyone in the system than by a concern for the inmates' welfare. No guard ever inter-
vened in any direct way on behalf of the prisoners, ever interfered with the orders of the
cruelest guards, or ever openly complained about the subhuman quality of life that characterized this prison.

Perhaps the most devastating impact of the more hostile guards was their creation of a
capricious, arbitrary environment. Over time the prisoners began to react passively. When
our mock prisoners asked questions, they got answers about half the time, but the rest of the
time they were insulted and punished—and it was not possible for them to predict which
would be the outcome. As they began to "toe the line," they stopped resisting, questioning
and, indeed, almost ceased responding altogether. There was a general decrease in all categories of response as they learned the safest strategy to use in an unpredictable, threatening
environment from which there is no physical escape—do nothing, except what is required.
Act not, want not, feel not, and you will not get into trouble in prisonlike situations.

Can it really be, you wonder, that intelligent, educated volunteers could have lost
sight of the reality that they were merely acting a part in an elaborate game that would
eventually end? There are many indications not only that they did, but that, in addition,
so did we and so did other apparently sensible, responsible adults.

Prisoner 819, who had gone into an uncontrollable crying fit, was about to be pre-
maturely released from the prison when a guard lined up the prisoners and had them chant
in unison, "819 is a bad prisoner. Because of what 819 did to prison property we all must
suffer. 819 is a bad prisoner." Over and over again. When we realized 819 might be over-
hearing this, we rushed into the room where 819 was supposed to be resting, only to find
him in tears, prepared to go back into the prison because he could not leave as long as the
others thought he was a "bad prisoner." Sick as he felt, he had to prove to them he was not
a "bad" prisoner. He had to be persuaded that he was not a prisoner at all, that the others
were also just students, that this was just an experiment and not a prison and the prison

staff were only research psychologists. A report from the warden notes, "While I believe that it was necessary for *staff* [me] to enact the warden role, at least some of the time, I am startled by the ease with which I could turn off my sensitivity and concern for others for 'a good cause.'"

Consider our overreaction to the rumor of a mass escape plot that one of the guards claimed to have overheard. It went as follows: Prisoner 8612, previously released for emotional disturbance, was only faking. He was going to round up a bunch of his friends, and they would storm the prison right after visiting hours. Instead of collecting data on the pattern of rumor transmission, we made plans to maintain the security of our institution. After putting a confederate informer into the cell 8612 had occupied to get specific information about the escape plans, the superintendent went back to the Palo Alto Police Department to request transfer of our prisoners to the old city jail. His impassioned plea was only turned down at the last minute when the problem of insurance and city liability for our prisoners was raised by a city official. Angered at this lack of cooperation, the staff formulated another plan. Our jail was dismantled, the prisoners, chained and blindfolded, were carted off to a remote storage room. When the conspirators arrived, they would be told the study was over, their friends had been sent home, there was nothing left to liberate. After they left, we would redouble the security features of our prison making any future escape attempts futile. We even planned to lure ex-prisoner 8612 back on some pretext and imprison him again, because he had been released on false pretenses! The rumor turned out to be just that—a full day had passed in which we collected little or no data, worked incredibly hard to tear down and then rebuild our prison. Our reaction, however, was as much one of relief and joy as of exhaustion and frustration.

When a former prison chaplain was invited to talk with the prisoners (the grievance committee had requested church services), he puzzled everyone by disparaging each inmate for not having taken any constructive action in order to get released. "Don't you know you must have a lawyer in order to get bail, or to appeal the charges against you?" Several of them accepted his invitation to contact their parents in order to secure the services of an attorney. The next night one of the parents stopped at the superintendent's office before visiting time and handed him the name and phone number of her cousin who was a public defender. She said that a priest had called her and suggested the need for a lawyer's services! We called the lawyer. He came, interviewed the prisoners, discussed sources of bail money, and promised to return again after the weekend.

But perhaps the most telling account of the insidious development of the new reality, of the gradual Kafkaesque metamorphosis of good into evil, appears in excerpts from the diary of one of the guards, Guard A:

Prior to start of experiment: *"As I am a pacifist and nonaggressive individual, I cannot see a time when I might guard and/or maltreat other living things."*
After an orientation meeting: *"Buying uniforms at the end of the meeting confirms the gamelike atmosphere of this thing. I doubt whether many of us share the expectations of 'seriousness' that the experimenters seem to have."*

First Day: *"Feel sure that the prisoners will make fun of my appearance and I evolve my first basic strategy—mainly not to smile at anything they say or do which would be admitting it's all only a game. . . . At cell 3 I stop and setting my voice hard and low say to 5486, 'What are you smiling at?' 'Nothing, Mr. Correctional Officer.' 'Well, see that you don't.' (As I walk off I feel stupid.)"*

Second Day: *"5704 asked for a cigarette and I ignored him—because I am a non-smoker and could not empathize. . . . Meanwhile since I was feeling empathetic towards 1037, I determined not to talk with him. . . . after we had count and lights out [Guard D] and I held a loud conversation about going home to our girl friends and what we were going to do to them."*

Third Day (preparing for the first visitors' night): *"After warning the prisoners not to make any complaints unless they wanted the visit terminated fast, we finally brought in the first parents. I made sure I was one of the guards on the yard, because this was my first chance for the type of manipulative power that I really like—being a very noticed figure with almost complete control over what is said or not. While the parents and prisoners sat in chairs, I sat on the end of the table dangling my feet and contradicting anything I felt like. This was the first part of the experiment I was really enjoying. . . . 817 is being obnoxious and bears watching."*

Fourth Day: *". . . The psychologist rebukes me for handcuffing and blindfolding a prisoner before leaving the [counseling] office, and I resentfully reply that it is both necessary security and my business anyway."*

Fifth Day: *"I harass 'Sarge' who continues to stubbornly overrespond to all commands. I have singled him out for the special abuse both because he begs for it and because I simply don't like him. The real trouble starts at dinner. The new prisoner (416) refuses to eat his sausage . . . we throw him into the Hole ordering him to hold sausages in each hand. We have a crisis of authority; this rebellious conduct potentially undermines the complete control we have over the others. We decide to play upon prisoner solidarity and tell the new one that all the others will be deprived of visitors if he does not eat his dinner. . . . I walk by and slam my stick into the Hole door. . . . I am very angry at this prisoner for causing discomfort and trouble for the others. I decided to force-feed him, but he wouldn't eat. I let the food slide down his face. I didn't believe it was me doing it. I hated myself for making him eat but I hated him more for not eating."*

Sixth Day: *"The experiment is over. I feel elated but am shocked to find some other guards disappointed somewhat because of the loss of money and some because they are enjoying themselves."*

We were no longer dealing with an intellectual exercise in which a hypothesis was being evaluated in the dispassionate manner dictated by the canons of the scientific method. We were caught up in the passion of the present, the suffering, the need to control people, not variables, the escalation of power, and all the unexpected things that were erupting around and within us. We had to end this experiment: So our planned two-week simulation was aborted after only six (was it only six?) days and nights.

Was it worth all the suffering just to prove what everybody knows—that some people are sadistic, others weak, and prisons are not beds of roses? If that is all we demonstrated in this research, then it was certainly not worth the anguish. We believe there are many significant implications to be derived from this experience, only a few of which can be suggested here.

The potential social value of this study derives precisely from the fact that normal, healthy, educated young men could be so radically transformed under the institutional pressures of a "prison environment." If this could happen in so short a time, without the excesses that are possible in real prisons, and if it could happen to the "cream-of-the-crop of American youth," then one can only shudder to imagine what society is doing both to the actual guards and prisoners who are at this very moment participating in that unnatural "social experiment."

The pathology observed in this study cannot be reasonably attributed in pre-existing personality differences of the subjects, that option being eliminated by our selection procedures and random assignment. Rather, the subjects' abnormal social and personal reactions are best seen as a product of their transaction with an environment that supported the behavior that would be pathological in other settings, but was "appropriate" in this prison. Had we observed comparable reactions in a real prison, the psychiatrist undoubtedly would have been able to attribute any prisoner's behavior to character defects or personality maladjustment, while critics of the prison system would have been quick to label the guards as "psychopathic." This tendency to locate the source of behavior disorders inside a particular person or group underestimates the power of situational forces.

Our colleague, David Rosenhan, has very convincingly shown that once a sane person (pretending to be insane) gets labeled as insane and committed to a mental hospital, it is the label that is the reality which is treated and not the person. This dehumanizing tendency to respond to other people according to socially determined labels and often arbitrarily assigned roles is also apparent in a recent "mock hospital" study designed by Norma Jean Orlando to extend the ideas in our research.

Personnel from the staff of Elgin State Hospital in Illinois role-played either mental patients or staff in a weekend simulation on a ward in the hospital. The mock mental patients soon displayed behavior indistinguishable from that we usually associate with the chronic pathological syndromes of acute mental patients: Incessant pacing, uncontrollable weeping, depression, hostility, fights, stealing from each other, complaining. Many of the "mock staff" took advantage of their power to act in ways comparable to our mock guards by dehumanizing their powerless victims.

During a series of encounter debriefing sessions immediately after our experiment, we all had an opportunity to vent our strong feelings and to reflect upon the moral and ethical issues each of us faced, and we considered how we might react more morally in future "real-life" analogues to this situation. Year-long follow-ups with our subjects via questionnaires, personal interviews, and group reunions indicate that their mental anguish was transient and situationally specific, but the self-knowledge gained has persisted.

By far the most disturbing implication of our research comes from the parallels between what occurred in that basement mock prison and daily experiences in our own lives—and we presume yours. The physical institution of prison is but a concrete and steel metaphor for the existence of more pervasive, albeit less obvious, prisons of the mind that all of us daily create, populate, and perpetuate. We speak here of the prisons of racism, sexism, despair, shyness, "neurotic hang-ups," and the like. The social convention of marriage, as one example, becomes for many couples a state of imprisonment in which one partner agrees to be prisoner or guard, forcing or allowing the other to play the reciprocal role—invariably without making the contract explicit.

To what extent do we allow ourselves to become imprisoned by docilely accepting the roles others assign us or, indeed, choose to remain prisoners because being passive and dependent frees us from the need to act and be responsible for our actions? The prison of fear constructed in the delusions of the paranoid is no less confining or less real than the cell that every shy person erects to limit his own freedom in anxious anticipation of being ridiculed and rejected by his guards—often guards of his own making.

 For Discussion:

1. Zimbardo writes, "in any real prison, it is impossible to separate what each individual brings into the prison from what the prison brings out in each person." Can you give examples of what you think Zimbardo means?
2. According to Zimbardo, the researchers did not train the "guards" for their role and that the guards instead mimicked the behavior of guards they had seen from the "media." What other social roles do people learn about, and perhaps even copy, from media representations?
3. Was the Stanford Prison Experiment ethical?
4. Do you agree with Zimbardo's argument that a personal relationship can become a type of mental prison?
5. Describe the profile of the research subjects. Do you think this profile influenced the nature or results of the study?

 For Fact-Finding, Research, and Writing:

1. Using a library database, find a recent study that cites Zimbardo's article. How does the recent study incorporate or comment on the findings of "The Stanford Prison Experiment"?
2. A film based on "The Stanford Prison Experiment" was released in 2001. Using a newspaper database, find a review of that film.

3.   One of the "prisons of the mind" Zimbardo mentions at the end of the article is shyness. Find one of Zimbardo's articles on shyness, and write an abstract of that article.

4.   Select one of the four epigraphs that open this article and explain in a paragraph how it pertains to the study.

Eric Schlosser, "Why McDonald's Fries Taste So Good"

Eric Schlosser works as a correspondent for *The Atlantic Monthly*, and has also written articles for *Rolling Stone* and *The New Yorker*. He has won the National Magazine Award, and his book *Fast Food Nation* was on the *New York Times* Bestseller list for over a year.

 Before You Read:

Do any of your favorite foods contain artificial flavors, colors, or other chemical additives? Does that bother you?

Why McDonald's Fries Taste So Good

Eric Schlosser

A trip to northern New Jersey, the home of natural flavors

The french fry was "almost sacrosanct for me," Ray Kroc, one of the founders of McDonald's, wrote in his autobiography, "its preparation a ritual to be followed religiously." During the chain's early years french fries were made from scratch every day. Russet Burbank potatoes were peeled, cut into shoestrings, and fried in McDonald's kitchens. As the chain expanded nationwide, in the mid-1960s, it sought to cut labor costs, reduce the number of suppliers, and ensure that its fries tasted the same at every restaurant. McDonald's began switching to frozen french fries in 1966—and few customers noticed the difference. Nevertheless, the change had a profound effect on the nation's agriculture and diet. A familiar food had been transformed into a highly processed industrial commodity. McDonald's fries now come from huge manufacturing plants that can peel, slice, cook, and freeze two million pounds of potatoes a day. The rapid expansion of McDonald's and the popularity of its low-cost, mass-produced fires changed the way Americans eat. In 1960 Americans consumed an average of about eighty-one pounds of fresh potatoes and four pounds of frozen french fries. In 2000 they consumed an average of about fifty pounds of fresh potatoes and thirty pounds of frozen fries. Today McDonald's is the largest buyer of potatoes in the United States.

The taste of McDonald's french fries played a crucial role in the chain's success—fries are much more profitable than hamburgers—and was long praised by customers, competitors, and even food critics. James Beard loved McDonald's fries. Their distinctive taste does not stem from the kind of potatoes that McDonald's buys, the technology that processes them, or the restaurant equipment that fries them: other chains use Russet Burbanks, buy their french fries from the same large processing companies, and have similar fryers in their restaurant kitchens. The taste of a french fry is largely determined by the cooking oil. For decades McDonald's cooked its french fries in a mixture of about seven percent cottonseed oil and 93 percent beef tallow. The mixture gave the fries their unique flavor—and more saturated beef fat per ounce than a McDonald's hamburger.

In 1990, amid a barrage of criticism over the amount of cholesterol in its fries, McDonald's switched to pure vegetable oil. This presented the company with a challenge: how to make fries that subtly taste like beef without cooking them in beef tallow. A look at the ingredients in McDonald's french fries suggests how the problem was solved. Toward the end of the list is a seemingly innocuous yet oddly mysterious phrase: "natural flavor." That ingredient helps to explain not only why the fries taste so good but also why most fast food—indeed, most of the food Americans eat today—tastes the way it does.

Open your refrigerator, your freezer, your kitchen cupboards, and look at the labels on your food. You'll find "natural flavor" or "artificial flavor" in just about every list of ingredients. The similarities between these two broad categories are far more significant than the differences. Both are man-made additives that give most processed food most of its taste. People usually buy a food item the first time because of its packaging or appearance. Taste usually determines whether they buy it again. About 90 percent of the money that Americans now spend on food goes to buy processed food. The canning, freezing, and dehydrating techniques used in processing destroy most of food's flavor—and so a vast industry has arisen in the United States to make processed food palatable. Without this flavor industry today's fast food would not exist. The names of the leading American fast-food chains and their best-selling menu items have become embedded in our popular culture and famous worldwide. But few people can name the companies that manufacture fast food's taste.

The flavor industry is highly secretive. Its leading companies will not divulge the precise formulas of flavor compounds or the identities of clients. The secrecy is deemed essential for protecting the reputations of beloved brands. The fast-food chains, understandably, would like the public to believe that the flavors of the food they sell somehow originate in their restaurant kitchens, not in distant factories run by other firms. A McDonald's french fry is one of countless foods whose flavor is just a component in a complex manufacturing process. The look and the taste of what we eat now are frequently deceiving—by design.

The Flavor Corridor

The New Jersey Turnpike runs through the heart of the flavor industry, an industrial corridor dotted with refineries and chemical plants. International Flavors & Fragrances (IFF), the world's largest flavor company, has a manufacturing facility off Exit 8A in Dayton, New Jersey; Givaudan, the world's second-largest flavor company, has a plant in East Hanover. Haarmann & Reimer, the largest German flavor company, has a plant in Teterboro, as does Takasago, the largest Japanese flavor company. Flavor Dynamics has a plant in South Plainfield; Frutarom is in North Bergen; Elan Chemical is in Newark. Dozens of companies manufacture flavors in the corridor between Teaneck and South Brunswick. Altogether the area produces about two thirds of the flavor additives sold in the United States.

The IFF plant in Dayton is a huge pale-blue building with a modern office complex attached to the front. It sits in an industrial park, not far from a BASF plastics factory, a Jolly French Toast factory, and a plant that manufactures Liz Claiborne cosmetics. Dozens of tractor-trailers were parked at the IFF loading dock the afternoon I visited, and a thin cloud of steam floated from a roof vent. Before entering the plant, I signed a nondisclosure form, promising not to reveal the brand names of foods that contain IFF flavors. The place reminded me of Willy Wonka's chocolate factory. Wonderful smells drifted through the hallways, men and women in neat white lab coats cheerfully went about their work, and hundreds of little glass bottles sat on laboratory tables and shelves. The bottles contained powerful but fragile flavor chemicals, shielded from light by brown glass and round white caps shut tight. The long chemical names on the little white labels were as mystifying to me as medieval Latin. These odd-sounding things would be mixed and poured and turned into new substances, like magic potions.

I was not invited into the manufacturing areas of the IFF plant, where, it was thought, I might discover trade secrets. Instead I toured various laboratories and pilot kitchens, where the flavors of well-established brands are tested or adjusted, and where whole new flavors are created. IFF's snack-and-savory lab is responsible for the flavors of potato chips, corn chips, breads, crackers, breakfast cereals, and pet food. The confectionery lab devises flavors for ice cream, cookies, candies, toothpastes, mouthwashes, and antacids. Everywhere I looked, I saw famous, widely advertised products sitting on laboratory desks and tables. The beverage lab was full of brightly colored liquids in clear bottles. It comes up with flavors for popular soft drinks, sports drinks, bottled teas, and wine coolers, for all-natural juice drinks, organic soy drinks, beers, and malt liquors. In one pilot kitchen I saw a dapper food technologist, a middle-aged man with an elegant tie beneath his crisp lab coat, carefully preparing a batch of cookies with white frosting and pink-and-white sprinkles. In another pilot kitchen I saw a pizza oven, a grill, a milk-shake machine, and a french fryer identical to those I'd seen at innumerable fast-food restaurants.

In addition to being the world's largest flavor company, IFF manufactures the smells of six of the ten best-selling fine perfumes in the United States, including Estée Lauder's Beautiful, Clinique's Happy, Lancôme's Trésor, and Calvin Klein's Eternity. It also makes the smells of household products such as deodorant, dishwashing detergent, bath soap, shampoo, furniture polish, and floor wax. All these aromas are made through essentially the same process: the manipulation of volatile chemicals. The basic science behind the scent of your shaving cream is the same as that governing the flavor of your TV dinner.

"Natural" and "Artificial"

Scientists now believe that human beings acquired the sense of taste as a way to avoid being poisoned. Edible plants generally taste sweet, harmful ones bitter. The taste buds on our tongues can detect the presence of half a dozen or so basic tastes, including sweet, sour, bitter, salty, astringent, and umami, a taste discovered by Japanese researchers—a rich and full sense of deliciousness triggered by amino acids in foods such as meat, shellfish, mushrooms, potatoes, and seaweed. Taste buds offer a limited means of detection, however, compared with the human olfactory system, which can perceive thousands of different chemical aromas. Indeed, "flavor" is primarily the smell of gases being released by the chemicals you've just put in your mouth. The aroma of a food can be responsible for as much as 90 percent of its taste.

The act of drinking, sucking, or chewing a substance releases its volatile gases. They flow out of your mouth and up your nostrils, or up the passageway in the back of your mouth, to a thin layer of nerve cells called the olfactory epithelium, located at the base of your nose, right between your eyes. Your brain combines the complex smell signals from your olfactory epithelium with the simple taste signals from your tongue, assigns a flavor to what's in your mouth, and decides if it's something you want to eat.

A person's food preferences, like his or her personality, are formed during the first few years of life, through a process of socialization. Babies innately prefer sweet tastes and reject bitter ones; toddlers can learn to enjoy hot and spicy food, bland health food, or fast food, depending on what the people around them eat. The human sense of smell is still not fully understood. It is greatly affected by psychological factors and expectations. The mind focuses intently on some of the aromas that surround us and filters out the overwhelming majority. People can grow accustomed to bad smells or good smells; they stop noticing what once seemed overpowering. Aroma and memory are somehow inextricably linked. A smell can suddenly evoke a long-forgotten moment. The flavors of childhood foods seem to leave an indelible mark, and adults often return to them, without always knowing why. These "comfort foods" become a source of pleasure and reassurance—a fact that fast-food chains use to their advantage. Childhood memories of Happy Meals, which come with french fries, can translate into frequent adult visits to McDonald's. On average, Americans now eat about four servings of french fries every week.

The human craving for flavor has been a largely unacknowledged and unexamined force in history. For millennia royal empires have been built, unexplored lands traversed, and great religions and philosophies forever changed by the spice trade. In 1492 Christopher Columbus set sail to find seasoning. Today the influence of flavor in the world marketplace is no less decisive. The rise and fall of corporate empires—of soft-drink companies, snack-food companies, and fast-food chains—is often determined by how their products taste.

The flavor industry emerged in the mid-nineteenth century, as processed foods began to be manufactured on a large scale. Recognizing the need for flavor additives, early food processors turned to perfume companies that had long experience working with essential oils and volatile aromas. The great perfume houses of England, France, and the Netherlands produced many of the first flavor compounds. In the early part of the twentieth century Germany took the technological lead in flavor production, owing to its powerful chemical industry. Legend has it that a German scientist discovered methyl anthranilate, one of the first artificial flavors, by accident while mixing chemicals in his laboratory. Suddenly the lab was filled with the sweet smell of grapes. Methyl anthranilate later became the chief flavor compound in grape Kool-Aid. After World War II much of the perfume industry shifted from Europe to the United States, settling in New York City near the garment district and the fashion houses. The flavor industry came with it, later moving to New Jersey for greater plant capacity. Man-made flavor additives were used mostly in baked goods, candies, and sodas until the 1950s, when sales of processed food began to soar. The invention of gas chromatographs and mass spectrometers—machines capable of detecting volatile gases at low levels—vastly increased the number of flavors that could be synthesized. By the mid-1960s flavor companies were churning out compounds to supply the taste of Pop Tarts, Bac-Os, Tab, Tang, Filet-O-Fish sandwiches, and literally thousands of other new foods.

The American flavor industry now has annual revenues of about $1.4 billion. Approximately 10,000 new processed-food products are introduced every year in the United States. Almost all of them require flavor additives. And about nine out of ten of these products fail. The latest flavor innovations and corporate realignments are heralded in publications such as *Chemical Market Reporter*, *Food Chemical News*, *Food Engineering*, and *Food Product Design*. The progress of IFF has mirrored that of the flavor industry as a whole. IFF was formed in 1958, through the merger of two small companies. Its annual revenues have grown almost fifteenfold since the early 1970s, and it currently has manufacturing facilities in twenty countries.

Today's sophisticated spectrometers, gas chromatographs, and headspace-vapor analyzers provide a detailed map of a food's flavor components, detecting chemical aromas present in amounts as low as one part per billion. The human nose, however, is even more sensitive. A nose can detect aromas present in quantities of a few parts per trillion—an amount equivalent to about 0.000000000003 percent. Complex aromas, such as those of coffee and roasted meat, are composed of volatile gases from nearly a thousand different chemicals. The smell of a strawberry arises from the interaction of about 350 chemicals that are present in minute amounts. The quality that people seek most of all in a food—flavor—is usually present in a quantity too infinitesimal to be measured in traditional culinary terms

such as ounces or teaspoons. The chemical that provides the dominant flavor of bell pepper can be tasted in amounts as low as 0.02 parts per billion; one drop is sufficient to add
flavor to five average-size swimming pools. The flavor additive usually comes next to last
in a processed food's list of ingredients and often costs less than its packaging. Soft drinks
contain a larger proportion of flavor additives than most products. The flavor in a twelve-
ounce can of Coke costs about half a cent.

The color additives in processed foods are usually present in even smaller amounts
than the flavor compounds. Many of New Jersey's flavor companies also manufacture these
color additives, which are used to make processed foods look fresh and appealing. Food
coloring serves many of the same decorative purposes as lipstick, eye shadow, mascara—
and is often made from the same pigments. Titanium dioxide, for example, has proved to
be an especially versatile mineral. It gives many processed candies, frostings, and icings
their bright white color; it is a common ingredient in women's cosmetics; and it is the pigment used in many white oil paints and house paints. At Burger King, Wendy's, and
McDonald's coloring agents have been added to many of the soft drinks, salad dressings,
cookies, condiments, chicken dishes, and sandwich buns.

Studies have found that the color of a food can greatly affect how its taste is perceived.
Brightly colored foods frequently seem to taste better than bland-looking foods, even when
the flavor compounds are identical. Foods that somehow look off-color often seem to have
off tastes. For thousands of years human beings have relied on visual cues to help determine
what is edible. The color of fruit suggests whether it is ripe, the color of meat whether it is
rancid. Flavor researchers sometimes use colored lights to modify the influence of visual
cues during taste tests. During one experiment in the early 1970s people were served an
oddly tinted meal of steak and french fries that appeared normal beneath colored lights.
Everyone thought the meal tasted fine until the lighting was changed. Once it became
apparent that the steak was actually blue and the fries were green, some people became ill.

The federal Food and Drug Administration does not require companies to disclose the
ingredients of their color or flavor additives so long as all the chemicals in them are considered by the agency to be GRAS ("generally recognized as safe"). This enables companies to maintain the secrecy of their formulas. It also hides the fact that flavor compounds
often contain more ingredients than the foods to which they give taste. The phrase "artificial strawberry flavor" gives little hint of the chemical wizardry and manufacturing skill
that can make a highly processed food taste like strawberries.

A typical artificial strawberry flavor, like the kind found in a Burger King strawberry
milk shake, contains the following ingredients: amyl acetate, amyl butyrate, amyl valerate,
anethol, anisyl formate, benzyl acetate, benzyl isobutyrate, butyric acid, cinnamyl
isobutyrate, cinnamyl valerate, cognac essential oil, diacetyl, dipropyl ketone, ethyl acetate,
ethyl amyl ketone, ethyl butyrate, ethyl cinnamate, ethyl heptanoate, ethyl heptylate, ethyl
lactate, ethyl methylphenylglycidate, ethyl nitrate, ethyl propionate, ethyl valerate, he-
liotropin, hydroxyphenyl-2-butanone (10 percent solution in alcohol), α-ionone, isobutyl
anthranilate, isobutyl butyrate, lemon essential oil, maltol, 4-methylacetophenone, methyl
anthranilate, methyl benzoate, methyl cinnamate, methyl heptine carbonate, methyl naph-

thyl ketone, methyl salicylate, mint essential oil, neroli essential oil, nerolin, neryl isobutyrate, orris butter, phenethyl alcohol, rose, rum ether, γ-undecalactone, vanillin, and solvent.

Although flavors usually arise from a mixture of many different volatile chemicals, often a single compound supplies the dominant aroma. Smelled alone, that chemical provides an unmistakable sense of the food. Ethyl-2-methyl butyrate, for example, smells just like an apple. Many of today's highly processed foods offer a blank palette: whatever chemicals are added to them will give them specific tastes. Adding methyl-2-pyridyl ketone makes something taste like popcorn. Adding ethyl-3-hydroxy butanoate makes it taste like marshmallow. The possibilities are now almost limitless. Without affecting appearance or nutritional value, processed foods could be made with aroma chemicals such as hexanal (the smell of freshly cut grass) or 3-methyl butanoic acid (the smell of body odor).

The 1960s were the heyday of artificial flavors in the United States. The synthetic versions of flavor compounds were not subtle, but they did not have to be, given the nature of most processed food. For the past twenty years food processors have tried hard to use only "natural flavors" in their products. According to the FDA, these must be derived entirely from natural sources—from herbs, spices, fruits, vegetables, beef, chicken, yeast, bark, roots, and so forth. Consumers prefer to see natural flavors on a label, out of a belief that they are more healthful. Distinctions between artificial and natural flavors can be arbitrary and somewhat absurd, based more on how the flavor has been made than on what it actually contains.

"A natural flavor," says Terry Acree, a professor of food science at Cornell University, "is a flavor that's been derived with an out-of-date technology." Natural flavors and artificial flavors sometimes contain exactly the same chemicals, produced through different methods. Amyl acetate, for example, provides the dominant note of banana flavor. When it is distilled from bananas with a solvent, amyl acetate is a natural flavor. When it is produced by mixing vinegar with amyl alcohol and adding sulfuric acid as a catalyst, amyl acetate is an artificial flavor. Either way it smells and tastes the same. "Natural flavor" is now listed among the ingredients of everything from Health Valley Blueberry Granola Bars to Taco Bell Hot Taco Sauce.

A natural flavor is not necessarily more healthful or purer than an artificial one. When almond flavor—benzaldehyde—is derived from natural sources, such as peach and apricot pits, it contains traces of hydrogen cyanide, a deadly poison. Benzaldehyde derived by mixing oil of clove and amyl acetate does not contain any cyanide. Nevertheless, it is legally considered an artificial flavor and sells at a much lower price. Natural and artificial flavors are now manufactured at the same chemical plants, places that few people would associate with Mother Nature.

A Trained Nose and a Poetic Sensibility

The small and elite group of scientists who create most of the flavor in most of the food now consumed in the United States are called "flavorists." They draw on a number of disciplines in their work: biology, psychology, physiology, and organic chemistry. A flavorist is a chemist with a trained nose and a poetic sensibility. Flavors are created by blending scores of different chemicals in tiny amounts—a process governed by scientific principles but demanding a fair amount of art. In an age when delicate aromas and microwave ovens do not easily co-exist, the job of the flavorist is to conjure illusions about processed food and, in the words of one flavor company's literature, to ensure "consumer likeability." The flavorists with whom I spoke were discreet, in keeping with the dictates of their trade. They were also charming, cosmopolitan, and ironic. They not only enjoyed fine wine but could identify the chemicals that give each grape its unique aroma. One flavorist compared his work to composing music. A well-made flavor compound will have a "top note" that is often followed by a "dry-down" and a "leveling-off," with different chemicals responsible for each stage. The taste of a food can be radically altered by minute changes in the flavoring combination. "A little odor goes a long way," one flavorist told me.

In order to give a processed food a taste that consumers will find appealing, a flavorist must always consider the food's "mouthfeel"—the unique combination of textures and chemical interactions that affect how the flavor is perceived. Mouthfeel can be adjusted through the use of various fats, gums, starches, emulsifiers, and stabilizers. The aroma chemicals in a food can be precisely analyzed, but the elements that make up mouthfeel are much harder to measure. How does one quantify a pretzel's hardness, a french fry's crispness? Food technologists are now conducting basic research in rheology, the branch of physics that examines the flow and deformation of materials. A number of companies sell sophisticated devices that attempt to measure mouthfeel. The TA.XT2i Texture Analyzer, produced by the Texture Technologies Corporation, of Scarsdale, New York, performs calculations based on data derived from as many as 250 separate probes. It is essentially a mechanical mouth. It gauges the most-important rheological properties of a food—bounce, creep, breaking point, density, crunchiness, chewiness, gumminess, lumpiness, rubberiness, springiness, slipperiness, smoothness, softness, wetness, juiciness, spreadability, springback, and tackiness.

Some of the most important advances in flavor manufacturing are now occurring in the field of biotechnology. Complex flavors are being made using enzyme reactions, fermentation, and fungal and tissue cultures. All the flavors created by these methods—including the ones being synthesized by fungi—are considered natural flavors by the FDA. The new enzyme-based processes are responsible for extremely true-to-life dairy flavors. One company now offers not just butter flavor but also fresh creamy butter, cheesy butter, milky butter, savory melted butter, and super-concentrated butter flavor, in liquid or powder form. The development of new fermentation techniques, along with new techniques for heating mixtures of sugar and amino acids, have led to the creation of much more realistic meat flavors.

The McDonald's Corporation most likely drew on these advances when it eliminated beef tallow from its french fries. The company will not reveal the exact origin of the natural flavor added to its fries. In response to inquiries from *Vegetarian Journal*, however, McDonald's did acknowledge that its fries derive some of their characteristic flavor from "an animal source." Beef is the probable source, although other meats cannot be ruled out. In France, for example, fries are sometimes cooked in duck fat or horse tallow.

Other popular fast foods derive their flavor from unexpected ingredients. McDonald's Chicken McNuggets contain beef extracts, as does Wendy's Grilled Chicken Sandwich. Burger King's BK Broiler Chicken Breast Patty contains "natural smoke flavor." A firm called Red Arrow Products specializes in smoke flavor, which is added to barbecue sauces, snack foods, and processed meats. Red Arrow manufactures natural smoke flavor by charring sawdust and capturing the aroma chemicals released into the air. The smoke is captured in water and then bottled, so that other companies can sell food that seems to have been cooked over a fire.

The Vegetarian Legal Action Network recently petitioned the FDA to issue new labeling requirements for foods that contain natural flavors. The group wants food processors to list the basic origins of their flavors on their labels. At the moment vegetarians often have no way of knowing whether a flavor additive contains beef, pork, poultry, or shellfish. One of the most widely used color additives—whose presence is often hidden by the phrase "color added"—violates a number of religious dietary restrictions, may cause allergic reactions in susceptible people, and comes from an unusual source. Cochineal extract (also known as carmine or carminic acid) is made from the desiccated bodies of female *Dactylopius coccus Costa*, a small insect harvested mainly in Peru and the Canary Islands. The bug feeds on red cactus berries, and color from the berries accumulates in the females and their unhatched larvae. The insects are collected, dried, and ground into a pigment. It takes about 70,000 of them to produce a pound of carmine, which is used to make processed foods look pink, red, or purple. Dannon strawberry yogurt gets its color from carmine, and so do many frozen fruit bars, candies, and fruit fillings, and Ocean Spray pink-grapefruit juice drink.

In a meeting room at IFF, Brian Grainger let me sample some of the company's flavors. It was an unusual taste test—there was no food to taste. Grainger is a senior flavorist at IFF, a soft-spoken chemist with graying hair, an English accent, and a fondness for understatement. He could easily be mistaken for a British diplomat or the owner of a West End brasserie with two Michelin stars. Like many in the flavor industry, he has an Old World, old-fashioned sensibility. When I suggested that IFF's policy of secrecy and discretion was out of step with our mass-marketing, brand-conscious, self-promoting age, and that the company should put its own logo on the countless products that bear its flavors, instead of allowing other companies to enjoy the consumer loyalty and affection inspired by those flavors, Grainger politely disagreed, assuring me that such a thing would never be done. In the absence of public credit or acclaim, the small and secretive fraternity of flavor chemists praise one another's work. By analyzing the flavor formula of a product, Grainger can often tell which of his counterparts at a rival firm devised it. Whenever he walks down a supermarket aisle, he takes a quiet pleasure in seeing the well-known foods that contain his flavors.

Grainger had brought a dozen small glass bottles from the lab. After he opened each bottle, I dipped a fragrance-testing filter into it—a long white strip of paper designed to absorb aroma chemicals without producing off notes. Before placing each strip of paper in front of my nose, I closed my eyes. Then I inhaled deeply, and one food after another was conjured from the glass bottles. I smelled fresh cherries, black olives, sautéed onions, and shrimp. Grainger's most remarkable creation took me by surprise. After closing my eyes, I suddenly smelled a grilled hamburger. The aroma was uncanny, almost miraculous—as if someone in the room were flipping burgers on a hot grill. But when I opened my eyes, I saw just a narrow strip of white paper and a flavorist with a grin.

 For Discussion:

1. How many foods do you eat that contain no artificial additives?
2. What is one of your favorite childhood foods? Do you still like that food today?
3. Can you think of any smells or flavors that trigger your memories?
4. Schlosser argues that, by manipulating the connection between childhood memories and adult food preferences, McDonald's "Happy Meals" actually keep people coming back to the restaurant as adults. Do you agree with this argument? If true, is this an ethical business practice?
5. Should food manufacturers be required to place the origins of so called "natural flavors" on product labels?

 For Fact-Finding, Research, and Writing:

1. Schlosser mentions that Japanese researchers discovered the taste, "umami." Through library databases, find recent articles discussing "umami" and explain how food companies take advantage of this taste in their products.
2. According to the article, many of the developments in the flavor industry are reported in the following publications: *Chemical Market Reporter*, *Food Chemical News*, *Food Engineering*, and *Food Product Design*. How many of these publications can you access from our library?
3. Using our library's resources answer these questions. Who were the first people to use the insect, cochineal (*Dactylopius coccus costa*) as a food additive? How is this insect harvested? List three recently published journal articles and/or books that discuss the use of this insect in food.
4. In this 2001 article, Schlosser mentions that the Vegetarian Legal Action Network asked the FDA to change its labeling requirements for companies that use "natural flavors." Find out how this issue was resolved.

CHAPTER THREE

Who Creates Culture?

Introduction

The last decades have brought remarkable technological and scientific advancements. We landed robots on Mars and sent probes into the nucleus of a comet, thus expanding our knowledge far beyond the borders of our planet. The Internet has revolutionized the way we communicate and receive information and connected people of all nations so that they can exchange information, ideas, and plans.

The history of technology is intertwined with culture and informs its development. The mission of this chapter is to explore the increasing connection between culture and technology, particularly as it affects issues of gender, education, language, and politics. Does our way of learning and thinking through technology isolate people, or does it provide for greater interaction among individuals and across cultures? How does technology contribute to our sense of identity (or lack of it)? Are we truly an educated nation, or have we become unable to truly think about the information with which we are bombarded? The texts in this section explore these important questions and confront the world's love affair with its evolving technologies and their effects on culture, as well as its fear of them.

Thomas de Zengotita "The Numbing of the American Mind: Culture as Anesthetic"

Thomas de Zengotita is a faculty member of New York University and holds a Ph.D. in anthropology from Columbia University. In recent years, he emerged as one of the most insightful and ambitious essayist of *Harper's Magazine*. de Zengotita's most recent book, *Mediated: How the Media Shapes Your World and the Way You Live in It*, discusses ways in which media affects our culture, our lives, and our choices.

 Before You Read:

Can our technological and information-saturated world numb our thoughts and feelings?

The Numbing of the American Mind: Culture as Anesthetic

Thomas de Zengotita

. . . the massive influx of impressions is so great; surprising, barbaric, and violent things press so overpoweringly—"balled up into hideous clumps"—in the youthful soul; that it can save itself only by taking recourse in premeditated stupidity.

—Friedrich Nietzsche

It was to have been the end of irony, remember? Superficial celebrity culture was over; a new age of seriousness was upon us. Of course, the way media celebrities focused on their own mood as the consequence of September 11 was in itself an irony so marvelous you knew immediately how wrong they were. And sure enough, the spotlight never wavered. It went on shining as it always had, on those it was meant for—on them. A guarantee of continuing superficiality right there, quite apart from unintended irony.

So we shared Dan Rather's pain, marveled at intrepid Ashleigh Banfield, scrutinizing those ferocious tribal fighters through her designer specs, and Tom Brokaw, arbiter of greatness among generations, took us on a tour of the real West Wing. But these iconic moments swam into focus only momentarily, soon to be swept away in a deluge of references, references so numerous, so relentlessly repeated, that they came at last to constitute a solid field, a new backdrop for all our public performances. How often did you hear, how often did you say, "Since the events of 9/11"? A new idiom had been deposited in the language, approaching the same plane of habituality as "by the way" or "on the other hand." And in the process we got past it after all. Six months or so was all it took. The holidays came and went, and—if you were not personally stricken by the terror of September—chances are you got over it. You moved on.

How is that possible?

Nietzsche was not thinking I.Q. or ignorance when he used the word "stupidity." He meant stupidity as in clogged, anesthetized. Numb. He thought people at the end of the *nineteenth* century were suffocating in a vast goo of meaningless stimulation. Ever notice how, when your hand is numb, everything feels thin? Even a solid block of wood lacks depth and texture. You can't feel the wood; your limb just encounters the interrupting surface. Well, numb is to the soul as thin is to a mediated world. Our guiding metaphor. And it isn't just youthful souls either.

Here's the basic situation. On the one hand: the Web, satellite cable TV, PalmPilot, DVD, Ethernet—Virtual Environments everywhere. On the other hand: cloning, genetic engineering, artificial intelligence, robotics—Virtual Beings everywhere. Someday, when people (or whatever they are) look back on our time, all this will appear as a single development, called something like "The Information Revolution," and the lesson of that revolution will have been this: what counts is the code. Silicon- or carbon-based. Artifact or animate. The difference between them is disappearing. This is not science fiction. This is really happening. Right now, in an Atlanta hospital, there is a quadriplegic with his brain directly wired to a computer. He can move the cursor with his thoughts.

The moving cursor doesn't really need explaining—it comes down to digital bytes and neurochemical spikes. What needs explaining is our equanimity in the face of staggering developments. How can we go about our business when things like this are happening? How can we just read the article, shake our heads, turn the page? If creatures from outer space sent a diplomatic mission to the U.N., how long would it be before we were taking that in stride? Before Comedy Central send-ups were more entertaining than the actual creatures? About six months?

Soap-opera politics. The therapy industry. Online communities. Digital effects. Workshops for every workplace. Viagra, Prozac, Ritalin. Reality TV. Complete makeovers. Someday, it will be obvious that all the content on our information platforms converges on this theme: there is no important difference between fabrication and reality, between a chemical a pill introduces and one your body produces, between role-playing in marital therapy and playing your role as a spouse, between selling and making, campaigning and governing, expressing and existing. And that is why we moved on after September 11, after an event that seemed so enormous, so horrific, so stark, that even the great blob of virtuality that is our public culture would be unable to absorb it. But it could. It has. Here's how.

Fabrication

Some people refuse to believe that reality has become indistinguishable from fabrication. But beliefs are crude reflections of the psychological processes that actually determine how we function. Fat people believe they are on the stocky side. Abject drunks believe they are poetical free spirits. Malicious prudes believe they are selfless do-gooders. And a lot of people still believe that, with some obvious exceptions involving hoaxes and errors, we know what's real and what's not. We can tell the difference between the *Kursk* and the *Titanic* (meaning the movie, of course), for example.

And maybe we can—when specifically focused on the issue. It might take a while, of course, because there *are* so many gradations when you stop to think about it. For example:

- Real real: You fall down the stairs. Stuff in your life that's so familiar you've forgotten the statement it makes.
- Observed real: You drive by a car wreck. Stuff in your life in which the image-statement is as salient as the function.
- Between real real and observed real: Stuff that oscillates between the first two categories. Like you're wearing something you usually take for granted but then you meet someone attractive.
- Edited real real: Shtick you have down so pat you don't know it's shtick anymore, but you definitely only use it in certain situations. Documentaries and videos in which people are unaware of the camera, though that's not easy to detect, actually. Candid photographs.
- Edited observed real: Other people's down-pat shtick. Shtick you are still working on. Documentaries in which people are accommodating the camera, which is actually a lot of the time, probably.
- Staged real: Formal events like weddings. Retail-clerk patter.
- Edited staged real: Pictures of the above. Homemade porn.
- Staged observed real unique: Al kisses Tipper. *Survivor*.
- Staged observed real repeated: Al kisses Tipper again and again. Anchor-desk and talkshow intros and segues. Weather Channel behavior.

(In the interests of time, we can skip the subtler middle range of distinctions and go to the other end of the spectrum:)

- Staged realistic: *The English Patient* and *NYPD Blue*.
- Staged hyperreal: Oliver Stone movies and *Malcolm in the Middle*.
- Overtly unreal realistic: S.U.V.'s climbing buildings. Digitized special effects in general, except when they are more or less undetectable.
- Covertly unreal realistic: Hair in shampoo ads. More or less undetectable digital effects, of which there are more every day.
- Between overtly and covertly unreal realistic: John Wayne in a beer ad (you have to know he's dead to know he isn't "really" in the ad).
- Real unreal: Robo-pets.
- Unreal real: Strawberries that won't freeze because they have fish genes in them.

See? No problem. The differences are perfectly clear.

But the issue isn't *can* we do it; it's *do* we do it—and the answer is, of course not. Our minds are the product of total immersion in a daily experience saturated with fabrications to a degree unprecedented in human history. People have never had to cope with so much stuff, so many choices. In kind and number.

Flood

And sheer quantity really matters, because here we collide with a real limit, one of the few that remain—namely, how much a person can register at a given instant. No innovation in techno-access or sensationalism can overcome this bottleneck. It determines the fundamental dynamic, the battle to secure attention, in every domain of our lives.

Compare, say, the cereal and juice sections of a supermarket today with those of years ago. For you youngsters out there, take it from Dad: it used to be Wheaties, Corn Flakes, Cheerios (oats), Rice Krispies—and that was about it. One for each grain, see? Same for fruit juice. But now? Pineapple/Banana/Grape or Strawberry/Orange/Kiwi anyone? And that's just a sample from Tropicana—check out Nantucket Nectars. Makes of cars? Types of sunglasses? Sneaker species? Pasta possibilities? On and on. It's all about options, as they say.

Umbrella brands toss off diverse and evolving lines of market-researched products for niches of self-inventing customers with continual access to every representational fabrication ever produced in the whole of human history. That's "the environment." You like Vedic ankle tattoos? 1930s cockney caps? Safari jackets? Inca ponchos? Victorian lace-up high-heel booties? Whatever.

No wonder that word caught on.

The moreness of everything ascends inevitably to a threshold in psychic life. A change of state takes place. The discrete display melts into a pudding, and the mind is forced to certain adaptations if it is to cohere at all.

When you find out about the moving cursor, or hear statistics about AIDS in Africa, or see your 947th picture of a weeping fireman, you can't help but become fundamentally indifferent because you are exposed to things like this all the time, just as you are to the rest of your options. Over breakfast. In the waiting room. Driving to work. At the checkout counter. *All the time.* I know you know this already. I'm just reminding you.

Which is not to say you aren't moved. On the contrary, you are moved, often deeply, very frequently—never more so, perhaps, than when you saw the footage of the towers coming down on 9/11. But you are so used to being moved by footage, by stories, by representations of all kinds—that's the point. It's not your fault that you are so used to being moved, you just are.

So it's not surprising that you have learned to move on so readily to the next, sometimes moving, moment. It's sink or surf. Spiritual numbness guarantees that your relations with the moving will pass. And the stuffed screen accommodates you with moving surfaces that assume you are numb enough to accommodate them. And so on, back and forth. The dialectic of postmodern life.

One might say, "Well, people didn't respond deeply to every development in the world 200 years ago either." And that's true, but it isn't an objection, it's a confirmation. Until the new media came along, people didn't even *know* about such developments, or not as quickly, and above all not as dramatically or frequently. Also, there weren't as many developments, period. This is crucial, another aspect of sheer moreness that gets overlooked. *Less was happening.*

The contrast is stark with, say, the Middle Ages. By the industrial era, a lot more was happening, and numbness became an issue then. Think of Baudelaire, adrift in the crowd, celebrating the artist for resisting numbness, for maintaining vulnerability—thus setting the standard for the genius of modernism. But a qualitative threshold has since been breached. Cities no longer belong to the soulful *flâneur* but to the wired-up voyeur in his sound-proofed Lexus. Behind his tinted windows, with his cell phone and CD player, he gets more input, with less static, from more and different channels, than Baudelaire ever dreamed of. But it's all insulational—as if the deities at Dreamworks were invisibly at work around us, touching up the canvas of reality with existential airbrushes. Everything has that edgeless quality, like the lobby of a high-end Marriott/Ramada/Sheraton. Whole neighborhoods feel like that now. And you can be sure that whatever they do at "the site" will feel like that, too. Even if they specifically set out to avoid having it feel like that—it will still feel like that. They can't control themselves. They can't stop.

Take the new Times Square, everybody's icon for this process. All the usual observations apply—and each contributes its iota to muffling what it meant to expose. But the point here is the way everything in that place is *aimed*. Everything is firing message modules, straight for your gonads, your taste buds, your vanities, your fears. These modules seek to penetrate, but in a passing way. A second of your attention is all they ask. Nothing is firing that rends or cuts. It's a massage, really, if you just go with it. And why not? Some of the most talented people on the planet have devoted their lives to creating this psychic sauna, just for you.

And it's not just the screens and billboards, the literal signs; it's absolutely everything you encounter. Except for the eyes of the people, shuffling along, and the poignant imperfections of their bodies; they are so manifestly unequal to the solicitations lavished upon them. No wonder they stuff themselves with junk—or, trying to live up to it all, enslave themselves to regimes of improvement.

Yes, there were ersatz environments and glitzy ads back in the fifties, but this is a new order of quality and saturation. Saying that it's just more of what we had before is like saying a hurricane is just more breeze. For here, too, there is a psychological threshold. Today, your brain is, as a matter of brute fact, full of stuff that was *designed* to affect you. As opposed to the scattered furniture of nature and history that people once registered just because it happened to be there. September 11 had to accommodate the fact that our inner lives are now largely constituted by effects.

To get relief, you have to stumble into the Greyhound bus station in Albany, or some old side-street barbershop that time forgot, into someplace not yet subjected to the renovating ministrations of the International Red Brick and Iron Filigree Restoration Corporation. And "stumble" is the key concept here. Accidental places are the only real places left.

That's why a couple of weeks out in Nature doesn't make it anymore. Even if you eschew the resonant clutter of The Tour and The Gear, you will virtualize everything you encounter anyway, all by yourself. You won't see wolves, you'll see "wolves." You'll be murmuring to yourself, at some level, "Wow, look, a real wolf, not in a cage, not on TV, I can't believe it."

That's right, you can't. Natural things have become their own icons.

And you will get restless really fast if that "wolf" doesn't do anything. The kids will start squirming in, like, five minutes; you'll probably need to pretend you're not getting bored for a while longer. But if that little smudge of canine out there in the distance continues to just loll around in the tall grass, and you don't have a really powerful tripod-supported telelens gizmo to play with, you will get bored. You will begin to appreciate how much technology and editing goes into making those nature shows. The truth is that if some no-account chipmunk just happens to come around your campsite every morning for crumbs from your picnic table, it will have meant more to you than any "wolf."

Precious accidents.

Back to the new Times Square—do you parse out the real from the fabricated in that mélange? Not *can* you, but *do* you. The Fox screen is showing Elián in his Cuban school uniform on the side of a building—real or not? Some glorious babe in her underwear is sprawled across 35 percent of your visual field. She's looking you right in the eye. You feel that old feeling—real or not? A fabulous man, sculpted to perfection by more time in the health club than most parents have for their kids, is gliding by on Day-Glo Rollerblades eight inches high. He's wearing Tex-tex gear so tight it looks like it's under his skin, and the logos festooning his figure emit meaning-beeps from every angle—real or not? What about the pumped-up biceps? If he uses steroids? But, once again, the issue isn't what you *can* do when I call your attention to it. The real issue is *do* you do it as a matter of routine processing? Or do you rely instead on a general immunity that only numbness can provide, an immunity that puts the whole flood in brackets and transforms it all into a play of surfaces—over which you hover and glide like a little god, dipping in here and there for the moving experience of your choice, with the ultimate reaches of your soul on permanent remote?

Finitude

What about that feeling that it's all been done? Not in the techie department, of course; there, the possibility of novelty seems to be unlimited. But in those areas occupied by what platform proprietors call "content providers." What a phrase! Could anything register devastation of the spirit more completely than that little generic? Could meaning suffer more complete evacuation? Not since we landed on the moon and found nothing has our cultural unconscious encountered so traumatic a void.

Maybe the postmodern taste for recycling and pastiche is more than a phase? Maybe it's necessity. Maybe more or less everything that can be done in the plastic arts, say, has been done? How many different ways can a finite set of shapes and colors be arranged in a finite space? We aren't talking infinitely divisible Platonic geometry here. Maybe there just isn't any really new way to put *x* shapes and *y* colors into *z* permutations. Maybe some day it will be obvious that the characteristic gestures of twentieth-century art were flailing against this fact. Cézanne's planes, Magritte's pipe, Pollock's swirls, Warhol's soup can, Christo's draperies, Serrano's piss, the "installations"—so many desperate efforts to elude the end of originality?

Likewise with music? How many distinguishable sounds can be put in how many patterns? There has to be some limit. After you've integrated techno and Brazilian-Afro and Tibetan monko and Hump-backed Whalo, at some point, surely there's going to be nothing left but play it again, Sam. Maybe that's why it's the age of the mix. And characters and plots, in stories and shows? What's the raw material? Sex, outlaws, illness, death, master villains, guilt, the fall of giants, fate, just deserts, the dark side, redemption by the little things, a few other themes—we all know the repertoire. Maybe it's just impossible to think of anything that couldn't be described, after the fashion of all contemporary pitches, as "It's *To the Lighthouse* meets *Married with Children*" or "It's Hannibal Lecter meets Peter Pan."

The prospect of finitude helps to account for the turn to sensation, as if intensity of presentation could make up for repetition. Of course, sensation is also a response to sheer clutter on the screen, a way to grab the most possible attention in the least amount of time. But that clutter also accounts for why everything's already been done, and so it cycles on relentlessly—fill the pages, fill the time slots, fill the channels, the websites, the roadsides, the building facades, the fronts and backs of shirts and caps, everything, everything must be saying something, every minute. But what? What's left to say? It doesn't matter. Cut to the response.

Zap. Whimper. Flinch. Cringe. Melt. Assert! Exult! Weep. Subside. Ahhh . . .

Eventually we can just wire our glands directly to a console of sensation buttons, platform to platform, and be done with this tiresome content altogether. Call it P2P communication. Talk about interactive. Thus will the human soul be compensated for the despair of finitude.

Fast

Remember that T-shirt from the eighties that said "High on Stress"? It was sort of true and sort of a way to bluff it out and sort of a protest—it had that "any number of meanings" quality we now prefer to depth. That's because the any-number-of-meanings quality keeps you in motion, but depth asks you to stop. Depth is to your life what dead air is to a talk show.

Being numb isn't antithetical to being totally stressed, 24-7—and asking for more. Over-scheduled busyness might seem like the opposite of numbness, but it is just the active aspect of living in a flood of fabricated surfaces. Consider the guiding metaphor again. The (absence of) sensation that is physical numbness is constituted by a multitude of thrills and tingles at a frequency beyond which you feel nothing. The numbness of busyness works on the same principle, but it relies upon its agents to abide by an agreement they must keep secret, even from themselves. The agreement is this: we will so conduct ourselves that everything becomes an emergency.

Under that agreement, stress is how reality feels. People addicted to busyness, people who don't just use their cell phones in public but display in every nuance of cell-phone deportment their sense of throbbing connectedness to Something Important—these people would suffocate like fish on a dock if they were cut off from the Flow of Events they have conspired with their fellows to create. To these plugged-in players, the rest of us look like zombies, coasting on fumes. For them, the feeling of being busy *is* the feeling of being alive.

Partly, it's a function of speed, like in those stress dramas that television provides to keep us virtually busy, even in our downtime. The bloody body wheeled into the ER, every personjack on the team yelling numbers from monitors, screaming for meds and equipment, especially for those heart-shocker pads—that's the paradigm scene. All the others derive from it: hostage-negotiator scenes, staffers pulling all-nighters in the West Wing, detectives sweeping out of the precinct, donning jackets, adjusting holsters, snapping wisecracks. Sheer speed and Lives on the Line. That's the recipe for feeling real.

The irony is that *after* we have worked really hard on something urgent for a long time, we do escape numbness for a while—stepping out of the building, noticing the breeze, the cracks in the sidewalk, the stillness of things in the shop window. During those accidental and transitional moments, we actually get the feeling of the real we were so frantically pursuing when we were busy. But we soon get restless. We can't take the input reduction. Our psychic metabolism craves more.

Actually, stress dramas are about the lives of the media people who make them. They purport to be about hospitals or law firms, but they are actually about what it is like to make TV shows, about high-stakes teamwork in the land of celebrity, where, by definition, everything matters more than it does anywhere else, a land that welcomes diversity and foibles as long as The Job Gets Done, a land where everything personal, unconditional, intimate—everything unbounded by the task—takes place on the side. That's why, in these shows through which the celebrated teach the rest of us how to be like them, the moments of heart-felt encounter that make it all worthwhile are stolen in the corridors of power, while the verdict is awaited. If we get that real-folks-rushing-to-get-out-of-the-house-in-the-morning scene, it's just to underscore the priority of the Flow of Events that protects the busy from being left alone in the stillness with what makes it all worthwhile. Lest direction be lost, motion must be maintained.

Moving On

So life in a flood of surfaces means a life of perpetual motion, and TV provides the model in other modes as well. Take the transitions from story to story in newscasts, that finishing-with-a-topic moment. "Whether these supplies, still piling up after weeks of intense effort by these humanitarian workers, will actually reach the victims (pause) remains to be seen." A hint of a sigh, a slight shake of the head, eyes down-turning; the note of seasoned resignation. Profound respect is conveyed for the abandoned topic even as a note of anticipation rises to greet the (also interesting, but less burdensome) next topic—and the new camera angle at the anchor desk makes it clear that stern and external necessity, rather than any human agency, governs the shift from two minutes on mass starvation to the next episode of The Fall of the House of Enron.

Judy Woodruff is especially good at this, her particular little head nod, or shake, as the case may be, and the way her lips tighten up a tad. "If it were up to me as a human being I would *never* leave this coverage of thousands of dying innocents, but, as a newscaster, of course, I have to." And her speaking voice says, "All right, Jim, we have to go to a break now, but we will be following this story as it develops—and thanks again." "Thank you, Judy," says Jim, echoing her gesture, and we understand that he, too, as a human being, would never allow us to move on from so ghastly and demanding a reality, but it isn't up to him as a human being either. It isn't up to anybody, actually. That's the one real reality. Moving on.

It would be irrelevant to object by asking, "Well, how else are we supposed to do it?" There isn't any other way to do it. That's the point. This isn't a consultant's memo. This is a serious diagnosis of a serious condition. Would we rather not know about it because it happens to be incurable? This goes much deeper than subject matter, or political bias, the usual fodder. It determines the way we frame everything. Like all that is most profound in human custom, this agreement is almost physical, an attunement, more music than semantics. It instills and expresses, moment by moment, the *attitude* we bring to living in this world of surfaces.

So, for example, you don't have to wait for the anchorperson to change the topic. You can change it yourself, and you don't have to sigh or tighten your lips as you make the transition. But you do. Monitor yourself next time you zap away from some disturbing something on *Lehrer* to catch the action on the *Law & Order* reruns. You mime those little gestures as you punch the buttons. These are the constituting habit structures of our culture.

And we've touched already on what awaits you when you join the gang on *Law & Order*. The stress drama re-creating, more elaborately, the basic gesture of the news show, the one you just performed when you slid away from those refugee visuals. Everything's in motion, elliptical, glancing, fungible. You see the sides of faces, the slope of shoulders, the beginnings of expressions but not the ends, the ends of expressions but not the beginnings. No matter the horror, no matter the injustice, no matter how passionate McCoy may feel, no matter how angry Bratt gets at Briscoe (actors or characters?), no matter how obnoxious the defense attorney or impatient the judge (especially in chambers), they all keep moving. And the camera keeps moving, too, gliding, peeking, glimpsing. Frightened witnesses, incoming lawyers, outgoing suspects, they're all moving—as is the traffic, the doors, hands, phones, everything. Meaningful personal encounters are bound to be interrupted, and the performers, like would-be fighters in a bar relying on friends to keep them apart, anticipate the interruption. Ferociously or tenderly, they emote in transitional interlude, awaiting inevitable rescue by events, and, gratefully regretting the passing of the moment of communion, they watch the D.A. step into the elevator and deliver the homily as the door slides shut across his grizzled visage, a homily that is never merely upbeat or despairing, never final or conclusive in any way. Because the one thing people in a TV series know is that tomorrow is another show, and they will be ready to roll. For they are pros, and pros know how to deal. It's not that they're indifferent or cynical. They care. Sometimes they win, sometimes they lose—but, either way, they move on. That's the lesson, the ultimate homily of all shows. The way we live now.

So, if we were spared a gaping wound in the flesh and blood of personal life, we inevitably moved on after September 11. We were carried off by endlessly proliferating representations of the event, and by an ever expanding horizon of associated stories and characters, and all of them, in their turn, represented endlessly, and the whole sweep of it driven by the rhythms of The Show—anthrax, postal workers, the Bronx lady, the Saddam connection, Osama tapes, Al Jazeera's commentary on Osama tapes, Christiane Amanpour's commentary on Al Jazeera's commentary on Osama tapes, a magazine story about Christiane Amanpour . . .

And that's just one thread in this tapestry of virtuality. The whole is so densely woven and finely stranded that no mind could possibly comprehend it, escape it, govern it. It's the dreamwork of culture. It just proceeds and we with it, each of us exposed to thousands, probably millions of 9/11-related representations—everything from the layout of the daily paper to rippling-flag logos to NYPD caps on tourists to ads for *Collateral Damage*. Conditioned thus relentlessly to move from representation to representation, we got past the thing itself as well; or rather, the thing itself was transformed into a sea of signs and upon it we were borne away from every shore, moving on, moving on.

What else could we do?

 For Discussion:

1. What evidence does de Zengotita offer to support his statement that "there is no important difference between fabrication and reality"?
2. Why do some people refuse to realize that reality is fabricated?
3. Do you agree with de Zengotita when he contends that we got over the events of 9/11 easily?
4. de Zengotita uses headlines such as "Fabrication," "Flood," "Finitude," "Fast," and "Moving On" to describe a condition of contemporary life. To what do these headlines refer specifically and how do they affect the numbing of our minds?

 For Fact-Finding, Research, and Writing:

1. Consult two journal articles and one book to define the term "pastiche" as it is used in contemporary analyses of culture or art.
2. de Zengotita opens his essay with a quote by Friedrich Nietzsche. Who is Nietzsche, what are his main works, and what ideas is he best known for?
3. Locate a book and a journal article on the idea of reality as fabrication. In what ways do the arguments of these works differ from those of de Zengotita?

Alleen Pace Nilsen, "Sexism in English: A 1990s Update"

Alleen Pace Nilsen is Professor of English Education at the University of Iowa. In the late 1960s, she and her family lived in Kabul, Afghanistan, where she became acutely aware of how sexism affects a society. In 1977, Nilsen published *Sexism and Language*, a pioneering study of sexism in everyday American speech and writing. The following article updates her findings.

 Before You Read:

What do you consider sexist language? Why is it important or unimportant to consider sexism in language?

"Sexism in English: A 1990s Update"

Alleen Pace Nilsen

Twenty years ago I embarked on a study of the sexism inherent in American English. I had just returned to Ann Arbor, Michigan, after living for two years (1967–69) in Kabul, Afghanistan, where I had begun to look critically at the role society assigned to women. The Afghan version of the *chaderi* prescribed for Moslem women was particularly confining. Afghan jokes and folklore were blatantly sexist, such as this proverb: "If you see an old man, sit down and take a lesson; if you see an old woman, throw a stone."

But it wasn't only the native culture that made me question women's roles, it was also the American community.

Most of the American women were like myself—wives and mothers whose husbands were either career diplomats, employees of USAID, or college professors who had been recruited to work on various contract teams. We were suddenly bereft of our traditional roles: some of us became alcoholics, others got very good at bridge, while still others searched desperately for ways to contribute either to our families or to the Afghans. The local economy provided few jobs for women and certainly none for foreigners; we were isolated from former friends and the social goals we had grown up with.

When I returned in the fall of 1969 to the University of Michigan in Ann Arbor, I was surprised to find that many other women were also questioning the expectations they had grown up with. In the spring of 1970, a women's conference was announced. I hired a babysitter and attended, but I returned home more troubled than ever. The militancy of these women frightened me. Since I wasn't ready for a revolution, I decided I would have my own feminist movement. I would study the English language and see what it could tell me about sexism. I started reading a desk dictionary and making notecards on every entry that seemed to tell something about male and female. I soon had a dog-eared dictionary, along with a collection of notecards filling two shoe boxes.

Ironically, I started reading the dictionary because I wanted to avoid getting involved in social issues, but what happened was that my notecards brought me right back to looking at society. Language and society are as intertwined as a chicken and an egg. The language a culture uses is telltale evidence of the values and beliefs of that culture. And because there is a lag in how fast a language changes—new words can easily be introduced, but it takes a long time for old words and usages to disappear—a careful look at English will reveal the attitudes that our ancestors held and that we as a culture are therefore predisposed to hold. My notecards revealed three major points. Friends have offered the opinion that I didn't need to read the dictionary to learn such obvious facts. Nevertheless, it was interesting to have linguistic evidence of sociological observations.

Women Are Sexy; Men Are Successful

First, in American culture a woman is valued for the attractiveness and sexiness of her body, while a man is valued for his physical strength and accomplishments. A woman is sexy. A man is successful.

A persuasive piece of evidence supporting this view are the eponyms—words that have come from someone's name—found in English. I had a two-and-a-half-inch stack of cards taken from men's names but less than a half-inch stack from women's names, and most of those came from Greek mythology. In the words that came into American English since we separated from Britain, there are many eponyms based on the names of famous American men: *Bartlett pear, boysenberry, diesel engine, Franklin stove, Ferris wheel, Gatling gun, mason jar, sideburns, sousaphone, Schick test,* and *Winchester rifle.* The only common eponyms taken from American women's names are *Alice blue* (after Alice Roosevelt Longworth), *bloomers* (after Amelia Jenks Bloomer), and *Mae West jacket* (after the buxom actress). Two out of the three feminine eponyms relate closely to a woman's physical anatomy, while the masculine eponyms (except for *sideburns* after General Burnsides) have nothing to do with the namesake's body but, instead, honor the man for an accomplishment of some kind.

Although in Greek mythology women played a bigger role than they did in the biblical stories of the Judeo-Christian cultures and so the names of goddesses are accepted parts of the language in such place names as *Pomona* from the goddess of fruit and *Athens* from Athena and in such common words as *cereal* from Ceres, *psychology* from Psyche, and *arachnoid* from Arachne, the same tendency to think of women in relation to sexuality is seen in the eponyms *aphrodisiac* from Aphrodite, the Greek name for the goddess of love and beauty, and *venereal disease* from Venus, the Roman name for Aphrodite.

Another interesting word from Greek mythology is *Amazon*. According to Greek folk etymology, the *a* means "without" as in *atypical* or *amoral*, while *mazon* comes from *mazos* meaning "breast" as still seen in *mastectomy*. In the Greek legend, Amazon women cut off their right breasts so that they could better shoot their bows. Apparently, the storytellers had a feeling that for women to play the active, "masculine" role the Amazons adopted for themselves, they had to trade in part of their femininity.

This preoccupation with women's breasts is not limited to ancient stories. As a volunteer for the University of Wisconsin's *Dictionary of American Regional English (DARE)*, I read a western trapper's diary from the 1930s. I was to make notes of any unusual usages or language patterns. My most interesting finding was that the trapper referred to a range of mountains as *The Teats*, a metaphor based on the similarity between the shapes of mountains and women's breasts. Because today we use the French wording, *The Grand Tetons*, the metaphor isn't as obvious, but I wrote to mapmakers and found the following listings: *Nippletop* and *Little Nipple Top* near Mount Marcy in the Adirondacks; *Nipple Mountain* in Archuleta County, Colorado; *Nipple Peak* in Coke County, Texas; *Nipple Butte* in Pennington, South Dakota; *Squaw Peak* in Placer County, California (and many other locations); *Maiden's Peak* and *Squaw Tit* (they're the same mountain) in the Cascade Range in Oregon; *Mary's Nipple* near Salt Lake City, Utah; and *Jane Russell Peaks* near Stark, New Hampshire.

Except for the movie star Jane Russell, the women being referred to are anonymous— it's only a sexual part of their body that is mentioned. When topographical features are named after men, it's probably not going to be to draw attention to a sexual part of their bodies but instead to honor individuals for an accomplishment. For example, no one thinks of a part of the male body when hearing a reference to Pike's Peak, Colorado, or Jackson Hole, Wyoming.

Going back to what I learned from my dictionary cards, I was surprised to realize how many pairs of words we have in which the feminine word has acquired sexual connotations while the masculine word retains a serious businesslike aura. For example, a *callboy* is the person who calls actors when it is time for them to go on stage, but a *callgirl* is a prostitute. Compare *sir* and *madam*. *Sir* is a term of respect, while *madam* has acquired the specialized meaning of a brothel manager. Something similar has happened to *master* and *mistress*. Would you rather have a painting by an *old master* or an *old mistress?*

It's because the word *woman* had sexual connotations, as in "She's his woman," that people began avoiding its use, hence such terminology as *ladies' room, lady of the house,* and *girls' school* or *school for young ladies.* Feminists, who ask that people use the term *woman* rather than *girl* or *lady,* are rejecting the idea that *woman* is primarily a sexual term. They have been at least partially successful in that today *woman* is commonly used to communicate gender without intending implications about sexuality.

I found two hundred pairs of words with masculine and feminine forms, e.g., *heir-heiress, hero-heroine, steward-stewardess, usher-usherette.* In nearly all such pairs, the masculine word is considered the base, with some kind of feminine suffix being added. The masculine form is the one from which compounds are made, e.g., from *king-queen* comes *kingdom* but not *queendom*, from *sportsman-sportslady* comes *sportsmanship* but not *sportsladyship*. There is one—and only one—semantic area in which the masculine word is not the base or more powerful word. This is in the area dealing with sex and marriage. When someone refers to a *virgin*, a listener will probably think of a female, unless the speaker specifies *male* or uses a masculine pronoun. The same is true for *prostitute*.

In relation to marriage, there is much linguistic evidence showing that weddings are more important to women than to men. A woman cherishes the wedding and is considered a bride for a whole year, but a man is referred to as a groom only on the day of the wedding. The word *bride* appears in *bridal attendant*, *bridal gown*, *bridesmaid*, *bridal shower*, and even *bridegroom*. Groom comes from the Middle English *groom*, meaning "man," and in the sense is seldom used outside of the wedding. With most pairs of male/female words, people habitually put the masculine word first, *Mr. and Mrs.*, *his and hers*, *boys and girls*, *men and women*, *kings and queens*, *brothers and sisters*, *guys and dolls*, and *host and hostess*, but it is the *bride and groom* who are talked about, not the *groom and bride*.

The importance of marriage to a woman is also shown by the fact that when a marriage ends in death, the woman gets the title of *widow*. A man gets the derived title of *widower*. This term is not used in other phrases or contexts, but *widow* is seen in *widowhood*, *widow's peak*, and *widow's walk*. A *widow* in a card game is an extra hand of cards, while in typesetting it is an extra line of type.

How changing cultural ideas bring changes to language is clearly visible in this semantic area. The feminist movement has caused the differences between the sexes to be downplayed, and since I did my dictionary study two decades ago, the word *singles* has largely replaced such sex specific and value-laden terms as *bachelor*, *old maid*, *spinster*, *divorcee*, *widow*, and *widower*. And in 1970 I wrote that when a man is called *a professional* he is thought to be a doctor or a lawyer, but when people hear a woman referred to as *a professional* they are likely to think of a prostitute. That's not as true today because so many women have become doctors and lawyers that it's no longer incongruous to think of women in those professional roles.

Another change that has taken place is in wedding announcements. They used to be sent out from the bride's parents and did not even give the name of the groom's parents. Today, most couples choose to list either all or none of the parents' names. Also it is now much more likely that both the bride and groom's picture will be in the newspaper, while a decade ago only the bride's picture was published on the "Women's" or the "Society" page. Even the traditional wording of the wedding ceremony is being changed. Many officials now pronounce the couple "husband and wife" instead of the old "man and wife," and they ask the bride if she promises to "love, honor, and cherish," instead of "to love, honor, and obey."

Women Are Passive; Men Are Active

The wording of the wedding ceremony also relates to the second point that my cards showed, which is that women are expected to play a passive or weak role while men play an active or strong role. In the traditional ceremony, the official asks, "Who gives the bride away?" and the father answers, "I do." Some fathers answer, "Her mother and I do," but that doesn't solve the problem inherent in the question. The idea that a bride is something to be handed over from one man to another bothers people because it goes back to the days when a man's servants, his children, and his wife were all considered to be his property. They were known by his name because they belonged to him, and he was responsible for their actions and their debts.

The grammar used in talking or writing about weddings as well as other sexual relationships shows the expectation of men playing the active role. Men *wed* women while women *become* brides of men. A man *possesses* a woman; he *deflowers* her; he *performs*; he *scores*; he *takes away* her virginity. Although a woman can *seduce* a man, she cannot offer him her virginity. When talking about virginity, the only way to make the woman the actor in the sentence is to say that "She lost her virginity," but people lose things by accident rather than by purposeful actions, and so she's only the grammatical, not the real-life, actor.

The reason that women tried to bring the term Ms. into the language to replace Miss or Mrs. relates to this point. Married women resent being identified only under their husband's names. For example, when Susan Glascoe did something newsworthy, she would be identified in the newspaper only as Mrs. John Glascoe. The dictionary cards showed what appeared to be an attitude on the part of the editors that it was almost indecent to let a respectable woman's name march unaccompanied across the pages of a dictionary. Women were listed with male names whether or not the male contributed to the woman's reason for being in the dictionary or in his own right was as famous as the woman. For example, Charlotte Bronte was identified as Mrs. Arthur B. Nicholls, Amelia Earhart as Mrs. George Palmer Putnam, Helen Hayes as Mrs. Charles MacArthur, Jenny Lind as Mme. Otto Goldschmit, Cornelia Otis Skinner as the daughter of Otis, Harriet Beecher Stowe as the sister of Henry Ward Beecher, and Edith Sitwell as the sister of Osbert and Sacheverell. A very small number of women got into the dictionary without the benefit of a masculine escort. They were rebels and crusaders: temperance leaders Frances Elizabeth Caroline Willard and Carry Nation, women's rights leaders Carrie Chapman Catt and Elizabeth Cady Stanton, birth control educator Margaret Sanger, religious leader Mary Baker Eddy, and slaves Harriet Tubman and Phillis Wheatley.

Etiquette books used to teach that if a woman had Mrs. in front of her name, then the husband's name should follow because Mrs. is an abbreviated form of Mistress and a woman couldn't be a mistress of herself. As with many arguments about "correct" language usage, this isn't very logical because Miss is also an abbreviation of Mistress. Feminists hoped to simplify matters by introducing Ms. as an alternative to both Mrs. and Miss, but what happened is that Ms. largely replaced Miss, to become a catch-all business title for women. Many married women still prefer the title Mrs., and some resent being addressed with the term Ms. As one frustrated newspaper reporter complained, "Before I can write about a woman, I have to know not only her marital status but also her political philosophy." The result of such complications may contribute to the demise of titles, which are already being ignored by many computer programmers who find it more efficient to simply use names, for example in a business letter: "Dear Joan Garcia," instead of "Dear Mrs. Joan Garcia," "Dear Ms. Garcia," or "Dear Mrs. Louis Garcia."

The titles given to royalty provide an example of how males can be disadvantaged by the assumption that they are always to play the more powerful role. In British royalty, when a male holds a title, his wife is automatically given the feminine equivalent. But the reverse is not true. For example, a *count* is a high political officer with a *countess* being his wife. The same is true for a *duke* and a *duchess* and a *king* and a *queen*. But when a female holds the royal title, the man she marries does not automatically acquire the matching title. For example, Queen Elizabeth's husband has the title of *prince* rather than *king*, but if Prince Charles should become king while he is still married to Lady or Princess Diana, she will be known as the queen. The reasoning appears to be that since masculine words are stronger, they are reserved for true heirs and withheld from males coming into the royal family by marriage. If Prince Phillip were called *King Phillip*, it would be much easier for British subjects to forget where the true power lies.

The names that people give their children show the hopes and dreams they have for them, and when we look at the differences between male and female names in a culture, we can see the cumulative expectations of that culture. In our culture girls often have names taken from small, aesthetically pleasing items, e.g., *Ruby, Jewel,* and *Pearl, Esther* and *Stella* mean "star," *Ada* means "ornament," and *Vanessa* means "butterfly." Boys are more likely to be given names with meanings of power and strength, e.g., *Neil* means "champion," *Martin* is from Mars, the God of War, *Raymond* means "wise protection," *Harold* means "chief of the army," *Ira* means "vigilant," *Rex* means "king," and *Richard* means "strong king."

We see similar differences in food metaphors. Food is a passive substance just sitting there waiting to be eaten. Many people have recognized this and so no longer feel comfortable describing women as "delectable morsels." However, when I was a teenager, it was considered a compliment to refer to a girl (we didn't call anyone a woman until she was middle-aged) as a *cute tomato, a peach, a dish, a cookie, honey, sugar,* or *sweetie-pie*. When being affectionate, women will occasionally call a man *honey* or *sweetie,* but in general, food metaphors are used much less often with men than with women. If a man is called a *fruit,* his masculinity is being questioned. But it's perfectly acceptable to use a food metaphor if the food is heavier and more substantive than that used for women. For example pin-up pictures of women have long been known as *cheesecake,* but when Burt Reynolds posed for a nude centerfold the picture was immediately dubbed *beefcake,* c.f., *a hunk of meat.* That such sexual references to men have come into the language is another reflection of how society is beginning to lessen the differences between their attitudes toward men and women.

Something similar to the *fruit* metaphor happens with references to plants. We insult a man by calling him a *pansy,* but it wasn't considered particularly insulting to talk about a girl being a *wallflower,* a *clinging vine,* or a *shrinking violet,* or to give girls such names as *Ivy, Rose, Lily, Iris, Daisy, Camellia, Heather,* and *Flora.* A plant metaphor can be used with a man if the plant is big and strong, for example, Andrew Jackson's nickname of *Old Hickory*. Also, the phrases *blooming idiots* and *budding geniuses* can be used with either sex, but notice how they are based on the most active thing a plant can do, which is to bloom or bud.

Animal metaphors also illustrate the different expectations for males and females. Men are referred to as *studs*, *bucks*, and *wolves* while women are referred to with such metaphors as *kitten*, *bunny*, *beaver*, *bird*, *chick*, and *lamb*. In the 1950s we said that boys went *tomcatting*, but today it's just *catting around* and both boys and girls do it. When the term *foxy*, meaning that someone was sexy, first became popular it was used only for girls, but now someone of either sex can be described as a *fox*. Some animal metaphors that are used predominantly with men have negative connotations based on the size and/or strength of the animals, e.g., *beast*, *bullheaded*, *jackass*, *rat*, *loanshark*, and *vulture*. Negative metaphors used with women are based on smaller animals, e.g., *social butterfly*, *mousy*, *catty*, and *vixen*. The feminine terms connote action, but not the same kind of large scale action as with the masculine terms.

Women Are Connected with Negative Connotations; Men with Positive Connotations

The final point that my notecards illustrated was how many positive connotations are associated with the concept of masculine, while there are either trivial or negative connotations connected with the corresponding feminine concept. An example from the animal metaphors makes a good illustration. The word *shrew* taken from the name of a small but especially vicious animal was defined in my dictionary as "an ill-tempered scolding woman," but the word *shrewd* taken from the same root was defined as "marked by clever, discerning awareness" and was illustrated with the phrase "a shrewd businessman."

Early in life, children are conditioned to the superiority of the masculine role. As child psychologists point out, little girls have much more freedom to experiment with sex roles than do little boys. If a little girl acts like a *tomboy*, most parents have mixed feelings, being at least partially proud. But if their little boy acts like a *sissy* (derived from *sister*), they call a psychologist. It's perfectly acceptable for a little girl to sleep in the crib that was purchased for her brother, to wear his hand-me-down jeans and shirts, and to ride the bicycle that he has outgrown. But few parents would put a boy baby in a white and gold crib decorated with frills and lace, and virtually no parents would have their little boy wear his sister's hand-me-down dresses, nor would they have their son ride a girl's pink bicycle with a flower-bedecked basket. The proper names given to girls and boys show this same attitude. Girls can have "boy" names—*Cris*, *Craig*, *Jo*, *Kelly*, *Shawn*, *Teri*, *Toni*, and *Sam*—but it doesn't work the other way around. A couple of generations ago, *Beverley*, *Frances*, *Hazel*, *Marion*, and *Shirley* were common boys' names. As parents gave these names to more and more girls, they fell into disuse for males, and some older men who have these names prefer to go by their initials or by such abbreviated forms as *Haze* or *Shirl*.

When a little girl is told to *be a lady*, she is being told to sit with her knees together and to be quiet and dainty. But when a little boy is told to *be a man* he is being told to be noble, strong, and virtuous—to have all the qualities that the speaker looks on as desirable. The concept of manliness has such positive connotations that it is used to be a compliment to call someone a *he-man*, to say that he was doubly a man. Today many people are more ambivalent about this term and respond to it much as they do to the word *macho*. But calling someone a *manly man* or a *virile man* is nearly ways meant as a compliment. *Virile* comes from the IndoEuropean *vir* meaning "man," which is also the basis for *virtuous*. Contrast the positive connotations of both *virile* and *virtuous* with the negative connotations of *hysterical*. The Greeks took this latter word from their name for *uterus* (as still seen in *hysterectomy*). They thought that women were the only ones who experienced uncontrolled emotional outbursts, and so the condition must have something to do with a part of the body that only women have.

Differences in the connotations between positive male and negative female connotations can be seen in several pairs of words that differ denotatively only in the matter of sex. *Bachelor* as compared to *spinster* or *old maid* has such positive connotations that women try to adopt them by using the term *bachelor-girl* or *bachelorette*. *Old maid* is so negative that it's the basis for metaphors: pretentious and fussy old men are called *old maids*, as are the leftover kernels of unpopped popcorn, and the last card in a popular children's game.

Patron and *matron* (Middle English for *father* and *mother*) have such different levels of prestige that women try to borrow the more positive masculine connotations with the word *patroness*, literally "female father." Such a peculiar term came about because of the high prestige attached to *patron* in such phrases as a *patron of the arts* or a *patron saint*. *Matron* is more apt to be used in talking about a woman in charge of a jail or a public restroom.

When men are doing jobs that women often do, we apparently try to pay the men extra by giving them fancy titles, for example, a male cook is more likely to be called a *chef* while a male seamstress will get the title of *tailor*. The armed forces have a special problem in that they recruit under such slogans as "The Marine Corps builds men!" and "Join the Army! Become a Man." Once the recruits are enlisted, they find themselves doing much of the work that has been traditionally thought of as "women's work." The solution to getting the work done and not insulting anyone's masculinity was to change the titles as shown below:

waitress	orderly
nurse	medic or corpsman
secretary	clerk-typist
assistant	adjutant
dishwasher or kitchen helper	KP (kitchen police)

Compare *brave* and *squaw*. Early settlers in America admired Indian men and hence named them with a word that carried connotations of youth, vigor, and courage. But they used the Algonquin's name for "woman" and over the years it developed almost opposite connotations to those of *brave*. *Wizard* and *witch* contrast almost as much. The masculine *wizard* implies skill and wisdom combined with magic, while the feminine *witch* implies evil intentions combined with magic. Part of the unattractiveness of both *witch* and *squaw* is that they have been used so often to refer to old women, something with which our culture is particularly uncomfortable, just as the Afghans were. Imagine my surprise when I ran across the phrases *grandfatherly advice* and *old wives' tales* and realized that the underlying implication is the same as the Afghan proverb about old men being worth listening to while old women talk only foolishness.

Other terms that show how negatively we view old women as compared to young women are *old nag* as compared to *filly*, *old crow* or *old bat* as compared to *bird*, and of being *catty* as compared to being *kittenish*. There is no matching set of metaphors for men. The chicken metaphor tells the whole story of a woman's life. In her youth she is a *chick*. Then she marries and begins *feathering her nest*. Soon she begins feeling *cooped up*, so she goes to *hen parties* where she *cackles* with her friends. Then she has her *brood*, begins to *henpeck* her husband, and finally turns into an *old biddy*.

I embarked on my study of the dictionary not with the intention of prescribing language change but simply to see what the language would tell me about sexism. Nevertheless I have been both surprised and pleased as I've watched the changes that have occurred over the past two decades. I'm one of those linguists who believes that new language customs will cause a new generation of speakers to grow up with different expectations. This is why I'm happy about people's efforts to use inclusive language, to say *he or she* or *they* when speaking about individuals who names they do not know. I'm glad that leading publishers have developed guidelines to help writers use language that is fair to both sexes, and I'm glad that most newspapers and magazines list women by their own names instead of only by their husbands' names and that educated and thoughtful people no longer begin their business letters with "Dear Sir" or "Gentlemen," but instead use a memo form or begin with such salutations as "Dear Colleagues," "Dear Reader," or "Dear Committee Members." I'm also glad that such words as *poetess, authoress, conductress*, and *aviatrix* now sound quaint and old-fashioned and that *chairman* is giving way to *chair* or *head*, *mailman* to *mail carrier*, *clergyman* to *clergy*, and *stewardess* to *flight attendant*. I was also pleased when the National Oceanic and Atmospheric Administration bowed to feminist complaints and in the late 1970s began to alternate men's and women's names for hurricanes. However, I wasn't so pleased to discover that the change did not immediately erase sexist thoughts from everyone's mind, as shown by a headline about Hurricane David in a 1979 New York tabloid, "David Rapes Virgin Islands." More recently a similar metaphor appeared in a headline in the *Arizona Republic* about Hurricane Charlie, "Charlie Quits Carolinas, Flirts with Virginia."

What these incidents show is that sexism is not something existing independently in American English or in the particular dictionary that I happened to read. Rather, it exists in people's minds. Language is like an X-ray in providing visible evidence of invisible thoughts. The best thing about people being interested in and discussing sexist language is that as they make conscious decisions about what pronouns they will use, what jokes they will tell or laugh at, how they will write their names, or how they will begin their letters, they are forced to think about the underlying issue of sexism. This is good because as a problem that begins in people's assumptions and expectations, it's a problem that will be solved only when a great many people have given it a great deal of thought.

 For Discussion:

1. Explain the connections Nilsen makes between language and society. How do words explain historical and social patterns?
2. Do you agree with Nilsen's statement that "in American culture a woman is valued for the attractiveness and sexiness of her body, while a man is valued for his physical strength and accomplishments? A woman is sexy. A man is successful"?
3. Comment on Nilsen's three major categories that resulted from her research. If possible, add more categories connected to sexism in the English language.
4. How can we avoid sexist language since "it exists in people's minds"? How should we raise and educate future generations?

 For Fact-Finding, Research, and Writing:

1. Use *Oxford English Dictionary* and an etymological dictionary and write the history and usage of three eponyms.
2. Using the library databases, find an article in a newspaper or magazine that includes occurrences of sexist language. Replace the examples of sexist language with non-sexist terminology.
3. Since sexism occurs in other aspects of life besides language, find two peer-reviewed scholarly journal articles that address sexism in various areas of our society and write an abstract of one.

Richard Hofstadter, "Democracy and Anti-Intellectualism in America"

Professor of American History at Columbia University, Richard Hofstadter (1916–1970) wrote two Pulitzer Prize winning books, *The Age of Reform* and *Anti-Intellectualism in American Life*, as well as *Social Darwinism in American Thought*, *The American Political Tradition*, and *The Paranoid Style in American Politics*.

Before You Read:

How would you define an "intellectual"? Do you want to become one?

Democracy and Anti-Intellectualism in America

Richard Hofstadter

Intellectualism and Democracy

American education today is in the midst of a great crisis, the general outlines of which I believe we can all recognize. About the first part of this crisis, its financial aspect, I shall have nothing to say. A second part of it comes from outside education, in the shape of tremendous pressures to conform, for we live in a society in which the most dynamic force is provided by a small group of politicians who seek to base careers upon the policing of opinion. About the problems of freedom and conformity, I will speak briefly. The third part of this crisis, which concerns me most, is internal; it is less dramatic and perceptible than the others and it has been going on for a longer time. It stems from an inner failure of nerve, for it is nothing less than the growing loss of confidence among educators in the importance and value of the life of the mind, a capitulation within the educational world—indeed, in many quarters an eager capitulation—to the non-intellectual or anti-intellectual criteria that many forces in our society wish to impose upon education and which we might well consider it the bounden duty of educators to resist. It is about this that I wish primarily to speak; and I hope to suggest some relations between this species of educational failure and our popular democracy.

Since I am speaking about education and intellectualism, I want to make it entirely clear that I do not make the mistake of identifying higher education in general with intellectualism. Quite the contrary; I propose to emphasize the extent to which anti-intellectualism is rampant within the educational community. But it is also probably true that in America the greater part of the leadership of those who can be called intellectuals lives and works in academic communities. And if higher education can be said to be under fire today, it can be said with greater certainty that the distinctively intellectual part of the educational community is the part that stands to lose most.

The crisis in higher education is also a crisis in the history of the intelligentsia. Today, everywhere in America, intellectuals are on the defensive. They have been identified with the now-defeated inheritance of the New Deal and the Fair Deal. That this identification should have been made is ironical, because the New Deal itself, for all its Brain Trusters, had its own streak of anti-intellectualism. But it has also been unfair: the intellectuals are never given credit for the successes of the New Deal, but they have had to take the blame for everything that has been charged up to the Democratic administrations of the past twenty years—with so-called creeping socialism, with the war, with the alleged failure at Yalta, even with treason. In the late presidential campaign a political leader who embodied the kind of traits that the intellectual would most like to see in our national leadership found the support of the intellectuals of slight value in overcoming the disadvantages of his party and his hour. During that campaign the nation also found the epithet for the intellectuals that it has so long wanted—"egg-heads."

Do not imagine, however, that the intellectual is going into permanent eclipse. He always has his day posthumously, for the very men who are most forward in proclaiming their dislike of living intellectuals are the most abject followers of the dead ones. They may not like contemporary intellectuals but they are often quite hypnotized by the intellectual leavings of Adam Smith or Herbert Spencer, or Edmund Burke, or Thomas Aquinas, or similar gods of the past. They have restored an old slogan of the frontiersman with a new meaning and a new object: "The only good intellectual is a dead intellectual."

But what is an intellectual, really? This is a problem of definition that I found, when I came to it, far more elusive than I had anticipated. A great deal of what might be called the journeyman's work of our culture—the work of engineers, physicians, newspapermen, and indeed of most professors—does not strike me as distinctively intellectual, although it is certainly work based in an important sense on ideas. The distinction that we must recognize, then, is one originally made by Max Weber between living *for* ideas and living *off* ideas. The intellectual lives for ideas; the journeyman lives off them. The engineer or the physician—I don't mean here to be invidious—needs to have a pretty considerable capital stock in frozen ideas to do his work; but they serve for him a purely instrumental purpose: he lives off them, not for them. Of course he may also be, in his private role and his personal ways of thought, an intellectual, but it is not necessary for him to be one in order to work at his profession. There is in fact no profession which demands that one be an intellectual. There do seem to be vocations, however, which almost demand that one be an anti-intellectual, in which those who live off ideas seem to have an implacable hatred for those who live for them. The marginal intellectual workers and the unfrocked intellectuals who work in journalism, advertising, and mass communication are the bitterest and most powerful among those who work at such vocations.

It will help, too, to make the further distinction between living for ideas and living for *an idea*. History is full of cases of great men with good minds, a capacity to deal with abstractions, and a desire to make systems of them—all qualities we associate with the intellectual. But when, as it has in many of them, this concern with ideas, no matter how dedicated and sincere, reduces in the end to the ingenious use of them for a central preconception, however grand, then I think we have very little intellectualism and a great deal of something else. A good historical illustration is that of Lenin, who, as his more theoretical works show, had in him a powerful element of intellectuality; but this intellectuality was rendered thin by his all-absorbing concern with certain very limiting political values. His book on philosophy, *Materialism and Empirio-Criticism*, a shrill work and an extremely depressing one to read, makes it altogether clear that the politician in him swallowed up the intellectual. I choose the illustration of Lenin because it helps me to make another point that seems unfortunately necessary because of the present tendency to identify intellectuals with subversives. That point is that the idea of a party line and political messianism is inherently inconsistent with intellectualism, and those few intellectuals who have in some way survived that tension are few, pitiable, and on the whole sterile.

The journeyman of ideas, and the janizary who makes a somewhat complicated but highly instrumental use of ideas, provide us with two illustrations of people who work with ideas but are not precisely intellectuals, as I understand the term. What, then, are the differences between the men who work with ideas but are *not* intellectuals and the men who work with ideas and *are* intellectuals?

Two things, that seems in fact to be mutually at odds, mark off the intellectual from the journeyman of ideas; one is playfulness, the other is piety.

Certainly the intellectual, if he is nothing else, is one who relishes *the play of the mind* for its own sake, for whom it is one of the major ends of life. The intellectual has a full quotient of what Veblen called "idle curiosity." His mind, instead of falling to rest when it has provided him with his girl and his automobile and his dinner, becomes even more active. Indeed if we had to define him in physiological terms, we might define him as the creature whose mind is *most* likely to be active after dinner.

I speak of playfulness too because of the peculiar nature of the relationship, in the intellectual's mind, between ideas and practicality. To the journeyman of ideas the be-all and end-all of ideas lies in their practical efficacy. Now the intellectual, by contrast, is not necessarily impractical; I can think of some intellectuals like Thomas Jefferson and Robert Owen and John Maynard Keynes who have been eminently practical, and I consider the notion that the intellectual is inherently impractical to be one of the most contemptible of the delusions with which the anti-intellectual quiets his envy—the intellectual is not impractical but primarily concerned with a quality of ideas that does not depend upon their practicality. He neither reveres nor disdains practical consequences; for him they are either marginal or irrelevant. And when he does talk about the practicality or the "relevance" of ideas, the kind of practicality that he is concerned with is itself somewhat different from the practicality of building a bridge, curing a disease, or making a profit—it is practical relevance to spiritual values themselves.

The best illustration of the intellectual's view of the purely practical that has recently come to my attention is the reaction of Clerk Maxwell, the great nineteenth-century mathematician and theoretical physicist, to the invention of the telephone. Maxwell was asked to give a lecture on the workings of this wonderful new instrument, which he began by saying how difficult it was to believe, when the word first came from America, that such a thing had actually been devised. But then, he said, "when at last this little instrument appeared, consisting, as it does, of parts, every one of which is familiar to us, and capable of being put together by an amateur, the disappointment arising from its humble appearance was only partially relieved on finding that it was really able to talk." Perhaps, then, this regrettable appearance of simplicity might be redeemed by the presence somewhere of "recondite physical principles, the study of which might worthily occupy an hour's time of an academic audience." But no; Maxwell had not met a single person who could not understand the physical processes involved, and even the science reporters for the daily press had almost got it right! The thing was a disappointing bore; it was not recondite, it was not profound, it was not complex, it was not *intellectually* new.

To be sure, what this illustration suggests is not merely that the telephone disappointed Maxwell as a pure scientist and an intellectual, but that the strain of intellectuality in him was not as broadly developed as it might have been. The telephone might well excite not merely the commercial imagination but the historical imagination. But my point is, after all, not that Maxwell was a universal intellectual, but that he was displaying the attitude of the intellectual in his particular sphere of interest.

The second element in intellectualism is its religious strain, the note of piety. What I mean by this is simply that for the intellectual the whole world of moral values becomes attached to ideas and to the life dedicated to ideas. The life given over to the search for truth takes on for him a primary moral significance. Intellectualism, although hardly confined to doubters, is often the sole piety of the skeptic. A few years ago a distinguished sociologist asked me to read a brief manuscript which he had written primarily for students planning to go on to advanced work in his field, the purpose of which was to illustrate various ways in which the life of the mind might be cultivated. The essay had about it a little too much of the how-to-do books, and my friend abandoned it. But the nub of the matter from the standpoint of our present problem was that I found myself to be reading a piece of devotional literature, comparable perhaps to Cotton Mather's *Essays to do Good* or Richard Steele's *The Tradesman's Calling*. My friend was trying to communicate his sense of dedication to the life of ideas, which he conceived much in the fashion of the old Protestant writers as a *calling*. To work is to pray. Yes, and for this kind of man, to think—really to think—is to pray. What he knows best, when he is at his best, is the pursuit of truth; but *easy* truths bore him. What he is certain of becomes unsatisfactory always; the meaning of his intellectual life lies in the quest for new uncertainties.

In a bygone day when men lived even more by dogma than they do now, there were two kinds of men whose special office it was to seek for and utter the truth; and they symbolize these two sides of the intellectual's nature. One was the angelic doctor, the learned schoolman, the conserver of old orthodoxies but also the maker of the new, and the prodder at the outer limits of received truths. The other was the jester, the professional fool, who had license to say on occasion for the purposes of amusement and release those things that bordered on lèse majesté and could not be uttered by others who were accounted serious men.

The fool and the schoolman are very far apart. No doubt you will ask whether there is not a contradiction between these two qualities of the intellectual, piety and playfulness.

Certainly there is great tension between them; human beings are tissues of contradictions, and the life even of the intellectual is not logic, to borrow from Holmes, but experience. If you will think of the intellectuals you know, some will occur to you in whom the note of playfulness seems stronger, others who are predominantly pious. But I believe that in all intellectuals who have any stability as intellectuals—and that includes the angelic doctors of the middle ages—each of these characteristics is at some point qualified by the other. Perhaps the tensile strength of the intellectual can be gauged by his ability to maintain a fair equipoise between these aspects of himself. At one end of the scale, an excess of play-fulness leads to triviality, to dilettantism, to cynicism, to the failure of all sustained creative effort. At the other, an excess of piety leads to fanaticism, to messianism, to ways of life that may be morally magnificent or morally mean, but in either case are not quite the ways of intellectualism. It is of the essence of the intellectual that he strikes a balance.

The widespread distrust of intellectuals in America reflects a tendency to depreciate their playfulness and distrust their piety. Ours is a society in which every form of play seems to be accepted by the majority except the play of the mind. It does not need to be explained to most people in America why sports, sex, liquor, gambling, motoring, and gourmandizing are all more or less legitimate forms of amusement for those who happen to find them amusing. The only forms of *mental* play that are similarly accepted and understood are those that do not involve the particular kinds of critical intelligence that are called into play by intellectualism; I refer, of course, to such highly cerebral amusements as bridge, chess, and the various forms of the crossword puzzle. I suppose that those who are inclined to find economic explanations will point out that the play of the mind, being the only kind that has not been susceptible to commercialization, has not been able to rally the support of a vested interest. I believe, however, that a large part of our common neglect of the humani-ties is attributable to the absence of a traditional and accepted leisure class which looks upon this kind of personal cultivation as a natural goal of life. The idea of leisured intel-lectual exercise, not put to the service of some external end, has been offensive to mass democracy. One of the best signs of this is the rhetoric adopted by college presidents and others who appeal to the public for support for education. Always these appeals tell how much education does for citizenship, science, technology, morals, or religion. Rarely do they point to the glories or pleasures of the human mind as an end in itself.

Just as the truly religious man is always a misfit in a secular society, so it is the piety of the intellectual that makes the greatest difficulties for him. Playfulness may be disdained or misunderstood, but it is not usually thought to be dangerous. Piety is another matter, for it is almost certain in the end to challenge something. It is the piety of the intellectual that puts iron into his nonconformism, if he happens to be a nonconformist. It is his piety that will make him, if anything does, a serious moral force in society. In our day the pressures operating against boldness in thought, as well as the sheer bureaucratization of intellectual life, bear hardest against the elements of piety in the intellectual. The temptation is very strong for some intellectuals to suppress the note of piety in themselves, to turn increas-ingly to the playful and generally more esoteric aspects of their work, to give up the office of spiritual leadership. Such self-suppression is psychologically and morally dangerous, and cannot be indulged in without paying a serious price. It does not become the intellectual, it is much too false to an important part of him, to give in altogether to playfulness and play the fool to the powerful. The jester had his prerogatives, to be sure, but we should also remember that he was usually a slave.

I have attempted thus far to define and elucidate intellectualism. Let me now explain what I mean by democracy when I say that in an important sense higher education and democracy have often been at odds. I do not mean by democracy simply the indispensable formal essentials of our society—constitutionalism, government by discussion, guarantees for the civil liberties of political minorities. These I neither challenge nor criticize; and I am sure that free higher education cannot in our time stand without them. But I do mean to criticize something that relates to the spirit of our politics, something that for lack of a better term I will call populistic democracy. Populistic democracy is neither progressive nor conservative, although it is in a perverse way equalitarian. Populistic democracy is the meeting ground, in fact, of the extreme left and the extreme right. It is government by or through the mass man, disguised behind the mask of an easy sentimentalization of the folk. It is the idea that anything done in the name of the people is *ipso facto* legitimate, even if the same act done in the name of a vested interest would be considered outrageous. It is the idea that a dozen postcards to a congressman from the wildest cranks should be given the same weight as a dozen reasoned letters from sober citizens. Transferred to the field of education, which is our concern, it is the idea that a university ought to cater to the needs of anybody who comes out of or pretends to represent the folk, whether or not he has any real need for or interest in the use of ideas. Put in terms of the state university, it is the idea that any graduate of the public high school should be accepted as a freshman no matter how dismal his prospects are as a student. Put in broader terms, it is the idea that any of the wants, real or fancied, of a mass society, should be absolute imperatives to its system of higher education.

We Americans are noted for our faith in both democracy and education. It has been our assumption that democracy and education, both being good, must be closely related and mutually reinforcing. We should have, it is argued, as much education and as much democracy as possible. It is also assumed that education serves democracy, and one of the most common shibboleths in our educational literature is the slogan "education for democracy." It is characteristically American that very few of us trouble to inquire whether democracy serves education. Whether it does indeed do so as fully and unambiguously as we might consider desirable is the question I insist we must face.

That there is any necessary relation between a vital system of higher education and a democratic society, one may readily deny on the basis of historical evidence. Two of the greatest periods in university history, that of the thirteenth and fourteenth centuries and that of the German universities in the nineteenth century, occurred in societies that were not notably democratic. In our own experience, I do not believe it incorrect to say that the great age of American university development from 1870 to 1910 was for the most part an age of political and economic oligarchy; and also that our finest universities and small colleges, by and large, have been those started and endowed by rich men and patronized chiefly by the upper classes.

All this does not mean, of course, that there is any necessary antagonism between democracy and higher education. Presumably there is no inherent or universally necessary opposition between a political democracy and a vital, respected, intellectually rich and alert university system. But I do wish to point out that there has been a historically persistent tension between our popular democracy and intellectualism that has been very sadly felt in the sphere of university and college life. The problem of how democracy and education can best serve and complement each other—as we would all, no doubt, like them to do—has not been nearly as constructively attacked as it might be for the simple reason that it has not often enough been candidly faced.

Long ago Tocqueville saw that the democratic culture that had emerged in the United States had brought with it pressures that were seriously hostile to the free use of the mind. He found that the democratic and equalitarian impulse had weakened the ability of the individual to resist the pressure of the opinion of the mass:

> The fact that the political laws of the Americans are such that the majority rules the community with sovereign sway, materially increases the power which that majority naturally exercises over the mind. For nothing is more customary in man than to recognise superior wisdom in the person of his oppressor. . . . The intellectual dominion of the greater number would probably be less absolute among a democratic people governed by a king than in the sphere of a pure democracy, but it will always be extremely absolute; and by whatever political laws men are governed in the ages of equality, it may be foreseen that faith in public opinion may become a species of religion there, and the majority its ministering prophet.
>
> Thus intellectual authority will be different, but it will not be diminished; and far from thinking that it will disappear, I augur that it may readily acquire too much preponderance and confine the action of private judgment within narrower limits than are suited either to the greatness or the happiness of the human race. In the principle of equality I very clearly discern two tendencies; the one leading the mind of every man to untried thoughts, the other inclined to prohibit him from thinking at all. And I perceive how, under the dominion of certain laws, democracy would extinguish that liberty of mind to which a democratic social condition is favourable; so that, after having broken all the bondage once imposed on it by ranks or by men, the human mind would be closely fettered to the general will of the greatest number.

Tocqueville found that in his time the most absolute monarchs in Europe were unable to prevent certain heretical notions from circulating through their dominions and even in their courts:

> Such is not the case in America; as long as the majority is still undecided, discussion is carried on; but as soon as its decision is irrevocably pronounced, a submissive silence

is observed, and the friends, as well as the opponents of the measure unite in assenting to its propriety. The reason of this is perfectly clear: no monarch is so absolute as to combine all the powers of society in his own hands, and to conquer all opposition with the energy of a majority which is invested with the right of making and of executing the laws. . . .

I know no country in which there is so little true independence of mind and freedom of discussion as in America. In any constitutional state in Europe every sort of religious and political theory may be advocated and propagated abroad; for there is no country in Europe so subdued by any single authority as not to contain citizens who are ready to protect the man who raises his voice in the cause of truth from the consequences of his hardihood. If he is unfortunate enough to live under an absolute government, the people is upon his side; if he inhabits a free country, he may find a shelter behind the authority of the throne, if he require one. The aristocratic part of society supports him in some countries and the democracy in others. But in a nation where democratic institutions exist, organized like those of the United States, there is but one sole authority, one single element of strength and of success, with nothing beyond it.

While I do believe that Tocqueville was exaggerating the case of the United States in 1835, he pointed to the heart of the problem of majority tyranny over the soul. It is a problem that has grown still more acute in our own age, an age of mass communications and the mass man; for now the tyranny of the majority can be spread uniformly over the surface of a great nation otherwise well suited by size and diversity to a multiplicity of opinions, and it can be to some degree forged and manipulated from a few centers. If there were any horrors in that spontaneous, grass-roots variety of popular tyranny, as Tocqueville saw it, they must be greatly compounded by the artificial and centralized means of manipulation that the communications technology of our time has made possible.

But has there been substantial historical evidence in the development of American higher education for the validity of Tocqueville's fear of mass tyranny? I believe there is certainly enough evidence to warrant a reconsideration of our views of the relation between democracy and university culture. I propose to argue that while populistic democracy has been on the side of many educational improvements and reforms, it has often been aligned as sharply with forces tending to constrain freedom in higher education and to lower its devotion to intellectual goals.

Democracy and Higher Education

There may have been some popular upsurges in our history that have been auspicious for intellectualism in general, and for higher education in particular; but the popular movements that have been notable for their failure to understand the place of learning in our culture, or even on occasion for their hostility to it, are quite numerous. One of the first, the Great Awakening of the mid-eighteenth century, was notable for its hostility to a free and liberal-minded theological education such as was emerging in the older colleges; and while the Awakening must be in the end credited for enlarging the number of colleges, the goal sought at first in these enterprises was not an enhancement of the sphere of free learning but simply the creation of schools that would teach the right brand of theology. Jeffersonian democracy was not, on the whole, what I call populistic—at least not in its leadership. Its most constructive work in education, the founding of a liberal university in Virginia, was the work of aristocratic leadership. Jacksonian democracy, whatever its benefits in other areas, was identified with a widespread deterioration in the standards of professional education, masquerading under the ideology that easier access to these privileged areas of life must be made available to the people.

The founding of early state universities was badly hampered by popular hostility to advanced education that was held to be of use chiefly to the aristocrats, who, in fact, usually provided the basic impetus to the cultivation of the higher learning, whether in state-founded or private institutions. The movement that destroyed the old classical curriculum and made American universities, especially our state universities, the nurseries of all kinds of subintellectual practical skills of less than university grade was in its impetus very largely a popular movement; and while many of the consequences of that movement must be set to its credit as compensations, the undercurrent of vocationalism and anti-intellectualism was undeniable. Our history books tell us—to come toward our own time—that during the Populist-Bryan period the university professors who failed to accept the gold-standard economics of the well-to-do classes were often victims of outrageous interference; they do not usually trouble to tell us that when the Populists captured Kansas they raised hob with the University of Kansas in much the same way that they complained of so bitterly when the shoe was on the other foot. One of the most genuinely popular, and I believe democratic, political leaders in our history was William Jennings Bryan; and the sort of respect he showed for science and academic freedom is familiar to you all. His concept of the rights of the dissenting teacher reduces to his famous comment: "A man cannot demand a salary for saying what his employers do not want said."

My aim in stressing these facts is not to cast discredit upon popular democracy, whose merit in our whole scheme of things must be weighed by taking into account all its achievements as well as its deficiencies; I am simply trying to suggest that many of us have in the past made a mystique of the masses and have tended too much to attribute all the villainy in our world to the machinations of vested interests. I find it rather suggestive that the sole ruling group in our history that could be called a vested intellectual interest of any considerable power—I refer, of course, to the early Puritan clergy—has suffered the fate of being scandalously libelled by our "liberal" historians who have written in the tradition of V.L. Parrington.

Why this persistent tension between popular democracy and free higher learning? Obviously it is to some degree an aspect of social striving: a college education is a privilege that has not been open to all. While it can open up otherwise unavailable opportunities to the children of the less favored classes, it can also confirm the privileges of the upper classes by adding to those social, political, and economic advantages which are theirs by birth and family, the advantages of a superior education. Much of the early opposition to state universities was based precisely upon this argument. Why tax the poor, it was repeatedly asked, to educate the sons of the rich? No doubt there is such an element of resentment on the part of the lower classes for the privileges and attainments of the upper classes. But this, to my mind, will not get us very far in explaining why the United States in particular has been a happy hunting ground for anti-intellectualism. Class divisions exist in all western societies. Moreover, of all western nations, the United States has given by far the greatest proportion of its total population an opportunity to have a college education. In our more than 1700 colleges, for instance, we offer higher education, or a reasonable facsimile thereof, to about ten times as large a portion of our population as is done in the British Isles. Moreover, while we have always had our class stratification, class lines have been less sharp in the United States, and mobility between classes somewhat easier, than in European countries. By the showing of these facts, the United States should, in accordance with the class envy theory, have much less resentment of higher education as a source of privilege than any other country on the globe.

The evidence is all to the contrary, and this is enough to give us pause. It remains to be explained why, in a culture that seems to value education very highly, that has provided an enormous apparatus for the collegiate education of its youth, the genuine intellectual content of higher education is so little esteemed, why the teacher in general and the college professor in particular has so much less social status than he does almost anywhere else. I believe that the problem of status is, indeed, quite crucial, but that the situation cannot be explained in terms of broad assertions about the envy of manual for intellectual labor, the poor for the well-to-do, or the middle classes for the leisure classes. We must look to some of the unique factors of American historical development for our answers.

From the beginning the American people were confronted with rich resources, an immense task of continental settlement, and a shortage of labor. Their culture thus came to set a premium on practical achievement, the manipulation of material reality, and quick decision. It did not encourage reflection or a respect for the ultimate and irreducible disagreements of life. On the contrary, it suggested that it was to everyone's interest to arrive at a quick consensus, general enough to get the work done, that any disagreement on details was, in the light of the rich potentialities of organized work, unimportant. The American still sets a very high premium on such a consensus; he implicitly approaches broad intellectual and philosophical problems with that model of prompt decision in mind. "What can we agree on?" he wants to know. The wonderful persistence of irreducible differences of opinion, of the plurality of human dreams and perspectives, the exchange or contemplation of differences as an exercise in mutual understanding—all these are likely to be dark mysteries to him. He makes an ideology of normality; he asks not "What am I?" but "What is it customary and proper to be around here?" He *thinks* he is an individualist because he does truly and genuinely resent any rude coercive efforts to make him conform, but he cannot realize that he spends half his time trying to figure out how he can conform "spontaneously." One of the most appalling things in American life is the failure of those who prate

most about individualism to develop any understanding of individuality. The loudest ho-
sannas to individualism to develop any understanding of individuality. The loudest hosan-
nas to individualism are sung by grim, regimented choruses.

The effects of our chronic shortage of labor have also struck quite directly at the
teaching profession from grammar schools to graduate schools. Our historic abundance of
land and other resources has continually beckoned to the inadequate resources of our labor power. The consequences of this for other areas of life than education have often been
noted. Our agriculture, for instance, was dedicated from the outset to extensive and waste-
ful cultivation and rapid mechanization rather than to intensive and careful cultivation and
farming as a settled way of life. Too little has been said about a similar trend in our educational history. I think we have cultivated man wastefully and mechanically too. The teaching of our young, for instance, has been all too regularly left over to those whose imagina-
tions and energies were not absorbed—or not yet absorbed—in the more exciting and
lucrative life of physical and economic conquest, or to those who for one reason or another
were altogether incapable of entering upon it. Ichabod Crane was, I suppose, the archetype
of the American schoolmaster—the timid misfit, the amiable failure, the man who was
scared out of town; and when Brom Bones chased him that terrible night through Sleepy
Hollow and frightened him almost to death with a pumpkin, he was passing upon him the
characteristic comment of the American philistine upon the American teacher. If the
teacher was not Ichabod Crane, then it was the lonely spinster, driven by desperation to
take up teaching when all else failed. If not the spinster, it was the young man who was
merely marking time, supporting himself before launching upon a more permanent career
in business or some really serious profession. "The men teachers," wrote an observer of early
Massachusetts schools—mind you, even Massachusetts schools—

> may be divided into three classes: (1) Those who think teaching is easier and possibly
> a little more remunerative than common labor. (2) Those who are acquiring, or have
> acquired, a good education, and who take up teaching as a temporary employment,
> either to earn money for pressing necessities or to give themselves time to choose delib-
> erately a regular profession. (3) Those who, conscious of weakness, despair of distinc-
> tion or even the means of subsistence by other means. . . .They are often very young,
> they are constantly changing their employment, and consequently can have but little
> experience; and what is worse than all, they have never had any direct preparation for
> their profession. . . . No standard of attainments is fixed . . . so that any one keeps
> school, which is a very different thing from teaching school, who wishes to do it, and
> can persuade by herself or her friends, a small district to employ her. And this is not a
> very difficult matter, especially when the renumeration for the employment is so very
> trifling. . . . If a young man be moral enough to keep out of State prison, he will find
> no difficulty in getting approbation for a schoolmaster.

An exaggeration? Possibly. But in 1930–31, even after much had been done to improve standards of teacher training in the United States, the National Survey of the Education of

Teachers showed that American teacher education, although only slightly inferior to that of England, was drastically inferior to that of France, Germany, and the Scandinavian countries. The teacher of a high school in the continental countries was found to be a much superior person, attracted by the relatively high social position, higher salaries, and advanced professional morale. And while I have been speaking here of the teaching profession below the university grade, most of what I have said will apply almost as well to American colleges down at least to the last three decades of the nineteenth century.

Let us look for a moment at those old colleges and the situation of their faculties. One of the first things that any observer of American higher education is struck by is the fact that the American professoriat is the only profession in the United States that is governed by laymen. Outside the continent of North America university faculties are nowhere governed, as they are here, by lay boards of trustees. Of course it is not easy to say whether the American professor lacks status because he is not self-governing or whether he has failed to get self-government in part because he lacks status. Genetically, however, it is not too difficult to explain how the curse of absentee government came to afflict American education. American colleges were called into existence before the community had the full means to support them amply, and indeed before there was a body of learned men professionally given to teaching. The great independent, self-governing universities of the middle ages, which established the pattern for early modern university government, came into existence only where there were well-established bodies of students and masters; they took their political form from the guild model of corporate self-control and the church's model of independence from the power of the state. The American colleges were founded in a Protestant milieu, which, no longer accepting the principles of hierarchy and corporate independence, had introduced lay government of churches. From this to lay government of colleges was a natural step, made the more natural by the fact that the greater part of the teaching personnel in early American colleges, for over a century and a half, consisted of young tutors, recent graduates, who were merely waiting and studying preparatory to entering the ministry. These men usually had no permanent interest in teaching as a profession, no permanent stake in its welfare. And they were considered by the philanthropic non-teachers who founded the colleges to be too young and too transient to be entrusted with the task of governing the colleges and managing their resources. Hence governmental powers were kept in the hands of trustees. The only working member of the college who held the full stature of a master of university learning was the president who, in the absence of the trustees, took over a larger and larger share of the task of determining college policy. Hence to this day the only person in the American community who enjoys a measure of prestige and respect comparable to that enjoyed by the university professor in most countries of Europe is our college or university president. Needless to say, with the development of the modern university, a great deal of the power to govern academic affairs has informally passed into the hands of faculties. But in almost all cases, such powers are delegated and may be legally retaken on any issue at any time by trustees. While few American university professors would argue for full self-government at this date, the legal inability of the American academic community to govern itself in matters bearing on academic freedom and tenure is a major disability in its struggle against the external forces of anti-intellectualism.

It may also be said in passing that the historic lack of prestige within the American academic community has tended to feed on itself. I am sure that no man anywhere whose primary desire is for a large share of the material goods of life enters the teaching profession with the idea that it will supply them with any abundance. He enters it because of other inducements: because he wants to pursue knowledge, because he values leisure (he will be lucky if he gets it), because he likes the idea of living in an academic community, or because of the prestige of the office. But American academic life, having so little prestige to offer, has failed to recruit a very large percentage of its professorial personnel from the upper classes, as does the professoriat in England or on the continent. The American college professor is characteristically drawn from the lower middle classes. I hope you will not imagine that I am being snobbish when I argue that this has been a signal disadvantage both to the freedom and the intellectualism of the academic community. Logan Wilson, in his study of *The Academic Man* in the United States, has pointed out that the recruit from the lower middle classes often comes from a background of cultural poverty in which, of necessity, the view taken of most things has to be profoundly affected by their material efficacy. I should also add that a man who comes from a well-established family with secure connections, and has perhaps in addition some personal resources to draw on, can confront the problems of free expression with far greater boldness than the man who feels that he must cling to his academic job at all costs. I have been impressed, in studying the development of a certain measure of liberalism in the American colleges of the eighteenth century, by the important role played by men who came to academic life from secure positions of social prestige, either in great commercial families or the ministry. One of the boldest men in early academic life was Professor John Winthrop, the great Harvard astronomer, and no little part of his boldness rested upon the security derived from the fact that he was, after all, a Winthrop in Massachusetts.

The low prestige of the professor in America was matched by the low prestige of the college itself. At the end of the eighteenth century and the beginning of the nineteenth, as the American population broke through the Allegheny mountains and began to spread across the continent, a process of educational fragmentation began which still profoundly afflicts our educational system. Every sect of Protestants wanted to have a little college to service every part of a great country. Localities thought that a community college would be good for local development. Parents welcomed the opportunity to educate their sons near at home in small schools whose annual tuition was often not much larger than the cost of transportation to a distant and perhaps more formidable seat of learning. They were advised, too, that the country college was socially democratic and that it protected their offspring from the corrupting atmosphere of great cities. This passion for breaking up the educational system into small units destroyed much of the potential strength and prestige of the old college. Where English colleges had clustered at a few university centers, American colleges were strewn across three thousand miles of continent. Innumerable colleges failed because they were so flimsily launched. Many that survived were much too tiny to maintain decent teaching staffs and adequate educational standards. It became a commonplace among serious educators before the Civil War that the American college was not, in the terms of international educational standards, a college at all, but a closer equivalent to the German gymnasium, the French lycée, the English public school.

After a time the old college became the butt of a great deal of criticism. It was, of course, devoted chiefly to the inherited classical curriculum, featuring Latin, Greek, and mathematics. This kind of schooling was increasingly held to be unadapted to the needs of American business, technology, and agriculture. It was held, and quite correctly, to be too limited and rigid to be adequate to the growing fund of human knowledge. Between the educational reformers, who were dissatisfied with the low level of work that the existing colleges were unable to transcend, and the practical reformers, who wanted to make American higher education work for the community in a clearer and more easily definable way, a curiously mixed transformation was finally effected in the last half of the nineteenth century. Universities, both state and private, were at last reared on adequate foundations; graduate and professional schools were created; schools of agriculture and engineering were founded; the curriculum was broadened; and the elective system was introduced.

Within only a few decades a curriculum system that had been too tight and too rigid was made too loose and too sprawling. All kinds of practical skills that had neither professional nor intellectual stature—no matter how necessary they might be to the community—were taught, or presumed to be taught, at universities. The president of a great state university was proud to say: "The state universities hold that there is no intellectual service too undignified for them to perform." Vast numbers of students without notable intellectual interests or skills flocked to the colleges and universities, availed themselves freely of the multitude of elective courses with little or no intellectual content, and passed out into the world with padded degrees. Much of the information thus inculcated may be thought to have no place in any system of formal education. A still larger part belongs to purely technical and mechanical education of the sort that can be properly taught in formal education but is not elsewhere considered proper to a university—the sort of thing that on the continent of Europe is to be found among the offerings of the German *technische Hochschule* and its many counterparts in other countries.

Now all this has taken place at serious cost to intellectualism. It is possible, of course, to argue that the professor of some field of pure learning is not interfered with in the pursuit of his work simply because his colleague in the school of agriculture is busy teaching farmers how to raise healthy pigs. Theoretically, no; but those who are familiar with the problems of university administration and finance know that these things have a way of pulling against or tripping over each other; and that when all kinds of skills of various levels are jumbled together and taught in one institution, the hierarchy of values that places intellectual accomplishment at the top, as one would expect to do in a university, is somehow broken and destroyed. Thus the universities, that we might have expected to stand as solid barriers against the undercurrents of American anti-intellectualism, have actually intensified the push of the stream. How they could have resisted it, I do not honestly know. For one thing, our system of higher education is, unlike all the other systems in the world, a system of mass education, that today enrolls about 3,000,000 people. In a way, that is a preposterous figure, and I suppose it is altogether unreasonable to expect that students in such numbers will all get anything that could be called a common liberal education. All kinds of things pass for a college education in this country and will no doubt continue to do so for a long time to come. The difficulty is that we now have an educational system which rarely produces educators who will themselves dare to defend an education whole-heartedly directed to the goal of increasing intellectual power. The famous report of the President's Commission on Higher Education published in 1948—a report prepared by a representative group of American educators and laymen interested in education—had this to say on the subject:

> We shall be denying educational opportunity to many young people as long as we main-tain the present orientation of higher education toward verbal skills and intellectual interest. Many young people have abilities of a different kind, and they cannot receive "education commensurate with their native capacities" in colleges and universities that recognize only one kind of educable intelligence.
>
> Traditionally the colleges have sifted out as their special clientele persons possess-ing verbal aptitudes and a capacity for grasping abstractions. But many other apti-tudes—such as social sensitivity and versatility, artistic ability, motor skill and dexter-ity, and mechanical aptitude and ingenuity—also should be cultivated in a society depending, as ours does, on the minute division of labor and at the same time upon the orchestration of an enormous variety of talents.

I can think of no more shameful capitulation than this to the canons of anti-intel-lectualism: a group of educators urging that our de-intellectualized colleges become still more de-intellectualized by giving up their alleged preoccupation with "verbal aptitudes" and "a capacity for grasping abstractions"—that is, the power to think and to express thought—for a motley batch of skills which, however valuable, one does not have to go to college to learn; for "social sensitivity" that no doubt includes ballroom dancing and par-lor games; for "motor skill and dexterity" that must clearly mean athletics if it does not mean the ability to wash dishes without dropping them; and for "mechanical aptitude and ingenuity" that may very well mean the ability to drive and repair an automobile. Worthy skills every single one of them, and no doubt a necessary part of our life; but why they have to be acquired in something that calls itself a college or university the Commission, whose business was supposed to be with *higher* education, did not take the trouble to explain. No doubt its members did not feel themselves to be on the defensive, for they were expressing the dominant point of view in American society.

At the top of our educational system this attitude threatens to weaken whatever intellec-tualism we have. At lower levels, in our grammar and high schools, it threatens to wipe out literacy altogether in the name of "progressive education" or education for "life adjustment." If you think I exaggerate, listen to the principal of a junior high school in Urbana, Illinois, speaking to a meeting of the National Association of Secondary-School Principals:

> *Through the years we've built a sort of halo around reading, writing, and arithmetic. We've said they were for everybody . . . rich and poor, brilliant and not-so-mentally endowed, ones who liked them and those who failed to go for them. Teacher has said that these were something "everyone should learn." The principal has remarked, "All educated people know how to write, spell, and read." When some child declared a dislike for a sacred subject, he was warned that, if he failed to master it, he would grow up to be a so-and-so.*
>
> *The Three R's for All Children and All Children for the Three R's! That was it.*
>
> *We've made some progress in getting rid of that slogan. But every now and then some mother with a Phi Beta Kappa award or some employer who has hired a girl who can't spell stirs up a fuss about the schools . . . and ground is lost. . . .*
>
> *When we come to the realization that not every child has to read, figure, write, and spell . . . that many of them either cannot or will not master these chores . . . then we shall be on the road to improving the junior high curriculum.*
>
> *Between this day and that a lot of selling must take place. But it's coming. We shall some day accept the thought that it is just as illogical to assume that every boy must be able to read as it is that each one must be able to perform on a violin, that it is no more reasonable to require that each girl shall spell well than it is that each one shall bake a good cherry pie. . . .*
>
> *When adults finally realize that fact, everyone will be happier . . . and schools will be nicer places in which to live. . . .*

Of course this speaker, unlike the President's Commission, does not seem to be entirely in harmony with the prevailing sentiments of the country—at least, not yet; for it is clear that he thinks himself to be a visionary whose notions are considerably in advance of the times but whose high ideals for the future of illiteracy will some fine day be realized. I must ask you, however, to try to envisage the minds of a generation of young Americans who receive their lower education under men of this stamp and their higher education under a regime fully conforming to the President's Commission's disdain for verbal aptitudes and abstractions.

 For Discussion:

1. What reasons does Hofstadter give for what he calls the educational crisis in the 1950s?
2. Explain Hofstadter's concepts: "living for ideas," "living for an idea," and "living off ideas."

3. Critiquing Americans' attitudes about forms of play, Hofstadter writes, "sports, sex, liquor, gambling, motoring, and gourmandizing are all more or less legitimate forms of amusement . . . [whereas] the play of the mind, being the only kind that has not been susceptible to commercialization, has not been able to rally the support of a vested interest." Do you agree? What evidence or reasons would you give for your perspective?

4. Hofstadter argues that in a culture that supposedly values education, the status of the genuine intellectual, the high school teacher, or the college professor is little esteemed. Do you think he is correct?

5. What role does Hofstadter feel democracy has played in education and anti-intellectualism in America? In what ways is this argument correct or incorrect?

 For Fact-Finding, Research, and Writing:

1. Using a library database, find another author who defines the concepts of intellectualism and anti-intellectualism and summarize his or her argument. Is the definition similar to Hofstadter's?

2. Who was Alexis de Tocqueville and what did he write about American democracy? Cite one journal article and a book in response to this question.

3. Consult two journal articles that describe the curriculum of the American college before and after the Civil War and summarize the main points of one.

Laura Miller, "Women and Children First: Gender and the Settling of the Electronic Frontier"

Laura Miller is Senior Editor at *Salon*, an Internet magazine of arts and ideas, and editor of *The Salon.com Reader's Guide to Contemporary* Author (2000). Prior to joining *Salon*, Miller wrote about books, movies, and digital culture for the *San Francisco Examiner* and such publications as *The New York Times Review of Books*, *Harper's*, and *Wired*. This essay originally appeared in *Resisting the Virtual Life: The Culture and Politics of Information* (1995).

 Before You Read:

What kinds of dangers are posed by the Internet? Do you think women are particularly endangered in any way by the Internet?

Women and Children First:
Gender and the Settling of the Electronic Frontier

Laura Miller

WHEN *NEWSWEEK* (May 16, 1994) ran an article entitled "Men, Women, and Computers," all hell broke out on the Net, particularly on the online service I've participated in for six years, the WELL (Whole Earth 'Lectronic Link). "Cyberspace, it turns out," declared *Newsweek*'s Nancy Kantrowitz, "isn't much of an Eden after all. It's marred by just as many sexist ruts and gender conflicts as the Real World. . . . Women often feel about as welcome as a system crash." "It was horrible. Awful, poorly researched, unsubstantiated drivel," one member wrote, a sentiment echoed throughout some 480 postings.

However egregious the errors in the article (some sources maintain that they were incorrectly quoted), it's only one of several mainstream media depictions of the Net as an environment hostile to women. Even women who had been complaining about online gender relations found themselves increasingly annoyed by what one WELL member termed the "cyberbabe harassment" angle that seems to typify media coverage of the issue. Reified in the pages of *Newsweek* and other journals, what had once been the topic of discussions by insiders—online commentary is informal, conversational, and often spontaneous—became a journalistic "fact" about the Net known by complete strangers and novices. In a matter of months, the airy stuff of bitch sessions became widespread, hardened stereotypes.

At the same time, the Internet has come under increasing scrutiny as it mutates from an obscure, freewheeling web of computer networks used by a small elite of academics, scientists, and hobbyists to . . . well, nobody seems to know exactly what. But the business press prints vague, fevered prophecies of fabulous wealth, and a bonanza mentality has blossomed. With it comes big business and the government, intent on regulating this amorphous medium into a manageable and profitable industry. The Net's history of informal self-regulation and its wide libertarian streak guarantee that battles like the one over the Clipper chip (a mandatory decoding device that would make all encrypted data readable by federal agents) will be only the first among many.

Yet the threat of regulation is built into the very mythos used to conceptualize the Net by its defenders—and gender plays a crucial role in that threat. However revolutionary the technologized interactions of online communities may seem, we understand them by deploying a set of very familiar metaphors from the rich figurative soup of American culture. Would different metaphors have allowed the Net a different, better historical trajectory? Perhaps not, but the way we choose to describe the Net now encourages us to see regulation as its inevitable fate. And, by examining how gender roles provide a foundation for the intensification of such social controls, we can illuminate the way those roles pro-scribe the freedoms of men as well as women.

For months I mistakenly referred to the EFF (an organization founded by John Perry Barlow and Lotus 1-2-3 designer Mitch Kapor to foster access to, and further the discur-sive freedom of, online communications) as "The Electronic Freedom Foundation," instead of by its actual name, "The Electronic Frontier Foundation." Once corrected, I was struck by how intimately related the ideas "frontier" and "freedom" are in the Western mythos. The *frontier*, as a realm of limitless possibilities and few social controls, hovers, grail-like, in the American psyche, the dream our national identity is based on, but a dream that's always, somehow, just vanishing away.

Once made, the choice to see the Net as a frontier feels unavoidable, but it's actually quite problematic. The word "frontier" has traditionally described a place, if not land then the limitless "final frontier" of space. The Net, on the other hand, occupies precisely no physical space (although the computers and phone lines that make it possible do). It is a completely bodiless, symbolic thing with no discernable boundaries or location. The land of the American frontier did not become a "frontier" until Europeans determined to con-quer it, but the continent existed before the intention to settle it. Unlike land, the Net was created by its pioneers.

Most peculiar, then, is the choice of the word "frontier" to describe an artifact so humanly constructed that it only exists as ideas or information. For central to the idea of the frontier is that it contains no (or very few) other people—fewer than two per square mile according to the nineteenth-century historian Frederick Turner. The freedom the frontier promises is a liberation from the demands of society, while the Net (I'm thinking now of Usenet) has nothing but society to offer. Without other people, news groups, mail-ing lists, and files simply wouldn't exist and e-mail would be purposeless. Unlike real space, cyberspace must be shared.

Nevertheless, the choice of a spatial metaphor (credited to the science-fiction nov-elist William Gibson, who coined the term "cyberspace"), however awkward, isn't surpris-ing. Psychologist Julian Jaynes has pointed out that geographical analogies have long pre-dominated humanity's efforts to conceptualize—map out—consciousness. Unfortunately, these analogies bring with them a heavy load of baggage comparable to Pandora's box: open it and a complex series of problems have come to stay.

The frontier exists beyond the edge of settled or owned land. As the land that doesn't belong to anybody (or to people who "don't count," like Native Americans), it is on the verge of being acquired; currently unowned, but still ownable. Just as the idea of chastity makes virginity sexually provocative, so does the unclaimed territory invite settlers, irre-sistibly so. Americans regard the lost geographical frontier with a melancholy, voluptuous fatalism—we had no choice but to advance upon it and it had no alternative but to sub-mit. When an EFF member compares the Clipper chip to barbed wire encroaching on the prairie, doesn't he realize the surrender implied in his metaphor?

The psychosexual undercurrents (if anyone still thinks of them as "under") in the idea of civilization's phallic intrusion into nature's passive, feminine space have been observed, exhaustively, elsewhere. The classic Western narrative is actually far more concerned with social relationships than conflicts between man and nature. In these stories, the frontier is a lawless society of men, a milieu in which physical strength, courage, and personal charisma supplant institutional authority and violent conflict is the accepted means of settling disputes. The Western narrative connects pleasurably with the American romance of individualistic masculinity; small wonder that the predominantly male founders of the Net's culture found it so appealing.

When civilization arrives on the frontier, it comes dressed in skirts and short pants. In the archetypal 1939 movie *Dodge City*, Wade Hatton (Errol Flynn) refuses to accept the position of marshal because he prefers the footloose life of a trail driver. Abbie Irving (Olivia de Haviland), a recent arrival from the civilized East, scolds him for his unwillingness to accept and advance the cause of law; she can't function (in her job as crusading journalist) in a town governed by brute force. It takes the accidental killing of a child in a street brawl for Hatton to realize that he must pin on the badge and clean up Dodge City.

In the Western mythos, civilization is necessary because women and children are victimized in conditions of freedom. Introduce women and children into a frontier town and the law must follow because women and children must be protected. Women, in fact, are usually the most vocal proponents of the conversion from frontier justice to civil society.

The imperiled women and children of the Western narrative make their appearance today in newspaper and magazine articles that focus on the intimidation and sexual harassment of women online and reports of pedophiles trolling for victims in computerized chat rooms. If online women successfully contest these attempts to depict them as the beleaguered prey of brutish men, expect the pedophile to assume a larger profile in arguments that the Net is out of control.

In the meantime, the media prefer to cast women as the victims, probably because many women actively participate in the call for greater regulation of online interactions, just as Abbie Irving urges Wade Hatton to bring the rule of law to Dodge City. These requests have a long cultural tradition, based on the idea that women, like children, constitute a peculiarly vulnerable class of people who require special protection from the elements of society men are expected to confront alone. In an insufficiently civilized society like the frontier, women, by virtue of this childlike vulnerability, are thought to live under the constant threat of kidnap, abuse, murder, and especially rape.

Women, who have every right to expect that crimes against their person will be rigorously prosecuted, should nevertheless regard the notion of special protections (chivalry, by another name) with suspicion. Based as it is on the idea that women are inherently weak and incapable of self-defense and that men are innately predatory, it actually reinforces the power imbalance between the sexes, with its roots in the concept of women as property, constantly under siege and requiring the vigilant protection of their male owners. If the romance of the frontier arises from the promise of vast stretches of unowned land, an escape from the restrictions of a society based on private property, the introduction of women spoils that dream by reintroducing the imperative of property in their own persons.

How does any of this relate to online interactions, which occur not on a desert landscape but in a complex, technological society where women are supposed to command equal status with men? It accompanies us as a set of unexamined assumptions about what it means to be male or female, assumptions that we believe are rooted in the imperatives of our bodies. These assumptions follow us into the bodiless realm of cyberspace, a forum where, as one scholar puts it "participants are washed clean of the stigmata of their real 'selves' and are free to invent new ones to their tastes." Perhaps some observers feel that the replication of gender roles in a context where the absence of bodies supposedly makes them superfluous proves exactly how innate those roles are. Instead, I see in the relentless attempts to interpret online interactions as highly gendered, an intimation of just how artificial, how created, our gender system is. If it comes "naturally," why does it need to be perpetually defended and reasserted?

Complaints about the treatment of women online fall into three categories: that women are subjected to excessive, unwanted sexual attention, that the prevailing style of online discussion turns women, off, and that women are singled out by male participants for exceptionally dismissive or hostile treatment. In making these assertions, the *Newsweek* article and other stories on the issue do echo grievances that some online women have made for years. And, without a doubt, people have encountered sexual come-ons, aggressive debating tactics, and ad hominem attacks on the Net. However, individual users interpret such events in widely different ways, and to generalize from those interpretations to describe the experiences of women and men as a whole is a rash leap indeed.

I am one of many women who don't recognize their own experience of the Net in the misogynist gauntlet described above. In researching this essay, I joined America Online and spent an hour or two "hanging out" in the real-time chat rooms reputed to be rife with sexual harassment. I received several "instant messages" from men, initiating private conversations with innocuous questions about my hometown and tenure on the service. One man politely inquired if I was interested in "hot phone talk" and just as politely bowed out when I declined. At no point did I feel harassed or treated with disrespect. If I ever want to find a phone-sex partner, I now know where to look but until then I probably won't frequent certain chat rooms.

Other women may experience a request for phone sex or even those tame instant messages as both intrusive and insulting (while still others maintain that they have received much more explicit messages and inquiries completely out of the blue). My point isn't that my reactions are the more correct, but rather that both are the reactions of women, and no journalist has any reason to believe that mine are the exception rather than the rule.

For me, the menace in sexual harassment comes from the underlying threat of rape or physical violence. I see my body as the site of my heightened vulnerability as a woman. But online—where I have no body and neither does anyone else—I consider rape to be impossible. Not everyone agrees. Julian Dibble, in an article for the *Village Voice*, describes the repercussions of a "rape" in a multiuser dimension, or MUD, in which one user employed a subprogram called a "voodoo doll" to cause the personae of other users to perform sexual acts. Citing the "conflation of speech and act that's inevitable in any computer-mediated world," he moved toward the conclusion that "since rape can occur without any physical pain or damage, then it must be classified as a crime against the mind." Therefore, the offending user had committed something on the same "conceptual continuum" as rape. Tellingly, the incident led to the formation of the first governmental entity on the MUD.

No doubt the cyber-rapist (who went by the nom de guerre Mr. Bungle) appreciated the elevation of his mischief-making to the rank of virtual felony: all of the outlaw glamour and none of the prison time (he was exiled from the MUD). Mr. Bungle limited his victims to personae created by women users, a choice that, in its obedience to prevailing gender roles, shaped the debate that followed his crimes. For, in accordance with the real-world understanding that women's smaller, physically weaker bodies and lower social status make them subject to violation by men, there's a troubling notion in the real and virtual worlds that women's minds are also more vulnerable to invasion, degradation, and abuse.

This sense of fragility extends beyond interactions with sexual overtones. The *Newsweek* article reports that women participants can't tolerate the harsh, contentious quality of online discussions, that they prefer mutual support to heated debate, and are retreating wholesale to women-only conferences and newsgroups. As someone who values online forums precisely because they mandate equal time for each user who chooses to take it and forestall various "alpha male" rhetorical tactics like interrupting, loudness, or exploiting the psychosocial advantages of greater size or a deeper voice, I find this perplexing and disturbing. In these laments I hear the reluctance of women to enter into the kind of robust debate that characterizes healthy public life, a willingness to let men bully us even when they've been relieved of most of their traditional advantages. Withdrawing into an electronic purdah where one will never be challenged or provoked, allowing the ludicrous ritual chest-thumping of some users to intimidate us into silence—surely women can come up with a more spirited response than this.

And of course they can, because besides being riddled with reductive stereotypes, media analyses like *Newsweek*'s simply aren't accurate. While the online population is predominantly male, a significant and vocal minority of women contribute regularly and more than manage to hold their own. Some of the WELL's most bombastic participants are women, just as there are many tactful and conciliatory men. At least, I think there are, because, ultimately, it's impossible to be sure of anyone's biological gender online. "Transpostites," people who pose as members of the opposite gender, are an established element of Net society, most famously a man who, pretending to be a disabled lesbian, built warm and intimate friendships with women on several CompuServe forums.

Perhaps what we should be examining is not the triumph of gender differences on the Net, but their potential blurring. In this light, *Newsweek*'s stout assertion that in cyberspace "the gender gap is real" begins to seem less objective than defensive, an insistence that online culture is "the same" as real life because the idea that it might be different, when it comes to gender, is too scary. If gender roles can be cast off so easily, they may be less deeply rooted, less "natural" than we believe. There may not actually be a "masculine" or "feminine" mind or outlook, but simply a conventional way of interpreting individuals that recognizes behavior seen as in accordance with their biological gender and ignores behavior that isn't.

For example, John Seabury wrote in *The New Yorker* (June 6, 1994) of his stricken reaction to his first "flame," a colorful slice of adolescent invective sent to him by an unnamed technology journalist. Reading it, he begins to "shiver" like a burn victim, an effect that worsens with repeated readings. He writes that "the technology greased the words . . . with a kind of immediacy that allowed them to slide easily into my brain." He tells his friends, his coworkers, his partner—even his mother—and, predictably, appeals to CompuServe's management for recourse—to no avail. Soon enough, he's talking about civilization and anarchy, how the liberating "lack of social barriers is also what is appalling about the Net," and calling for regulation.

As a newcomer, Seabury was chided for brooding over a missive that most Net veterans would have dismissed and forgotten as the crude potshot of an envious jerk. (I can't help wondering if my fellow journalist never received hate mail in response to his other writings; this bit of e-mail seems comparable, par for the course when one assumes a public profile.) What nobody did was observe that Seabury's reaction—the shock, the feelings of violation, the appeals to his family and support network, the bootless complaints to the authorities—reads exactly like many horror stories about women's trials on the Net. Yet, because Seabury is a man, no one attributes the attack to his gender or suggests that the Net has proven an environment hostile to men. Furthermore, the idea that the Net must be more strictly governed to prevent the abuse of guys who write for *The New Yorker* seems laughable—though who's to say that Seabury's pain is less than any woman's? Who can doubt that, were he a woman, his tribulations would be seen as compelling evidence of Internet sexism?

The idea that women merit special protections in an environment as incorporeal as the Net is intimately bound up with the idea that women's minds are weak, fragile, and unsuited to the rough and tumble of public discourse. It's an argument that women should recognize with profound mistrust and resist, especially when we are used as rhetorical pawns in a battle to regulate a rare (if elite) space of gender ambiguity. When the mainstream media generalize about women's experiences on line in ways that just happen to uphold the most conventional and pernicious gender stereotypes, they can expect to be greeted with howls of disapproval from women who refuse to acquiesce in these roles and pass them on to other women.

And there are plenty of us, as the WELL's response to the *Newsweek* article indicates. Women have always participated in online communications, women whose chosen careers in technology and the sciences have already marked them as gender-role resisters. As the schoolmarms arrive on the electronic frontier, their female predecessors find themselves cast in the role of saloon girls, their willingness to engage in "masculine" activities like verbal aggression, debate, or sexual experimentation marking them as insufficiently feminine, or "bad" women. "If that's what women online are like, I must be a Martian," one WELL woman wrote in response to the shrinking female technophobes depicted in the *Newsweek* article. Rather than relegating so many people to the status of gender aliens, we ought to reconsider how adequate those roles are to the task of describing real human beings.

For Discussion:

1. Explain Miller's reasons for arguing against the accuracy of the frontier as a metaphor for the Internet. What merits or faults do you see in her argument?
2. Do you agree with Miller when she contends: "But online—where I have no body and neither does anyone else—I consider rape to be impossible"?
3. Do you think that the flow of information on the Net should be controlled and regulated? If yes, do you think that women need protection?
4. Does Miller claim that the Internet is not particularly problematic for women, or does she argue that women should learn to live with the problems?

 For Fact-Finding, Research, and Writing:

1. Miller alludes to an article from *Newsweek*. Find the article, summarize its main points, and explain whether or not she has used it fairly.
2. Create an alternate email address (an alias) and log onto a chat room. (For your own protection, avoid chat rooms with obviously offensive names). How are gender roles represented? How do your findings affect your reading of Miller's essay?
3. Using the Statistical Lexis-Nexis database, find current figures about the gender of Internet users.
4. Are there laws controlling Internet harassment? Are they adequate? Unnecessary?

Mike Godwin, "Hollywood vs. the Internet"

A graduate of the University of Texas School of Law, Godwin currently serves as a policy fellow for the Center for Democracy and Technology in Washington, DC. He is also Chief Correspondent for IP Worldwide and a columnist for *American Lawyer* magazine. He served on the Massachusetts Computer Crime Commission and appeared as co-counsel for the plaintiffs in the Supreme Court case, Reno v. ACLU. In addition to his 1998 book, *Cyber Rights: Defending Free Speech in the Digital Age*, he has published numerous articles on both legal and social issues raised in cyberspace communication. This selection was first published by *Reason*, a monthly magazine published by the Reason Foundation, a research and educational organization in Los Angeles.

 Before You Read:

Should there be different copyright standards for different communication venues such as print, broadcast, motion picture, and recording industries?

Hollywood vs. the Internet

Mike Godwin

IF YOU HAVE a fast computer and a fast Internet connection, you make Hollywood nervous. Movie and TV studios are worried not because of what you're doing now, but because of what you might do in the near future: grab digital content with your computer and rebroadcast it online.

Which is why the studios, along with other content providers, have begun a campaign to stop you from ever being able to do such a thing. As music software designer Selene Makarios puts it, this effort represents "little less than an attempt to outlaw general-purpose computers."

Maybe you loved Napster or maybe you hated it, but the right to start a Napster, or to infringe copyright and get away with it, is not what's at issue here. At some date in the near future, perhaps as early as 2010, people may no longer be able to do the kinds of things they routinely do with their digital tools today. They may no longer be able, for example, to move music or video files easily from one of their computers to another, even if the other is a few feet away in the same house. Their music collections, reduced to MP3s, may be movable to a limited extent, unless their hardware doesn't allow it. The digital videos they shot in 1999 may be unplayable on their desktop and laptop computers.

Programmers trying to come up with, say, the next great version of the Linux operating system may find their development efforts put them at risk of civil and criminal penalties. Indeed, their sons and daughters in grade school computer classes may face similar risks if the broadest of the changes now being proposed—a ban on software, hardware, and any other digital-transmission technology that does not incorporate copyright protection—becomes law.

Whether this scenario comes to pass depends mainly on the outcome of an emerging struggle between the content industries and the information technology industries. The Content Faction includes copyright holders such as movie and Tv studios, record companies, and book publishers. The Tech Faction includes computer makers, software companies, and manufacturers of related devices such as CD burners, MP3 players, and Internet routers. In this war over the future shape of digital technology, it's computer users who may suffer the collateral damage.

Digital television will be the first battleground. Unlike DVD movies, which are encrypted on the disk and decrypted every time they're played, digital broadcast television has to be unencrypted. For one thing, the Federal Communications Commission requires that broadcast television be sent "in the clear." (The rationale is that broadcasters are custodians of a public resource—the part of the electromagnetic spectrum used for television—and therefore have to make whatever they pump into that spectrum available to everyone.) Then, too, digital TV has to reach existing digital television sets, which cannot decode encrypted broadcasts.

The lack of encryption, coupled with digital TV's high quality, poses a problem for copyright holders. If a home viewer can find a way to copy the content of a digital broadcast, he or she can reproduce it digitally over the Internet (or elsewhere), and everybody can get that high-quality digital content for free. This possibility worries the movie and TV studios, which repackage old television shows for sale to individuals as DVDs or videotapes and sell cable channels and broadcast stations the right to air reruns. Who is going to buy DVDs or tapes of TV shows or movies they can get for free online through peer-to-peer file sharing? And if everybody is trading high-quality digital copies of Buffy the Vampire Slayer or Law & Order over the Internet, who's going to watch the reruns on, respectively, Fox's F/X network or the Arts & Entertainment channel? What advertisers are going to sponsor those shows when their complete runs are available online to viewers, commercial-free, through some successor to Napster or Gnutella?

The Content Faction has a plan to prevent this situation from developing—a plan Hollywood's copyright holders hope will work for music and every other kind of content. The first part of the plan involves incorporating a "watermark" into digital TV signals. Invisible to viewers, the watermark would contain information telling home entertainment systems whether to allow copying and, if so, how much. But the watermark won't work without home entertainment equipment that is designed to understand the information and limit copying accordingly. Such a system has not been developed yet, but in theory it could apply to all digital media.

There are some problems with this scheme. If Princeton computer scientist Edward Felten is right, a watermark that's invisible to the audience yet easily detected by machines will be relatively easy to remove. To put it simply, if you can't see it, you won't miss it when it's gone. Which is why the components of new home entertainment systems probably would have to be designed not to play unwatermarked content. Otherwise, all you've done is develop an incentive for both inquisitive hackers and copyright "pirates" to find a way to strip out the watermarks. But if the new entertainment systems won't play content without watermarks, they won't work with old digital videos or MP3s.

The implications of a watermark system extend beyond the standard components of today's home entertainment systems: VCRs, CD and DVD players, TV and radio receivers, amplifiers, and speakers. What tech industry pundits call "convergence" means that one other component is increasingly likely to be part of home entertainment setups: the personal computer. Says Emery Simon, special counsel to the Business Software Alliance (an anti-piracy trade group), "That's the multipurpose device that has them terrified, that will result in leaking [copyrighted content] all over the world."

This prospect is what Disney CEO Michael Eisner had in mind when, in a 2000 speech to Congress, he warned of "the perilous irony of the digital age." Eisner's view of the problem is shared by virtually everybody in the movie industry: "Just as computers make it possible to create remarkably pristine images, they also make it possible to make remark-ably pristine copies."

Because computers are potentially very efficient copying machines, and because the Internet is potentially a very efficient distribution mechanism, the Content Faction has set out to restructure the digital world. It wants to change not just the Internet but every com-puter and digital tool, online or off, that might be used to make unauthorized copies. It wants all such technologies to incorporate "digital rights management" (DRM)—features that prevent copyright infringement.

At stake in this campaign, according to Eisner, is "the future of the American enter-tainment industry, the future of American consumers, the future of America's balance of international trade." Lobbyists at News Corporation, Vivendi Universal S.A., and pretty much every other company whose chief product is content agree with Eisner, the Content Faction's acknowledged leader, about the magnitude of the issue (although foreign-based companies such as Bertelsmann A.G. are understandably less concerned about the U.S. balance of trade). All of them tend to talk about the problems posed by computers, digital technology, and the Internet in apocalyptic terms.

The companies whose bailiwick is computers, digital technology, and the Internet tend to take a different view. Of course, Tech Faction members, which include Microsoft, IBM, Hewlett-Packard, Cisco Systems, and Adobe, also value copyright. (Adobe, for in-stance, last year instigated the prosecution of a Russian computer programmer who cracked the company's encryption-based e-book security scheme.) And many of them—especially those who have been developing their own DRM technologies—want to see a world in which copyrighted works are reasonably well-protected. Yet if you ask them what they think of the Content Faction's agenda for the digital world, you invariably get something similar to the position expressed by Emery Simon of the Business Software Alliance (BSA), a group that includes the Tech Faction's major players: "We are strongly antipiracy, but we think mandating these protections is an abysmally stupid idea."

The two factions' agreement about the importance of protecting copyrighted works online makes them uncomfortable to be on opposite sides now. The Tech Faction and the Content Faction both supported the Digital Millennium Copyright Act (DMCA) of 1998, and both like it pretty much as it is. The DMCA prohibits the creation, dissemination, and use of tools that circumvent DRM technologies.

Where the two factions differ is on the issue of whether the DMCA is enough. The BSA's Simon views the DMCA as a well-crafted piece of legislation but thinks efforts to build DRM into every digital device are overreaching. And in taped remarks at a Decem-ber business technology conference in Washington, D.C., Intel CEO Craig Barrett spoke out against a bill proposed (but not yet formally introduced) by Sen. Ernest "Fritz" Hollings (D-S.C.) that would mandate a national copyright protection standard. The Content Fac-tion says it needs such a standard to survive.

A few companies are so big and diverse that they don't fall easily into either faction. Take AOL Time Warner. The movie studios and other content producers under its um-brella tend to favor efforts that lock down cyberspace, but AOL itself, along with some of the company's cable subsidiaries, tends to resist any effort to mandate universal DRM. "We like the DMCA," says Jill Lesser, AOL Time Warner's senior vice president for domestic public policy. "There isn't from our perspective a need for additional remedies." AOL's reluctance to embrace the Hollings legislation explains why the Motion Picture Association of America, of which AOL Time Warner is a prominent member, remains officially neutral on the bill.

But Lesser needs only to take a breath before she adds that something like the Hollings bill, at least with regard to digital TV, may be a good idea. Industry progress toward an agreement for copyright protection in digital television hasn't proceeded as quickly as the content companies would like. "Maybe a mandate is the way to get there more quickly," she says.

Napster is the specter that's haunting the Content Faction. Although the free version of Napster has been essentially wiped out by music-company litigation (a new version of the file sharing system is being developed by Bertelsmann A.G.), the Napster phenomenon still casts a long shadow. One technologist for News Corporation who is working on a watermark-based DRM scheme says he thinks Napster signals the end of the music industry. He argues that since record companies generally have most of their catalogs available on unprotected CDs, which can be "ripped" and duplicated with CD burners or distributed over the Internet as MP3 files, music lovers already have gotten out of the habit of paying for records, which means an end to big profits and thus an end to big record companies. "Within five years," he says, "the music industry will be a cottage industry."

Matthew Gerson, vice president for public policy at Vivendi Universal, which produces and sells both music (Universal Music Group) and movies (Universal Studios), is quick to dispute such predictions. "We know that if we build a safe, consumer-friendly site that has all the bells and whistles and features that music fans want, it will flourish," he says. "My hunch is that fans will have no trouble paying for the music that they love and compensating the artists who bring it to them—established stars as well as the new voices the labels introduce year after year."

But maintaining that model, in which big music companies play an important filtering role for audiences, depends both on large streams of revenue and on control of copyrighted works. The Internet and digital technology could change all that, cutting off the revenue stream by moving music consumers to a world in which trading music online for free is the norm. (Some recording artists, including Don Henley and Courtney Love, might welcome the change. They question whether the music companies truly serve artists' interests as well as they serve their own corporate interests.) At the same time, a technical/legal scheme that perfects control of digital content creates new revenue opportunities: The music companies, for example, could "rent" or "license" music to us in a protected format rather than sell copies outright.

The Hollings legislation, dubbed the Security Systems Standards and Certification Act, is designed to help content companies turn the potential peril of digital technology into profits. In the drafts available last fall, the bill would make it a civil offense for anyone to develop a new computer or operating system (or any other digital tool that makes copies) that does not incorporate a federally approved security standard preventing unlicensed copying. The bill would set up a scheme under which private companies met and approved the security standard. It would require that the standard be adopted within 18 months; if that deadline passed without agreement on a standard, the government would step in and impose one. In at least one version, the bill would also make it a felony to remove the watermark from copyrighted content or to connect a computer that sidesteps DRM technology to the Internet.

The Hollings bill applies to any digital technology, not just TV. It's clear why the bill's supporters want its scope to be so broad: If the watermark scheme works for digital TV, creating a system for labeling copyrighted works and for designing consumer electronics to prevent unlicensed copying, it should be possible to make it work for the rest of the digital world, including the Internet.

According to Capitol Hill sources, the Hollings bill was inspired by Eisner's 2000 speech to Congress. The people who had a hand in drawing up the legislation do not describe it in terms of protecting embattled copyright interests. Instead, they say it's a proactive measure designed to promote both digital content and increased use of high-speed Internet services. They note that consumer adoption of broadband services (such as cable modems and DSL) has been slower than predicted. Consequently, the cable and phone companies have too small a consumer base to justify building out their broadband capacity very quickly or very far. But if Hollywood could be assured that its content would be protected on the broadband Internet, the theory goes, it would offer more compelling online content, which would inspire greater consumer demand for high-speed service.

This theory, which assumes that what people really want from the Internet is more TV and movies, is questionable, but it has a lot of currency in Washington. And as the debate over broadband deregulation shows, Congress wants to find a way to take credit for a quicker rollout of faster Internet service.

It was the Hollings bill that brought the war between the Content Faction and the Tech Faction out into the open. And in the near term it's the Hollings bill that is likely to be the flash point for the debate about copyright protection standards. A congressional hearing on Hollings' proposal was held in late February, but no bill has been formally introduced.

One way to understand the conflict between the Content Faction and the Tech Faction is to look at how they describe their customers. For the content industries, they're "consumers." By contrast, the information technology companies talk about "users."

If you see people as consumers, you control access to what you offer, and you do everything you can to prevent theft, for the same reason supermarkets have cameras by the door and bookstores have electronic theft detectors. Allowing people to take stuff for free is inconsistent with your business model.

But if you see people as users, you want to give them more features and power at cheaper prices. The impulse to empower users was at the heart of the microcomputer revolution: Steve Jobs and Steve Wozniak wanted to put computing power into ordinary people's hands, and that's why they founded Apple Computer. If this is your approach—enabling people to do new things—it's hard to adjust to the idea of building in limitations.

In a basic sense, moving bits around from hard drives to RAM to screen and back again, with 100 percent accuracy in copying, is simply what computers do. To the Tech Faction, building DRM into computers, limiting how they perform their basic functions, means turning them into special-purpose appliances, something like a toaster. This approach is anathema to the user empowerment philosophy that drove the PC revolution.

The Tech Faction believes people should be able to do whatever they want with their digital tools, except to the extent that copyrighted works are walled off by DRM. The Content Faction believes the digital world isn't safe unless every tool also functions as a copyright policeman.

At the heart of this argument are two questions: whether computer users can continue to enjoy the capabilities computers have had since their invention, and whether the content companies can survive in a world where users have those capabilities. What's been missing from the debate so far has been the users themselves, although some public interest groups are gearing up to tackle the issue. Users may well take the approach I would take: If computers and software start shipping in a hamstrung form, mandated by government, I'll quit buying new equipment. Why trade in last year's feature-rich laptop for a new one that, while faster, has fewer capabilities?

The Content Faction may be right that what people really want is compelling content over broadband. It may even be the case that, if they were asked, most people would be willing to trade the open, robust, relatively simple tools they now have for a more constrained digital world in which they have more content choices. But for now, nobody's asking ordinary people what they want.

 For Discussion:

1. What is the difference between "consumers" and "users"?
2. What is DRM? What are the issues raised by the use of DRMs?
3. Godwin discusses the disagreements between the Tech faction and the Content faction. What is the third faction he acknowledges? Where does this third faction fit into the ongoing argument?
4. What action does Godwin suggest for computer owners? Will this action resolve the problems he has outlined?

 For Fact-Finding, Research, and Writing:

1. Locate a copy of the Hollings Bill and transcriptions of the debate it created. Who made the most effective argument for or against the bill? Why?
2. When were the first copyright laws enacted in the United States? Prior to that time, what rights of ownership did authors enjoy? What problems did authors face before copyright laws were enforced?

3. Find a list of contributors to the Center for Democracy and Technology. What can you infer from these funding sources?
4. Read the mission statement of the Reason Foundation. What are the implications of this organization's goals?

Don DeLillo, "Videotape"

Don DeLillo, a winner of the National Book Award and the PEN/Faulkner Award for fiction, is the author of twelve novels. Born in 1936, he worked at an advertising agency after graduating from Fordham University. In 1964, he became a freelance writer and published his first novel, *Americana*, in 1971. Although he was long a critically acclaimed author, *White Noise* (1985) was his first commercially successful work. "Videotape" first appeared in *Antaeus* in 1994, has been frequently reprinted and appears in the opening chapter of Part 2 of his novel *Underworld* (1997). He has described this short story as being "about reliving things. . . . Fiction is about reliving things. It is our second chance." Some of his work "relives" historical events such as the assassination of John F. Kennedy *(Libra)*. DeLillo's work examines cultural production and the consumption of culture—how the world around us is presented and represented, and how we receive and use those representations. Although he may write about computers and other technological advances, he uses a manual typewriter to create his fiction.

 Before You Read:

DeLillo writes, "You know about families and their video cameras." What do you know about camcorders in the hands of a family member? Why have some families scrapped their photo albums for video recordings?

Videotape

Don DeLillo

IT SHOWS A man driving a car. It is the simplest sort of family video. You see a man at the wheel of a medium Dodge.

It is just a kid aiming her camera through the rear window of the family car at the windshield of the car behind her.

You know about families and their video cameras. You know how kids get involved, how the camera shows them that every subject is potentially charged, a million things they never see with the unaided eye. They investigate the meaning of inert objects and dumb pets and they poke at family privacy. They learn to see things twice.

It is the kid's own privacy that is being protected here. She is twelve years old and her name is being withheld even though she is neither the victim nor the perpetrator of the crime but only the means of recording it.

It shows a man in a sport shirt at the wheel of his car. There is nothing else to see. The car approaches briefly, then falls back.

You know how children with cameras learn to work the exposed moments that define the family cluster. They break every trust, spy out the undefended space, catching Mom coming out of the bathroom in her cumbrous robe and turbaned towel, looking bloodless and plucked. It is not a joke. They will shoot you sitting on the pot if they can manage a suitable vantage.

The tape has the jostled sort of noneventness that marks the family product. Of course the man in this case is not a member of the family but a stranger in a car, a random figure, someone who has happened along in the slow lane.

It shows a man in his forties wearing a pale shirt open at the throat, the image washed by reflections and sunglint, with many jostled moments.

It is not just another video homicide. It is a homicide recorded by a child who thought she was doing something simple and maybe halfway clever, shooting some tape of a man in a car.

He sees the girl and waves briefly, wagging a hand without taking it off the wheel— an underplayed reaction that makes you like him.

It is unrelenting footage that rolls on and on. It has an aimless determination, a persistence that lives outside the subject matter. You are looking into the mind of home video. It is innocent, it is aimless, it is determined, it is real.

He is bald up the middle of his head, a nice guy in his forties whose whole life seems open to the hand-held camera.

But there is also an element of suspense. You keep on looking not because you know something is going to happen—of course you do know something is going to happen and you do look for that reason but you might also keep on looking if you came across this footage for the first time without knowing the outcome. There is a crude power operating here. You keep on looking because things combine to hold you fast—a sense of the random, the amateurish, the accidental, the impending. You don't think of the tape as boring or interesting. It is crude, it is blunt, it is relentless. It is the jostled part of your mind, the film that runs through your hotel brain under all the thoughts you know you're thinking.

The world is lurking in the camera, already framed, waiting for the boy or girl who will come along and take up the device, learn the instrument, shooting old Granddad at breakfast, all stroked out so his nostrils gape, the cereal spoon baby-gripped in his pale fist.

It shows a man alone in a medium Dodge. It seems to go on forever.

There's something about the nature of the tape, the grain of the image, the sputtering black-and-white tones, the starkness—you think this is more real, truer-to-life, than anything around you. The things around you have a rehearsed and layered and cosmetic look. The tape is superreal, or maybe underreal is the way you want to put it. It is what lies at the scraped bottom of all the layers you have added. And this is another reason why you keep on looking. The tape has a searing realness.

It shows him giving an abbreviated wave, stiff-palmed, like a signal flag at a siding.

You know how families make up games. This is just another game in which the child invents the rules as she goes along. She likes the idea of videotaping a man in his car. She has probably never done it before and she sees no reason to vary the format or terminate early or pan to another car. This is her game and she is learning it and playing it at the same time. She feels halfway clever and inventive and maybe slightly intrusive as well, a little bit of brazenness that spices any game.

And you keep on looking. You look because this is the nature of the footage, to make a channeled path through time, to give things a shape and a destiny.

Of course if she had panned to another car, the right car at the precise time, she would have caught the gunman as he fired.

The chance quality of the encounter. The victim, the killer, and the child with a camera. Random energies that approach a common point. There's something here that speaks to you directly, saying terrible things about forces beyond your control, lines of intersection that cut through history and logic and every reasonable layer of human expectation.

She wandered into it. The girl got lost and wandered clear-eyed into horror. This is a children's story about straying too far from home. But it isn't the family car that serves as the instrument of the child's curiosity, her inclination to explore. It is the camera that puts her in the tale.

You know about holidays and family celebrations and how somebody shows up with a camcorder and the relatives stand around and barely react because they're numbingly accustomed to the process of being taped and decked and shown on the VCR with the coffee and cake.

He is hit soon after. If you've seen the tape many times you know from the handwave exactly when he will be hit. It is something, naturally, that you wait for. You say to your wife, if you're at home and she is there, Now here is where he gets it. You say, Janet, hurry up, this is where it happens.

Now here is where he gets it. You see him jolted, sort of wire-shocked—then he seizes up and falls toward the door or maybe leans or slides into the door is the proper way to put it. It is awful and unremarkable at the same time. The car stays in the slow lane. It approaches briefly, then falls back.

You don't usually call your wife over to the TV set. She has her programs, you have yours. But there's a certain urgency here. You want her to see how it looks. The tape has been running forever and now the thing is finally going to happen and you want her to be here when he's shot.

Here it comes, all right. He is shot, head-shot, and the camera reacts, the child reacts—there is a jolting movement but she keeps on taping, there is a sympathetic response, a nerve response, her heart is beating faster but she keeps the camera trained on the subject as he slides into the door and even as you see him die you're thinking of the girl. At some level the girl has to be present here, watching what you're watching, unprepared —the girl is seeing this cold and you have to marvel at the fact that she keeps the tape rolling.

It shows something awful and unaccompanied. You want your wife to see it because it is real this time, not fancy movie violence—the realness beneath the layers of cosmetic perception. Hurry up, Janet, here it comes. He dies so fast. There is no accompaniment of any kind. It is very stripped. You want to tell her it is realer than real but then she will ask what that means.

The way the camera reacts to the gunshot—a startled reaction that brings pity and terror into the frame, the girl's own shock, the girl's identification with the victim.

You don't see the blood, which is probably trickling behind his ear and down the back of his neck. The way his head is twisted away from the door, the twist of the head gives you only a partial profile and it's the wrong side, it's not the side where he was hit.

And maybe you're being a little aggressive here, practically forcing your wife to watch. Why? What are you telling her? Are you making a little statement? Like I'm going to ruin your day out of ordinary spite. Or a big statement? Like this is the risk of existing. Either way you're rubbing her face in this tape and you don't know why.

It shows the car drifting toward the guardrail and then there's a jostling sense of two other lanes and part of another car, a split-second blur, and the tape ends here, either because the girl stopped shooting or because some central authority, the police or the district attorney or the TV station, decided there was nothing else you had to see.

This is either the tenth or eleventh homicide committed by the Texas Highway Killer. The number is uncertain because the police believe that one of the shootings may have been a copycat crime.

And there is something about videotape, isn't there, and this particular kind of serial crime? This is a crime designed for random taping and immediate playing. You sit there and wonder if this kind of crime became more possible when the means of taping and playing an event—playing it immediately after the taping—became part of the culture. The principal doesn't necessarily commit the sequence of crimes in order to see them taped and played. He commits the crimes as if they were a form of taped-and-played event. The crimes are inseparable from the idea of taping and playing. You sit there thinking that this is a crime that has found its medium, or vice versa—cheap mass production, the sequence of repeated images and victims, stark and glary and more or less unremarkable.

It shows very little in the end. It is a famous murder because it is on tape and because the murderer has done it many times and because the crime was recorded by a child. So the child is involved, the Video Kid as she is sometimes called because they have to call her something. The tape is famous and so is she. She is famous in the modern manner of people whose names are strategically withheld. They are famous without names or faces, spirits living apart from their bodies, the victims and witnesses, the underage criminals, out there somewhere at the edges of perception.

Seeing someone at the moment he dies, dying unexpectedly. This is reason alone to stay fixed to the screen. It is instructional, watching a man shot dead as he drives along on a sunny day. It demonstrates an elemental truth, that every breath you take has two possible endings. And that's another thing. There's a joke locked away here, a note of cruel slapstick that you are completely willing to appreciate. Maybe the victim's a chump, a dope, classically unlucky. He had it coming, in a way, like an innocent fool in a silent movie.

You don't want Janet to give you any crap about it's on all the time, they show it a thousand times a day. They show it because it exists, because they have to show it, because this is why they're out there. The horror freezes your soul but this doesn't mean that you want them to stop.

 For Discussion:

1. DeLillo describes the videotape as, "more real, truer-to-life, than anything around you." What do you think such a statement implies about our world?
2. Why do you think this is a "famous murder"? Why might the young girl be called "The Video Kid"?
3. What might the videotape reveal if an adult had operated the camera? Why?
4. For what purpose would television stations air this video "all the time"?
5. How would you characterize the narrator and Janet as television news consumers? What do their responses suggest about American television audiences?
6. How is DeLillo's story related to the essay of de Zengotita?

 For Fact-Finding, Research, and Writing:

1. Is there any "central authority" in the United States that monitors what video footage reaches an audience?
2. Using a newspaper or news magazine database, look up information about a specific instance of violent news footage aired in the United States. What was the public reaction to repeated broadcast of it?
3. What standards are in place for violent material broadcast on television? Print or copy the standards you locate and analyze the guidelines you have found. Are the goals ethical or commercial?
4. How has the federal government addressed the issues of representing violence on television? What government agencies would be concerned with this issue, and why?

CHAPTER FOUR

What's in the Future?

Introduction

It is certain that advances in information technology will influence our future. Unfortunately, determining the shape of this future is not easy to predict. This section explores how current ideas and systems may affect our future lives and the course of both humankind and the planet we inhabit. There is no shortage of futuristic visions; speculations about the future come from not only science fiction writers but from lawyers, engineers, environmental scientists, economists, and even cartoonists. The years 1984 and 2001 have passed without fulfilling the dire projections wrought by George Orwell and Stanley Kubrick, but we remain uncertain as to what's in store down the line.

Our world continues to change as the way we process, evaluate and use information replaces older methods. These solutions may lead to phenomenal advances, but as anyone who has ever felt a pang of dread during a science fiction film knows, there may be equally phenomenal risks and sometimes those risks outweigh the rewards. Each vision of the future raises questions of ethics: how can we create a more just and peaceful world in which fundamental rights to health, education, and self-determination may be respected? What do we value most about our lives on Earth? The question we face as we advance deeper into the twenty-first century is often not *if* we can do something, but *should* we?

Monsters, Androids, and Corporations

An anonymous staff writer reviewed Per Schelde's book on science fiction film for the magazine, *The Futurist*. It is published by The World Future Society, a non-profit organization of scientists and social analysts interested in all facets of futuristic research. Its membership has included such diverse thinkers as Margaret Mead, Al Gore, Carl Sagan, B. F. Skinner, and Buckminster Fuller.

 Before You Read:

Think about the science fiction or futuristic films you have seen. Which did you find most frightening and why?

Monsters, Androids, and Corporations

Images of the future flashing across movie screens consist of aliens out to destroy humans, androids out to replace humans, and various monsters wreaking havoc unforeseen by their mad scientist creators. But, as stories set sometime in the future, do these images really reflect our views of the future?

Probably not, says Per Schelde, a linguistic anthropologist and folklorist. Rather, these movie monsters can be viewed as extensions of creatures from folklore, like dwarfs, trolls, and pixies. Folklore is traditionally used to explain unknown powers and forces. The science-fiction monsters of today emerge from our new "unknowns"—outer space and faraway planets. Science fiction (sf) also deals with disasters wrought on Earth, usually the result of science and technology out of control. The images we see on the screen are frightening because they depict "a reality which the people who created them have, in effect, no power to influence," says Schelde.

The author notes that sf movies have little in common with sf literature and appeal to different audiences. The sf movie audience is drawn more from the general public, whereas sf readers tend to be more interested in intellectual speculation. "Sf movies assiduously (with few exceptions) avoid being intellectual and speculative. The focus is not the 'what ifs' of science, technology, and the future. The sf film focus is on the effects of science, on the junction where what science has created (usually a monster) meets people going about living their lives. Sf science does not have to be logical. All that is required is a scary monster. How the monster came to be or where it came from is, if not irrelevant, peripheral."

This is not to say that sf movies have not provided some lessons about ourselves and about society's direction. For example, one of the most dangerous movie "monsters" depicted in recent years is the giant corporation, Schelde argues. In *Robocop*, "the Bad Guys are two corporation executives who control the scientists and pit their 'monsters' against each other." At the end of the twentieth century, the multinational corporation has become the monster in movie metaphor, like communism in the middle of the century.

Taking the images on the screen too seriously has dangers, according to Schelde. Because movies rely on conflict, the only vision of a utopia that is filmable is one in disarray. A conflict-free society is uninteresting, so the reasons for the lack of conflict must be sinister—perhaps the destruction of freedom, human individuality, and creativity, as in *The Handmaid's Tale* and *Brazil*. And, unlike real life, movies solve the conflict within a couple of hours. The heroes win, the bad guys are killed.

Schelde argues that, in some ways, movies may desensitize us to the dystopian futures they depict. "Sf shows us what to expect, gets us used to it. In the end sf becomes point man for the *Brave New World*: the movies get us accustomed to the dystopia. When the police state is in place, we will recognize it and be almost relieved because we were expecting it. And the police state, the Corporate Empire, will come. It is happening, not overnight and suddenly, as in the movies, but slowly and imperceptibly. Sf makes us blind to the slow, creeping changes, because we are looking for the sudden, the dramatic."

Androids, Humanoids, and Other Science Fiction Monsters covers such wildly different films as the classic *2001: A Space Odyssey, E.T.: The Extraterrestrial, Blade Runner*, and *Twins*, the comic takeoff on genetic engineering (with Danny DeVito and Arnold Schwarzenegger as twin brothers). The book is written with insight and clarity by a scholar willing to venture out of the ivory tower to sit in a lot of darkened theaters.

 For Discussion:

1. If you read or were told fairytales as a child, you may remember some of the creatures imagined in them. What comparisons would you make between those figures and the science-fiction monsters of today's films? Do you think Schelde is correct that our nightmares in film are simply new versions of the monsters of old?

2. Do you agree that "the multinational corporation has become the monster in movie metaphor"? Why might this be true or untrue?

3. Is it possible that viewing dystopian visions of the future will blind us to "the slow creeping changes" of our time or numb us to the horror of a dystopian present? Or does that seem unlikely?

4. This review may resemble the abstracts you are being asked to write for your own annotated bibliography. What are some of the major differences and similarities between this review and the abstracts you've been assigned?

 For Fact-Finding, Research, and Writing:

1. Find a peer-reviewed article on a major dystopian film like *Blade Runner, Alien, Akira,* or *Robocop* and a review of the same film in a publication intended for a general audience. What is the thesis of each, and what differences do you see in their approach to their subject?
2. Using the OSU library webpage or an internet search engine, find a definition of "cyberpunk" that distinguishes it from horror or futuristic film. Evaluate the credibility of the source using the guidelines in *Writing Worth Reading*, pages 355–59.
3. Find a book in the library catalogue by one of the persons listed in the head note to this reading selection. Using the clickable subject headings located directly under the publication data, find another book on a related subject.

Sherry Turkle, "Cyberspace and Identity"

Sherry Turkle is Abby Rockefeller Mauzé Professor in the Program in Science, Technology, and Society at the Massachusetts Institute of Technology (MIT). She is also the founder and director of the MIT Initiative on Technology and Self. She is considered one of the foremost experts on the psychological and sociological impacts of computational technology. Her books include *Psychoanalytic Politics: Jacques Lacan and Freud's French Revolution* (1978), *The Second Self: Computers and the Human Spirit* (1984), and *Life on the Screen: Identity in the Age of the Internet* (1995), from which this essay is excerpted.

 Before You Read:

Do you have different personalities you use to handle certain people or occasions? Do you ever wish you were someone else? What might change about you if you had a different name, or even a different face or body? If you chat online, what are some differences between your real identity and your online identity? If you have never chatted online, what might you leave out of a personal description?

Cyberspace and Identity

Sherry Turkle

WE COME TO SEE ourselves differently as we catch sight of our images in the mirror of the machine. Over a decade ago, when I first called the computer a "second self" (1984), these identity-transforming relationships were most usually one-on-one, a person alone with a machine. This is no longer the case. A rapidly expanding system of networks, collectively known as the Internet, links millions of people together in new spaces that are changing the way we think, the nature of our sexuality, the form of our communities, our very identities. In cyberspace, we are learning to live in virtual worlds. We may find ourselves alone as we navigate virtual oceans, unravel virtual mysteries, and engineer virtual skyscrapers. But increasingly, when we step through the looking glass, other people are there as well.

Over the past decade, I have been engaged in the ethnographic and clinical study of how people negotiate the virtual and the "real" as they represent themselves on computer screens linked through the Internet. For many people, such experiences challenge what they have traditionally called "identity," which they are moved to recast in terms of multiple windows and parallel lives. Online life is not the only factor that is pushing them in this direction; there is no simple sense in which computers are causing a shift in notions of identity. It is, rather, that today's life on the screen dramatizes and concretizes a range of cultural trends that encourage us to think of identity in terms of multiplicity and flexibility.

Virtual Personae

In this essay, I focus on one key element of online life and its impact on identity, the creation and projection of constructed personae into virtual space. In cyberspace, it is well known, one's body can be represented by one's own textual description: The obese can be slender, the beautiful plain. The fact that self-presentation is written in text means that there is time to reflect upon and edit one's "composition," which makes it easier for the shy to be outgoing, the "nerdy" sophisticated. The relative anonymity of life on the screen—one has the choice of being known only by one's chosen "handle" or online name—gives people the chance to express often unexplored aspects of the self. Additionally, multiple aspects of self can be explored in parallel. Online services offer their users the opportunity to be known by several different names. For example, it is not unusual for someone to be BroncoBill in one online community, ArmaniBoy in another, and MrSensitive in a third.

The online exercise of playing with identity and trying out new identities is perhaps most explicit in "role playing" virtual communities (such as Multi-User Domains, or MUDs) where participation literally begins with the creation of a persona (or several); but it is by no means confined to these somewhat exotic locations. In bulletin boards, newsgroups, and chat rooms, the creation of personae may be less explicit than on MUDs, but it is no less psychologically real. One IRC (Internet Relay Chat) participant describes her experience of online talk: "I go from channel to channel depending on my mood. . . . I actually feel a part of several of the channels, several conversations . . . I'm different in the different chats. They bring out different things in me." Identity play can happen by changing names and by changing places.

For many people, joining online communities means crossing a boundary into highly charged territory. Some feel an uncomfortable sense of fragmentation, some a sense of relief. Some sense the possibilities for self-discovery. A 26-year-old graduate student in history says, "When I log on to a new community and I create a character and know I have to start typing my description, I always feel a sense of panic. Like I could find out something I don't want to know." A woman in her late thirties who just got an account with America Online used the fact that she could create five "names" for herself on her account as a chance to "lay out all the moods I'm in—all the ways I want to be in different places on the system."

The creation of site-specific online personae depends not only on adopting a new name. Shifting of personae happens with a change of virtual place. Cycling through virtual environments is made possible by the existence of what have come to be called "windows" in modern computing environments. Windows are a way to work with a computer that makes it possible for the machine to place you in several contexts at the same time. As a user, you are attentive to just one of the windows on your screen at any given moment, but in a certain sense, you are a presence in all of them at all times. You might be writing a paper in bacteriology and using your computer in several ways to help you: You are "present" to a word processing program on which you are taking notes and collecting thoughts, you are "present" to communications software that is in touch with a distant computer for collecting reference materials, you are "present" to a simulation program that is charting the growth of bacterial colonies when a new organism enters their ecology, and you are "present" to an online chat session where participants are discussing recent research in the field. Each of these activities takes place in a "window," and your identity on the computer is the sum of your distributed presence.

The development of the windows metaphor for computer interfaces was a technical innovation motivated by the desire to get people working more efficiently by "cycling through" different applications, much as time-sharing computers cycle through the computing needs of different people. But in practice, windows have become a potent metaphor for thinking about the self as a multiple, distributed, "time-sharing" system.

The self no longer simply plays different roles in different settings—something that people experience when, for example, one wakes up as a lover; makes breakfast as a mother; and drives to work as a lawyer. The windows metaphor suggests a distributed self that exists in many worlds and plays many roles at the same time. The "windows" enabled by a computer operating system support the metaphor, and cyberspace raises the experience to a higher power by translating the metaphor into a life experience of "cycling through."

Identity, Moratoria, and Play

Cyberspace, like all complex phenomena, has a range of psychological effects. For some people, it is a place to "act out" unresolved conflicts, to play and replay characterological difficulties on a new and exotic stage. For others, it provides an opportunity to "work through" significant personal issues, to use the new materials of cybersociality to reach for new resolutions. These more positive identity effects follow from the fact that for some, cyberspace provides what Erik Erikson ([1950] 1963) would have called a "psychosocial moratorium," a central element in how he thought about identity development in adolescence. Although the term moratorium implies a "time out," what Erikson had in mind was not withdrawal. On the contrary, the adolescent moratorium is a time of intense interaction with people and ideas. It is a time of passionate friendships and experimentation. The adolescent falls in and out of love with people and ideas. Erikson's notion of the moratorium was not a "hold" on significant experiences but on their consequences. It is a time during which one's actions are, in a certain sense, not counted as they will be later in life. They are not given as much weight, not given the force of full judgment. In this context, experimentation can become the norm rather than a brave departure. Relatively consequence-free experimentation facilitates the development of a "core self," a personal sense of what gives life meaning that Erikson called "identity."

Erikson developed these ideas about the importance of a moratorium during the late 1950s and early 1960s. At that time, the notion corresponded to a common understanding of what "the college years" were about. Today, 30 years later, the idea of the college years as a consequence-free "time out" seems of another era. College is pre-professional, and AIDS has made consequence-free sexual experimentation an impossibility. The years associated with adolescence no longer seem a "time out." But if our culture no longer offers an adolescent moratorium, virtual communities often do. It is part of what makes them seem so attractive.

Erikson's ideas about stages did not suggest rigid sequences. His stages describe what people need to achieve before they can move ahead easily to another developmental task. For example, Erikson pointed out that successful intimacy in young adulthood is difficult if one does not come to it with a sense of who one is, the challenge of adolescent identity building. In real life, however, people frequently move on with serious deficits. With incompletely resolved "stages," they simply do the best they can. They use whatever materials they have at hand to get as much as they can of what they have missed. Now virtual social life can play a role in these dramas of self-reparation. Time in cyberspace reworks the notion of the moratorium because it may now exist on an always-available "window."

Expanding One's Range in the Real

Case, a 34-year-old industrial designer happily married to a female co-worker, describes his real-life (RL) persons as a "nice guy," a "Jimmy Stewart type like my father." He describes his outgoing, assertive mother as a "Katharine Hepburn type." For Case, who views assertiveness through the prism of this Jimmy Stewart/Katharine Hepburn dichotomy, an assertive man is quickly perceived as "being a bastard." An assertive woman, in contrast, is perceived as being "modern and together." Case says that although he is comfortable with his temperament and loves and respects his father, he feels he pays a high price for his own low-key ways. In particular, he feels at a loss when it comes to confrontation, both at home and at work. Online, in a wide range of virtual communities, Case presents himself as females whom he calls his "Katharine Hepburn types." These are strong, dynamic, "out there" women who remind Case of his mother, who "says exactly what's on her mind." He tells me that presenting himself as a woman online has brought him to a point where he is more comfortable with confrontation in his RL as a man.

Case describes his Katharine Hepburn personae as "externalizations of a part of myself." In one interview with him, I used the expression "aspects of the self," and he picked it up eagerly, for his online life reminds him of how Hindu gods could have different aspects or subpersonalities, all the while being a whole self. In response to my question "Do you feel that you call upon your personae in real life?" Case responded:

> Yes, an aspect sort of clears its throat and says, "I can do this. You are being so amazingly conflicted over this and I know exactly what to do. Why don't you just let me do it?" . . . In real life, I tend to be extremely diplomatic, nonconfrontational. I don't like to ram my ideas down anyone's throat. [Online] I can be, "Take it or leave it." All of my Hepburn characters are that way. That's probably why I play them. Because they are smart-mouthed, they will not sugarcoat their words.

In some ways, Case's description of his inner world of actors who address him and are able to take over negotiations is reminiscent of the language of people with multiple-personality disorder. But the contrast is significant: Case's inner actors are not split off from each other or from his sense of "himself." He experiences himself very much as a collective self, not feeling that he must goad or repress this or that aspect of himself into conformity. He is at ease, cycling through from Katharine Hepburn to Jimmy Stewart. To use analyst Philip Bromberg's language (1994), online life has helped Case learn how to "stand in the spaces between selves and still feel one, to see the multiplicity and still feel a unity." To use computer scientist Marvin Minsky's (1987) phrase, Case feels at ease cycling through his "society of mind," a notion of identity as distributed and heterogeneous. Identity, from the Latin *idem*, has been used habitually to refer to the sameness between two qualities. On the Internet, however, one can be many, and one usually is.

An Object to Think with for Thinking about Identity

In the late 1960s and early 1970s, I was first exposed to notions of identity and multiplicity. These ideas—most notably that there is no such thing as "the ego," that each of us is a multiplicity of parts, fragments, and desiring connections—surfaced in the intellectual hothouse of Paris; they presented the world according to such authors as Jacques Lacan, Gilles Deleuze, and Felix Guattari. But despite such ideal conditions for absorbing theory, my "French lessons" remained abstract exercises. These theorists of poststructuralism spoke words that addressed the relationship between mind and body, but from my point of view had little to do with my own.

In my lack of personal connection with these ideas, I was not alone. To take one example, for many people it is hard to accept any challenge to the idea of an autonomous ego. While in recent years, many psychologists, social theorists, psychoanalysts, and philosophers have argued that the self should be thought of as essentially decentered, the normal requirements of everyday life exert strong pressure on people to take responsibility for their actions and to see themselves as unitary actors. This disjuncture between theory (the unitary self is an illusion) and lived experience (the unitary self is the most basic reality) is one of the main reasons why multiple and decentered theories have been slow to catch on—or when they do, why we tend to settle back quickly into older, centralized ways of looking at things.

When, 20 years later, I used my personal computer and modem to join online communities, I had an experience of this theoretical perspective which brought it shockingly down to earth. I used language to create several characters. My textual actions are my actions—my words make things happen. I created selves that were made and transformed by language. And different personae were exploring different aspects of the self. The notion of a decentered identity was concretized by experiences on a computer screen. In this way, cyberspace becomes an object to think with for thinking about identity—an element of cultural bricolage.

Appropriable theories—ideas that capture the imagination of the culture at large—tend to be those with which people can become actively involved. They tend to be theories that can be "played" with. So one way to think about the social appropriability of a given theory is to ask whether it is accompanied by its own objects-to-think-with that can help it move out beyond intellectual circles.

For example, the popular appropriation of Freudian ideas had little to do with scientific demonstrations of their validity. Freudian ideas passed into the popular culture because they offered robust and down-to-earth objects to think with. The objects were not physical but almost-tangible ideas, such as dreams and slips of the tongue. People were able to play with such Freudian "objects." They became used to looking for them and manipulating them, both seriously and not so seriously. And as they did so, the idea that slips and dreams betray an unconscious began to feel natural.

In Freud's work, dreams and slips of the tongue carried the theory. Today, life on the computer screen carries theory. People decide that they want to interact with others on a computer network. They get an account on a commercial service. They think that this will provide them with new access to people and information, and of course it does. But it does more. When they log on, they may find themselves playing multiple roles; they may find themselves playing characters of the opposite sex. In this way, they are swept up by experiences that enable them to explore previously unexamined aspects of their sexuality or that challenge their ideas about a unitary self. The instrumental computer, the computer that does things for us, has revealed another side: a subjective computer that does things *to* us as people, to our view of ourselves and our relationships, to our ways of looking at our minds. In simulation, identity can be fluid and multiple, a signifier no longer clearly points to a thing that is signified, and understanding is less likely to proceed through analysis than by navigation through virtual space.

Within the psychoanalytic tradition, many "schools" have departed from a unitary view of identity, among these the Jungian, object-relations, and Lacanian. In different ways, each of these groups of analysts was banished from the ranks of orthodox Freudians for such suggestions, or somehow relegated to the margins. As the United States became the center of psychoanalytic politics in the mid-twentieth century, ideas about a robust executive ego began to constitute the psychoanalytic mainstream.

But today, the pendulum has swung away from that complacent view of a unitary self. Through the fragmented selves presented by patients and through theories that stress the decentered subject contemporary social and psychological thinkers are confronting what has been left out of theories of the unitary self. It is asking such questions as, What is the self when it functions as a society? What is the self when it divides its labors among its constituent "alters"? Those burdened by posttraumatic dissociative disorders suffer these questions; I am suggesting that inhabitants of virtual communities play with them. In our lives on the screen, people are developing ideas about identity as multiplicity through new social *practices* of identity as multiplicity.

With these remarks, I am not implying that chat rooms or MUDs or the option to declare multiple user names on America Online are causally implicated in the dramatic increase of people who exhibit symptoms of multiple-personality disorder (MPD), or that people on MUDs have MPD, or that MUDding (or online chatting) is like having MPD. I am saying that the many manifestations of multiplicity in our culture, including the adoption of online personae, are contributing to a general reconsideration of traditional, unitary notions of identity. Online experiences with "parallel lives" are part of the significant cultural context that supports new theorizing about nonpathological, indeed healthy, multiple selves.

In thinking about the self, *multiplicity* is a term that carries with it several centuries of negative associations, but such authors as Kenneth Gergen (1991), Emily Martin (1994), and Robert Jay Lifton (1993) speak in positive terms of an adaptive, "flexible" self. The flexible self is not unitary, nor are its parts stable entities. A person cycles through its aspects, and these are themselves ever-changing and in constant communication with each other. Daniel Dennett (1991) speaks of the flexible self by using the metaphor of consciousness as multiple drafts, analogous to the experience of several versions of a document open on a computer screen, where the user is able to move between them at will. For Dennett, knowledge of these drafts encourages a respect for the many different versions, while it imposes a certain distance from them. Donna Haraway (1991), picking up on this theme of how a distance between self states may be salutory, equates a "split and contradictory self" with a "knowing self." She is optimistic about its possibilities: "The knowing self is partial in all its guises, never finished, whole, simply there and original; it is always constricted and stitched together imperfectly; and therefore able to join with another to see together without claiming to be another." What most characterizes Haraway's and Dennett's models of a knowing self is that the lines of communication between its various aspects are open. The open communication encourages an attitude of respect for the many within us and the many within others.

Increasingly, social theorists and philosophers are being joined by psychoanalytic theorists in efforts to think about healthy selves whose resilience and capacity for joy comes from having access to their many aspects. For example, Philip Bromberg (1994) insists that our ways of describing "good parenting" must now shift away from an emphasis on confirming a child in a "core self" and onto helping a child develop the capacity to negotiate fluid transitions between self states. The healthy individual knows how to be many but to smooth out the moments of transition between states of self. Bromberg says: "Health is when you are multiple but feel a unity. Health is when different aspects of self can get to know each other and reflect upon each other." Here, within the psychoanalytic tradition, is a model of multiplicity as a state of easy traffic across selves, a conscious, highly articulated "cycling through."

From a Psychoanalytic to a Computer Culture?

Having literally written our online personae into existence, they can be a kind of Rorschach test. We can use them to become more aware of what we project into everyday life. We can use the virtual to reflect constructively on the real. Cyberspace opens the possibility for identity play, but it is very serious play. People who cultivate an awareness of what stands behind their screen personae are the ones most likely to succeed in using virtual experience for personal and social transformation. And the people who make the most of their lives on the screen are those who are able to approach it in a spirit of self-reflection. What does my behavior in cyberspace tell me about what I want, who I am, what I may not be getting in the rest of my life?

As a culture, we are at the end of the Freudian century. Freud, after all, was a child of the nineteenth century; of course, he was carrying the baggage of a very different scientific sensibility than our own. But faced with the challenges of cyberspace, our need for a practical philosophy of self-knowledge, one that does not shy away from issues of multiplicity, complexity, and ambivalence, that does not shy away from the power of symbolism, from the power of the word, from the power of identity play, has never been greater as we struggle to make meaning from our lives on the screen. It is fashionable to think that we have passed from a psychoanalytic culture to a computer culture—that we no longer need to think in terms of Freudian slips but rather of information processing errors. But the reality is more complex. It is time to rethink our relationship to the computer culture and psychoanalytic culture as a proudly held joint citizenship.

References

Bromberg, Philip. 1994. "Speak that I May See You: Some Reflections on Dissociation, Reality, and Psychoanalytic Listening." *Psychoanalytic Dialogues* 4 (4): 517–47.

Dennett, Daniel. 1991. *Consciousness Explained.* Boston: Little, Brown.

Erikson, Erik. [1950] 1963. *Childhood and Society,* 2nd Ed. New York: Norton.

Haraway, Donna. 1991. "The Actors are Cyborg, Nature is Coyote, and the Geography is Elsewhere: Postscript to 'Cyborgs at Large.'" In *Technoculture,* edited by Constance Penley and Andrew Ross. Minneapolis: University of Minnesota Press.

Gergen, Kenneth. 1991. *The Saturated Self-Dilemmas of Identity in Contemporary Life.* New York: Basic Books.

Lifton, Robert Jay. 1993. *The Protean Self: Human Resilience in an Age of Fragmentation.* New York: Basic Books.

Martin, Emily. 1994. *Flexible Bodies: Tracking Immunity in American Culture from the Days of Polio to the Days of AIDS.* Boston: Beacon Press.

Minsky, Martin. 1987. *The Society of Mind.* New York: Simon & Schuster.

Turkle, Sherry. [1978] 1990. *Psychoanalytic Politics: Jacques Lacan and Freud's French Revolution.* 2nd Ed. New York: Guilford Press.

———— 1984. *The Second Self: Computers and the Human Spirit.* New York: Simon & Schuster.

———— 1995. *Life on the Screen: Identity in the Age of the Internet.* New York: Simon & Schuster.

 For Discussion:

1. Turkle writes that "your identity on the computer is the sum of your distributed presence." Using yourself as an example, list some ways that you see yourself fragmented in this way. What does this mean? If you cannot come up with any, what do you think this says about your identity?

2. Turkle argues that healthy people use multiple identities to deal with a variety of situations. She further argues that these people differ from those with multiple-personality disorder (MPD) because their various selves never disassociate them from the whole. Do you agree or disagree with this idea?

3. A writer might create a story, poem, or song from the perspective of someone other than him or herself. What's different about doing that and speaking from multiple identities in the way Turkle describes? Or is there a difference?

 For Fact-Finding, Research, and Writing:

1. In discussing the concept of *multiplicity,* Turkle cites five other sources that deal with the topic. Using the library, locate two of the sources she mentions and paraphrase how they define the term *multiplicity.* To what extent do you agree with these definitions? How would you modify them?

2. Turkle builds her argument on the ideas of the influential psychologist Erik Erikson. Who is he, and what ideas is he best known for?

3. In what ways does Turkle's essay echo Plato's argument about the need to come out of the cave?

Chris Hables Gray, "Citizenship in the Age of Electronic Reproduction"

Chris Hables Gray received his B.A. from Stanford University and his Ph.D. from the University of California, Santa Cruz. Currently Associate Professor of Computer Science at the University of Great Falls, Gray is an internationally recognized scholar of cybernetics and cyberculture. A frequent consultant to the computer industry, he is the author or editor of four books: *Technohistory* (1996), *The Cyborg Handbook* (1996), *Postmodern War* (1997), and *Cyborg Citizen* (2002).

 Before You Read:

What traits do you believe must be present before someone can be considered human? In your view, are human rights different from the rights afforded to citizens of a nation?

Citizenship in the Age of Electronic Reproduction

Chris Hables Gray

[I]t is no longer enough to feel represented by a government (if it ever was); now a citizen of the cybernetic political world inhabits various bodies interfaced more or less intimately with various prosthetics, all models for political structures that subject and partially construct us.

—Chris Hables Gray and Steven Mentor

Who or What Is a Citizen?

IN AN EPISODE of *Star Trek: The Next Generation*, Data the android is put on trial to determine whether he is property or a citizen. *ST:TNG* is full of cyborgs: Geordi La Forge with his visor, Riker with his transporter clone, Worf with an artificial spine, Pecard with an artificial heart, various holographic characters who come to life, and, in several episodes, the ship itself. And there are the Borg, the evil, black-leather-clad cyborg group mind. But Data is a particularly interesting cyborg because his cyborgization is based on two very unrelated technologies. First, his skin is a biological construction. Second, his consciousness arises from patterns extracted from the memories of humans in the colony where he was built. Technically it is far from clear that Data is anything more than a very sophisticated robot with some borrowings from the organic world. But he longs to be human.

Data's trial results from the machinations of an ambitious scientist from the United Federation of Planets who wants to deconstruct Data to see how he works. Data's friends testify but they are far from convincing. Finally Data takes the stand. In his testimony he reveals that he keeps a hologram of Tasha Yar, the butch, blonde security chief who died engulfed in an evil ink blot on an earlier episode. Data confesses that he had sex with Tasha once when the whole crew was exposed to an aphrodisiac ("I am fully functional," he told her when she propositioned him), and so he is deemed a citizen after all.

The ability to have sex with a human may seem like a strange criterion for citizenship, but it is actually the ability to have sex *and talk about it* that saves Data. The definition of citizenship is freeing itself from gender-, race-, and class-based criteria and becoming an issue of competent participation in what some philosophers call a discourse community but what most of us would just label a meaningful conversation. The communication need not be speech or writing, as Helen Keller proved, but there must be communication for political participation. This perspective helps us think about cyborg citizenship just as it has helped define intelligence through the Turing test. We will return to the Turing test and the cyborg citizen below, but first a few more things need to be said about citizenship itself.

The idea of citizenship has been growing more powerful as the world transforms into a cyborged society. Consider the alternatives. Would you rather be a subject? An employee? A tribal member? The role of tribal member is much more nuanced than some might think and is quite different from "citizen." But while some coherent tribes remain strong institutions that people gladly subsume their individuality to because of long-standing blood ties and links to specific land, for most people being a tribal member is not an option. And for many tribal members it is an option that is refused. What is popular is citizenship.

The word "citizen" comes from "cities," and the first citizens were in the Greek city-states. They were male, adult, property-owning members who fought in the military; non-members, women, children, and the poor were not citizens and had few rights. Originally, in the Massachusetts Bay Colony, a citizen had to be a landowner or ranked as a master craftsman, a member of the Puritan Church, white, male, and an oath-swearer to the Crown. Even now, the U.S. Constitution says that the president must be a "natural-born citizen," which excludes "naturalized" citizens, of course; but does it also mean a test-tube baby cannot grow up to be president?

Some theorists still link the idea of citizenship to membership in a state and, like the Australian political scientist Jan Pakulski, they worry that the postmodern "weakening of the state and the erosion of state legitimacy will ultimately arrest the process of citizenship extension." Pakulski notes that more and more rights are being linked to a person's status as a human being (as in the UN's Declaration of Human Rights) and not to their membership in a state.

For me this is not a problem. I trace my citizenship to my consent to be governed, in the formulation of John Locke, and that stems from my ability to be part of the polis, the political entity that humans and cyborgs (and in the future who knows what else) share through our ability to communicate together about political issues, sex, and whether or not Madonna has talent. Let me stress that I reject the patriarchal and classist assumptions that mar Locke's work and that do not follow logically. But the fundamental premise of Locke (and of the American and French revolutions and many more besides) is that the governed must consent to be governed or the state is not legitimate. Postmodern citizenship is more diffuse and proactive, as consent and allegiance can be granted to more than just nation-states; (bio)regions, cities, and the world as a whole can claim part of the citizen's allegiance. This is not so much a matter of political theory as it is of political practice, and as long as enough of us are willing to put our lives and our sacred honor on the line for this idea of conscious and proactive citizenship, it will remain true.

Pakulski makes much of the state as "the monopolistic enforcer of rights," but it is my reading of history that individuals and groups have to struggle mightily, often against states, to acquire and defend their rights. Sometimes this is to establish or change states so that they are more amenable to human rights, but even then the natural tendency of even the most revolutionary and limited government is to grow in power (the iron law of bureaucracy) and start usurping people's freedoms. Thomas Jefferson stressed that it takes continual effort to keep our freedom. He phrased it in more colorful language, advocating perpetual revolutions every 20 years because: "The tree of liberty must be refreshed from time to time with the blood of patriots and tyrants." Such enthusiasm is probably why I am happy to call myself a Jeffersonian anarchist; after all, his disciple John L. O'Sullivan pointed out that "the government that governs least governs best," which has a nice logic to it.

Since nation-states are contingent, based on belief and history (some political scientists call them "imaginary communities"), there is no reason not to imagine a polity of the world. World citizenship makes much more political and ecological sense than does citizenship in nation-states. Aspects of national citizenship, such as those discussed by Bryan Turner in the premier issue of a journal called *Citizenship Studies*—legal rights, political rights, social rights—can be applied to world citizenship. But global citizenship offers the opportunity of combining human rights with these rights—and the concurrent obligations—of national citizens.

I am in sympathy with Pakulski's call for a "cultural citizenship" that expands the individual's rights and obligations to include economic and cultural dimensions as well as freedom and equality in the political process. Citizenship is clearly changing, as the very ground of politics shifts through the globalization of human culture and the other aspects of postmodernity that our ever-expanding technosciences are driving. But what will citizenship in the twenty-first century look like?

However citizenship may evolve, technology will play a major role. Langdon Winner, for one, has argued that technologies can be autonomous, that artifacts have politics of their own. Thus certain technologies may be inherently authoritarian, and real citizenship might be accorded only to those individuals who gain knowledge, control, or access as a result of their relationships to complex technologies. Those without are doomed to become "technopeasants" or, as my graduate student Katie Meyers wrote in an unpublished short story, "technotards." There is certainly the possibility that the expansion of citizenship might be reversed by differentiated access to technologies, especially health, information, and power. Cyborgization contains this danger as well. Yet the dynamics of cyborg citizenship are more complex than a simple accounting of haves and have-nots.

Engin Isin, a Canadian academic, has explored this issue in his article "Who Is the New Citizen?" He documents the rise of "new knowledge workers" and other shifts in the political landscape, including the development of a new "professional-citizen." This leads him to ask: What are the new political and moral obligations that will inevitably arise with new types of citizenship? The new citizenship must stem not just from the economic changes we are now experiencing but also from the actual changes our bodies are undergoing through cyborgization. We have to think in terms of the cyborg citizen, and that means we have to decide who qualifies.

The complications of cyborg citizenship call for a cyborg citizen Turing test to determine which entities can actually participate in our discourse community and which cannot. The Turing test is a very pragmatic exercise that has long been useful to scientists and writers trying to determine if a computer is intelligent. The test was first proposed by Alan Turing, the homosexual English computer scientist who died mysteriously in the 1950s after apparently biting a poisoned apple; whether it was suicide or the state solving a security risk we may never know. Turing, who played a fundamental role in developing the computer while he was building code-breaking machines during World War II, based his test on a party game called "the imitation game."

In the original "party" version, a man and a woman are given the same set of questions, which they then take to a separate room. One of them replies on a typed sheet, and the party guests try to guess if it is the man's or the woman's reply.

Turing proposed that a machine be substituted for one of the humans, and then argued that since intelligence is an operational concept, not an absolute, the best way to judge it is by testing whether or not the entity in question could carry on an intelligent conversation with an intelligent human for a serious length of time. If it could, then even a machine should be considered intelligent, at least as intelligent as many humans.

The value of Turing's test—and its use for determining cyborg citizenship—is its insight that intelligence, like citizenship, is a working idea, not an abstract universal value. Citizenship is based on assumptions about the consent of the governed, the relationship between responsibility and rights, and the autonomy of individuals. Historically, criteria for citizenship have ranged from gender and class, through literacy, to the current system in which birthright assures eventual citizenship unless it is abrogated through misdeeds. But beneath these shifting rules one can discern that the idea of a discourse community has always been the basic ground. Western political communities may have been limited in earlier days by political goals of racial, gender, or class domination, but among their approved citizens the ideal has always been equal discourse. The polis is a discourse community, after all, and every historical expansion of it has been predicated on arguments about the participation of new individuals in that discourse. Today, as we are faced with a whole range of complex and difficult decisions about who should be and who can be citizens, it seems wise to stay within this framework.

Currently, judgments about the suitability for citizenship of individual humans and cyborgs are made on the grounds of their ability to take part in the discourse of the polis, either by assumptions about age or by the evaluation of experts. Many of the more difficult cases are of actual cyborgs: humans linked to machines that keep them alive or humans who maintain autonomy only through drugs and other technointerventions. Instead of a jury of one's peers, the decision usually results from a negotiation between doctors, social workers, lawyers, and judges. Even in such cases, the criterion is operational. For example, in the United States, the National Council of State Boards of Nursing defines competence as "the application of knowledge and the interpersonal, decision-making, and psychomotor skills expected." If people are going to be judged on what is "expected," maybe that determination should be made by their peers.

Let us take such power away from the "soft" police and return it to the polis at large, in the form of juries of peers conducting their own rough Turing tests. An entity must convince a simple majority of twelve other citizens that it can be part of their conversation. This requirement should prevent refusals of citizenship on the basis of racism or other prejudices. The point is not to exclude those who are already citizens, as literacy and property laws were designed to do. And the point is not to include pets or fetuses or corporate entities. If such entities deserve rights and protection, they can be granted in other ways than citizenship.

The beauty of the Turing test is that it escapes the straitjacket of arbitrary standards and static definitions. Flexible though it is, it does not cast out all values; instead it focuses on the core of politics—communication—and enshrines that as the ultimate value. Also it implies strongly that citizenship is embodied, whether the body be organic, machinic, or both, ambiguous or not, constructed or not.

The Cyborg Bill of Rights

Donna Haraway's "A Manifesto for Cyborgs" is the founding document of cyborg politics. Republished dozens of times since 1985, it has inspired, outraged, and befuddled countless readers. Since then there has been a proliferation of cyber-manifestos. It almost seems as if most things written now about "cyber" anything are in the style of a manifesto. Which would be appropriate, since, according to Steven Mentor:

All manifestos are cyborgs. That is, they fit Donna Haraway's use of this term in her own "A Manifesto for Cyborgs"—manifestos are hybrids, chimeras, boundary-confusing technologies. They combine and confuse popular genres and political discourses, borrow from critical theory and advertising, serve as would be control systems for the larger social technologies their authors hope to manufacture.

Among the more interesting cyber-manifestos are the "Mutant Manifesto," Stelarc's "Cyborg Manifesto," "The Magna Carta for the Knowledge Age," and a number of proclamations from the Extropians. Many of these are based on earlier manifestos from the late 1700s. Other manifestos include "The Declaration of the Independence of Cyberspace" announced by cyber-libertarians in 1996, and the "Bill of Gender Rights" from the Second International Conference on Transgender Law and Employment Policy in 1993. This bill of rights includes "the right to control and change one's own body," the "right to medical and professional care," and the "right to freedom from psychiatric treatment." Manifestos seem to break the ground for new rights, which are sometimes then codified into texts that seem like technologies.

Bills of rights, and the constitutions they are prosthetics for, are technically called "written instruments" and they are indeed technologies. They are supposed to help us govern ourselves. While my particular Cyborg Bill of Rights is designed as amendments to the U.S. Constitution, the ideas in it are relevant to all postmodern democracies. Many constitutions draw from the U.S. version, as Japan's and South Africa's do. The U.S. Constitution comes out of English common law, French political thinking, and Greek, Roman, and Native American governing traditions. This is not a proposal aimed just at the United States. All cyborg citizens need their rights defended. So, in the hope of making a modest improvement in the human political condition, I propose this *Cyborg Bill of Rights*.

One last point. Despite some strange rulings in the past by the U.S. Supreme Court, it is explicitly stated in this new Bill of Rights that:

Business corporations and other bureaucracies are not citizens or individuals, nor shall they ever be.

As it is now, corporations have many of the rights of citizens but few of the obligations. In the future there might be "corporate" cyborgs with multiple or distributed intelligence. Without some level of unitary identity, such a cyborg will not have the ability to act coherently. But, perhaps some cyborg of the far future will be multiple but coherent enough to be capable of casting one vote. Still there is no reason to allow business corporations to keep their quasi-citizen status. Even without it they have too much power.

The ten amendments are as follows:

1. *Freedom of Travel.* Citizens shall have the right to travel anywhere, virtually or in the flesh, at their own risk and expense.
2. *Freedom of Electronic Speech.* Electronic and other nonphysical forms of transmitting information are protected by the Constitution's First Amendment.

3. *The Right of Electronic Privacy.* Electronic and other nonmaterial forms of property and personhood shall be accorded the protection of the Fourth Amendment.

4. *Freedom of Consciousness.* The consciousness of the citizen shall be protected by the First, Fourth, and Eighth Amendments. Unreasonable search and seizure of this, the most sacred and private part of an individual citizen, is absolutely prohibited. Individuals shall retain all rights to modify their consciousness through psychopharmological, medical, genetic, spiritual, and other practices, insofar as they do not threaten the fundamental rights of other individuals and citizens, and that they do so at their own risk and expense.

5. *Right to Life.* The body of the citizen shall be protected by the First, Fourth, and Eighth Amendments. Unreasonable search and seizure of this sacred and private part of an individual citizen shall be absolutely prohibited. Individuals shall retain all rights to modify their bodies, at their own risk and expense, through psychopharmological, medical, genetic, spiritual, and other practices, insofar as they do not threaten the fundamental rights of other individuals and citizens.

6. *Right to Death.* Every citizen and individual shall have the right to end their life, at their own risk and expense, in the manner of their own choice, as long as it does not infringe upon the fundamental rights of other citizens and individuals.

7. *Right to Political Equality.* The political power of every citizen should be determined by the quality of his or her arguments, example, energy, and single vote, not based on his or her economic holdings or social standing. Congress shall permit no electoral system that favors wealth, coercion, or criminal behavior to the detriment of political equality.

8. *Freedom of Information.* Citizens shall have access to all information held about them by governments or other bureaucracies. Citizens shall have the right to correct all information held on them by governments and other bureaucracies at the expense of these bureaucracies. Institutional and corporate use of information to coerce or otherwise illegally manipulate or act upon citizens shall be absolutely forbidden.

9. *Freedom of Family, Sexuality, and Gender.* Citizens and individuals have the right to determine their own sexual and gender orientations, at their own risk and expense, including matrimonial and other forms of alliance. Congress shall make no law arbitrarily restricting the definition of the family, of marriage, or of parenthood.

10. *Right to Peace.* Citizens and individuals have a right to freedom from war and violence. War shall be a last resort and must be declared by a two thirds vote of Congress when proposed by the president. The Third Amendment shall not be construed as permitting citizens and individuals to own all types of weapons. Freedom from governmental tyranny will not be safeguarded through local militia or individual violence. Only solidarity, tolerance, sacrifice, and an equitable political system will guarantee freedom. Nonetheless, citizens and individuals shall have the right to defend themselves with deadly force, at their own risk and expense, if their fundamental rights are being abridged.

These amendments are important, but alone they cannot protect us. We need active citizens and new political technologies to protect our rights from the relentless changes that cyborgian technoscience is producing.

I have assumed here that cyborg citizens are real political bodies and therefore they need real political rights instantiated in technologies such as constitutions and operational tests of citizenship. The individual needs real political protection in this age of new powerful technosciences and the systems they make possible. Without such protection, corporations, parties, bureaus of police, governments, and wealthy families will achieve hegemony, and the vast majority of us will lose all political power.

Citizenship will always be embodied in some sense, although not necessarily in living flesh. Many theorists, and I am one of them, think intelligence itself is inherently embodied. A disembodied intelligence, if it were even possible, might very well not be interested in our definition of citizenship. Our political system (indeed our existence) is based on embodiment.

It is feminist philosophy that has made the embodiment of citizenship undeniable in the postmodern era, through an examination of the dangers of disembodied philosophies that make hyperrationality the measure of all things and through many case studies of the role of bodies in real politics. For example, Elaine Scarry's *Bodies in Pain* details how bodies are the ground for both war and the coercive power of government. Different philosophies have put forward many other possible bases for political principles—the soul, the race, the nation—but in real terms it is the action of, and on, bodies that is the basis of politics. This explains the crucial political importance of cyborgs.

Donna Haraway points out that cyborg politics are not inevitably liberatory. Far from it. They offer a chance for sustaining, even extending, democracy, but also the equally real chance of ultimate oppression, especially if we subscribe to illusions of "total theory," "pure information," and "perfect communication" and deny the messy reality of machinic and organic bodies and their rights.

An example of where such illusions might lead can be found in Bruno Latour's political thinking, especially in his 1993 book *We Have Never Been Modern*. Latour, an aristocratic French scholar, has argued that science is a collaborative construction involving alliances between institutions, rhetorics, technologies, artifacts, and humans. On the surface it might seem that his argument parallels the one here. He denounces totalitarian rationality-is-everything narratives and urges a reconciliation between nature and technology. But Latour's advocacy for granting rights to nonhuman, nonliving objects and implementing a "Parliament of Things" is profoundly problematic on several levels. First, the argument is couched in abstract and symbolic terms. Secondly, it depends on a series of oversimplified dichotomies, such as the alienation of modernism from nature and the domination of human(ism) over the rest of reality. Finally, it is based on illusions about agency and causality that in actuality would make working politics impossible.

That artifacts have politics does not mean that they have agency. Certainly, cyborgs (or "hybrids," in Latour's formulation) demonstrate that organic embodiment is not the final arbitrator of agency, but that does not mean that anything can be an actor ("actant" for Latour). That everything can be called a system does not mean that all systems can think, or act, or practice politics in any real way.

The dangers of Latour's schema becomes apparent when one looks closely at his Parliament:

> Let one of the representatives talk, for instance, about the ozone hole, another represent the Monsanto chemical industry, a third the workers of the same chemical industry, another the voters of New Hampshire, a fifth the meteorology of the polar regions; let still another speak in the name of the State; what does it matter, so long as they are all talking about the same thing, about a quasi-object they have all created, the object-discourse-nature-society whose new properties astound us all and whose network extends from my refrigerator to the Antarctic by way of chemistry, law, the State, the economy and satellites.

All of this "speaking" for others reminds me of vanguard parties speaking for the working class. Elites have a funny way of helping themselves while they speak for others. This diffusion of representation based on Latour's totalizing theories about binary reality and his assumptions about perfect communication and pure information (both necessary for all this "speaking for," unless the meteorology of the polar regions suddenly does become articulate on its own) paves the way for the end of real representative government.

Citizens need representation, holes in the ozone layer and chemical companies do not. Chemical companies will look after themselves, unfortunately. That is why we have an ozone hole that threatens us, after all. It is living intelligence (whether human, cyborg, or purely artificial as may someday happen) that must be empowered, not every quasi-object we can count dancing on a pinhead.

"Lives are at stake," Donna Haraway reminds us, "in curious quasi-objects like databases. . . ." *Lives*, not objects, quasi or otherwise. Of course it is in the long-term interest of citizens to recognize how interdependent we all are, how much a part of nature we are. And it is in our interest to do more than theorize about old and new dichotomies. We have to get political, down and dirty, and mess with the cyborgian machinery of government. As Haraway also says:

> Undoubtedly, we will have to do more than mutate the stories and the figures if the cyborg citizens of the third planet from the sun are to enjoy something better than the deadly transgressive flexibility of the New World Order.

Accepting ourselves as cyborgs can be liberating and empowering. We can choose how we construct ourselves. We can resist. But we must go beyond resistance. The long degradation of representation can be reversed if we reject calls such as Latour's for its elitist reconstruction. If autonomy is to avoid becoming automaton, we must make cyborg citizenship real, and defend it and expand it, in every way we can. Hence my ironic but serious proposal for a Cyborg Bill of Rights and a Turing test for citizenship. The threat to our freedoms and to justice from the megacyborgs of governments, corporations, and the superwealthy is very real indeed.

Cyborgian Justice: Panopticons versus Cyborg Death Cults

> *I believe the fundamental bioethical imperative for behavioral scientists today is to have the courage to renounce all collaboration with forces seeking to "control" or "modify" or "engineer" human responses.*
>
> —Dr. Richard Restak

He would carry a gold-plated ice pick in a velvet case. After applying a mild local anesthetic, he would drive the ice pick into the patient's skull through the edge of one of the eye sockets, severing the nerve connections to the thalamus and producing, in many cases, zombielike behavior along with convulsive seizures, intellectual impairment to the point of severe retardation, and the loss of all emotions. He did this more than 3,500 times. He was Dr. Walter Freeman, a neurologist at George Washington University Hospital in Washington, D.C., and was, along with James Watts, the inventor of the lobotomy.

Controlling human behavior through psychosurgery or other means is an old dream dating at least back to the ancient Romans, who noticed that sword wounds in the head sometimes cured mental illness. But only in the late twentieth century did it become a massive industry with a tremendous amount of government support, often framed in the language of cybernetics, the science of control.

Ice picks and other surgical implements passed out of favor with the advent of powerful drugs that offered the potential for "chemical" lobotomies. Thorazine and other tranquilizers are used massively today to control violent or just annoying mental patients, even though their long-term effects are sometimes just as damaging as the gold-plated ice pick. Behavior modification scientists have gone much further, researching electrical brain implants, studying military brainwashing techniques to see how they can be applied to criminals, and even inventing their own torture devices.

In the 1960s, the staff at Atascadero and Vacaville, prisons for the criminally insane in California, used the drug succinylcholine to "modify" patient behavior. Since the drug paralyzes the whole body, including the lungs, but leaves the victim conscious as they suffocate, it was considered ideal for convincing prisoners to change their behavior.

Fortunately, legal interventions stopped these "experiments" and also ended other programs, such as the one where doctors coerced patients to agree to psychosurgery by administering brain shocks and then forcibly operated on them even though they had later recanted their earlier approval. The U.S. courts ruled that prisoners and patients could not be forced to undergo irreversible treatments and that in many cases noncoerced consent was impossible. However, reversible interventions, illegal experiments (some no doubt undertaken by the government), and studies outside North America and Europe, where patients' rights are protected to some extent, undoubtably continue.

In his book *Pre-Meditated Man*, Richard Restak reviews this history and looks at a number of other areas where biotechnology is impacting society, such a genetic engineering. The key issue, he decides, is power. Who has the power to decide? Transplant programs, kidney machine use, and behavior and genetic modifications "are not questions of 'ethics,' they are questions of power." As a physician and scientist himself, he stresses that we cannot rely upon scientists to be the ultimate judges. Society must decide in general, and individual patients must have the power in particular. And, he warns, we cannot assume the government is a disinterested mediator of what the people want. It has interests of its own. He also argues that the power of new technologies for behavioral and genetic modification and the ever-quickening rate of innovation in these areas means that the amount of time society has to respond to them grow shorter while the consequences of mistakes grows heavier. Every time we do not get it right there is a wave of deaths, deformations, and other horrific consequences, as with the thalidomide babies.

Some people just aspire to control people directly. Consider Dr. Jose M. R. Delgado, author of *Physical Control of the Mind*. A distinguished professor at Madrid University, UCLA, and Yale, he implanted electrodes in the brains of animals to control them. Donna Haraway describes Delgado's joint project with Nathan Kline and leading primatologists to manipulate gibbons through brain stimulation:

> The proposed research was a straightforward extension of work Delgado had done for over twenty years. He had been instrumental in developing the multichannel radio stimulator, the programmed stimulator, the stimoceiver, the transdermal brain stimulator, a mobility recorder, chemitrodes, external dialtrodes, and subcutaneous dialtrodes. These were cyborg organs within cybernetic functionalism.

The cyborgs are animal-machines, experimental objects for perfecting cybernetic control. Along with the animals, the behavioral observations were automated as much as possible using a mobile telemetry system that, when analyzed by computer, would produce suggested medication levels. As Haraway notes, the "structure of a command-control-communication system pervades the discourse of Delgado and his community, whether or not explicit military metaphors or social ties appear." Command, control, and communication do not apply just to military units now; they are what governments want to exercise on citizen-subjects who otherwise might run out of control.

It is an old fear of rulers. How do we control the masses? More subtle approaches than those discussed here often work, but sometimes the powers-that-be feel that extreme measures are necessary. Technoscience has gifted us with incredible destructive powers. What do we do when they are used by small groups of clever nuts who have been driven insane by society's rapid transitions?

Today's body politic is clearly uncomfortable when it contemplates its progressing cyborgization. There is good reason to fear that there will be pathological reactions. The Aum group from Japan, famous around the world for its nerve gas attacks, was in many ways the first cyborg death cult. Along with the typical trappings of insane death cults (a guru, a bizarre eschatology, and an internal dynamic of oppression and conformity), cult members had also totally embraced the idea that they were cyborg supermen who would save the world from the apocalypse of the current world ecological crisis.

Aum's worldview was shaped equally by science fiction (the work of Isaac Asimov), Buddhism, and its leaders' dreams of commanding and controlling its members though perfect communication. World domination was their goal, nothing less. Aum devotees wore special six-volt electrode shock caps (four volts for children) that were meant to synchronize the wearers' brains to their guru's brain waves, which were continuously broadcast into their heads. They were called Perfect Salvation Initiation machines and they cost initiates about $7,000 dollars a month to use. Aum's security/medical team treated dissenters with electroshock and psychopharmacology. The executed were literally microwaved into ash. Cult members were told that they were superhumans capable of resisting nuclear blasts and plasma rays, thanks to a combination of cyborg technologies (such as the shock caps and drugs) and meditation. Aum's many young scientists not only manufactured small arms but also produced a wide range of biological and chemical weapons, including the sarin used in the Tokyo subway attacks that killed 12 and injured thousands. They had been trying to buy nuclear weapons and develop laser and microwave weapons as well. Fortunately, this particular cyborg microculture collapsed into self-destructive paranoia before it could effectively incorporate mass-death weapons.

The danger of groups like Aum is real. But perhaps the "cure" for such terrorism is just as dangerous as the disease. Using high technology to combat the threat of high-technology terrorism has tremendously corrosive effects on our freedoms, especially from government coercion and surveillance. Video systems have proliferated. They can be found in most stores now, in many workplaces, and on thousands of street corners. The government installs them not only to capture street crimes on tape, but traffic violations as well. Less obvious but perhaps even more intrusive is the explosive growth of databases full of information about the average citizen. A whole range of companies, from marketing to insurance, are creating profiles of millions of potential customers to maximize their advertising budgets or vet potential insurers. Much of this information is illegally acquired, inaccurate, or both.

Meanwhile, new surveillance technologies are introduced all the time. For example, police now possess a device that can detect electromagnetic radiation with such sensitivity that they can tell who is carrying a gun—or wearing a colostomy bag—without a direct search. There are also thermal-imaging devices that can track large mammals from the sky, gamma-ray scanners that can look inside trucks, X-ray technology and computer-aided metal detectors that can reveal items hidden under clothing up to 60 feet away, and ion sniffers that sample the air around someone's skin for chemical traces of cocaine and other naughty things.

Drug tests are used by many corporations and government agencies, from the short-term and inaccurate (but cheap) urine tests to the expensive hair analysis that can detect drug use from years before. Despite the many false-positives such tests produce (do not eat poppy-seed muffins before hand!), their popularity is increasing. Managers find the superficial clarity of such measures reassuring, and for this same reason they have begun to use various personality profiles to cull potentially bad employees and even resort to lie-detector tests for important positions.

A universal infallible lie detector such as the one imagined in James Halperin's novel *The Truth Machine* might seem like a beneficial development at first glance, but not upon reflection. No machine would be 100 percent accurate, only 99.999 percent at best, because there will always be a few sociopaths who can beat it. In the story, the inventor, who programmed it, can also outsmart it. Who watches the watcher? Then there is always the problem of people who are mistaken. They think they are telling the truth but they are wrong, which actually happens with many eyewitness identifications today. Even if the machine were perfectly accurate, is it really what we want? Sure, most of the criminals would be caught and most of the innocent freed, and most politicians and lawyers would be out of a job. But every insincere compliment, every stray politically incorrect thought, every incomplete self-deception could potentially be exposed. In the novel no wedding, no hiring, no contract, no graduation takes place without a truth test, and it fundamentally reorganizes society.

While a perfect truth machine might never be possible, more accurate lie detectors will eventually be built because our understanding of cognition and physiology continues to improve. Do we want a lie detector of 98 percent accuracy, for example, admitted into court? There is always that 2 percent, but most people do not seem to care. Even now, the use of our current horribly inaccurate lie detectors is spreading. Society loves technological solutions to political problems; look at the popularity of "electronic" arrest.

Since 1983 many convicted minor criminals, such as habitual drunk-driving offenders, have been held under "house" arrest by electronic "leashes" that are cuffed to their wrists or ankles and linked to their phones. A simple call from the probation department can verify if the convict—or at least the leash—is at home.

The system is being adapted for more dangerous criminals, such as Wesley Miller, who killed and mutilated a high school classmate in 1982. Three different systems monitor Miller: the ankle cuff, a global positioning system (GPS) satellite link on his other ankle, and a pager that he must answer immediately so that a computer can verify his identity with voice-recognition software. The satellite link insures that he will not go to any forbidden locations. Texas monitors over 1,000 high-risk parolees using these systems, but Miller is the first to have all three. He will not be the last.

A whole range of such cyborg containment technologies are being developed, including chips to be implanted in the flesh. They give the government and other big bureaucracies unprecedented power to control the population. Private security firms sell much of the actual equipment and expertise to the highest bidder, so we are beginning to experience a privitized version of *1984*. "I want to thank George Orwell for having the depth and foresight to plan my career," remarked Richard Chace of the Security Industry Association, an organization that promotes closed-circuit television security systems.

But is privacy overrated? David Brin, a physics professor and brilliant science-fiction writer, has explored the idea that privacy may be a problem. In his novel *Earth*, the nations of the world have attacked Switzerland in a nuclear Helvetian War to expose the secrets and the fruits of governmental and corporate abuse hidden in Swiss banks. His novel explores the politics of privacy in great detail (along with a dozen other fascinating themes, some of them quite cyborgian), and, to his credit, he does not simplify the issues. Surprisingly, he comes down unequivocally *against* privacy. He argues that "secrecy has always favored the mighty." Today the powerful benefit from secrecy; they can buy the most impenetrable privacy and they can also "get around whatever pathetic barriers you or I erect." So "privacy laws and codes will protect those at the top."

His answer is not "more fog, but more light: transparency." He admits that the average citizen would sacrifice something, but "we'll have something precious to help make up for lost privacy: freedom." Brin proposes to do away aggressively with privacy altogether. No secret bank accounts, no hidden files, free access by anyone to any camera anywhere! If the police have a surveillance system, the citizen should be able to view it. The weakness of this proposal is that it would take a world war to implement. Until then, do we really want to live in a totally surveilled society, inside the panopticon?

Jeremy Bentham coined the term "panopticon" for a prison he designed with his brother in which jailers could always observe the inmates. A key to the success of the panopticon is that the inmates would not know if they were being watched or not, just that they might be. The same can be said of the ubiquitous video cameras spreading through contemporary society. You can never know if someone is watching the monitor or might view the tape later.

The effect of this uncertainty is very wearying. Have you ever been watched? During my years as a political organizer, I was photographed at scores of demonstrations, visited by the FBI and Secret Service, had my phone tapped more than I probably know, and was jailed 10 times. Once, when asked how it felt to get out of jail, I replied: "It feels the same out here"—which was an exaggeration, of course. Still, I have seldom felt that the outside world was fundamentally different from jail. Our culture disturbingly resembles *The Truman Show*, where the unsuspecting Truman had his whole life broadcast live on television. As the actor who plays the actor playing Truman's best friend explains, the set of the Truman Show is "real, it is merely controlled." Our real world seems quite controlled. It is becoming more and more like the panopticon designed by the Bentham brothers. The difference between the two is shrinking at an alarming rate.

Is this what cyborg society inevitably leads to—a commanded and controlled body politic? A consumer-friendly police state? Do cyborg technologies offer only potential threats to our freedoms? Many people would argue that the reverse is true. Cyberdemocracy is true democracy, they claim. We shall see.

 For Discussion:

1. Gray begins his essay by introducing definitions of citizenship. What forms of citizenship besides "membership in a state" does he suggest? Which ones seem most important to you?

2. Using the example of Mr. Data, Gray argues that one's right to citizenship should be based on abilities? Do you agree? What could happen if some people have greater access to the means of discourse, while others remain "technopeasants"?

3. According to what criteria are citizen's rights, human rights, and the rights of non-human life defined in futuristic fiction novels and films with which you are familiar? Are there conflicting definitions?

4. What dangers does Gray see in "cyborg containment technologies"? Will enhanced privacy laws protect us sufficiently? Compare his vision of the future with Lucas D. Introna's analysis of privacy issues in the present.

5. Some of Gray's sentences require slow, careful reading. Choose a sentence you found difficult and work through it with a partner or as a class to establish a clear paraphrase.

 For Fact-Finding, Research, and Writing:

1. Find the United Nations declaration on human rights. Which points are similar to those proposed by the Cyborg Bill of Rights and the Turing test for citizenship? Is the U.N. declaration broader or narrower?

2. The government of the United States has not recognized the prisoners at Guantanamo Bay as citizens of any country. In what ways does their status compare to or contrast with that of U.S. citizens who have been arrested and/or convicted? Is there any governing body or declaration that protects their human rights?

3. Gray mentions the Extropians in his discussion of the Cyborg Bill of Rights. What is Extropianism? Use the databases on the library website to find an article by an Extropian that is related to one of the issues raised by Chris Hables Gray.

Robert Reich, "Why the Rich Are Getting Richer and the Poor Are Getting Poorer"

Secretary of Labor in the first Clinton administration, Robert Reich now teaches at Brandeis University. A former Rhodes Scholar and graduate of Yale Law School, Reich continues to publish prolifically on economic and political questions. In his books, Reich has attempted to reach beyond specialists in Economics to a general educated readership. This essay is taken from his 1991 book, *The Work of Nations.*

Before You Read:

The average yearly income in the United States is $37, 610, whereas that of the world's poorest country is less than $100. How do you feel about this?

Why the Rich Are Getting Richer and the Poor Are Getting Poorer

Robert Reich

The division of labour is limited by the extent of the market.

—Adam Smith
An Inquiry into the Nature and Causes of the
Wealth of Nations (1776)

Regardless of how your job is officially classified (manufacturing, service, managerial, technical, secretarial, and so on), or the industry in which you work (automotive, steel, computer, advertising, finance, food processing), your real competitive position in the world economy is coming to depend on the function you perform in it. Herein lies the basic reason why incomes are diverging. The fortunes of routine producers are declining. In-person servers are also becoming poorer, although their fates are less clear-cut. But symbolic analysts—who solve, identify, and broker new problems—are, by and large, succeeding in the world economy.

All Americans used to be in roughly the same economic boat. Most rose or fell together as the corporations in which they were employed, the industries comprising such corporations, and the national economy as a whole became more productive—or languished. But national borders no longer define our economic fates. We are now in different boats, one sinking rapidly, one sinking more slowly, and the third rising steadily.

The boat containing routine producers is sinking rapidly. Recall that by midcentury routine production workers in the United States were paid relatively well. The giant pyramidlike organizations at the core of each major industry coordinated their prices and investments—avoiding the harsh winds of competition and thus maintaining healthy earnings. Some of these earnings, in turn, were reinvested in new plant and equipment (yielding ever-larger-scale economies); another portion went to top managers and investors. But a large and increasing portion went to middle managers and production workers. Work stoppages posed such a threat to high-volume production that organized labor was able to exact an ever-larger premium for its cooperation. And the pattern of wages established within the core corporations influenced the pattern throughout the national economy. Thus the growth of a relatively affluent middle class, able to purchase all the wondrous things produced in high volume by the core corporations.

But, as has been observed, the core is rapidly breaking down into global webs which earn their largest profits from clever problem-solving, -identifying, and brokering. As the costs of transporting standard things and of communicating information about them continue to drop, profit margins on high-volume, standardized production are thinning, because there are few barriers to entry. Modern factories and state-of-the-art machinery can be installed almost anywhere on the globe. Routine producers in the United States, then, are in direct competition with millions of routine producers in other nations. Twelve thousand people are added to the world's population every hour, most of whom, eventually, will happily work for a small fraction of the wages of routine producers in America.[1]

The consequence is clearest in older, heavy industries, where high-volume, standardized production continues its ineluctable move to where labor is cheapest and most accessible around the world. Thus, for example, the Maquiladora factories cluttered along the Mexican side of the U.S. border in the sprawling shanty towns of Tijuana, Mexicali, Nogales, Agua Prieta, and Ciudad Juárez—factories owned mostly by Americans, but increasingly by Japanese—in which more than a half million routine producers assemble parts into finished goods to be shipped into the United States.

The same story is unfolding worldwide. Until the late 1970s, AT&T had depended on routine producers in Shreveport, Louisiana, to assemble standard telephones. It then discovered that routine producers in Singapore would perform the same tasks at a far lower cost. Facing intense competition from other global webs, AT&T's strategic brokers felt compelled to switch. So in the early 1980s they stopped hiring routine producers in Shreveport and began hiring cheaper routine producers in Singapore. But under this kind of pressure for ever-lower high-volume production costs, today's Singaporean can easily end up as yesterday's Louisianan. By the late 1980s, AT&T's strategic brokers found that routine producers in Thailand were eager to assemble telephones for a small fraction of the wages of routine producers in Singapore. Thus, in 1989, AT&T stopped hiring Singaporeans to make telephones and began hiring even cheaper routine producers in Thailand.

The search for ever-lower wages has not been confined to heavy industry. Routine data processing is equally footloose. Keypunch operators located anywhere around the world can enter data into computers, linked by satellite or transoceanic fiber-optic cable, and take it out again. As the rates charged by satellite networks continue to drop, and as more satellites and fiber-optic cables become available (reducing communication costs still further), routine data processors in the United States find themselves in ever more direct competition with their counterparts abroad, who are often eager to work for far less.

By 1990, keypunch operators in the United States were earning, at most, $6.50 per hour. But keypunch operators throughout the rest of the world were willing to work for a fraction of this. Thus, many potential American data-processing jobs were disappearing, and the wages and benefits of the remaining ones were in decline. Typical was Saztec International, a $20-million-a-year data-processing firm headquartered in Kansas City, whose American strategic brokers contracted with routine data processors in Manila and with American-owned firms that needed such data-processing services. Compared with the average Philippine income of $1,700 per year, data-entry operators working for Saztec earn the princely sum of $2,650. The remainder of Saztec's employees were American problem-solvers and -identifiers, searching for ways to improve the worldwide system and find new uses to which it could be put.[2]

By 1990, American Airlines was employing over 1,000 data processors in Barbados and the Dominican Republic to enter names and flight numbers from used airline tickets (flown daily to Barbados from airports around the United States) into a giant computer bank located in Dallas. Chicago publisher R. R. Donnelley was sending entire manuscripts to Barbados for entry into computers in preparation for printing. The New York Life Insurance Company was dispatching insurance claims to Castleisland, Ireland, where routine producers, guided by simple directions, entered the claims and determined the amounts due, then instantly transmitted the computations back to the United States. (When the firm advertised in Ireland for twenty-five data-processing jobs, it received six hundred applications.) And McGraw-Hill was processing subscription renewal and marketing information for its magazines in nearby Galway. Indeed, literally millions of routine workers around the world were receiving information, converting it into computer-readable form, and then sending it back—at the speed of electronic impulses—whence it came.

The simple coding of computer software has also entered into world commerce. India, with a large English-speaking population of technicians happy to do routine programming cheaply, is proving to be particularly attractive to global webs in need of this service. By 1990, Texas Instruments maintained a software development facility in Bangalore, linking fifty Indian programmers by satellite to TI's Dallas headquarters. Spurred by this and similar ventures, the Indian government was building a teleport in Poona, intended to make it easier and less expensive for many other firms to send their routine software design specifications for coding.[3]

This shift of routine production jobs from advanced to developing nations is a great boon to many workers in such nations who otherwise would be jobless or working for much lower wages. These workers, in turn, now have more money with which to purchase symbolic-analytic services from advanced nations (often embedded within all sorts of complex products). The trend is also beneficial to everyone around the world who can now obtain high-volume, standardized products (including information and software) more cheaply than before.

But these benefits do not come without certain costs. In particular the burden is borne by those who no longer have good-paying routine production jobs within advanced economies like the United States. Many of these people used to belong to unions or at least benefited from prevailing wage rates established in collective bargaining agreements. But as the old corporate bureaucracies have flattened into global webs, bargaining leverage has been lost. Indeed, the tacit national bargain is no more.

Despite the growth in the number of new jobs in the United States, union member-ship has withered. In 1960, 35 percent of all nonagricultural workers in America belonged to a union. But by 1980 that portion had fallen to just under a quarter, and by 1989 to about 17 percent. Excluding government employees, union membership was down to 13.4 per-cent.[4] This was a smaller proportion even than in the early 1930s, before the National Labor Relations Act created a legally protected right to labor representation. The drop in membership has been accompanied by a growing number of collective bargaining agree-ments to freeze wages at current levels, reduce wage levels of entering workers, or reduce wages overall. This is an important reason why the long economic recovery that began in 1982 produced a smaller rise in unit labor costs than any of the eight recoveries since World War II—the low rate of unemployment during its course notwithstanding.

Routine production jobs have vanished fastest in traditional unionized industries (au-tos, steel, and rubber, for example), where average wages have kept up with inflation. This is because the jobs of older workers in such industries are protected by seniority; the young-est workers are the first to be laid off. Faced with a choice of cutting wages or cutting the number of jobs, a majority of union members (secure in the knowledge that there are many who are junior to them who will be laid off first) often have voted for the latter.

Thus the decline in union membership has been most striking among young men entering the work force without a college education. In the early 1950s, more than 40 per-cent of this group joined unions; by the late 1980s, less than 20 percent (if public employ-ees are excluded, less than 10 percent).[5] In steelmaking, for example, although many older workers remained employed, almost half of all routine steelmaking jobs in America van-ished between 1974 and 1988 (from 480,000 to 260,000). Similarly with automobiles: During the 1980s, the United Auto Workers lost 500,000 members—one-third of their total at the start of the decade. General Motors alone cut 150,000 American production jobs during the 1980s (even as it added employment abroad). Another consequence of the same phenomenon: the gap between the average wages of unionized and nonunionized workers widened dramatically—from 14.6 percent in 1973 to 20.4 percent by end of the 1980s.[6] The lesson is clear. If you drop out of high school or have no more than a high school diploma, do not expect a good routine production job to be awaiting you.

Also vanishing are lower- and middle-level management jobs involving routine pro-duction. Between 1981 and 1986, more than 780,000 foremen, supervisors, and section chiefs lost their jobs through plant closings and layoffs.[7] Large numbers of assistant divi-sion heads, assistant directors, assistant managers, and vice presidents also found themselves jobless. GM shed more than 40,000 white-collar employees and planned to eliminate an-other 25,000 by the mid-1990s.[8] As America's core pyramids metamorphosed into global webs, many middle-level routine producers were as obsolete as routine workers on the line.

As has been noted, foreign-owned webs are hiring some Americans to do routine pro-duction in the United States. Philips, Sony, and Toyota factories are popping up all over—to the self-congratulatory applause of the nation's governors and mayors, who have lured them with promises of tax abatements and new sewers, among other amenities. But as these ebullient politicians will soon discover, the foreign-owned factories are highly automated and will become far more so in years to come. Routine production jobs account for a small fraction of the cost of producing most items in the United States and other advanced nations, and this fraction will continue to decline sharply as computer-integrated robots take over. In 1977 it took routine producers thirty-five hours to assemble an automobile in the United States; it is estimated that by the mid-1990s, Japanese-owned factories in America will be producing finished automobiles using only eight hours of a routine producer's time.[9]

The productivity and resulting wages of American workers who run such robotic machinery may be relatively high, but there may not be many such jobs to go around. A case in point: in the late 1980s, Nippon Steel joined with America's ailing Inland Steel to build a new $400 million cold-rolling mill fifty miles west of Gary, Indiana. The mill was celebrated for its state-of-the-art technology, which cut the time to produce a coil of steel from twelve days to about one hour. In fact, the entire plant could be run by a small team of technicians, which became clear when Inland subsequently closed two of its old cold-rolling mills, laying off hundreds of routine workers. Governors and mayors take note: your much-bally-hooed foreign factories may end up employing distressingly few of your constituents.

Overall, the decline in routine jobs has hurt men more than women. This is because the routine production jobs held by men in high-volume metal-bending manufacturing industries had paid higher wages than the routine production jobs held by women in textiles and data processing. As both sets of jobs have been lost, American women in routine production have gained more equal footing with American men—equally poor footing, that is. This is a major reason why the gender gap between male and female wages began to close during the 1980s.

The second of the three boats, carrying in-person servers, is sinking as well, but somewhat more slowly and unevenly. Most in-person servers are paid at or just slightly above the minimum wage and many work only part-time, with the result that their take-home pay is modest, to say the least. Nor do they typically receive all the benefits (health care, life insurance, disability, and so forth) garnered by routine producers in large manufacturing corporations or by symbolic analysts affiliated with the more affluent threads of global webs.[10] In-person servers are sheltered from the direct effects of global competition and, like everyone else, benefit from access to lower-cost products from around the world. But they are not immune to its indirect effects.

For one thing, in-person servers increasingly compete with former routine production workers, who, no longer able to find well-paying routine production jobs, have few alternatives but to seek in-person service jobs. The Bureau of Labor Statistics estimates that of the 2.8 million manufacturing workers who lost their jobs during the early 1980s, fully one-third were rehired in service jobs paying at least 20 percent less.[11] In-person servers must also compete with high school graduates and dropouts who years before had moved easily into routine production jobs but no longer can. And if demographic predictions about the American work force in the first decades of the twenty-first century are correct (and they are likely to be, since most of the people who will comprise the work force are already identifiable), most new entrants into the job market will be black or Hispanic men, or women—

groups that in years past have possessed relatively weak technical skills. This will result in an even larger number of people crowding into in-person services. Finally, in-person servers will be competing with growing numbers of immigrants, both legal and illegal, for whom in-person services will comprise the most accessible jobs. (It is estimated that between the mid-1980s and the end of the century, about a quarter of all workers entering the American labor force will be immigrants.[12])

Perhaps the fiercest competition that in-person servers face comes from labor-saving machinery (much of it invented, designed, fabricated, or assembled in other nations, of course). Automated tellers, computerized cashiers, automatic car washes, robotized vending machines, self-service gasoline pumps, and all similar gadgets substitute for the human beings that customers once encountered. Even telephone operators are fast disappearing, as electronic sensors and voice simulators become capable of carrying on conversations that are reasonably intelligent and always polite. Retail sales workers—among the largest groups of in-person servers—are similarly imperiled. Through personal computers linked to television screens, tomorrow's consumers will be able to buy furniture, appliances, and all sorts of electronic toys from their living rooms—examining the merchandise from all angles, selecting whatever color, size, special features, and price seem most appealing, and then transmitting the order instantly to warehouses from which the selections will be shipped directly to their homes. So, too, with financial transactions, airline and hotel reservations, rental car agreements, and similar contracts, which will be executed between consumers in their homes and computer banks somewhere else on the globe.[13]

Advanced economies like the United States will continue to generate sizable numbers of new in-person service jobs, of course, the automation of older ones notwithstanding. For every bank teller who loses her job to an automated teller, three new jobs open for aerobics instructors. Human beings, it seems, have an almost insatiable desire for personal attention. But the intense competition nevertheless ensures that the wages of in-person servers will remain relatively low. In-person servers—working on their own, or else dispersed widely amid many small establishments, filling all sorts of personal-care niches—cannot readily organize themselves into labor unions or create powerful lobbies to limit the impact of such competition.

In two respects, demographics will work in favor of in-person servers, buoying their collective boat slightly. First, as has been noted, the rate of growth of the American work force is slowing. In particular, the number of young workers is shrinking. Between 1985 and 1995, the number of the eighteen- to twenty-four-year-olds will have declined by 17.5 percent. Thus, employers will have more incentive to hire and train in-person servers whom they might previously have avoided. But this demographic relief from the competitive pressures will be only temporary. The cumulative procreative energies of the postwar baby-boomers (born between 1946 and 1964) will result in a new surge of workers by 2010 or thereabouts.[14] And immigration—both legal and illegal—shows every sign of increasing in years to come.

Next, by the second decade of the twenty-first century, the number of Americans aged sixty-five and over will be rising precipitously, as the baby-boomers reach retirement age and live longer. Their life expectancies will lengthen not just because fewer of them will have smoked their way to their graves and more will have eaten better than their parents, but also because they will receive all sorts of expensive drugs and therapies designed to keep them alive—barely. By 2035, twice as many Americans will be elderly as in 1988, and the number of octogenarians is expected to triple. As these decaying baby-boomers ingest all the chemicals and receive all the treatments, they will need a great deal of personal attention. Millions of deteriorating bodies will require nurses, nursing-home operators, hospital administrators, orderlies, home-care providers, hospice aides, and technicians to operate and maintain all the expensive machinery that will monitor and temporarily stave off final disintegration. There might even be a booming market for euthanasia specialists. In-person servers catering to the old and ailing will be in strong demand.[15]

One small problem: the decaying baby-boomers will not have enough money to pay for these services. They will have used up their personal savings years before. Their Social Security payments will, of course, have been used by the government to pay for the previous generation's retirement and to finance much of the budget deficits of the 1980s. Moreover, with relatively fewer young Americans in the population, the supply of housing will likely exceed the demand, with the result that the boomers' major investments—their homes—will be worth less (in inflation-adjusted dollars) when they retire than they planned for. In consequence, the huge cost of caring for the graying boomers will fall on many of the same people who will be paid to care for them. It will be like a great sump pump: in-person servers of the twenty-first century will have an abundance of health-care jobs, but a large portion of their earnings will be devoted to Social Security payments and income taxes, which will in turn be used to pay their salaries. The net result: no real improvement in their standard of living.

The standard of living of in-person servers also depends, indirectly, on the standard of living of the Americans they serve who are engaged in world commerce. To the extent that these Americans are richly rewarded by the rest of the world for what they contribute, they will have more money to lavish upon in-person services. Here we find the only form of "trickle-down" economics that has a basis in reality. A waitress in a town whose major factory has just been closed is unlikely to earn a high wage or enjoy much job security; in a swank resort populated by film producers and banking moguls, she is apt to do reasonably well. So, too, with nations. In-person servers in Bangladesh may spend their days performing roughly the same tasks as in-person servers in the United States, but have a far lower standard of living for their efforts. The difference comes in the value that their customers add to the world economy.

Unlike the boats of routine producers and in-person servers, however, the vessel containing America's symbolic analysts is rising. Worldwide demand for their insights is growing as the ease and speed of communicating them steadily increases. Not every symbolic analyst is rising as quickly or as dramatically as every other, of course; symbolic analysts at the low end are barely holding their own in the world economy. But symbolic analysts at the top are in such great demand worldwide that they have difficulty keeping track of all their earnings. Never before in history has opulence on such a scale been gained by people who have earned it, and done so legally.

Among symbolic analysts in the middle range are American scientists and researchers who are busily selling their discoveries to global enterprise webs. They are not limited to American customers. If the strategic brokers in General Motors' headquarters refuse to pay a high price for a new means of making high-strength ceramic engines dreamed up by a team of engineers affiliated with Carnegie Mellon University in Pittsburgh, the strategic brokers of Honda or Mercedes-Benz are likely to be more than willing.

So, too, with the insights of America's ubiquitous management consultants, which are being sold for large sums to eager entrepreneurs in Europe and Latin America. Also, the insights of America's energy consultants, sold for even larger sums to Arab sheikhs. American design engineers are providing insights to Olivetti, Mazda, Siemens, and other global webs; American marketers, techniques for learning what worldwide consumers will buy; American advertisers, ploys for ensuring that they actually do. American architects are issuing designs and blueprints for opera houses, art galleries, museums, luxury hotels, and residential complexes in the world's major cities; American commercial property developers, marketing these properties to worldwide investors and purchasers.

Americans who specialize in the gentle art of public relations are in demand by corporations, governments, and politicians in virtually every nation. So, too, are American political consultants, some of whom, at this writing, are advising the Hungarian Socialist Party, the remnant of Hungary's ruling Communists, on how to salvage a few parliamentary seats in the nation's first free election in more than forty years. Also at this writing, a team of American agricultural consultants is advising the managers of a Soviet farm collective employing 1,700 Russians eighty miles outside Moscow. As noted, American investment bankers and lawyers specializing in financial circumnavigations are selling their insights to Asians and Europeans who are eager to discover how to make large amounts of money by moving large amounts of money.

Developing nations, meanwhile, are hiring American civil engineers to advise on building roads and dams. The present thaw in the Cold War will no doubt expand these opportunities. American engineers from Bechtel (a global firm notable for having employed both Caspar Weinberger and George Shultz for much larger sums than either earned in the Reagan administration) have begun helping the Soviets design and install a new generation of nuclear reactors. Nations also are hiring American bankers and lawyers to help them renegotiate the terms of their loans with global banks, and Washington lobbyists to help them with Congress, the Treasury, the World Bank, the IMF, and other politically sensitive institutions. In fits of obvious desperation, several nations emerging from communism have even hired American economists to teach them about capitalism.

Almost everyone around the world is buying the skills and insights of Americans who manipulate oral and visual symbols—musicians, sound engineers, film producers, makeup artists, directors, cinematographers, actors and actresses, boxers, scriptwriters, songwriters, and set designers. Among the wealthiest of symbolic analysts are Steven Spielberg, Bill Cosby, Charles Schulz, Eddie Murphy, Sylvester Stallone, Madonna, and other star directors and performers—who are almost as well known on the streets of Dresden and Tokyo as in the Back Bay of Boston. Less well rewarded but no less renowned are the unctuous anchors on Turner Broadcasting's Cable News, who appear daily, via satellite, in places ranging from Vietnam to Nigeria. Vanna White is the world's most-watched game-show hostess. Behind each of these familiar faces is a collection of American problem-solvers, -identifiers, and brokers who train, coach, advise, promote, amplify, direct, groom, represent, and otherwise add value to their talents.[16]

There are also the insights of senior American executives who occupy the world headquarters of global "American" corporations and the national or regional headquarters of global "foreign" corporations. Their insights are duly exported to the rest of the world through the webs of global enterprise. IBM does not export many machines from the United States, for example. Big Blue makes machines all over the globe and services them on the spot. Its prime American exports are symbolic and analytic. From IBM's world headquarters in Armonk, New York, emanate strategic brokerage and related management services bound for the rest of the world. In return, IBM's top executives are generously rewarded.

The most important reason for this expanding world market and increasing global demand for the symbolic and analytic insights of Americans has been the dramatic improvement in worldwide communication and transportation technologies. Designs, instructions, advice, and visual and audio symbols can be communicated more and more rapidly around the globe, with ever-greater precision and at ever-lower cost. Madonna's voice can be transported to billions of listeners, with perfect clarity, on digital compact discs. A new invention emanating from engineers in Battelle's laboratory in Columbus, Ohio, can be sent almost anywhere via modem, in a form that will allow others to examine it in three dimensions through enhanced computer graphics. When face-to-face meetings are still required—and videoconferencing will not suffice—it is relatively easy for designers, consultants, advisers, artists, and executives to board supersonic jets and, in a matter of hours, meet directly with their worldwide clients, customers, audiences, and employees.

With rising demand comes rising compensation. Whether in the form of licensing fees, fees for service, salaries, or shares in final profits, the economic result is much the same. There are also nonpecuniary rewards. One of the best-kept secrets among symbolic analysts is that so many of them enjoy their work. In fact, much of it does not count as work at all, in the traditional sense. The work of routine producers and in-person servers is typically monotonous; it causes muscles to tire or weaken and involves little independence or discretion. The "work" of symbolic analysts, by contrast, often involves puzzles, experiments, games, a significant amount of chatter, and substantial discretion over what to do next. Few routine producers or in-person servers would "work" if they did not need to earn the money. Many symbolic analysts would "work" even if money were no object.

At midcentury, when America was a national market dominated by core pyramid-shaped corporations, there were constraints on the earnings of people at the highest rungs. First and most obviously, the market for their services was largely limited to the borders of the nation. In addition, whatever conceptual value they might contribute was small relative to the value gleaned from large scale—and it was dependent on large scale for whatever income it was to summon. Most of the problems to be identified and solved had to do with enhancing the efficiency of production and improving the flow of materials, parts, assembly, and distribution. Inventors searched for the rare breakthrough revealing an entirely new product to be made in high volume; management consultants, executives, and engineers thereafter tried to speed and synchronize its manufacture, to better achieve scale efficiencies; advertisers and marketers sought then to whet the public's appetite for the standard item that emerged. Since white-collar earnings increased with larger scale, there was considerable incentive to expand the firm; indeed, many of America's core corporations grew far larger than scale economies would appear to have justified.

By the 1990s, in contrast, the earnings of symbolic analysts were limited neither by the size of the national market nor by the volume of production of the firms with which they were affiliated. The marketplace was worldwide, and conceptual value was high relative to value added from scale efficiencies.

There had been another constraint on high earnings, which also gave way by the 1990s. At midcentury, the compensation awarded to top executives and advisers of the largest of America's core corporations could not be grossly out of proportion to that of low-level production workers. It would be unseemly for executives who engaged in highly visible rounds of bargaining with labor unions, and who routinely responded to government requests to moderate prices, to take home wages and benefits wildly in excess of what other Americans earned. Unless white-collar executives restrained themselves, moreover, blue-collar production workers could not be expected to restrain their own demands for higher wages. Unless both groups exercised restraint, the government could not be expected to forbear from imposing direct controls and regulations.

At the same time, the wages of production workers could not be allowed to sink too low, lest there be insufficient purchasing power in the economy. After all, who would buy all the goods flowing out of American factories if not American workers? This, too, was part of the tacit bargain struck between American managers and their workers.

Recall the oft-repeated corporate platitude of the era about the chief executive's responsibility to carefully weigh and balance the interests of the corporation's disparate stakeholders. Under the stewardship of the corporate statesman, no set of stakeholders—least of all white-collar executives—was to gain a disproportionately large share of the benefits of corporate activity; nor was any stakeholder—especially the average worker—to be left with a share that was disproportionately small. Banal though it was, this idea helped to maintain the legitimacy of the core American corporation in the eyes of most Americans, and to ensure continued economic growth.

But by the 1990s, these informal norms were evaporating, just as (and largely because) the core American corporation was vanishing. The links between top executives and the American production worker were fading: an ever-increasing number of subordinates and contractees were foreign, and a steadily growing number of American routine producers were working for foreign-owned firms. An entire cohort of middle-level managers, who had once been deemed "white collar," had disappeared; and, increasingly, American executives were exporting their insights to global enterprise webs.

As the American corporation itself became a global web almost indistinguishable from any other, its stakeholders were turning into a large and diffuse group, spread over the world. Such global stakeholders were less visible, and far less noisy, than national stakeholders. And as the American corporation sold its goods and services all over the world, the purchasing power of American workers became far less relevant to its economic survival.

Thus have the inhibitions been removed. The salaries and benefits of America's top executives, and many of their advisers and consultants, have soared to what years before would have been unimaginable heights, even as those of other Americans have declined.

Notes

1. The reader should note, of course, that lower wages in other areas of the world are of no particular attraction to global capital unless workers there are sufficiently productive to make the labor cost of producing *each unit* lower there than in higher-wage regions. Productivity in many low-wage areas of the world has improved due to the ease with which state-of-the-art factories and equipment can be installed there. [Reich's note]
2. John Maxwell Hamilton, "A Bit Player Buys into the Computer Age," *New York Times Business World*, December 3, 1989, p. 14. [Reich's note]
3. Udayan Gupta, "U.S.-Indian Satellite Link Stands to Cut Software Costs," *Wall Street Journal*, March 6, 1989, p. B2. [Reich's note]
4. *Statistical Abstract of the United States* (Washington, D.C.: U.S. Government Printing Office, 1989), p. 416, table 684. [Reich's note]
5. Calculations from Current Population Surveys by L. Katz and A. Revenga, "Changes in the Structure of Wages: U.S. and Japan," National Bureau of Economic Research, September 1989. [Reich's note]
6. U.S. Department of Commerce, Bureau of Labor Statistics, "Wages of Unionized and Non-Unionized Workers," various issues. [Reich's note]
7. U.S. Department of Labor, Bureau of Labor Statistics, "Reemployment Increases Among Displaced Workers," *BLS News*, USDL 86-414, October 14, 1986, table 6. [Reich's note]
8. *Wall Street Journal*, February 16, 1990, p. A5. [Reich's note]
9. Figures from the International Motor Vehicles Program, Massachusetts Institute of Technology, 1989. [Reich's note]
10. The growing portion of the American labor force engaged in in-person services, relative to routine production, thus helps explain why the number of Americans lacking health insurance increased by at least 6 million during the 1980s. [Reich's note]
11. U.S. Department of Labor, Bureau of Labor Statistics, "Reemployment Increases Among Disabled Workers," October 14, 1986. [Reich's note]
12. Federal Immigration and Naturalization Service, *Statistical Yearbook* (Washington, D.C.: U.S. Government Printing Office, 1986, 1987). [Reich's note]
13. See Claudia H. Deutsch, "The Powerful Push for Self-Service," *New York Times*, April 9, 1989, section 3, p. 1. [Reich's note]
14. U.S. Bureau of the Census, Current Population Reports, Series P-23, no. 138, tables 2-1, 4-6. See W. Johnson, A. Packer, et al., *Workforce 2000: Work and Workers for the 21st Century* (Indianapolis: Hudson Institute, 1987). [Reich's note]
15. The Census Bureau estimates that by the year 2000, at least 12 million Americans will work in health services—well over 6 percent of the total work force. [Reich's note]
16. In 1989, the entertainment business summoned to the United States $5.5 billion in foreign earnings—making it among the nation's largest export industries, just behind aerospace. U.S. Department of Commerce, International Trade Commission, "Composition of U.S. Exports," various issues. [Reich's note]

For Discussion:

1. Define each of the key terms in Reich's essay: routine producers, in-person servers, and symbolic analysts. Then give examples of each of these kinds of workers in your own community.
2. List the changes Reich notes in the American economy since 1960. Have those changes affected people you know? Have those changes been for better or for worse? Reich makes a clear link between advanced education and wealth. Based on your observations, do you think he is correct?
3. Many people simply prefer to work with their hands, and many people are not able to do the intellectual work associated with higher learning. What will their future be in the world Reich predicts?

 For Fact-Finding, Research, and Writing:

1. Locate Reich's book on the Chrysler Corporation in the library catalogue. Using the related subject headings situated under the publisher's name, find a book on U.S. industrial policy in the 19th century. Then use the subject headings under that book to find one more title on 19th century American industrial policy.
2. Use the Country Profiles feature of the British Broadcasting System's news website to find the country in Europe with the lowest GNI per capita. Skim the information given in the Profile and write in two or three sentences an explanation for its poverty.
3. Do literacy rates always correspond to GNI rates? Find statistics to suggest an answer.

The Technology Timeline

TECHNOLOGICAL DEVELOPMENT is ever accelerating, bringing new products onto the market. To help understand the range of innovations emerging and their potential impacts, researchers at British Telecommunications began the Technology Timeline in 1991 under the direction of Paul McIlroy. Since then, futurist Ian Pearson of BTexact Technologies, BT's business division, has updated the timeline about once every two or three years.

The timeline presented here is drawn from the 2002 edition of the full timeline developed by Pearson with Ian Neild, which is available on BTexact's Web site. The timeline also incorporates several possible "wild cards," based on *Out of the Blue* by John L. Petersen of the Arlington Institute.

"What must be remembered by anyone preparing for the future is that technology change isn't very important in itself," says Pearson, "What matters is what this change enables or destroys." Thus, the timeline is potentially useful not only to BT's business customers, but also to government, the media, and private individuals.

"The intention of the timeline is to illustrate the potential for beneficial technologies," says Pearson. "We will have more variety of entertainment, better health, greater wealth, and probably better social well-being."

2005

ARTIFICIAL INTELLIGENCE AND LIFE	Toys with network based intelligence, 2004 Confessions to AI priest, 2004 Behavior alarms based on human mistake recognition, 2006 AI chatbots indistinguishable from people. 2005
BIOTECHNOLOGY: HEALTH AND MEDICINE	Retinal implants linked to external video cameras, 2004 Designer babies, 2005 All patients tagged in hospitals, 2005
BUSINESS AND EDUCATION	80% of U.S. homes have PCs, 2005 Virtual reality is used to teach science, art, history, etc. 2005
COMPUTING POWER	100-teraflop computer, 2004 **CAMERAS RECORD VISUAL EXPERIENCES BY 2004.**
ENVIRONMENT AND RESOURCES	Clothes collect and store solar power, 2005
HOME AND LEISURE	Smart paint containing computer chips is available, 2004 Fiber-optic plants used in gardens, 2005 Living rooms decorated with virtual reality scenes, 2005
MACHINE-HUMAN INTERFACE	Tactile sensors comparable to human sensation, 2004 Voice synthesis quality up to human standard, 2005 Voice control of many household gadgets, 2005
ROBOTICS	Robotic space vehicles and facilities, 2005
SECURITY, LAW, WAR	People's courts on Internet for minor disputes, 2004 VR routinely used in courtrooms for evidence presentation, 2005 Soldiers' weapons fired remotely, 2005
SPACE	Space tugs take satellites into high orbits, 2005 **Wild Card: Major genetic engineering accident, 2005**
TRAVEL AND TRANSPORTATION	Hydrogen-fueled executive jets (cryoplanes), 2005 Assisted lane-keeping systems used in trucks and buses, 2005
WEARABLE AND PERSONAL TECHNOLOGY	Cameras built into glasses record what we see, 2004 Polymer video screens built into clothes. 2005

2010

ARTIFICIAL INTELLIGENCE AND LIFE	Software is trained rather than written, 2006 Artificial nervous system for autonomous robots, 2010 25% of TV celebrities are synthetic, 2010
BIOTECHNOLOGY: HEALTH AND MEDICINE	Artificial heart (lab-cultured or entirely synthetic), 2010
BUSINESS AND EDUCATION	All government services delivered electronically, 2008
COMPUTING POWER	Optical neurocomputers, 2007 Quantum computer, 2007 Supercomputer as fast as human brain, 2010
ENVIRONMENT AND RESOURCES	Multilayer solar cells with efficiency of more than 50%, 2006 Effective prediction of most natural disasters, 2010
HOME AND LEISURE	Cybercommunity attains population of 100 million, 2010 Mood-sensitive light bulbs developed, 2010 Chips in packaging control cooking, 2010
MACHINE-HUMAN INTERFACE	Emotionally responsive toys and robots, 2006 Voice interface for home appliances, 2010
ROBOTICS	Robotic security and fire guards, 2008 Self-monitoring infrastructures use smart materials, sensors, 2010
SECURITY, LAW, WAR	First Net war fought between cybercommunities, 2007 Logic checkers highlight contradictory evidence, 2008
SPACE	Next-generation space telescope launched, 2007
TRAVEL AND TRANSPORTATION	Pollution-monitor chips are built into cars, 2008 Cars with automatic steering, 2008 GPS and engine-management systems limit speed automatically, 2010
WEARABLE AND PERSONAL TECHNOLOGY	Portable translation device for simple conversation, 2007 Video tattoos, 2010

Wild Card: Viruses immune to known treatments, 2010

2015

ARTIFICIAL INTELLIGENCE AND LIFE	Satellite location devices implanted into pets, 2015
BIOTECHNOLOGY: HEALTH AND MEDICINE	Some implants seen as status symbols, 2015 Shower body scan, 2015 Artificial lungs, kidneys, 2015
BUSINESS AND EDUCATION	Purely electronic companies exist with minimal human involvement, 2012 3-D video conferencing, 2015
COMPUTING POWER	DNA computer, 2012 Desktop computer as fast as human brain, 2015
ENVIRONMENT AND RESOURCES	Insect-like robots used for crop pollination, 2012 Commercial magma power stations, 2012
HOME AND LEISURE	Holographic windows redirect sunlight, 2015 Dual geo/cybernationality recognized internationally, 2015
MACHINE-HUMAN INTERFACE	**COMPUTER SCREENS IN CLOTHES BY 2005.**
ROBOTICS	Robots for almost any job in homes or hospitals, 2012 Reconfigurable buildings, 2015
SECURITY, LAW, WAR	ID cards replaced by biometric scanning, 2015
SPACE	First manned mission to Mars, 2015 Space hotel accommodates 350 guests, 2015 Near-Earth space tours, 2015
TRAVEL AND TRANSPORTATION	*Wild Card: Self-aware machine intelligence, 2015*
WEARABLE AND PERSONAL TECHNOLOGY	

2020

ARTIFICIAL INTELLIGENCE AND LIFE	Machine knowledge exceeds human knowledge, 2017 Electronic life form given basic rights, 2020 Artificial insects and small animals with artificial brains, 2025
BIOTECHNOLOGY: HEALTH AND MEDICINE	Artificial liver, 2020 Only 15% of deaths worldwide due to infectious diseases, 2020 Nanobots in toothpaste attack plaque, 2020
BUSINESS AND EDUCATION	
COMPUTING POWER	AI technology imitates thinking processes of the brain, 2018
ENVIRONMENT AND RESOURCES	Sensors widely used in countryside to monitor environment, 2020 Systems based on biochemical storage of solar energy, 2020
HOME AND LEISURE	Kaleidoscopic flowers using electronic inks, 2020 Digital image overlays enhance relationships, 2020 Bore filter screens dullards out of digital communications, 2020
MACHINE-HUMAN INTERFACE	Computers linked to biological sensory organs, 2018
ROBOTICS	Self-diagnostic, self-repairing robots, 2017 Robotic mail delivery, 2020
SECURITY, LAW, WAR	
SPACE	Regular manned missions to Mars, 2020
TRAVEL AND TRANSPORTATION	Driverless truck convoys using electronic towbar, 2020 Reservations required to use some key roads, 2020
WEARABLE AND PERSONAL TECHNOLOGY	Computer-enhanced dreaming, 2020

Wild Card: Rise of a global machine dictator, 2020

NEAR-EARTH SPACE TOURS BY 2015.

2025

ARTIFICIAL INTELLIGENCE AND LIFE	
BIOTECHNOLOGY: HEALTH AND MEDICINE	Fully functioning artificial eyes, 2024 Artificial peripheral nerves, 2025 Artificial legs, 2025
BUSINESS AND EDUCATION	Learning superseded by transparent interface to smart computers, 2025
COMPUTING POWER	
ENVIRONMENT AND RESOURCES	ROBOTS SURPASS DEVELOPED-WORLD POPULATION BY 2025.
HOME AND LEISURE	Holographic TV, 2025 VR becomes popular entertainment in nursing homes, 2025
MACHINE-HUMAN INTERFACE	Thought recognition becomes everyday input means, 2025
ROBOTICS	Cybernetic gladiators, 2025
SECURITY, LAW, WAR	*Wild Card: Conscious networks won't cooperate, 2025*
SPACE	Space factories for commercial production, 2025 Antimatter production and storage becomes feasible, 2025
TRAVEL AND TRANSPORTATION	
WEARABLE AND PERSONAL TECHNOLOGY	

2030

ARTIFICIAL INTELLIGENCE AND LIFE	Robots are physically and mentally superior to humans, 2030
BIOTECHNOLOGY: HEALTH AND MEDICINE	First Bionic Olympics, 2020
BUSINESS AND EDUCATION	
COMPUTING POWER	Library of Congress contents available in sugar-cube-sized device, 2030
ENVIRONMENT AND RESOURCES	Space solar power stations, 2030 Carbon dioxide fixation technologies for environmental protection, 2030
HOME AND LEISURE	
MACHINE-HUMAN INTERFACE	Full direct brain link, 2030
ROBOTICS	
SECURITY, LAW, WAR	Emotion control chips used to control criminals, 2030
SPACE	Start of construction of manned Mars laboratory, 2030 Use of human hibernation in space travel, 2030
TRAVEL AND TRANSPORTATION	
WEARABLE AND PERSONAL TECHNOLOGY	Dream-linking technology built for nighttime networking, 2030

Wild Card: Nanotechnology war, 2030

2040

ARTIFICIAL INTELLIGENCE AND LIFE	Living genetically engineered electronic toy/pet developed, 2040
BIOTECHNOLOGY: HEALTH AND MEDICINE	Artificial brain, 2035
BUSINESS AND EDUCATION	
COMPUTING POWER	**ASTEROID DIVERSION TECHNOLOGY USED AS WEAPON BY 2040**
ENVIRONMENT AND RESOURCES	Artificial precipitation induction and control, 2035 Wave energy provides up to 50% of UK requirements, 2040
HOME AND LEISURE	Experience-recording technology developed, 2035 Realistic nanotech toy soldiers are built, 2035
MACHINE-HUMAN INTERFACE	**MOON BASE SIZE OF SMALL VILLAGE BUILT BY 2040**
ROBOTICS	
SECURITY, LAW, WAR	Asteroid diversion technology used as weapon, 2040
SPACE	Moon base the size of small village is built, 2040
TRAVEL AND TRANSPORTATION	*Wild Card: Electromagnetic communications disrupted, 2040*
WEARABLE AND PERSONAL TECHNOLOGY	